I0890234

LOGICAL PERSPECTIVES ON LANGUAGE AND INFORMATION

LOGICAL PERSPECTIVES ON LANGUAGE AND INFORMATION

edited by
Cleo Condoravdi
Gerard Renardel de Lavalette

CSLI
PUBLICATIONS
Center for the Study of
Language and Information
Stanford, California

Center for the Study of Language and Information
Leland Stanford Junior University
Printed in the United States
05 04 03 02 01   1 2 3 4 5

Library of Congress Cataloging-in-Publication Data

Logical perspectives on language and information / [edited by] Cleo Condoravdi, Gerard Renardel de Lavalette.
p. cm. -- (CSLI lecture notes ; no. 120)
Proceedings of the 5th Workshop on Logic, Language, and Cognition, held May 31–June 2, 1996 at Stanford University.
Includes bibliographical references and index.
ISBN 1-57586-284-0 (paper : alk. paper) -- ISBN 1-57586-283-2 (cloth : alk. paper)
1. Language and logic--Congresses. I. Condoravdi, Cleo A., 1962–
II. Renardel de Lavalette, Gerard. III. Workshop on Logic, Language, and Cognition (5th : 1996 : Stanford University) IV. Series.
P39 .L5967 2002
160--dc21

2001043321

∞ The acid-free paper used in this book meets the minimum requirements of the American National Standard for Information Sciences—Permanence of Paper for Printed Library Materials, ANSI Z39.48-1984.

Please visit our web site at
http://cslipublications.stanford.edu/
for comments on this and other titles, as well as for changes and corrections by the author and publisher.

Contents

Contributors

TOM COSTELLO was at the Computer Science Department of Stanford University when writing the paper published here. He is currently working at the IBM Almaden Research Center.

JAAP VAN DER DOES presently works for ABN AMRO Bank at Amstelveen (the Netherlands). His research interests include the semantics of natural language, in particular determiner logics.

DONKA FARKAS is professor of Linguistics at the University of California, Santa Cruz.

JEAN MARK GAWRON is professor of Computational Linguistics San Diego State University.

YOOKYUNG KIM earned her Ph.D. in Linguistics at Stanford University in 1997 and she was a post-doctoral fellow at CSLI (Center for the Study of Language and Information) for two years. Currently she is pursuing an MSCS at Stanford.

MANFRED KRIFKA is professor of Linguistics at the Humboldt University in Berlin.

MICHIEL VAN LAMBALGEN is at the Institute for Logic, Language and Computation at the University of Amsterdam. His research interests include mathematical logic, psychology of perception and reasoning, and the semantics of time and aspect in natural language.

ZOHAR MANNA is at the Computer Science Department of Stanford University.

GERARD RENARDEL DE LAVALETTE is full professor in theoretical computing science and mathematical logic af Groningen University. His research interests include modal logic and proof theory.

HENNY SIPMA is at the Computer Science Department of Stanford University.

TOMÁS URIBE is at the Computer Science Department of Stanford University.

Preface

The 5th Workshop on Logic, Language and Cognition (LLC5) took place on May 31 - June 2, 1996 at the Center for the Study of Language and Information (CSLI) at Stanford University. The organisers were Johan van Benthem, Henriëtte de Swart, Rob van Glabbeek, and Jean Braithwaite. The workshop was sponsored by the School of Humanities and Sciences, the Center for the Study of Language and Information, the Department of Philosophy, Professor Vaughan Pratt, Professor John Mitchell (all at Stanford University), and by the Dutch Research School in Logic.

Like its predecessors, the aim of LLC5 was to bring together scholars having an interest in logic – philosophers, linguists and computer scientists – with the overall aim of facilitating interdisciplinary interaction. It succeeded in doing so by presenting a program of 24 presentations by researchers from the United States, Netherlands and Spain, on a diversity of topics ranging from the role of negation in child language via dynamic epistemic logic to deductive modelchecking.

Some authors were invited after the workshop to contribute a paper related to their talk to the workshop bundle you are reading now. Each of their submissions underwent a thorough reviewing process involving two referees and one of the editors of the bundle. We thank all those who contributed to the refereeing process.

By a variety of reasons, the time lag between the workshop and the publication of this bundle extended far beyond our intentions. However, we think that the contents of each of the papers have not lost much of their interest, and we can recommend a closer study. In the sequel of this Introduction, we tell you more about their contents.

Circumscription, introduced by John McCarthy in 1977, is a form of nonmonotonic reasoning, based on minimising the extension of a predicate. In his paper *Cofinal circumscription*, Tom Costello addresses a serious problem with circumscription: in many examples of commonsense reasoning, straightforward formalisation leads to theories that become inconsistent after applying circumscription. He goes on to propose cofinal circumscription, which turns out to preserve consistency. It is based on the mathematical notion of density, intended to capture the notion of 'reasonable belief'.

In 1982, David Marr published a seminal book on the psychology of perception. In his models, perception is a multi-layered and essentially approximative process. Building on Marr's model of perception, Michiel van Lambalgen and Jaap van der Does present in their paper *A Logic of Vision: Preliminaries* a semantics based on sequences of approximations, partially ordered by a relation of refinement or decomposition. As a consequence, reality becomes an inverse limit of such a sequence. Both the limit and the approximations are first-order models, and existing model-theoretic (and topological) machinery can be used (with some adaptations). A novel notion of generalized quantification is used to express 'blurring' of reality. The semantics is then applied to familiar observations concerning perceptual reports in natural language.

It is a common fact that most things around us are subject to change. This observation justifies the 'dynamic turn' in logic, which aims to develop logical systems that reflect this dynamic character of the objects we may reason about. An early example is V. Pratt's Quantified Dynamic Logic. In his paper *A Logic of Modification and Creation*, Gerard Renardel generalises Pratt's and other dynamic logics and tries to unify related systems like Evolving Algebras and Database Logic.

Computer aided verification aims to develop methods to verify that certain digital systems (usually given as programs) satisfy certain properties (usually given as a specification). Due to the complexity of this task, the help of a computer is indispensable. The paper *Model Checking and Deduction for Infinite-State Systems* by Henny Sipma, Tomás Uribe and Zohar Manna addresses the verification of temporal properties of reactive systems (i.e. systems with an ongoing interaction with their environment). The temporal properties are expressed in temporal logic. Parallel to the logical duality between proofs and models, there are traditionally two complementary styles of verification: one via deduction, the other via model checking. The paper contains an overview of both styles, and proposes a combination called deductive model checking that aims to combine the best of both.

Cleo Condoravdi
Gerard Renardel de Lavalette

1

Non-novel Indefinites in Adverbial Quantification

MANFRED KRIFKA

1.1 Introduction

Adverbial quantification is sensitive to accent. Take the following example that characterizes the headgear habits on an American campus (acute accent marks the location of the main accent, usually a high-fall.)

(1) a. A freshman usually wears a báseball cap.
'Most freshmen wear a baseball cap.'
b. A fréshman usually wears a baseball cap.
'Most wearers of baseball caps are freshmen.'

This influence of accent has been taken as evidence that adverbial quantification is focus sensitive (cf. Rooth (1985)) or presupposition sensitive (cf. von Fintel (1994), Rooth (1995)). I will discuss a problem that has been identified by von Fintel and Rooth, the **requantification problem**. Roughly stated, standard accounts of indefinites as NPs that introduce new discourse referents are at odds with standard accounts of the focus sensitivity or presupposition sensitivity of (1), which force us to assume that indefinites may pick up existing discourse referents and "requantify" over them. I will argue for a special class of indefinites that pick up existing discourse referents, which I will call **non-novel indefinites**, to explain the nature

*Precursors of this paper were presented at the Conference on Non-Narrative Texts, Austin, February 1998, organized by Carlota Smith, and at a talk at MIT in April 1998. Thanks to the audiences for helpful comments at these occasions, in particular Irene Heim and Kai von Fintel, to Cleo Condoravdi, and to an anonymous reviewer.

Logical Perspectives on Language and Information.
Cleo Condoravdi and Gerard Renardel de Lavalette (eds.).

of quantification in cases like (1). I will discuss additional evidence for this class of indefinites, in particular the influence of accent on indefinite NPs in the protasis of conditionals, as in the following case discussed by Kadmon (1987) and Chierchia (1992):

(2) a. If a farmer owns a dónkey, he usually béats it.
   'Most farmers that own a donkey beat it.'
 b. If a fármer owns a donkey, he usually béats it.
   'Most donkeys owned by a farmer are beaten by him.'

2.1 Standard Accounts of Adverbial Quantification

Rooth (1985) treats the impact of accent on the interpretation of adverbially quantified statements such as in (1) as an instance of **association with focus**. In his early work, Rooth did not deal with cases that contained indefinite NPs, and to illustrate the basic property of his analysis, I will also start with an example in which the introduction of discourse referents can be neglected.

(3) a. Mary usually took Jóhn to the movies.
   'Most of the time when M. took someone to the movies, it was J.'
 b. Máry usually took John to the movies.
   'Most of the time when someone took J. to the movies, it was M.'

The adverbial quantifier *usually* is an operator that applies to a clause. An episodic clause like *Mary took John to the movies* is analyzed as a predicate of situations — the situations in which Mary took John to the movies. Accent marks the expression in focus. Focus, represented by a feature F, indicates that alternatives to the meaning of the expressions are to be considered (hence the term "Alternative Semantics"). We distinguish between the ordinary interpretation, $[\![\alpha]\!]$, and a set of alternatives, $[\![\alpha]\!]_A$.

(4) a. $[\![$*Mary took Jóhn*$_F$ *to the movies*$]\!]$
   $= \{s \mid \text{Mary took John to the movies in } s\}$
 b. $[\![$*Mary took Jóhn*$_F$ *to the movies*$]\!]_A$
   $= \{\{s \mid \text{Mary took x to the movies in } s\} \mid x \in \text{ALT(John)}\}$

ALT(John) is the set of contextually salient alternatives of John. If Bill is the only proper alternative to John, then ALT(John) = {John, Bill}. In this case (4.b) is a set that contains two sets of situations,

$$\{\{s \mid \text{Mary took John to the movies in } s\},\ \{s \mid \text{Mary took Bill to the movies in } s\}\}$$

Focus-sensitive adverbial quantifiers make use of the alternative meanings introduced by focus. In Rooth's theory, the alternative meanings supply the domain of quantification, which is simply the union of the alternatives. Example (6) illustrates this for *usually*, which is interpreted as the generalized quantifier MOST, cf. (5).

(5) $[\![\textit{usually}\ \Phi]\!] = \text{MOST}(\cup[\![\Phi]\!]_A, [\![\Phi]\!])$,
where $\text{MOST}(A, B)$ iff $\#(A \cap B) > \#(A - B)$

(6) $[\![$*Mary usually took Jóhn*$_F$ *to the movies*$]\!]$
= MOST(∪{{s | Mary took x to the movies in s} | x ∈ ALT(John)},
{s | Mary took John to the movies in s})
= MOST({s | ∃x∈ ALT(John)[Mary took x to the movies in s]},
{s | Mary took John to the movies in s})

If ALT(John) = {John, Bill}, this amounts to the following:

= MOST({s | Mary took John or Bill to the movies in s},
{s | Mary took John to the movies in s})

That is, in most cases in which Mary took John or Bill to the movies, she took John to the movies.

The generality of Rooth's solution of the influence of accent on quantification has been questioned, though. It has been argued that adverbial quantification is not sensitive to focus, but rather to **presuppositions**. Examples to that point have been adduced by Schubert & Pelletier (1989):

(7) a. Cats always land on their feet.
'If a cat touches ground when falling, it always lands on its feet.'
b. Robin Hood never misses.
'If Robin Hood tries to hit something, he never misses (it).'

These sentences can be understood as quantifications over situations that satisfy their presuppositions. The relevant presuppositions are the lexical presuppositions of *land* and *miss*. For example, any situation in which the issue arises whether *land on its feet* can or cannot be applied to an entity is one in which this entity touches ground at the end of a fall. In non-falling situations it would be infelicitous to talk about landing on one's feet. Kasper (1992) has observed a similar phenomenon with modals:

(8) Mary would have solved the problem.
'If Mary were confronted with the problem, she would have solved it.'

The modal statement in (8) cannot be taken as absolute, but has to be relativized to certain conditions. These conditions are at least partly given by the presuppositions of the sentence. In the case at hand, to solve a problem presupposes one's being confronted with it.

Hence the domain of an adverbial quantifier may be supplied by the presuppositions of a sentence, an idea proposed by Berman (1987) and von Fintel (1994). It can be motivated as follows: When a sentence is combined with an adverbial quantifier, the quantifier specifies to which extent the sentence is true (always, usually, sometimes or never). But the issue whether or not a sentence is true arises only when the presuppositions of the sentence are satisfied. This leads to the following schematic meaning rule for adverbial quantifiers, illustrated here for *usually*, where Pres(Φ) identifies the (conjunction of the) presuppositions of Φ:

(9) ⟦*usually* Φ⟧ = MOST(Pres(Φ), ⟦Φ⟧)

We have the following analysis of (7.b), where NO(A, B) expresses that the sets A and B have an empty intersection.

(10) a. ⟦*Robin Hood misses*⟧ = {s | Robin Hood misses in s}
b. Pres(*Robin Hood misses*) = {s | RH. tries to hit something in s}
c. ⟦*Robin Hood never misses*⟧
= NO({s |RH tries to hit something in s}, {s |RH misses (it) in s})

We have now two distinct rules for adverbial quantifiers: Rules of type (5) that treat them as sensitive to focus, and rules of type (9) that treat them as sensitive to presuppositions. This is not a desirable state of affairs: That adverbial quantifiers in English show both types of sensitivity would be a quirk of the English language, and we should expect that in other languages there are some quantifiers that are presupposition sensitive, and others that are focus-sensitive. This has never been reported. It is thus an appealing idea to conflate presupposition-sensitivity and focus-sensitivity of adverbial quantification and analyze it as one and the same phenomenon. This could be done in two ways: Either we reduce presupposition-sensitivity to focus-sensitivity, or we reduce focus-sensitivity to presupposition-sensitivity.

The first strategy, reduction to focus-sensitivity, would imply that instances that appear to be presupposition-sensitive expressions actually are focus-sensitive. This is convincing in some cases. For example, (7.a) is naturally read with main accent on *feet*, which is compatible with focus on *on their feet*. The alternatives on the level of the VP meaning then would be 'land on their feet', 'land on their back', etc. The sentence then would express that, in situations in which cats land on their feet or land on their back etc., they land on their feet. We get this type of interpretation if (7.a) is an answer to a question like *On what do cats land?* However, (7.a) can also answer a general question about the properties of a cat, e.g., *What properties do cats have?* This suggests that the whole VP, *land on their feet*, is in focus, and we cannot appeal to focus as the force that partitions a domain into a restrictor and a nuclear scope. Also, this strategy is not particularly convincing for (7.b). It is quite unnatural to assume that this sentence has to be read with a focus on *misses* that would introduce alternatives such as *hits*.

The other strategy is to assume that focalization leads to a presupposition, so that cases like (3.a,b), analyzed as focus sensitive before, actually can be seen as instances of presupposition sensitivity. The obvious candidate for a presupposition is an **existential** presupposition. If sentence (3.a) would generate the presupposition that Mary took *someone* to the movies, we would arrive at the same result as before, but now under the interpretation of *usually* as a presupposition-sensitive operator as in (9):

(11) a. ⟦*Mary took Jóhn*$_F$ *to the movies*⟧
= {s | Mary took John to the movies in s}
b. Pres(*Mary took Jóhn*$_F$ *to the movies*)
= {s | ∃x[Mary took x to the movies in s]}
c. ⟦*Mary usually took Jóhn to the movies*⟧
= MOST({s | ∃x[Mary took x to the movies in s]},
{s | Mary took John to the movies in s})

There is quite convincing evidence for focus as a device that introduces existential presuppositions. It comes from one of the primary uses of focus, namely, as a device to identify felicitous answers to questions. The question-answer pairs in (12.a,b) are felicitous, but notice that (12.a.B) could not answer (12.b.A), and neither could (12.b.B) answer (12.a.A).

(12) a. A: Who did Mary take to the movies?
B: Mary took Jóhn$_F$ to the movies.
b. A: Who took John to the movies?
B: Máry$_F$ took John to the movies.

Now, constituent questions have often been analyzed as introducing an existence presupposition. For example, (12.a.A) can be seen as presupposing that Mary took someone to the movies. A speaker that is in doubt about this has no business asking such a question. So we may assume that the answers to such questions have the same existential presupposition: A sentence like (12.a.B) presupposes that Mary took someone to the movies, just like the question, and supplies as new information that it was John.

However, there is an apparent problem with this. The questions of (12) can be reformulated in a way that they don't have an existential presupposition, e.g., *Who, if anyone, did Mary take to the movies?* Consequently, the answers should not come with an existential presupposition either. Furthermore, answers like *Mary didn't take anyone to the movies* are possible answers to the original question, (12.a.A). But we may apply some dialectic reasoning in this case and take negative quantifiers as possible alternatives of an expression in focus, a move that was suggested by Rooth (1994). This has consequences for the case considered here, sentences with adverbial quantifiers. For if we assume that *nobody* is an alternative to *John*, the paraphrase of (3.a) would be inadequate, and should rather be 'Most of the time, if Mary went to the movies, she took John with her'. The sentence, under the indicated accent, appears to have this interpretation. We can ascribe this to the fact that the range of alternatives is open to contextual influences; if it happens to include the negative quantifier, then we get the interpretation discussed here.

There are other ways to reconcile the apparent focus-sensitivity and the presupposition-sensitivity of adverbial quantifiers. Rooth (1992) and von Fintel (1994) develop a theory in which focus-sensitive operators are dependent on a domain C, which in turn depends on the focus of the expression in the scope of the operator. C is not fully determined by focus, but is subject to additional restrictions. It is natural to assume that C can also be constrained by the presuppositions of that expression.

3.1 Standard Account of Indefinites in Quantification

So far we have considered instances of adverbial quantification in which indefinite NPs don't play any role. Our examples consisted of an adverbial quantifier combined with an episodic sentence that was analyzed as a predicate over situations; the quantifier quantified over such situations. But there are cases in which the variable over which the quantifier ranges is supplied by an indefinite NP. Consider our initial examples (1); in (1.a) we have a quantification over freshmen, and in (1.b) over (wearers of) baseball caps. Such cases clearly require a theory of indefinites that shows how they introduce variables that can be quantified over. This type of theory was conceived by Karttunen (1976) and further developed in Kamp (1981), which initiated Discourse Representation Theory, and Heim (1982), especially chapter III, which developed into models of direct dynamic interpretation.

Let me outline here a simple framework for dynamic interpretation. It is a fairly standard account that just takes care of the change of the available discourse referents and the way they are anchored to entities. It suppresses the encoding of other factual information, for which we would have to include sets of possible worlds in the notion of a context.

Discourse referents are represented as natural numbers; I will use variables i, i′, etc. **Assignments** are partial functions from discourse referents to entities. I will use variables g, h, k, etc. Instead of g(i), I will write g_i, and say that the discourse referent i is **anchored** by g to the individual g_i. DOM(g) is the domain of assignment g. **Contexts** (common grounds) are sets of assignments, for which I will use variables like c, c′ etc. One requirement for contexts is that their assignments all have the same domain; I write DOM(c) for the domain of the assignments of c. **Clause meanings** are **context-change potentials**, that is, functions from an **input context** to an **output context.** I will use variables like α, β etc. for context-change potentials. For the **update** of a context c by a clause meaning α I write $c + \alpha$, instead of $\alpha(c)$. The definition of an **extension** of an assignment g for a particular index i resulting in an assignment h is given in (13). That is, h differs from g insofar as it assigns an entity to the discourse referent i.

(13) $g <_i h$ iff $g \subset h$ and
$\text{DOM}(h) = \text{DOM}(g) \cup \{i\}$ (where g, h are assignments)

Consider now the treatment of a simple sentence with an indefinite and the interpretation of a text consisting of two sentences. I take as the input of interpretation a level of Logical Form in which NPs are scoped and coindexed with their traces.

(14) a. *A man came in.*
b. LF: [*a man*]$_1$ [t$_1$ *came in*]
c. Interpretation with respect to an input context c_0:
$c_0 + [\![a\ man_1]\!] + [\![t_1\ came\ in]\!]$
$= c_0 + \lambda c\{h \mid \exists g \in c[g <_1 h \wedge \text{MN}(h_1)]\} + \lambda c\{g \in c \mid \text{CI}(g_1)\}$
$= \{h \mid \exists g \in c_0[g <_1 h \wedge \text{MN}(h_1)]\} + \lambda c\{g \in c \mid \text{CI}(g_1)\}$
$= \{g \in \{h \mid \exists g \in c_0[g <_1 h \wedge \text{MN}(h_1)]\} \mid \text{CI}(g_1)\}$
$= \{h \mid \exists g \in c_0[g <_1 h \wedge \text{MN}(h_1) \wedge \text{CI}(h_1)]\}$

That is, the LF [*a man*]$_1$ [t$_1$ *came in*] is a context-change potential that, when applied to an input context c_0, changes it to an output context that contains the set of assignments h that are like an assignment g in c_0, except that h maps the discourse referent 1 to an entity that is a man and to an entity that came in. The condition $g <_1 h$ enforces that the discourse referent 1 is neither in the domain of g nor, as all the assignments in a context have the same domain, in the domain of the input context c_0. That is, the condition expresses that the discourse referent is **novel.**

Consider now a small text. Notice that pronouns pick up an index.

(15) a. *A man came in. He smoked a cigar.*
b. LF: [*a man*]$_1$ [t$_1$ *came in*] [*a cigar*]$_2$ [*he*$_1$ *smoked* t$_2$]
c. $c_0 + [\![a\ man_1]\!] + [\![t_1\ came\ in]\!] + [\![a\ cigar_2]\!] + [\![he_1\ smoked\ t_2]\!]$
$= \{h \mid \exists g \in c_0[g <_1 h \wedge \text{MN}(h_1) \wedge \text{CI}(h_1)]\}$
$+ \lambda c\{h \mid \exists g \in c[g <_2 h \wedge \text{CG}(h_2)]\} + \lambda c\{g \in c \mid \text{SM}(g_1, g_2)]\}$
$= \{h \mid \exists g \in c_0[g <_{1,2} h \wedge \text{MN}(h_1) \wedge \text{CI}(h_1) \wedge \text{CG}(h_2) \wedge \text{SM}(h_1, h_2)]\}$

Here, $g <_{1,2} h$ abbreviates $\exists k[g <_1 k \wedge k <_2 h]$. We get as output context the set of assignments h that extend the assignments g in the input context c_0 insofar as they map the discourse referents 1 and 2 to entities, where 1 is mapped to a man that came in, and 2 is mapped to a cigar that 1 smoked.

This treatment of indefinites pays off not only for intersentential anaphora, but also for indefinites in sentences with adverbial or nominal quantifiers. Let me show this with the following example:

(16) Always, if a man came in, he smoked a cigar.
'Every man that came in smoked a cigar.'

This is the classical interpretation of adverbial quantifiers in Kamp (1981) and Heim (1982):

(17) $\text{ALWAYS}(\alpha, \beta) = \lambda c\{g \in c \mid \forall h[h \in \{g\}+\alpha \rightarrow \exists k[k \in \{h\}+\beta]]\}$

The quantifier takes a context-change potential α as restrictor, and another one β as nuclear scope. It says that every way h of extending an assignment g of the input context c with the restrictor α can be extended further to an assignment k that also satisfies the nuclear scope. As I defined updates with respect to contexts and not to single assignments, we have to write $\{g\}+\alpha$ instead of $g+\alpha$ here. Take a look at an example:

(18) $c_0 + [\![\textit{always} [\textit{a man}_1\ [t_1\ \textit{came in}]]\ [\textit{a cigar}_2\ [\textit{he}_1\ \textit{smoked}\ t_2]]]\!]$
$= c_0 + \text{ALWAYS}([\![\textit{a man}_1\ [t_1\ \textit{came in}]]\!], [\![\textit{a cigar}_2\ [\textit{he}_1\ \textit{smoked}\ t_2]]\!])$
$= \{g \in c_0 | \forall h[h \in \{g\}+[\![\textit{a man}_1\ [t_1\ \textit{came in}]]\!] \rightarrow$
$\exists k[k \in \{h\}+[\![\textit{a cigar}_2\ [\textit{he}_1\ \textit{smoked}\ t_2]]\!]]]\}$
$= \{g \in c_0 | \forall h[g <_1 h \wedge \text{MN}(h_1) \wedge \text{CI}(h_1) \rightarrow$
$\exists k[h <_2 k \wedge \text{CG}(k_2) \wedge \text{SM}(k_1,k_2)]]\}$

This formula accepts input contexts c_0 whose assignments g have the following property: Whenever g is extended to h which differs from g insofar as h maps a new discourse referent 1 to a man that came in, then h can be extended further to a k that differs from h insofar as k maps a new discourse referent 2 to a cigar that 1 smoked.

The rule for ALWAYS given in (17) needs to be refined, as rules of this type will not work for most other quantifiers. The following interpretation rule (19), illustrated with the quantifier *usually*, is based on the fact that natural language quantifiers are conservative, that is, we have $Q(A, B) \Leftrightarrow Q(A, A \cap B)$ for natural-language quantifiers Q (cf. Krifka (1992) and Chierchia (1992)):

(19) $\text{USUALLY}(\alpha, \beta)$
$= \lambda c\{g \in c \mid \text{MOST}(\{h \mid \{g\} + \alpha = \{g\&h\}\}, \{h \mid \{g\&h\} + \beta \neq \varnothing\})\}$

Where "g&h" stands for the **increment of assignment** of g with h, defined as the union of the assignments g and h, provided that their domains do not overlap:

(20) $g\&h = g \cup h$, if $\mathrm{DOM}(g) \cap \mathrm{DOM}(h) = \emptyset$, else undefined.

Expressions of the form $c + \alpha \neq \emptyset$ mean that the context c supports the context-change potential α in the sense that there is a non-empty context c' with $c + \alpha = c'$.

To see the meaning rule of *usually* at work in a case in which the restrictor and the nuclear scope are given explicitly, consider the following:

(21) Usually, if a man came in, he smoked a cigar.

$c_0 + [\![\textit{usually}\ [\textit{a man}_1\ [t_1\ \textit{came in}]]\ [\textit{a cigar}_2\ [\textit{he}_1\ \textit{smoked}\ t_2]]]\!]$

$= c_0 + \text{USUALLY}([\![\textit{a man}_1\ [t_1\ \textit{came in}]]\!], [\![\textit{a cigar}_2\ [\textit{he}_1\ \textit{smoked}\ t_2]]\!])$

$= \{g \in c_0 \mid \text{MOST}(\{h \mid \{g\} + [\![\textit{a man}_1\ [t_1\ \textit{came in}]]\!] = \{g\&h\}\},$
$\{h \mid \{g\&h\} + [\![\textit{a cigar}_2\ [\textit{he}_1\ \textit{smoked}\ t_2]]\!] \neq \emptyset\})\}$

$= \{g \in c_0 \mid \text{MOST}(\{h \mid g <_1 g\&h \wedge \text{MN}(g\&h_1) \wedge \text{CI}(g\&h_1)\},$
$\{h \mid \exists k[\{g\&h\} <_2 k \wedge \text{CG}(k_2) \wedge \text{SM}(k_1, k_2)]\})\}$

This says that the resulting context contains those assignments g of the input context c_0 such that most increments h that extend g insofar as they map the index 1 to a man that came in are also increments that can be extended to an assignment k that map the index 2 to a cigar such that 1 smoked 2. This gives us, effectively, quantification over incoming men.

4.1 The Requantification Problem

We are now ready to discuss the treatment of indefinites in sentences with adverbial quantifiers that are sensitive to accent variations, such as in (1). Let us start with a somewhat simpler sentence:

(22) A green-eyed dog is usually intélligent.
'Most green-eyed dogs are intelligent.'

Let me first analyze this sentence as an instance of focus-sensitive quantification. Combining alternative semantics with dynamic interpretation as in Rooth (1995), we get the following analysis:

(23) a. $[\![\textit{a dog}_1\ [t_1\ [\textit{is intélligent}]_F]]\!]$
$= \lambda c\{h \mid \exists g \in c[g <_1 h \wedge \text{DG}(h_1) \wedge \text{IN}(h_1)]\}$

b. $[\![\textit{a dog}\ [t_1\ [\textit{is intélligent}]_F]]\!]_A$
$= \{\lambda c\{h \mid \exists g \in c[g <_1 h \wedge \text{DG}(h_1) \wedge P(h_1)]\} \mid P \in \text{ALT}(\text{IN})\}$

Here, (23.a) is the ordinary meaning, and (23.b) is the set of alternatives. The ordinary meaning is a context-change potential that changes an input context c to the set of all assignments h that differ from assignments g in c insofar as they map the new discourse referent 1 to a dog that is intelligent.

The alternatives are a set of such context-change potentials; they all change an input context c to the set of all assignments h that differ from assignments g in c insofar as they map the new discourse referent 1 to a dog that has some property P, where P is an alternative to the property of being intelligent.[2] Assume that the only alternative to being intelligent is being dumb (DU); then the alternative meaning is the following set of two context-change potentials:

(23) c. If $\text{ALT}(\text{IN}) = \{\text{IN}, \text{DU}\}$:
$$= \{\lambda c\{h \mid \exists g \in c[g <_1 h \wedge \text{DG}(h_1) \wedge \text{IN}(h_1)]\},\ \lambda c\{h \mid \exists g \in c[g <_1 h \wedge \text{DG}(h_1) \wedge \text{DU}(h_1)]\}\}$$

Adverbial quantifiers are interpreted just as in the static model, as quantification over the union of the alternatives (cf. (5) for *usually*). But what is the union of a set of context-change potentials? We expect it to be a context-change potential as well, but note that this is not guaranteed if we require context-change potentials to be functions. The set-theoretic union

$$\{\langle c_0, c_0'\rangle, \langle c_1, c_1'\rangle\} \cup \{\langle c_0, c_0''\rangle, \langle c_1, c_1''\rangle\} = \{\langle c_0, c_0'\rangle, \langle c_1, c_1'\rangle, \langle c_0, c_0''\rangle, \langle c_1, c_1''\rangle\}$$

is not a function, as it violates right-uniqueness. Rather, we want the set

$$\{\langle c_0, c_0' \cup c_0''\rangle, \langle c_1, c_1' \cup c_1''\rangle\},$$

which can be obtained by the pointwise union of the values of the original context-change potential. Let us define this notion of union as follows:

(24) If A is a set of context-change potentials that have the same domain (input contexts),
then $\bigcup A = \{\langle c, c'\rangle \mid c \in \text{DOM}(A) \wedge c' = \cup\{c + \alpha \mid \alpha \in A\}\}$

For example, we have

$$\bigcup(23.c) = \lambda c\{h \mid \exists g \in c[g <_1 h \wedge \text{DG}(h_1) \wedge [\text{IN}(h_1) \vee \text{DU}(h_1)]]\},$$

which maps input contexts c to sets of assignments h that extend assignments g in c insofar as they assign the index 1 to an entity and express that h_1 is a dog that is either intelligent or dumb.

Now we can give a dynamic meaning rule for *usually*, which corresponds to the static rule of (5) (cf. Rooth 1995:296 for a corresponding rule for *always*, based on the simpler rule given in (17)).

---

[2] We must ensure that the alternatives are dynamically closed, that is, that they do not introduce discourse referents (cf. Rooth 1995: 295). This issue does not arise with focus on an adjective as in the present case, as adjectives, nouns and verbs are dynamically closed anyway. But focus may be on a constituent that includes, say, an indefinite NP, as in *Mary usually takes* [*a friend*]$_F$ *to the movies*, and therefore we must build an operation of dynamic closure into the interpretation rule for focused expression. See Krifka (1993) and Rooth (1995) for details of the compositional derivation of dynamic meanings of focused expressions in two different approaches.

(25) $[\![usually\ \Phi]\!] = \text{USUALLY}(\bigcup[\![\Phi]\!]_A, [\![\Phi]\!])$

Example (22) will get the following interpretation:

(26) $[\![usually\ [a\ dog_1\ [t_1\ [is\ intelligent]_F]]]\!]$
If ALT(IN) = {IN, DU}:
$= \text{USUALLY}(\{\lambda c\{h \mid \exists g\in c[g <_1 h \wedge \text{DG}(h_1) \wedge [\text{IN}(h_1) \vee \text{DU}(h_1)]]\},$
$\{\lambda c\{h \mid \exists g\in c[g <_1 h \wedge \text{DG}(h_1) \wedge \text{IN}(h_1)]\})$

Is this the interpretation we want? No, there is a problem when we interpret USUALLY as in (19), as this will give us the following result:

(27) $\lambda c\{g\in c \mid$
$\text{MOST}(\{h \mid \{g\} + \lambda c\{h \mid \exists g\in c[g <_1 h \wedge \text{DG}(h_1) \wedge$
$[\text{IN}(h_1) \vee \text{DU}(h_1)]] = \{g\&h\}\},$
$\{h \mid \{g\&h\} + \lambda c\{h \mid \exists g\in c[g <_1 h \wedge \text{DG}(h_1) \wedge \text{IN}(h_1)]\} \neq \varnothing\})\}$
$= \lambda c\{g\in c \mid$
$\text{MOST}(\{h \mid \mathbf{g <_1 g\&h} \wedge \text{DG}(g\&h_1) \wedge [\text{IN}(g\&h_1) \vee \text{DU}(g\&h_1)]\},$
$\{h \mid \exists k[\mathbf{g\&h <_1 k} \wedge \text{DG}(k_1) \wedge \text{IN}(k_1)]\})\}$

The problem is that $g <_1 g\&h$ and $g\&h <_1 k$ cannot hold both: One condition says that $1\in \text{DOM}(g\&h)$, but the other requires that $1\notin \text{DOM}(g\&h)$. We cannot requantify over the same index. I will call this the **requantification problem**, following von Fintel (1994).

The problem of requantification was observed in Rooth (1995) (the first version of which was circulated in 1991). Rooth's proposal to deal with it, which he calls the **domain regulator theory**, consists in the following: We should give up the novelty condition for indefinites, which we incorporated in the definition of $g <_i h$ (see (13)), and assume that the index of indefinites may be new or old. All that an indefinite does is to guarantee that its index will be in the output context. Hence the interpretation of an indefinite is not based on the extension relation < defined in (13), but rather on the relation ≤ defined in (28) below:

(28) a. $g \leq_i h$ iff $g \subseteq h$ and $i \in \text{DOM}(h)$
b. $[\![[a\ dog]_1]\!] = \lambda c\{h \mid \exists g\in c[g \leq_1 h \wedge \text{DG}(h_1)]\}$

This would of course allow for an analysis along the lines of (27), as the formula $g\&h \leq_1 k$ does not presuppose anymore that the discourse referent 1 is not an element of the domain of k.

There is an obvious problem with this. Once we give up the novelty condition for indefinites, they can pick up existing discourse referents. Coindexations like the one in (29.a) would become possible, with the same interpretation as in (29.b).

(29) a. A man_1 came in. A man_1 sat down.
b. A man_1 came in. He_1 sat down.

Perhaps we can exclude (29.a) by independent principles. The prospects for this actually look quite good. The difference between indefinite NPs on the one hand and pronouns and definite NPs on the other appears to be as follows: Indefinite NPs leave it open whether their index exists in the domain of the input context, whereas pronouns and definite NPs presuppose that it exists. Hence the following pragmatic division of labor arises: Whenever the speaker wants to pick up an existing discourse referent, she will choose a definite NP or a pronoun, because these expressions presuppose the existence of an index. And whenever the speaker wants to introduce a new index, she will use an indefinite NP, knowing that the hearer will conclude from the fact that the speaker avoided the more specific form of a pronoun or a definite NP that these types of NPs are not applicable. This is a classical instance of a **quantity implicature**.

Notice that it is not excluded that indefinite NPs pick up existing indices, just as with standard examples of quantity implicatures, which can be canceled. Cases like (22) are precisely of this form: Indefiniteness is motivated because the quantification should not re-use an existing index, which would enforce coreference to an accessible discourse referent. But if the way focus-sensitive quantification is interpreted requires coreference, and if the sentence itself does not provide any other NP to perform that job, an indefinite NP with an old index can be employed.[3]

Von Fintel's proposal to deal with the requantification problem starts with a redefinition of the semantics of adverbial quantifiers (cf. von Fintel 1994: 63ff, von Fintel 1997). He interprets adverbial quantification as quantification over situations, following Berman (1987). A sentence like (16) would be interpreted as: Every minimal situation s in which there is a man that came in can be extended to a situation s′ in which he smoked a cigar. This leads to the requantification problem when we combine it with Rooth's analysis of focus-sensitive quantification. A sentence like (22) would receive the interpretation: Most minimal situations s that contain a green-eyed dog can be extended to a situation s′ that contains a green-eyed dog that is intelligent. But notice that this does not guarantee that the second occurrence of *green-eyed dog* in this paraphrase refers to the same dog as the first occurrence. In a sense, if we assume that every situation can be extended to the

[3] This reasoning is reminiscent of the explanation of the distribution of pronominal forms in Horn (1984) and Levinson (1987, 1991). For example, Levinson argues that Binding Principle B, which prohibits binding of pronouns within a clause, is superfluous: In typical cases, reflexives will occupy this semantic niche, thus leaving pronouns for cases in which the binding is from outside the clause.

whole world of that situation, the existence of a single intelligent green-eyed dog would be sufficient to make sentence (22) true. Von Fintel proposes a change in the meaning rule of quantifiers that would give us the following truth condition for (22): Most minimal situations that contain a green-eyed dog are part of a **minimal** situation that contain a green-eyed dog that is intelligent. This enforces that the two occurrences of *a green-eyed dog* refer to the same dog.

However, von Fintel points out a problem with this solution: It would imply that a sentence like

(30) Usually, if a cat is hungry, a cat cries

means the same as 'Usually, if a cat is hungry, it cries'. We would have to impose some sort of novelty condition for indefinites over and above the situation-based semantics given by von Fintel. This also means that we have to prevent the application of the novelty condition in cases in which the double occurrence of the NP just arises due to the interpretation rule of focus-sensitive adverbial quantifiers. It is unclear what we have gained with the reformulation of the meaning rule for adverbial quantifiers, and so I will not dicuss this line of argumentation any further.

A radical solution to the requantification problem has been proposed by Percus (1997, 1998). Percus argues that indefinites have a uniqueness presupposition. This is how Percus analyzes (22):

(31) A green-eyed dog is usually intelligent.
'For most situations s, *the unique green-eyed dog* in s is intelligent.'

The sentence expresses a quantification over situations. The domain of quantification can be accommodated. The uniqueness condition that comes with indefinites will enforce a domain of quantification over situations in which each situation contains one, and only one, green-eyed dog. By this one-to-one mapping between green-eyed dogs and situations in the domain of quantification, the quantification over situations is truth-conditionally equivalent to a quantification over green-eyed dogs.

There are at least two problems with this account, both acknowledged by Percus. First, there are cases where uniqueness is clearly absent:

(32) A bìshop usually agrées with a bìshop.
'For most situations s that contain a bishop *and another bishop* s, the first bishop agrees with the second.'

The second problem is that it is unclear what the difference between definite NPs and indefinite NPs should be if both come with a uniqueness presupposition.

We have discussed the problem of requantification on the assumption that adverbial quantifiers are focus sensitive. In section 2 we have considered evidence that leads to a different theory, namely, that the domain of adverbial quantifiers is determined by the presuppositions of a sentence, and that focus only has an indirect effect by triggering an existential presupposition. The question then arises whether we can circumvent the requantification problem by following this latter analysis.

It is difficult to see how this could be the case. The reason is that adverbial quantifiers, analyzed as focus-sensitive or as sensitive to existential presuppositions triggered by focus, have very similar properties; only the mechanics of how the focus information is used makes a difference. The existential presupposition triggered by the focus in an expression α is simply the union of the alternative meanings, $\bigcup[\![\alpha]\!]_A$. Hence the only change between the two formats is how the pieces are glued together:

(33) a. Focus-sensitive quantification:
$[\![usually\ \Phi]\!] = \text{USUALLY}(\bigcup[\![\Phi]\!]_A, [\![\Phi]\!])$
b. Presupposition-sensitive quantification,
where the presupposition is triggered by focus:
$[\![usually\ \Phi]\!] = \text{USUALLY}(\text{Pres}(\Phi), [\![\Phi]\!])$, where $\text{Pres}(\Phi) = \bigcup[\![\Phi]\!]_A$.

In the next section I will develop an alternative solution that assumes that adverbial quantification is presupposition-sensitive. However, I will propose that the presupposition in question is not an existential presupposition introduced by focus, but rather a givenness presupposition introduced by indefinite NPs that are outside of the focus.

5.1 Non-novel Indefinites and their Accommodation

Let us assume that the accent distribution is not (necessarily) due to focus assignment, but to assignment of a **non-novelty** feature NN. The effect of non-novelty is that it prevents an item from receiving the main accent. This means that accent has to be realized elsewhere, an instance of **default accent** as discussed in Ladd (1980). The NP with the feature NN is deaccented or has a secondary accent realized as low-rise, which I will mark with a grave accent. The stress pattern that we observe in these examples then comes out as follows:

(34) Usually, $[$a green-eyed dòg$]_{NN}$ is intélligent.

(35) a. [A frèshman]$_{NN}$ usually wears a báseball cap.
'Most freshmen wear a baseball cap.'
b. A fréshman usually wears [a bàseball cap]$_{NN}$.
'Most baseball caps are worn by freshmen',
'Most baseball cap wearers are freshmen'

In (34) the NP *a green-eyed dog* is non-novel and gets destressed. This means that the complement expression, *is intelligent*, is accented. In (35.a), the phrase *a freshman* is non-novel, receiving secondary accent and deflecting the main accent on the complement expression, where it ends up on *a baseball cap*. The situation is just the reverse in (35.b).

This is not to say that focus plays no role in accentuation. If we take the accent of answers to constituent questions as indicative for focus, then we must assume that focus accent can be superimposed on the accentuation introduced by non-novelty. This is well-known from cases in which pronouns, which normally are deaccented, are in focus:

(36) A: Who do you like best, him or her?
B: I like [hér$_{NN}$]$_F$ best.

The same phenomenon can be observed with focus in quantified sentences. While the accentuation of (37) is similar to (35.b), its interpretation is rather the one of (35.a).

(37) A: Who wears usually a báseball cap on this campus?
B: [[A fréshman]$_{NN}$]$_F$ usually wears a bàseball cap.

What then is the effect of non-novel indefinites? I suggest that they come with the presupposition that their **index is presupposed**, that is, it exists in the input context. In addition, the descriptive part of the indefinite is presupposed as well.[4] I furthermore suggest that this presupposition is typically **accommodated**.

I follow here the account of accommodation developed in Karttunen (1974) and Stalnaker (1974). If a context c cannot be updated with a context-change potential α because α has a presupposition that is not satisfied in α (technically, c + α would result in the empty context, $\emptyset$), c can be changed minimally to a c′ such that c′ can be updated with α, provided the informational difference between c and c′ is uncontroversial.

---

[4] A related but different notion has been proposed by Condoravdi (1992, 1994) under the term **weakly novel indefinites**. These are indefinites whose indices are new, but which come with a presupposition that the enitites they refer to exist. Condoravdi treats *students* in the following text as a weakly novel indefinite: *In 1985 there was a serial killer haunting the campus. Students were aware of the danger*. Here, *students* is understood as 'the students of the campus'. In contrast, the notion of non-novel indefinites assumes that the index is old.

Non-novel indefinites can be analyzed as in (38). The NP $[a\ dog]_{1,\mathrm{NN}}$ expresses the requirement that the index 1 is in the domain of the input context, and is anchored to some dog or other.

(38) $[\![[a\ dog]_{1,\mathrm{NN}}]\!] = \lambda c\{g \in c \mid \forall g \in c[\mathrm{DG}(g_1)]\}$

We must of course define what a minimal change is. This is captured by the notion of a proper extension of a context, defined below.

(39) a. c′ **extends** c, **satisfying** (the presuppositions of) α, iff
— $c' + \alpha \neq \varnothing$
— $\forall h \in c'\ \exists g \in c[g \sqsubseteq h]$
b. c′ **extends** c **minimally, satisfying** α, iff
— c′ extends c, satisfying α,
— there is no c″, c″ ≠ c′, such that
c″ extends c, satisfying α, and
c′ extends c″, satisfying α.
c. c′ **extends** c **properly, satisfying** α (rendered as $c \leq c'[\alpha]$)
iff $c' = \cup\{c'' \mid c''$ extends c minimally, satisfying $\alpha\}$

That is, if $c + \alpha = \varnothing$ and $c \leq c'[\alpha]$, then c′ is the most conservative change of c that satisfies the presuppositions of α. In particular, c′ contains what is necessary to satisfy the presuppositions of α (39.a), but does not contain any excess information. This means that it does not introduce any unnecessary indices (39.b), and it does not make any unnecessarily specific claims about how the indices are anchored (39.c). We have the following fact:[5]

(40) If $1 \notin \mathrm{DOM}(c)$ and $c \leq c'[[\![[a\ dog]_{1,\mathrm{NN}}]\!]]$, then $c' = c + [\![[a\ dog]_1]\!]$

That is, if the discourse referent 1 is not in the domain of c, and if c′ extends c properly, satisfying $[\![[a\ dog]_{1,\mathrm{NN}}]\!]$, then c′ is the update of c with the simple indefinite, $[\![[a\ dog]_1]\!]$.

We can now formulate the interpretation of an adverbial quantifier Q along the following scheme:

(41) c + Q(Φ)
= c + Q-many ways in which c can be accommodated
to satisfy the presuppositions of Φ
are also ways that support the truth of Φ

---

[5] Proof: If $1 \notin \mathrm{DOM}(c)$ and $c \leq c'[[\![[a\ dog_{1,\mathrm{NN}}]]\!]]$, then c′ must satisfy the following requirements: First, $1 \in \mathrm{DOM}(c')$ and $\forall g \in c'[\mathrm{DG}(g_1)]$, due to the first condition of (39.a). Second, no other index is introduced, that is, $\mathrm{DOM}(c') = \mathrm{DOM}(c) \cup \{1\}$, due to (39.b). Third, every assignment h in c′ is an extension of an assignment g in c, with $g <_1 h$ and $\mathrm{DG}(h_1)$, due to the second condition of (39.a). Fourth, c′ contains all extensions h of g that satisfy the condition that there is a g in c and $g <_1 h \wedge \mathrm{DG}(h_1)$, due to (39.c). But this is exactly the c′ that we get by updating c with $[\![[a\ dog]_1]\!]$, namely $\{h \mid \exists g \in c[g <_1 h \wedge \mathrm{DG}(h_1)]\}$.

More precisely, for the interpretation of *usually*:

(42) $\text{USUALLY}(\alpha) = \lambda c\{g \in c \mid \text{MOST}(\{h \mid \{g\} \leq \{g\&h\}[\alpha]\}, \{h \mid \{g\&h\} + \alpha \neq \varnothing\})$

The condition $\{g\&h\} + \alpha \neq \varnothing$ amounts to: $\exists k[k \in \{g\&h\}+\alpha]$. Let me illustrate this rule with example (35.a).

(43) a. $[\![[a\ baseball\ cap]_2\ [t_1\ wears\ t_2]]\!]$
$= \lambda c\{h \mid \exists g \in c[g <_2 h \wedge \text{CP}(h_2) \wedge \text{WR}(h_1, h_2)]\}$
$[\![[a\ freshman]_{1,NN}]\!] = \lambda c\{g \in c \mid \forall g \in c[\text{FM}(g_1)]\}$
$[\![[a\ freshman]_{1,NN}\ [a\ baseball\ cap]_2\ [t_1\ wears\ t_2]]\!]$
$= \lambda c\{h \mid \forall g \in c[\text{FM}(g_1)] \wedge \exists g \in c[g <_2 h \wedge \text{CP}(h_2) \wedge \text{WR}(h_1, h_2)]\}$
$= \text{①}$

b. $[\![usually\ [a\ freshman]_{1,NN}\ [a\ baseball\ cap]_2\ [t_1\ wears\ t_2]]\!]$
$= \text{USUALLY}(\text{①})$
$= \lambda c\{g \in c \mid \text{MOST}(\{h \mid \{g\} \leq \{g\&h\}[\text{①}]\}, \{h \mid \exists k[k \in \{g\&h\}+\text{①}]\})$

c. If $1 \notin \text{DOM}(\{g\})$:
$\{g\} \leq \{g\&h\}[\text{①}]$ if, and only if, $g <_1 g\&h \wedge \text{FM}(h_1)$

d. If $g <_1 g\&h \wedge \text{FM}(h_1)$:
$\{g\&h\} + \text{①}$
$= \{k \mid \boldsymbol{\forall g' \in \{g\&h\}[\text{FM}(g'_1)]} \wedge g\&h <_2 k \wedge \text{CP}(k_2) \wedge \text{WR}(k_1, k_2)\}$

The boldfaced condition is now redundant, as it is guaranteed to be satisfied in $\{g\&h\}$. Hence (d) can be simplified to:

d′. If $g <_1 g\&h \wedge \text{FM}(h_1)$:
$\{g\&h\} + \text{①} = \{k \mid g\&h <_2 k \wedge \text{CP}(k_2) \wedge \text{WR}(k_1, k_2)\}$

Putting things together and assuming that $1, 2 \notin \text{DOM}(c)$:

e. $\text{USUALLY}(\text{①})$
$= \lambda c\{g \in c \mid \text{MOST}(\{h \mid g <_1 g\&h \wedge \text{FM}(h_1)\}, \{h \mid \exists k[\{g\&h\} <_2 k \wedge \text{CP}(k_2) \wedge \text{WR}(k_1, k_2)]\})\}$

This gives us the right interpretation. When applied to an input context c_0, we will get back c_0 if most increments h of assignments g of c_0 where 1 is anchored to a freshman are such that they in turn can be extended to a k that contains the new discourse referent 2 in its domain such that k_2 is a baseball cap, and k_1 (= h_1) wears k_2.

A condition for this analysis is that the input context c_0 does not contain the index 1. We can assume that non-novel indefinites in general are not used to pick up an existing discourse referent, for pragmatic reasons similar to the one that explained why coindexations as in (29.a) should be impossible. That is, definite NPs are better suited for this job, and therefore the use of an indefinite will implicate that the NP does not pick up an existing index. To substantiate that, let us discuss how definite NPs are interpreted. I cannot deliver here a full-fledged discussion of definite NPs; all that I can hope for is to make this pragmatic story reasonably plausible.

As a first try, definite NPs can be interpreted as in (44.b), in contrast to non-novel indefinites in (44.a):

(44) a. $[\![[a\ dog]_{1,NN}]\!] = \lambda c\{g \in c \mid \forall g \in c[\mathrm{DG}(g_1)]\}$

b. $[\![[the\ dog]_1]\!]$
$= \lambda c\{g \in c \mid \forall g \in c[\mathrm{DG}(g_1) \wedge \forall i \in \mathrm{DOM}(g)[\mathrm{DG}(g_i) \rightarrow g_i = g_1]]\}$

A non-novel indefinite NP presupposes that its discourse referent is introduced and satisfies the description. A definite NP comes with this presupposition as well, but in addition presupposes that the input context contains the reference to a unique entity under the given description. That is, all discourse referents i that are anchored to a dog by an assignment g are anchored by g to the same dog. Which means that only one dog is referenced by g, and this will naturally be satisfied if only one such discourse referent was introduced.

Notice that definite NPs are more specific than non-novel indefinites under this description; they express a tighter restriction on suitable input contexts. Also, definite NPs are better suited to pick out a particular existing discourse referent. To see this, consider the fact that indices are not part of the surface structure or the phonological form; they don't get "pronounced" publicly in a conversation. Rather, speaker and hearer have to supply indices (and consequently, discourse referents) on their own, following certain principles that guarantee the coherence of the semantic representation of a text. The mental models of the information contained in a text that arise for the speaker and for the hearer therefore are never exact copies; they will be alphabetical variants at best, identical up to the choice of indices and discourse referents. For example, the information state that represents the common ground of the hearer and of the speaker after the text (45) may be as follows (here, c_A is the common ground in the perspective of the speaker, and c_B is the common ground in the perspective of the hearer):

(45) a. A, to B: *A man went in. And then a man came out.*[6]

b. $c_A' = \{h \mid \exists g \in c_A[g <_{38,39} h \wedge \mathrm{MN}(h_{38}) \wedge \mathrm{WI}(h_{38}) \wedge \mathrm{MN}(h_{39}) \wedge \mathrm{CO}(h_{39})]\}$

c. $c_B' = \{h \mid \exists g \in c_B[g <_{74,75} h \wedge \mathrm{MN}(h_{74}) \wedge \mathrm{WI}(h_{74}) \wedge \mathrm{MN}(h_{75}) \wedge \mathrm{CO}(h_{75})]\}$

---

[6] In this example the second occurrence of *a man* is naturally deaccented. This does not have to be interpreted as a sign for non-novelty, though. Deaccenting can affect an expression simply because the same expression was used in the immediately preceding context.

If the speaker now wants to refer to the man that went in, the non-novel NP [*a man*]$_{NN}$ obviously would not suffice. It would be acceptable, but there is no guarantee that it picks out the right man. Even the definite NP [*the man*]$_{NN}$ would not be acceptable in this situation, as its uniqueness condition would result in a presupposition violation for any index. The non-novel indefinite NP [*a man that went in*]$_{NN}$ would perhaps be sufficient, but just by accident, because it happens to be the case that no other man that went in was mentioned. The definite NP *the man that went in* would certainly be the best choice because it explicitly **requires** that only one man that went in was introduced, that is, that all the indices in an assignment g that satisfy this description refer to the same entity. If speaker and hearer want to satisfy this requirement, they would have to choose this index, or one of these indices. Hence if the speaker wants the hearer to pick up the right index, a definite NP with an appropriate description is clearly the best choice. Consequently, whenever a speaker uses a non-novel indefinite NP, it will be implicated that the NP is not meant to pick out an index that actually has been introduced before.

This is just the beginning of an in-depth comparison of the relation between non-novel indefinites and definites. One important qualification is that not all definites are anaphoric. There are definites like *the oldest living person* that are motivated because their predicate applies to a unique entity. It should be possible to generalize the uniqueness condition so that it can either apply to entities in the world or to indices, under a given description. I think that this can be done, but I will not attempt to do it here.

6.1 A Comparison of Theories and New Evidence

We now have discussed two ways to circumvent the requantification problem in sentences with adverbial quantifiers. In sections 2 and 3 I have treated adverbial quantification as focus sensitive, or alternatively as sensitive to existential presuppositions that are introduced by focus. I will call this the **focus theory**. In section 5 I have treated adverbial quantification as sensitive to non-novelty, that is, to constituents that presuppose the existence of their discourse referent. I will call this the **non-novelty theory**.

The two theories have certain features in common. In particular, the domain regulator version of the focus theory, which says that the discourse referent of indefinites may be new or old, predicts that indefinite NPs can be used to pick up an existing discourse referent, just like the non-novelty theory. Both theories have to tell the same pragmatic story why indefinite NPs are normally not used for this purpose; namely, definite NPs are better suited to perform this task.

One important difference between the two theories lies in the way they explain the accent facts in our examples. The focus theory assumes that accent is motivated by focusing. It does not make use of any deaccenting rules, but is of course compatible with such rules. The non-novelty theory, on the other hand, makes crucial use of deaccenting rules, as it says that non-novel indefinites are deaccented. But again, it is compatible with accent rules for the purpose of focusing. In both cases, we can assume two constraints: (i) accent if [F], (ii) deaccent if [NN], with the first rule taking priority over the second.

It would seem that examples like (37) argue for the non-novelty theory, as they involve a focus that does not influence the domain of quantification. However, this conclusion would be premature, as we can assume that foci may be associated with different operators. For (37), we can assume a focus on *a baseball cap* that is associated with the quantificational adverbial, and a focus on *a freshman* that is associated with the answer or assertion operator. An illocutionary operator, it has scope over everything else in the clause, and in particular over the adverbial quantifier. These scopal relationships may account for the fact that the focus of the illocutionary operator is more prominent than the focus of the quantificational adverbial.[7]

There is one substantial difference between the two theories, namely, in the way indefinites are analyzed. According to the domain regulator theory there is only one type of indefinites. Indefinites just make sure that their index is defined in the output context; they don't care whether it is defined for the input context or not. The non-novelty theory, on the other hand, distinguishes between two types of indefinites, one that presupposes that its index is old, and another one that presupposes that its index is new. Hence evidence for a distinction between two classes of indefinites should, prima facie, be seen as evidence for the non-novelty theory.

Non-novel indefinites in English are sometimes marked by *a given*, an expression whose etymology is revealing for the current proposal. This is the case in the following two examples from the British National Corpus:

(46) a. But, however suggestive it may be, the fact that a given phenomenon is successfully predicted by a theory does not prove the theory to be correct.

b. What limits a teacher wishes to set will depend entirely on her own intentions for a given student.

(46.a) expresses a quantification over phenomena, and (b) a quantification over students, as predicted. However, *a given* is certainly not necessary for

[7] See Jacobs (1991) for a theory that relates scopal relations between focus-sensitive operators to the strength of the realization of their foci.

the interpretation of indefinites as non-novel. For example, (46.a) also expresses a quantification over theories, and (b) a quantification over teachers. Furthermore, *a given* can also be used in non-quantificational contexts to mark specific NPs, as in the following example which does not quantify over amounts of time. (I will return to specific indefinites shortly.)

(47) The students spend a given amount of time per week for a period of months (...)

I do not know of a language that marks the distinction between non-novel indefinites and regular indefinites in a consistent way. But consider the fact that we have to distinguish between at least three referential types: (i) definites, characterized by a uniqueness presupposition; (ii) non-novel indefinites, characterized by a presupposition that their index is given; and (iii) regular indefinites, which presuppose that their index is new. English is fairly consistent in differentiating (i) from (ii) and (iii) by the use of the definite vs. the indefinite article. There is evidence for languages that instead group (i) and (ii) together and mark non-novel indefinites like definites. This has been reported for Modern Greek (cf. Newton (1979)) and Spanish (cf. Laca (1990) for the data):

(48) a. Los vaqueros mascan tabaco.
the cowboys chew tobacco
'Cowboys usually chew tobacco.'
b. Los vaqueros mascan el tabaco.
the cowboys chew the tobacco
'What cowboys usually do with tobacco is: they chew it.'

Notice that in (48.a) *tabaco* lacks an article, just like other indefinite mass nouns, and is not in the restrictor of the generic quantifier; in (b) *el tabaco* is marked by the definite article and is in the restrictor of the generic quantifier.

As is well known, many languages do not mark definites vs. indefinites in a consistent way but use other means that clarify the interpretation of an NP. One example is Japanese, a language in which topic marking often indicates definiteness. Now, it is interesting to notice that indefinite NPs in the restrictor of adverbial quantifiers are marked as topics.[8]

(49) Taitei, midori no me o shita inu wa rikou de aru.
usually, green of eye Acc did dog(s) Top intelligent Decl is/are
'Usually, a green-eyed dòg is intélligent.'

[8] Thanks to Katsuhiko Yabushita, who provided me with these examples.

(50) a. Shin-nyuu-sei wa taitei yakyuu bou o kabu-tte iru.
newly-enter-student/s Top usually baseball cap/s Acc wear is/are
'Most freshmen wear a baseball cap.'

b. Yakyuu bou wa taitei shin-nyuu-sei ga kabu-tte iru.
baseball cap/s Top usually newly.enter-student/s Nom wear is/are
'Most baseball caps are worn by a freshmen.'

There is of course a natural connection between novelty and topicality: Topical NPs refer to entities that are established already in the context, and hence will be non-novel. This could be seen as a point in favor of the non-novelty theory. But the focus theory can explain the influence of topichood as well, as focused NPs cannot be topics.

But the following data point to a difference between the two theories. The meaning of (50.a) can also be expressed in the following way, in which 'a freshman' does not have a topic marker:

(51) Shin-nyuu-sei ga taitei yakyuu bou o kabu-tte iru.
newly-enter-student/s Nom usually baseball cap/s Acc wear is/are
'A fréshman usually wears a baseball cap.'

It is then understood as an answer to a question like the following:

(52) Douyuu hito/Dare ga taitei yakyuu bou o kabu-tte imasu ka.
what-kind-of people/who Nom usually baseball cap Acc wear is/are Q
'Who usually wears a baseball cap?'

The lack of topic marking of the subject NP in (51) is motivated here by the more pressing need to mark this NP as the focus of the utterance, which is incompatible with topic marking. This is similar to the English example (37). What is interesting in the Japanese case is that (51) cannot be used to express the meaning of (50.b), in any context. This comes as a surprise for theories that assume that adverbial quantifiers are directly or indirectly (by existential presuppositions) associated with focus.

Another type of evidence comes from languages with optional object NP markers, like Turkish or Persian. These markers are typically used for definite or specific NPs. Interestingly, they are also used to mark NPs in the restrictor of a quantifier, which we analyze as non-novel indefinites. For example, the following two sentences in Persian differ insofar as in (53.a) the object NP, which lacks the object marker *-ra*, is not part of the restrictor of the generic quantifier, whereas in (53.b) the *-ra* marked object is part of the restrictor.[9]

[9] Thanks to Ezat Karimi, who provided me with this example.

(53) a. Kowboyeeha tanbako mijavand.
cowboys tobacco chew
'Cowboys usually chew tobacco.'
b. Kowboyeeha tanbako-ra mijavand.
cowboys tobacco-OM chew
'What cowboys usually do with tobacco is: they chew it.'

Objects marked by *–ra* can be focused or non-focused. Hence the Persian data suggest that focusation is not a factor; rather, *-ra* is a marker of non-novelty.

Another property of non-novel indefinites is that they can undergo scrambling in languages that have this type of movement, like German. This is in contrast to regular indefinites, which do not scramble. Compare the following two examples, which I give in a verb-final construction:

(54) a. weil einer alten Dàme$_{1,NN}$ gewöhnlich eine Kátze t_1 gehört
because an old lady (DAT) usually a cat (NOM) belongs
'because most old ladies own a cat'
b. weil eine Kàtze$_{2,NN}$ gewöhnlich t_2 einer alten Dáme gehört
because a cat (NOM) usually an old lady (DAT) belongs
'because most cats belong to an old lady'

Non-novel indefinites share this property with definites. However, it so happens that expressions in focus do not undergo scrambling either, and so it seems that the data in (54) could equally well be explained within the focus theory, according to which *eine Katze* is in focus in (54.a), and *einer alten Dame* is in focus in (54.b).

There is another approach that was developed to deal with the effect of scrambling on quantification, namely, Diesing (1992). Diesing analyzes scrambling as having an immediate effect on quantification. It is assumed that we have existential closure over the VP and that scrambling moves constituents outside of the VP. As a result, the variable of an indefinite that is scrambled will not be bound by the existential closure over the VP, and hence can be bound by an adverbial quantifier:

(55) [eine Katze]$_2$ gewöhnlich $\exists$ [$_{VP}$ t_2 [einer alten Dame]$_2$ gehört]
usually(cat(x), $\exists$y[old lady(y) $\wedge$ belong-to(x,y)])

One problem this theory shares with the analysis in terms of association with focus is that we would be forced to treat the influence of presuppositions, as in (7), as a different phenomenon. And a specific problem of this theory is that it does not account for the fact that deaccented indefinites that apparently are in situ, that is, within the VP, can provide the variable for the adverbial quantifier:

(56) weil das Tierschutzheim gewöhnlich (ja doch) eine Kàtze
because the animal shelter usually PARTICLE a.ACC cat
einer alten Dáme anbietet.
a.DAT old lady offers
'because the animal shelter offers most cats to old ladies'

If the adverbial *gewöhnlich* marks the VP (a function that Diesing claims for modal particles like *ja doch*, which can occur at this position as well), then *eine Katze* is within the VP, but it nevertheless provides the variable for the quantifier.

I would also like to mention here the explanation for deaccenting of indefinite NPs proposed by Bartels & Merin (1997). The general function of what I have called deaccenting and what Bartels & Merin identified as L^*H^- tone is to indicate, roughly, a transfer of authority of referent choice from the speaker to the hearer. In the case of indefinites this means that it is granted to the hearer to select an entity that satisfies the description. This relates to the way universal statements are analyzed in game-theoretic semantics: To prove $\forall x\Phi[x]$, the speaker has to prove $\Phi[a]$ for some object *a* that can be chosen by a malevolent hearer, or "nature". This idea can be generalized for other quantificational forces. For example, to prove USUALLY$(x)\Phi[x]$, the speaker has to prove that $\Phi[a]$, where *a* is chosen by the opponent, is true for most choices of *a*. In contrast, for the existential interpretation $\exists x\Phi[x]$ it remains in the authority of the speaker to choose an instantiation *a* such that $\Phi[a]$, and this situation is not marked by L^*H^- but by H^*L^-.

This type of explanation shares certain features with the one developed here. In particular, it assumes that some feature of the indefinite NP is responsible for the selection of the variables for an adverbial quantifier. Also, the distinction between speaker-based choice and hearer-based choice has a parallel in the theory proposed here: New discourse referents are introduced through the authority of the speaker, whereas if the speaker wants to refer to an old discourse referent he has to appeal to the hearer to choose one from the discourse referents that are already part of the common ground, which is at the disposal of the hearer.

Non-novel indefinites compete with other NP types, in particular regular indefinites and definites. They have a *raison d'être* in the scope of adverbial quantifiers, but the question arises whether there are other ecological niches that they might occupy. What about the introduction of new discourse referents? Non-novel indefinites could do this by way of accommodation: They presuppose that their discourse referent is old, but at the same time cannot pick up a particular discourse referent (for this a definite NP would have been used). Hence the presupposition can only be satisfied by accommodating it, that is, by introducing a new discourse referent under the given description. Normally this is done by regular indefinites, that is, by regular update of a context, and regular update should be favored over accommodation, everything else being equal. So this does not appear to be a good niche for non-novel indefinites either. But accommodation has at least one important property in which it differs from regular update: It tends to be global, that is, it tends to happen before a sentence is interpreted (cf. Heim 1983, van der Sandt 1992)[10]. This means that an accommodated non-novel indefinite may have wider scope than a non-accommodated regular indefinite.

Now, it is well-known that **specific** indefinites can have wider scope than we would expect if they were regular quantificational NPs. Fodor & Sag (1982) show that such NPs can scope out of syntactic islands and claim that they are referential and hence appear to have widest scope:

(57) Each teacher overheard the rumor that *a student of mine* was called before the dean.
'There is a student of mine x, and each teacher overheard the rumor that x was called before the dean.'

Abusch (1994) argues that the referential analysis of specific indefinites cannot be correct, as there are readings in which they are still in the scope of another operator:

(58) Every professor rewarded every student who read *a book he had recommended.*
'For every professor x: There is a book that x recommended, y, and x rewarded every student that read y.'

Cresti (1995) has developed an analysis of specific NPs as **topical**, where topichood introduces a certain **presupposition**, and this presupposition can be **accommodated** globally, as in (57), or on an intermediate level, as in (58). In any case, presupposition projection is not subject to syntactic island conditions, which explains the apparent wide-scope phenomena of specific indefinites. The presupposition introduced by an indefinite specific NP like $[\textit{a student}]_i$ is essentially that the variable assignment must satisfy the condition $[\![\textit{student}]\!](x_i)$, where x_i is the variable corresponding to the index i (see Cresti 1995 p. 164 for details). What this means is, essentially, that the variable x_i is already available, and that it is established that x_i is a student. Details of implementation aside, this is similar to the proposal developed here for non-novel indefinites, which presupposes that their index is given. Cresti does not apply her theory to the solution of the requantifica-

10 See section 8 for a discussion of mechanisms for global accommodation.

tion problem, but what we have suggested here appears to be a natural extension of her approach.

The assumption that non-novel indefinite NPs are topical is quite natural.[11] We have seen that the topic marker in Japanese (examples (49) and (50)) can identify non-novel indefinite NPs, and topics certainly are generally deaccented, just like non-novel indefinites. In earlier presentations of the material discussed here I called non-novel indefinites "topical indefinites". I ultimately abstained from that because languages with topic markers like Japanese do not mark every non-novel indefinite NP (for example, in case there is more than one non-novel indefinite NP, as in (32)) or when it occurs in the protasis of a conditional, a case which I will discuss in the next section.

7.1 Non-novel Indefinites in Conditionals

In this section I will discuss another type of evidence for non-novel indefinites within quantificational structures. So far we were mainly concerned with indefinites in the scope of an adverbial quantifier in which the domain was not explicitly marked. One way of marking the domain is by an *if*-clause or *when*-clause (i.e., the protasis of the conditional sentence):

(59) If it is raining, Mary usually stays home.
'Most cases in which it is raining are such that Mary stays home.'

If indefinite NPs occur within the protasis, accentuation influences the truth conditions, as observed first by Kadmon (1987) and Kadmon (1990); cf. also Heim (1990).

(60) a. If a fàrmer owns a dónkey, he usually béats it.
'Most farmers that own a donkey beat it.'
b. If a fármer owns a dònkey, he usually béats it.
'Most donkeys owned by a farmer are beaten by him.'

Kadmon calls (60.a) the subject-asymmetric reading (quantification is over the variable associated with the subject NP, *a farmer*), and (60.b) the object-asymmetric reading (quantification is over the variable associated with the object NP, *a donkey*).

In Krifka (1992) I have treated the selection of subject-asymmetric and object-asymmetric readings as a consequence of focusing, assuming that

[11] Beaver (1994) has argued that the domain of quantification can be implicitly restricted by topichood. He analyses a sentence like *all Itálians use their càrs to go to wórk* as a sentence about car-owning Italians, where the destressed *their cars* helps determine the topic. Beaver contrasts the idea that the domain of quantification is formed by topichood and the idea that it is formed by presuppositions.

focus in the case of (60.a) is on *owns a donkey*, and in (60.b) on *a farmer*. The interpretation rule for an adverbial quantifier that scopes over a conditional clause makes sure that the discourse referent of the non-focused indefinite NP in the protasis is affected by the meaning of the quantifier. An alternative account proposed by Chierchia (1992) assumes that quantification is only over the "topical" parts in the protasis, that is *a farmer* in (60.a) and *a donkey* in (60.b). I had two objections: First, in languages that mark topic, like Japanese, contrasts as the one between (60.a) and (b) cannot be expressed by differences in topic marking within the *if*-clause. Second, it is generally assumed that there can be only one topic per sentence; for example, Japanese allows for only one *wa*-phrase per sentence. But in addition to the asymmetric readings discussed in (60) there are also symmetric readings, as in (61). Chierchia would have to assume here that both *a farmer* and *a donkey* are topical, hence, that the protasis has two topics.

(61) If a fàrmer ówns a dònkey, he usually takes cáre of it.
'Most farmer-donkey pairs x,y such that x owns y are such that x takes care of y.'

Chierchia (1995), chapter (2.4), provides a technical solution which involves coindexation of the quantifier with the NPs and the device of existential disclosure proposed in Dekker (1993). But it is not motivated there why existential disclosure is related to deaccentuation.

Alternatively, I assume that it is the non-novelty of indefinite NPs that distinguishes readings like (60.a,b). This eliminates the problems that an account in terms of topicality raises: While topical indefinite NPs are non-novel (cf. the discussion of the Japanese examples in (49) and (50)), we don't have to assume that EVERY non-novel indefinite NP is topical. The fact that we do not find topic-marked NPs within the protasis of a conditional in Japanese presumably shows that the topic marker identifies the topic of the whole sentence, and hence cannot occur within an embedded clause.[12] Also, there is no problem with the assumption that one sentence may contain more than one non-novel indefinite NP.

Take the basic interpretation scheme for adverbial quantifiers applied to a conditional clause with a protasis α and an apodosis β:

(62) $c + Q(\alpha, \beta)$
$= c +$ Q-many ways in which c can be updated so that it entails α are also ways that, when updated with α, entail β.

[12] Following Haiman (1978), it is the protasis itself that is the topic of the conditional sentence.

Where c entails α iff $c + \alpha = c$. Here the updates of c with α define the domain of quantification. If α contains presuppositions, then the domain should be restricted further:

(63) $c + Q(\alpha, \beta)$
= c + Q-many ways in which c can be accommodated to satisfy the presuppositions of α so that the result entails β
are also ways that, when updated with α, entail β

More specifically for *usually* (cf. the definition (42) for comparison):

(64) $[\![usually]\!](\alpha, \beta)$
$= \lambda c\{g \in c \mid \text{MOST}(\{h \mid \{g\} \leq \{g\&h\}[\alpha] \wedge \exists k[k \in [\{g\&h\} + \alpha]]\},$
$\{h \mid \exists k[k \in [\{g\&h\} + \alpha + \beta]]\})$

To illustrate, consider the following derivation of an example that is slightly more complex than the object-asymmetric interpretation of (60):

(65) a. If a fármer owns a dònkey$_{NN}$, he usually béats it with a stíck$_3$.
b. *usually* [*a farmer*$_1$ [*a donkey*$_{NN,2}$ [t_1 *own* t_2]],
[*a stick*$_3$ [*he*$_1$ *beats it*$_2$ *with* t_3]]]
c. ⟦*a farmer*$_1$ [*a donkey*$_{NN,2}$ [t_1 *own* t_2]]⟧
$= \lambda c\{h \mid \forall g \in c[\text{DK}(g_2)] \wedge \exists g \in c[g <_1 h \wedge \text{FR}(h_1) \wedge \text{OW}(h_1, h_2)]\},$
$= \textcircled{1}$
d. ⟦*a stick*$_3$ [*he*$_1$ *beats it*$_2$ *with* t_3]⟧
$= \lambda c\{h \mid \exists g \in c[g <_3 h \wedge \text{ST}(h_3) \wedge \text{BT}(h_1,h_2,h_3)]\},$
$= \textcircled{2}$
e. ⟦*usually* [*a farmer*$_1$ [*a donkey*$_{NNOP,2}$ [t_1 *own* t_2]]],
[*a stick*$_3$ [*he*$_1$ *beat it*$_2$ *with* t_3]]]⟧
$= \lambda c\{g \in c \mid \text{MOST}(\{h \mid \{g\} \leq \{g\&h\}[\textcircled{1}] \wedge \exists k[k \in \{g\&h\} + \textcircled{1}]\},$
$\{h \mid \exists k[k \in \{g\&h\} + \textcircled{1} + \textcircled{2}\}])$
$= \lambda c\{g \in c \mid$
$\text{MOST}(\{h \mid g <_2 g\&h \wedge \text{DK}(h_2) \wedge \exists k[g\&h <_1 k \wedge \text{FR}(k_1) \wedge \text{OW}(k_1,k_2)]\}$
$\{h \mid \exists k[g\&h <_{1,3} k \wedge \text{FR}(k_1) \wedge \text{DK}(k_2) \wedge \text{OW}(k_1,k_2)$
$\wedge \text{ST}(k_3) \wedge \text{BT}(k_1,k_2,k_3)]\})\}$

This is true in a context c_0 iff all assignments g in c_0 have the following properties:

- most increments h of g such that h_2 is a donkey and there is a farmer that owns h_2
- also have the property that there is a farmer that owns h_2 and that there is a stick with which the farmer beats h_2.

That is, 'most donkeys that are owned by a farmer are beaten with a stick by a farmer that owns them'. This is a correct interpretation of the so-called "weak" reading of (65.a). It appears plausible enough for the current case because we typically don't think of joint ownership of a donkey. See Rooth (1987), Chierchia (1995) for so-called "strong" readings, which I will not implement here for reasons of space, and Krifka (1996) for a discussion of the pragmatic principle governing weak vs. strong readings.

We have discussed the interpretation of quantificational adverbials in two types of contexts: When they are applied to a simple sentence, and when they are applied to a conditional. In the first case, the quantificational domain is formed by the discourse referents of the presuppositions of the sentence that have the properties expressed by the presuppositions of the sentence. In the second case, we have assumed that the domain of quantification is formed by the discourse referents of the presuppositions of the protasis that fall under the description of the protasis. The question arises how the presuppositions of the apodosis, the main clause, come into play. If they behave like the presuppositions of a simple clause, then we should assume that they influence the quantificational domain as well.

This is certainly the case. First consider an example in which the apodosis does not contain a presuppositional indefinite. The following sentence arguably has two readings:

(66) If a càt is heálthy, it usually lands on its féet.
 a. 'For every cat x that is healthy: Most situations s in which x touches ground are such that it lands on its feet.'
 b. 'For most pairs of situations s and healthy cats x in which x touches ground it holds that x lands on its feet in s.'

The reading (66.a) is easy to derive: A conditional with non-overt universal or generic quantifier embeds a simple sentence with an adverbial quantifier. This case combines the rule for *always,* or the generic quantifier for *if*-clauses, and the rule (43) for *usually*. In the case of (66.b). we have only one quantificational domain, over pairs, and the presuppositions of the apodosis are merged with the ones of the protasis. We have the same two types of readings in the following example, in which the discourse referents are introduced by indefinite NPs; I only specify the pair reading here:

(67) If an influential polìtician is on the board of trustees of a heálth organization, a well-informed nèwspaper reader usually knóws about it.

 Pair reading: 'Most pairs x, y, where x is an influential politician on the board of trustees of a health organization and y is a well-informed newspaper reader are such that y knows that x is on the board of trustees of the health organization.'

This suggests an analysis of quantificational adverbials along the following lines:

(68) c + Q(α, β)
= c + Q-many ways in which c can be accommodated to satisfy the presuppositions of "α and β" so that the result entails α are also ways that, when updated with α, entail β.

This leads to the following meaning rule for *usually* (cf. (64) for comparison). Here "α;β" stands for the composition of the context-change potential α with the context-change potential β, that is, for λc[c + α + β].

(69) USUALLY(α, β)
$= \lambda c\{g \in c | \text{MOST}(\{h | \{g\} \leq \{g\&h\}[\alpha;\beta] \wedge \exists k[k \in [\{g\&h\} + \alpha]]\}, \{h \mid \exists k[k \in [\{g\&h\} + \alpha + \beta]]\})$

In (67) the protasis and the apodosis will each supply the presupposition that a discourse referent is introduced (say, 1 and 2). The sentence will then quantify over increments h that map these two discourse referents to entities such that 1 is an influential politician and 2 is a well-informed newspaper reader (by accommodation), and that 1 is on the board of trustees of a health organization.

The assumption that the presuppositions of non-novel indefinites are accommodated can account for certain effects of accentuation on the availability of discourse referents as antecedents for pronouns. For example, von Fintel (1994) observes a contrast involving *unless*-conditionals that can be also observed with regular conditionals.

(70) a. Unless Pedro ówns a dònkey, he doesn't beat it.
b. *Unless Pedro owns a dónkey, he doesn't beat it.

(71) a. If Pedro doesn't ówn a dònkey, he doesn't beat it.
b. *If Pedro doesn't own a dónkey, he doesn't beat it.

The ungrammaticality of the (b) examples follows from standard assmptions if we assume that negation limits the life span of discourse referents introduced in their scope, and if we analyze *unless* as *if not*. The grammaticality of the (a) examples follows if we assume that *a donkey*, which is destressed, comes with a non-novelty presupposition that is, like other presuppositions, not affected by negation.

The assumption that the presuppositions of the apodosis get accommodated can be used to explain why we find backward anaphora as in the following examples (they are taken from Chierchia (1995), chapter 3; I have supplied the prosodic markers).

(72) If it_1 is overcóoked, a hàmburger_1 usually doesn't táste good.

(73) If a bòy$_1$ líes to her$_2$, a gìrl$_2$ won't trúst him$_1$ anymore.

Notice that the indefinite NPs in the main clause are necessarily deaccented. Consequently, they should be interpreted as non-novel indefinites. But then they become available as antecedents for the pronouns. For example, in the case of (73) the local input context {g} is accommodated to {g&h} at which point the following context change potential can be interpreted:

(74) $[\![[a\ boy]_{1,NN}\ lies\ to\ her_2]\!]; [\![[a\ girl]_{2,NN}\ doesn't\ trust\ him_1]\!]$
$= \lambda c\{g\in c \mid \forall g\in c[\text{BO}(g_1)] \wedge \forall g\in c[\text{FEM}(g_2)] \wedge \text{LT}(g_1, g_2)$
$\wedge \forall g\in c[\text{GI}(g_2)] \wedge \forall g[\text{MALE}(g_1)] \wedge \neg\text{TR}(g_2, g_1)\}$

By the pragmatic argument given in the discussion of examples (44.a,b), the input context must not contain the indices 1 and 2 yet (in this case definite NPs, *the boy* and *the girl*, would have been used instead). This means that these two indices must be accommodated, together with the presupposed information that 1 is anchored to a boy and 2 is anchored to a girl. That is, if {g}≤{g&h}[(74)], we have DOM(h) = {1, 2}, and h_1 is a boy and h_2 is a girl. The domain of quantification is further determined by using {g&h} as an input context for the protasis, which will restrict h further to cases in which h_1 lies to h_2. The quantification then states that most such increments h are such that {g&h} supports the truth of the protasis (which is trivially satisfied, due to conservativity) and of the apodosis, in this case, that h_2 is a girl (which is already guaranteed by accommodation) and that h_2 does not trust h_1.

Chierchia (1995), chapter 3, has treated examples like (72) and (73) by assuming reconstruction of the protasis into a position in which the subject c-commands its antecedent and hence can bind it. He works with reconstructed forms like the following (where GEN stands for the generic operator):

(75) a. a hamburger$_1$ [[usually [doesn't taste good]] if it$_1$ is overcooked]
b. a girl$_2$ [[GEN [won't trust him$_1$ anymore]] if a boy$_1$ lies to her$_2$]

A problem with this account is that it does not relate the availability of structures like (72) and (73) with the observed prosodic patterns[13]. The im-

---

[13] If anything, Chierchia's theory would predict that the NPs in question would NOT have to be deaccented. For (72) he argues for a structure as given in (75.a), and against the following structure, as this would result in a weak crossover violation after the *if*-clause is fronted from its original position:

(i) a hamburger$_1$ [[usually [t$_1$ doesn't taste good]] if it$_1$ is overcooked]

If *usually* is adjoined to IP, then *a hamburger* is interpreted IP-internally in (75.a). But if we want to make a structural distinction between topical NPs and non-topical NPs at all, then we will have to assume that topical NPs are interpreted IP-externally, that is, as in the problematic structure (i).

portance of prosody is particularly obvious when the full NP is in object position:

(76) a. If he_1 líes to her_2, a boy_1 risks lósing a gìrlfriend$_2$.
b. *If he_1 líes to her_2, a boy_1 risks losing a gírlfriend$_2$.

As an argument in favor of his reconstruction theory, Chierchia adduces the observation that sentences with a pronominal main clause subject are bad (cf. (77.a)). This is to be expected in his theory, as reconstruction would lead to a principle C violation:[14] (cf. (77.a)).

(77) a. *If a boy_1 lies to her_2, he_1 risks loosing a girlfriend$_2$.
b. *he_1 [risks [losing a girlfriend$_2$]] if a boy_1 lies to her_2]

However, such sentences need not be ungrammatical if the indefinite object NP is deaccented, which makes them similar in acceptability to (73).[15]

(78) If a boy líes to her, he risks lósing a gìrlfriend.

This comes as a surprise for Chierchia's theory, but can be explained in the theory developed here: An indefinite in the apodosis can be antecedent to a pronoun in the protasis only if it is non-novel, and non-novelty is marked by deaccenting.

8.1 Accommodation by Rule or by Principle

When we discussed the influence of the presuppositions in cases like *Usually, a green-eyed dòg is intélligent*, we proposed interpretation rules like (42), repeated here:

(79) USUALLY(β)
$= \lambda c\{g \in c \mid \text{MOST}(\{h \mid \{g\} \leq \{g\&h\}[\beta]\}, \{h \mid \{g\&h\} + \beta \neq \varnothing\})$

This says that most ways in which c can be accommodated to satisfy the presuppositions of β are also ways that support the truth of β. And when we discussed the influence of presuppositions in cases like *if a fármer owns a dònkey, he usually béats it*, we proposed interpretation rules like (69), represented here in the same format:

---

14 A standard donkey sentence like *If a boy lies to a girlfriend, he usually loses her* is fine because the protasis can be base-generated in situ. This option is impossible if the protasis contains pronouns with antecedents in the main clause.

15 The conditions under which backward anaphora are possible need further testing. While accentuation clearly plays a role along the lines suggested here, there seem to be additional factors that decrease grammaticality. Also, I have found relatively little agreement between speakers in judgements in preliminary testing.

(80) USUALLY(α, β)
$$= \lambda c\{g \in c \mid \text{MOST}(\{h \mid \{g\} \leq \{g\&h\}[\alpha;\beta] \wedge \exists k[k \in [\{g\&h\} + \alpha]]\},$$
$$\{h \mid \exists k[k \in \{\{g\&h\} + \alpha + \beta]]\})$$

That is, most ways in which c can be accommodated to satisfy the presuppositions of α and β so that the result entails α are also ways that, when updated with α, entail β.

How are (79) and (80) related to each other? Ideally, the former should be a simplified version of the latter, with an empty restrictor α. The empty context-change potential, for which I write 0, is the identity function $\lambda c[c]$, which leaves a context unchanged:

(81) $c + 0 = c$.

Another, even more important issue is the following:[16] Rules like (79) and (80) appear suspicious because they make explicit reference to accommodation. Usually, accommodation is seen as a repair strategy in case something goes wrong with the application of the interpretation rules. But here we have a semantic RULE that unabashedly appeals to repairs! It would clearly be preferably to have an interpretation rule for adverbial quantifiers that necessitates accommodation for independent reasons, following the general repair strategies outlined by Heim (1983) and, in more detail, van der Sandt (1992).

The rules presented in (79) and (80) can be reformulated in a way that their connection becomes evident, and which does not make explicit reference to accommodation. Let me assume the following principle for the semantic analysis for quantificational adverbials:

(82) c + Q(α, β)
= c + Q-many ways in which c entails α
are ways in which c entails α and β.

This principle does not make explicit reference to presuppositions. I will implement it by assuming a meaning of quantificational adverbials based on relations between an input assignment, a protasis context and an apodosis context. This is illustrated here with the operator MOST*, which will be employed for our analysis of *usually*:

(83) MOST*(g)(c′,c″) is defined iff $\forall h \in c'[g \subseteq h]$ and $\forall k \in c'' \exists h \in c'[h \subseteq k]$.
If defined, it holds iff $\text{MOST}(\{h \mid \exists k \in c'[g\&h = k]\}, \{h \mid \exists i \in c''[h \subseteq i]\})$

That is, MOST* is interpreted with respect to an input assignment g, and establishes a relation between two contexts c′ and c″, where the assignments in c′ are extensions of g, and the assignments in c″ are extensions of c′. The

[16] Thanks to Kai von Fintel, who got me thinking about this issue.

relation holds if most increments h by which the assignments in c′ differ from g are contained in the assignments in c″.

It is useful to introduce one last piece of notation. If c is a context and α a context-change potential, let c\α stand for {g∈c | {g}+α ≠ ∅}, that is, c\α reduces c to those assignments that support α, without changing those assignments. Now the interpretation of *usually* can be given as follows:

(84) c + USUALLY(α, β) = {g∈c | MOST*(g)({g}\α)({g}\[α;β])}

This captures (82) quite closely: If an input context c is updated with *usually α β*, then it will be restricted to those input assignments g for which it holds that most ways in which {g} supports α are also ways in which {g} supports α and β.

Now, if {g} supports α then {g}\α = {g}, and if {g} doesn't support α then {g}\α = ∅. In either case, there is no increment between the input assignment g and the assignments in {g} or ∅. This does not satisfy the requirements of MOST. A remedy in this situation is that presuppositions in α or β get accommodated in appropriate places. Let us first look at the presuppositions of the apodosis, β, in case the restrictor is empty. There are three points at which accommodation can take place: globally, intermediately, or locally (cf. van der Sandt 1992, Geurts 1995). I will write "ιc′[c≤c′[α]]" for the context that we get from c if the presuppositions of α are accommodated.

(85) c + USUALLY(0, β) = {g∈c | MOST*(g)({g}\0)({g}\[0;β])}
= {g∈c | MOST*(g)({g})({g}\β)}

presuppositions of β are not satisfied in {g}\β, which requires computation of {g}+β.

a. Global accommodation:
ιc′[c≤c′[β]] + USUALLY(0, β)
= {g∈ιc′[c≤c′[β]] | MOST*(g)({g})({g}\β)}

b. Local accommodation:
{g∈c | MOST*(g)({g})(ιc′[{g}≤c′[β]]\β)}

c. Intermediate accommodation:
{g∈c | MOST*(g)(ιc′[{g}≤c′[β]])(ιc′[{g}≤c′[β]]\β)}

Global accommodation, which changes the input context c to ιc′[c≤c′[β]], is of no use: The restrictor of the quantifier MOST* remains problematic. The same holds for local accommodation, in which the context in which β is interpreted within the apodosis is changed. But intermediate accommodation helps: The context of the protasis, {g}, is changed to the accommodated context ιc′[{g}≤c′[β]], and g and the elements in ιc′[{g}≤c′[β]] will differ if the accommodation involves the introduction of new discourse referents. (85.c) amounts to the following, according to (83):

(85) c′. $\{g \in c \mid \text{MOST}(\{h \mid \exists k \in \iota c'[\{g\} \leq c'[\beta]][g+h = k]\},$
$\{h \mid \exists i \in [\iota c'[\{g\} \leq c'[\beta]] \backslash \beta][h \subseteq i]\})\}$

That is, most increments h of g such that h satisfies the presuppositions of β are contained in the assignments that satisfy β. This is essentially what the original rule (79) said, now without explicit reference to accommodation.

In case the context-change potential β contains more than one non-novel indefinite NP, additional possibilities arise. It is sufficient that one non-novel indefinite is accommodated in the protasis; the other can be accommodated globally, leading to a specific interpretation, if we follow Cresti (1995). This is exemplified by the prominent reading of the following sentence:

(86) A frìend of mine$_{NN}$ usually is afráid of a dòg$_{NN}$.
'There is a friend of mine x, and for most dogs y: x is afraid of y.'

However, our way of representing presuppositions does not allow for such differential treatment. The context-change potential of the underlying sentence does not make a distinction between the two indefinites:

(87) A frìend of mine$_{NN,1}$ usually is afráid of a dòg$_{NN.2}$.
$\lambda c\{g \in c \mid \forall g \in c[\text{FR}(g_1)] \wedge \forall g \in c[\text{DG}(g_2)] \wedge \text{AF}(g_1, g_2)\}$

This can be only interpreted with contexts c that assign g_1 to a friend of mine, and g_2 to a dog. What we need here is a way to access presuppositions directly. Within the representational framework of DRT, this has been done by van der Sandt (1992) and Geurts (1995); an alternative, developed in Yeom (1998), makes use of a storage device. I will not implement direct access to presuppositions here.

Consider now cases in which the restrictor is not empty. Several possibilities arise: The presuppositions of the protasis could be accommodated locally or globally, and the presuppositions of the apodosis could be accommodated globally, intermediately, or locally. In order to satisfy the requirements for the quantifier, at least one presupposition has to be accommodated within the protasis. Also, if presuppositions of both the protasis and the apodosis are accommodated within the protasis, the order in which the accommodations are carried out may differ. Our original rule (80), in which both presuppositions are accommodated within the protasis, and the accommodation of the presuppositions of the protasis preceded the accommodation of the presuppositions of the apodosis, amounts to the following:

(88) a. $c + \text{USUALLY}(\alpha, \beta)$
$= \{g \in c \mid \text{MOST}^*(g)(\{g\} \backslash \alpha)(\{g\} \backslash [\alpha;\beta])\}$

b. Accommodation of $\{g\}$ to $\iota c''[\iota c'[\{g\} \leq c'[\alpha]] \leq c''[\beta]]$, = ①:
$c + \text{USUALLY}(\alpha, \beta)$
$= \{g \in c | \text{MOST}^*(g)(① \backslash \alpha)(① \backslash [\alpha;\beta])\}$
$= \{g \in c | \text{MOST}(\{h | \exists k \in ① \backslash \alpha [g+h = k]\}, \{h \mid \exists i \in [① \backslash [\alpha;\beta]][h \subseteq i]\})\}$

That is, most increments h of g such that h satisfies the presuppositions of α and β and where g+h actually makes α true are contained in assignments that make α and β true as well. This is what the original rule (80) said, without explicit mentioning of presuppositions. However, notice that (80) now represents just one of several possibilities of how to satisfy the requirement that a presupposition is accommodated in the protasis.

The interpretation rule (84) may still appear dubious. True, it does not mention accommodation, but it will never lead to an acceptable result except through the accommodation of presuppositions that introduce discourse referents. But I think that we have to live with that if we assume that adverbial quantification is indeed presupposition-sensitive. Also, one might raise objections against it for empirical reasons. After all, there are cases where we appear to quantify over constituents that are not introduced by non-novel indefinites:

(89) If a mán came in, he usually took off his hát.

In this sentence, *a man* bears accent and is presumably not a non-novel NP; still it appears to quantify over men than came in. However, I think that there is evidence that (89), with an eventive sentence as a protasis, does not quantify over men, but over situations; a man that came in twice would have to count twice. But then we can assume that the protasis clause is about situations, and that the discourse referent of the situation is introduced via accommodation

9.1 Conclusion

Let us summarize. In this paper I have argued for a novel type of indefinites, namely, non-novel indefinites. They presuppose that their discourse referent is given, but they differ from standard definites insofar as they do not come with a uniqueness presupposition, or some equivalent thereof. This is the reason why they are not used as anaphoric expressions. But they are used in the context of adverbial quantification. The domain of adverbial quantification is supplied by presuppositions, and non-novel indefinites supply their indices by this mechanism to the domain of quantification. This allows us to circumvent a problem that appears in previous accounts of indefinites in the scope of adverbial quantification in terms of focus sensitivity, the requantification problem. We have also discussed the influence of non-novel indefinites in the protasis of conditional clauses. We have argued that they have a similar function there, namely to restrict the domain of quantification, and we have discussed how non-novel indefinites in the protasis and the apodosis collaborate in this task.

References

Abusch, Dorit. 1994. The scope of indefinites. *Natural Language Semantics* 2, 83-136.

Bartels, Christine & Arthur Merin. 1997. Decision-theoretic semantics for intonation. Unpublished manuscript.

Beaver, David. 1994. Accommodating topics. P. Bosch & R. van der Sandt (eds.), *Focus and Natural Language Processing*, Vol. 3, 439-448. Schloss Wolfsbrunnen: IBM Deutschland Informationssysteme, Scientific Centre, Institute for Logic and Linguistics.

Beaver, David. 1992. *The kinematics of presupposition*. University of Amsterdam.

Berman, Stephen. 1987. Situation-based semantics for adverbs of quantification. In J. Blevins & A. Vainikka (eds.), *University of Massachusetts Occasional Papers 12*. Amherst: University of Massachusetts.

Chierchia, Gennaro. 1992. Anaphora and dynamic binding. *Linguistics and Philosophy* 15, 111-184.

Chierchia, Gennaro. 1995. *Dynamics of meaning. Anaphora, presupposition, and the theory of grammar*. Chicago: University of Chicago Press.

Condoravdi, Cleo. 1992. Weakly and Strongly Novel Noun Phrases. In Chris Barker & David Dowty (eds.), *Proceedings of the Second Conference on Semantics and Linguistic Analysis, Ohio State University*. Columbus, Ohio.

Condoravdi, Cleo. 1994. *Descriptions in context*. Ph.D. dissertation, Yale University. Published by Garland, New York.

Cresti, Diana. 1995. *Indefinite topics*. Ph.D. dissertation, Massachusetts Institute of Technology.

Dekker, Paul. 1993. Existential Disclosure. *Linguistics and Philosophy* 16, 561-588.

Diesing, Molly. 1992. *Indefinites*. Cambridge, MA: MIT Press.

Ebert, Karen. 1971. *Reference, Sprechsituation und die bestimmten Artikel in einem nordfriesischen Dialekt (Fering)*. Bredstedt: Nordfriisk Instituut.

Fodor, Jean D. & Ivan A. Sag. 1982. Referential and quantificational indefinites, *Linguistics and Philosophy*, 5, 355-398.

Geurts, Bart. 1995. *On Presupposing.* Ph.D. dissertation, University of Stuttgart.

Haiman, John. 1978. Conditionals are topics. *Language* 54, 564-589.

Heim, Irene. 1982. *The semantics of definite and indefinite noun phrases.* Ph.D. dissertation, University of Massachusetts at Amherst. Published by Garland, New York.

Heim, Irene. 1983. On the projection problem for presuppostions. M. Barlow, D. Flickinger & M. Wescoat (eds.), *West Coast Conference on Formal Linguistics*, Vol. 2, 114-125. Stanford Linguistics Association.

Heim, Irene. 1990. E-type pronouns and donkey anaphora. *Linguistics and Philosophy* 13, 137-179.

Jacobs, Joachim. 1991. Focus ambiguities. *Journal of Semantics* 8, 1-36.

Kadmon, Nirit. 1987. *On unique and non-unique reference and asymmetric quantification.* Ph.D. dissertation, University of Massachusetts at Amherst.

Kadmon, Nirit. 1990. Uniqueness. *Linguistics and Philosophy* 13, 273-324.

Kamp, Hans. 1981. A theory of truth and semantic representation. In J.A.G. Groenendijk, T.M.V. Janssen & M.B.J. Stokhof (eds.), *Formal Methods in the Study of Language,* 277-322. Amsterdam: Mathematical Centre Tracts 135.

Karttunen, Lauri. 1974. Presuppositions and linguistic context. *Theoretical Linguistics* 1, 181-194.

Karttunen, Lauri. 1976. Discourse referents. In J. McCawley (ed.), *Syntax and Semantics 7: Notes from the Linguistic Underground,* 363-385. New York: Academic Press.

Kasper, Walter. 1992. Presupposition, composition, and simple subjunctives. *Journal of Semantics* 9, 307-331.

Krifka, Manfred. 1992. A framework for focus-sensitive quantification. In Chris Barker & David Dowty (eds.), *Proceedings of the Second Conference on Semantics and Linguistic Analysis, Ohio State University.* Columbus, Ohio.

Krifka, Manfred. 1993. Focus and presupposition in dynamic interpretation. *Journal of Semantics* 10, 269-300.

Krifka, Manfred. 1996. Pragmatic strengthening in donkey sentences and plural predications. T. Galloway & J. Spence (eds.), *SALT 6,* 136-153. Rutgers University: CLC Publications, Morrill Hall, Cornell University.

Laca, Brenda. 1990. Generic objects: Some more pieces of the puzzle. *Lingua* 81, 25-46.

Ladd, D. Robert. 1980. *The structure of intonational meaning: Evidence from English.* Bloomington: Indiana University Press.

Ladusaw, William A. 1994. Thetic and categorical, stage and individual, weak and strong. M. Harvey & L. Santelmann (eds.), *Proceedings of SALT IV,* 220-229: Cornell University DMLL.

Lappin, Shalom. 1989. Donkey pronouns unbound. *Theoretical Linguistics* 15, 263-289.

Link, Godehard. 1983. The logical analysis of plurals and mass terms: A lattice-theoretical approach. In R. Bäuerle, C. Schwarze & A. von Stechow (eds.), *Meaning, use and the interpretation of language*, 303-323. Berlin, New York: Walter de Gruyter.

Newton, Brian. 1979. Scenarios, modality and verbal aspect in Modern Greek. *Language* 55, 139-167.

Percus, Orin. 1997. *Aspects of A.* Ph.D. dissertation, Massachusetts Institute of Technology.

Percus, Orin. 1998. A somewhat more definite article: Indefinites and quantificational variability. *Proceedings of SALT VIII.* CDC Publications, Cornell University.

Rooth, Mats. 1985. *Association with focus*. Ph.D. dissertation, University of Massachusetts at Amherst.

Rooth, Mats. 1987. Noun phrase interpretation in Montague Grammar, File Change Semantics, and Situation Semantics. In Peter Gärdenfors (ed.), *Generalized quantifiers. Linguistic and logical approaches.* 237-268. Dordrecht: Reidel.

Rooth, Mats. 1992. A theory of focus interpretation. *Natural Language Semantics* 1, 75-116.

Rooth, Mats. 1994. Association with focus or association with presupposition? Peter Bosch & Rob van der Sandt (eds.), *Focus and Natural Language Processing*, Vol. 2: Semantics, 389-398: IBM Deutschland Informationssysteme, Scientific Centre, Institute for Logic and Linguistics, Heidelberg.

Rooth, Mats. 1995. Indefinites, adverbs of quantification and focus semantics. In Gregory N. Carlson & Francis Jeffry Pelletier (eds.), *The Generic Book*, 265-291. Chicago: Chicago University Press.

Schubert, Lenhart K. & Jeffry Pelletier. 1989. Generically speaking; or, using Discourse Representation Theory to interpret generics. In Gennaro Chierchia, Barbara H. Partee & Raymond Turner (eds.), *Properties, types and meanings II: Semantic issues,* 193-268. Dordrecht: Kluwer.

Stalnaker, Robert. 1974. Pragmatic presuppositions. In M. Munitz & P. Unger (eds.), *Semantics and Philosophy*, 197-213. New York: New York University Press.

van der Sandt, Rob. 1992. Presupposition projection as anaphora resolution. *Journal of Semantics* 9, 332-377.

von Fintel, Kai-Uwe. 1994. *Restrictions on quantifier domains*. Ph.D. dissertation, University of Massachusetts at Amherst.

von Fintel, Kai-Uwe. 1997. A minimal theory of adverbial quantification. In Hans Kamp & Barbara Partee (eds), *Context-Dependence and Linguistic Meaning*, Vol. 1, 153-194. IMS, University of Stuttgart.

Yeom, Jae-Il. 1998. *A presuppositional analysis of specific indefinites. Common grounds as structured information states.* Ph.D. dissertation, University of Texas at Austin. Published by Garland, New York.

Yoon, Youngeun. 1996. Total and partial predicates and the weak and strong interpretation. *Natural Language Semantics* 4, 217-236.

2

Dependent Indefinites and Direct Scope

DONKA F. FARKAS

2.1 Introduction

This paper has two aims: (i) to put forth a direct theory of scope in which scopal dependencies are not reducible to structural configuration, and (ii) to present an account of the distribution and interpretation of a particular noun phrase type in Hungarian, namely indefinites whose D(eterminer) reduplicates. The discussion of the Hungarian facts rests on the distinctions drawn in the first part of the paper, and therefore supports the approach developed there. Indefinites with reduplicated Ds in Hungarian turn out to be further relevant to at least the following two theoretical considerations that are independent of the particulars of the scope theory one adopts: (a) the necessity of accommodating both situations and worlds in the model, and (b) the question of what drives noun phrase interpretation in general, and the interpretation of indefinites in particular. With respect to the first issue, recall that classical model theoretical semantics made use of worlds only; classical situation semantics replaced worlds with situations. The data to be discussed here provide an affirmative answer to the question of whether there are linguistic facts whose account necessitates a model that uses both these theoretical constructs. The second issue is part of a family of questions concerning the semantic typology of noun phrases, which have been central to much work in natural language semantics in the last two decades.

The paper is divided into three parts. The first lays out assumptions about the model and about quantification; the second presents the treatment of scope

*I wish to thank Cleo Condoravdi for comments and suggestions whose thoroughness went well beyond an editor's responsibility.

Logical Perspectives on Language and Information.
Cleo Condoravdi and Gerard R. Renardel de Lavalette.

and scopal dependencies I am proposing, and the third deals with D-reduplication in Hungarian. Section 2.2 reviews and extends material presented in Farkas 1993 and Farkas 1997.

2.1.1 General Assumptions

I assume that semantic interpretation involves two closely related levels of representation, syntactic structure, and semantic structure, or l(ogical) f(orm). The latter determines the satisfaction conditions of an expression relative to a context *c* and a model *M*. The satisfaction conditions of a complex expression are the result of conditions contributed by its parts, and their mode of combination.

The model *M* is, minimally, a triplet, $\langle W, U, V\rangle$, where *W* is a set of worlds, *U* is a set of entities, and *V* is a valuation function that assigns intensions to constants. Following Kratzer 1989, I take situations to be parts of worlds. I assume that worlds determine their own extensional model, where the set of situations in a world plays the role of worlds in intensional models. Thus, for every world $w \in W$, M_w is the extensional model of w such that $M_w = \langle S_w, U_w, V_w\rangle$, where S_w is the set of situations in w, U_w is the set of individuals in w, and V_w assigns values to constants in each $s \in S_w$.

Logical form, or semantic structure, is a structured set of conditions on the model. Its content is essentially the same as the information that appears in DRT boxes but since I will make minimal use of structure at this level the analysis is closer in spirit to Dynamic Predicate Logic (see Groenendjik and Stokhof 1991).

Expressions at this level, called lfs, are allowed to contain free variables. Most generally, the satisfaction conditions for an lf α are as in [1]:

[1] α is satisfied in w wrt *M* and *c* iff there is an assignment function *f* such that α is satisfied relative to *f* in w and *c*, to be abbreviated as $(\alpha)_{f,w,c}$.

What conditions α imposes depends on its form and content.

I turn now to a brief discussion of three properties of expressions at lf that are relevant for present purposes.

(a) Lfs contain sorted variables, also known as *discourse referents*. In what follows, the sorts we distinguish between are individual, situational and world variables. The latter two are special in that they may not function as arguments of predicates but only as parameters of evaluation. Individual variables themselves may be of different sorts—individual proper or kind-level, and atomic or group-level. Variables may be 'free,' in the sense that their quantificational force is determined by the satisfaction conditions of the expressions in which they appear, in the manner of Heim 1982, Chapter 3, and standard DRT. Crucially, no existential closure rules of any sort are needed. Indefinite, as well as definite noun phrases, contribute such free variables.

(b) The logical language in which lfs are expressed uses restricted variables in the sense that predicative expressions have the following two distinct functions: (i) a *main predicative function*, as in standard systems, and (ii) a *restrictive function*, in which case they specify the domain from which a variable may be given values. The main advantage of using restricted variables when dealing with natural language is that it allows one to distinguish the role of the D(escriptive) C(ontent) of noun phrases, which contribute restrictive expressions, from the role of main predicates. (For discussion, see McCawley 1980.)[1] Given (a) and (b), the components of the logical form of [2a] are as in [2b],

[2] a. A man left.
b. *x: man(x) leave(x)*

where *x* is an individual discourse referent, *man(x)* is the restrictive expression that restricts the allowed value assignments for *x* to individuals who are men, and *leave(x)* is the main predication. Restrictive expressions are separated from the variable they restrict by a semi-colon. The variable and its restrictive expression are contributed by the indefinite noun phrase; the main predication by the predicate. I follow Heim 1982 in assuming that definite and indefinite noun phrases differ only with respect to conditions concerning familiarity/novelty (and perhaps uniqueness) of the discourse referent introduced. Assuming that [2b] is interpreted relative to some world *w* and some context *c*, its satisfaction conditions are as in [3], where α is the expression in [2b]:

[3] α is satisfied in w wrt *M* and *c* iff there is an *f* such that $(\alpha)_{f,w,c}$. This condition is met iff (i) $f(x) \in V(man,w)$, and (ii) $f(x) \in V(leave,w)$.

The first part of the condition in [3] is contributed by the restrictive expression in [2b], and the second, by the main predication.

(c) Finally, lfs contain evaluation indices à la Kaplan, which specify the parameters with respect to which a particular expression has to be interpreted. Thus, the modal index of a predicative expression specifies in what worlds the expression has to be satisfied; the functional index of a variable specifies which function (or set of functions) assigns it values. Evaluation indices play a crucial role in the theory of scope to be presented below.

The use of the intermediate level of lf for present purposes is quite limited. It has not been dispensed with because it allows one to capture what is common to a variety of types of quantification in natural language. Specifically, I will refer crucially to the articulation of any quantificational expression into a R(estrictor), a N(uclear) S(cope) and a Q(uantifier). This is the crucial

[1] The effect of using restricted variables can also be achieved using sorted variables, as in Szabolcsi 1997a, where restrictive expressions specify sorts. The advantage of the present system is that it does not need infinite sorts, and that it uses sorts for the traditional task of distinguishing between coarser types.

structural consideration at this level that is relevant to the proposed approach to scope. Let us turn now to a more detailed discussion of quantification.

2.1.2 Quantification

Common to all types of quantification is that at lf it involves tripartite structures as in [4]:

[4] Q_v $[\ldots v \ldots]_R$ $[\ldots]_{NS}$

where the quantifier, *Q*, is subscripted for the variable it must bind. The expression in R, henceforth e_R, defines a set of cases, assumed to be non-empty, that form the domain of quantification; the expression in the NS, henceforth e_{NS}, is predicated of this set. In Aristotelean terms, the cases defined by R are the logical subject of the predication expressed in the NS. A welcome consequence of this assumption is that it entails that R is prior (or accessible) to the NS. The predication relation between R and the NS may in principle be distributive or collective. Most generally, the satisfaction conditions imposed by expressions of the form in [4] are as in [5]:

[5] A quantificational expression α is satisfied in w wrt *M* and *c* iff there is an *f* such that $(\alpha)_{f,w,c}$. This condition is met iff Q-many ways of satisfying e_R relative to f, w, c are ways of satisfying e_{NS} relative to f, w, c.

The 'ways of satisfying R' give us the cases that form the domain of quantification. The cases in question may be worlds, situations or individual assignments, depending on the type of quantification involved. Quantification over worlds is illustrated in [6], by a modal sentence and an afactual conditional.

[6] a. Martin may be sick.
b. If Martin were sick, he'd be in bed.

Quantification over situations is illustrated in [7], by a sentence involving adverbs of quantification, and by a factual conditional,

[7] a. Often/Always, when Martin is hungry, he is grouchy.
b. If Martin is hungry, he is grouchy.

Quantification over individuals is illustrated in [8] by a sentence involving D(eterminer)-Quantification:

[8] Every student left.

The details of the satisfaction conditions will differ depending on the type of quantification involved. Each type will be briefly discussed below.

Quantification over individuals

This type of quantification is triggered by D-quantification. The quantifier in this case is subscripted by the variable introduced by the quantificational noun phrase that contributes it. The general form of such expressions is as in [9]:

[9] Q_x [... x ...]$_R$ [...]$_{NS}$

A way of satisfying R in the case of quantification over individuals amounts to choosing an evaluation function that assigns to x a value that meets its DC condition. Thus, when one checks whether some function f satisfies e_R one has to consider alternative ways of assigning values to x, i.e., one has to consider assignment functions f' that assign to x values that meet the DC contributed by the quantificational noun phrases.

I assume here that assignment functions assign values to all variables. The notion of a function f' being a variant of another function f with respect to a set of variables X is defined in [10]:

[10] *Variant of a function*
A function f' is a variant of a function f with respect to a (possibly empty) set of variables X iff f' agrees with f on all assignments except possibly for the variables in X. If X is empty, f' is a trivial variant of f. The function f is the *domain function* for f', and X is the *variant set* of f'.

The expression $f'(f/x)$ will be used to indicate that f' is a variant of f and x is the only element in the variant set of f'.

Returning now to [9], in checking whether the expression in R is satisfied relative to f, w, c one has to check whether it is satisfied relative to a set of functions F' such that every $f' \in F'$ is such that $f'(f/x)$ and $f'(x)$ meets the DC condition. When one looks at ways of satisfying e_{NS} relative to f, w, c one has to consider a set of functions F'' such that every $f'' \in F''$ is a variant of a different function in F' and $(e_{NS})_{f'',w,c}$. An expression of the form in [9] then is satisfied relative to f, w, c iff Q-many functions in F' have variant functions in F''. The condition is stated in [11]:

[11] Let α be an expression of the form in [9]. α is satisfied in w wrt M and c iff there is an assignment function f such that $(\alpha)_{f,w,c}$. This condition is met iff there are Q-many functions $f'(f/x)$ such that $(e_R)_{f',w,c}$, such that each f' has a (possibly trivial) variant f'' such that $(e_{NS})_{f'',w,c}$.[2]

According to [11], [9] is satisfied in w, c iff there is an assignment function f such that Q-many variants of f that satisfy R in w, c have variants that satisfy the NS in w, c.

Let us call the function (or set thereof) that has to satisfy an expression e the base function of e. Taking α to be [9], the initial function f is the base function for α; the functions in F' are the base functions for e_R and the functions in F'' are the base functions for e_{NS}. The functions in F'' *depend* on the functions

[2]Evaluation functions here play the role of sequences in Heim 1982.

in F' because they are defined by associating to every $f' \in F'$ a function f''. The functions F' are determined by R; their dependents, F'', are determined by the NS.

To exemplify, the lf of [8] is as in [12], and its satisfation conditions are as in [13], under the assumption that modal indices are set to *w*, the default value:

[12] $\forall_x$ [*x: student(x)*]$_R$ [*leave(x)*]$_{NS}$

[13] [12] is satisfied in *w* wrt *M* and *c* iff there is some *f* with the following property: every $f'(f/x)$ such that $f'(x) \in$ *V(student,w)* has the property of having a trivial variant f'' such that $f''(x) \in$ *V(leave,w)*.

The conditions in [13] require that every individual in the set of students be in the set of individuals who left.

Note that the variable *x* must be in the variant set of f' because *x* is contributed by the quantificational noun phrase *every student*, and therefore Q is subscripted by *x*. The contribution of noun phrases whose determiner is *every* to the lf of the expressions in which they appear is the following: (i) a universal quantifier; (ii) an individual variable in R subscripted to (and therefore bound by) Q. This amounts to requiring *x* to be in the variant set of f'; (iii) the specification that the predication relation between R and the NS be distributive;[3] (iv) a restrictive expression on the variable contributed by the DC of the noun phrase.[4]

Note that the complex satisfaction conditions in [13] extend the general schema in [5], which in turn extends the schema in [1]. They are compositionally derived from the contribution of the components of the expression in [12]: the NS constrains its base functions to those which assign to *x* a value in the set of people who left; R constrains its base functions to those which assign to *x* a value in the set of students. What the base functions are and how they are related is determined by the fact that [12] is an instance of [9], and therefore its conditions are determined by [11], and by the fact that *x* is contributed by a noun phrase whose D is *every*.

Concerning distributivity, I follow Roberts 1991 in treating it as a mode of predication involving universal quantification over the parts of the logical subject, the key, in the terminology of Gil 1995. The key then contributes R in the universal quantification structure associated with distributivity. Following Kamp and Reyle 1993 I take it that plural or coordinate noun phrases may play the role of key contributors in the distributive readings of sentences such as [14]:

---

[3]I assume that the universal quantifier in [12] specifies both universal force (namely that *all* relevant assignments have to be considered) and distributivity (namely that the Restrictor is to serve as 'key' and the NS as 'share').

[4]Following Szabolcsi 1997a, I am also assuming that such noun phrases introduce a set-level referent, namely the set of individuals who meet the DC condition but since this is not relevant to present purposes, it will be ignored in what follows.

[14] The children/Bill and Sue carried the suitcase upstairs.

Following Roberts 1991, I assume that the subject noun phrase in the distributive reading of [14] introduces an i-sum referent whose i-parts form the domain over which the distributive predication ranges. The predicate distributes over each i-part of its logical subject. Any argument of a predicate may in principle contribute the key over which the predication distributes.

Under these assumptions, the distributive/collective interpretation is a function of the interpretation of the predication relation between the logical subject and the logical predicate. Whether the predication relation is understood as distributive or collective may depend on both properties of the logical subject and properties of the predicate. The choice between distributive and collective predication may be forced by properties of the logical subject (the choice of *every*, or *each* forces a distributive reading), or by the choice of predicate (the predicate *gather* forces a collective reading), or it may be left open, as in [14] above.[5] With respect to distributivity, noun phrases fall into the following two categories: (i) obligatory key introducers: noun phrases whose D is *every* or *each*; (ii) optional key introducers: plural and coordinate noun phrases, noun phrases whose determiner is *all*, and cardinal noun phrases. Note that the noun phrases in (ii) pattern together with respect to the difficulty with which they take inverse scope over the noun phrases in (i).

Quantification over worlds

The interpretation of modalized sentences and afactual conditionals involves quantification over worlds. In this case Q is subscripted by a world-level variable that ranges over $W' \subseteq W$; W' is the domain over which one quantifies. In the case of modalized sentences W' is the set of worlds in what Kratzer 1980 calls the modal base. I follow Kratzer in assuming that the worlds that form the modal base are determined by the context and the particular modal used. The quantifier is universal or existential depending on the choice of modal. The lfs of such expressions are satisfied if the NS (the lf in the scope of the modal) is satisfied relative to one or all $w' \in W'$.

With afactual conditionals W' is established on the basis of the antecedent, which contributes the expression in R. The general form of such expressions is as in [15], where e_R is the lf of the antecedent, and e_{NS} is the lf of the consequent:

[5] With respect to the difference between *every* and *each*, I assume that the former contributes a universal quantifier and the requirement that the predication relation be distributive; the latter is a key introducer, whose universal force is merely a consequence of the fact that distributivity involves universal quantification. This explains the contrast between (i) and (ii) below:

(i) Almost every student left.

(ii) *Almost each student left.

For discussion, see Vendler 1967, and more recently, Beghelli and Stowell 1997.

[15] $Q_{w'}$ $[e_R]_{w'}$ $[e_{NS}]_{w'}$

Taking this expression to be α in [5], its satisfaction conditions relative to w and c require there to be an f such that $(\alpha)_{f,w,c}$, i.e., Q-many ways of satisfying e_R relative to f, w, c must be ways of satisfying e_{NS} relative to f, w, c. A way of satisfying e_R relative to f, w, c amounts to satisfying e_R relative to f, w', c, where w' is close to w.[6] Thus, when one checks whether $(e_R)_{f,w,c}$ one has to consider whether $(e_R)_{f,w',c}$. An expression of the form in [15] then is satisfied relative to *f,w,c* iff Q-many worlds w' close to w such that $(e_R)_{f,w',c}$ are such that $(e_{NS})_{f,w',c}$. The satisfaction conditions for expressions of the form in [15] are given in [16].

[16] Let α be of the form in [15]. α is satisfied in w, c iff there is an f such that $(\alpha)_{f,w,c}$. This condition is met iff Q-many worlds w' close to w such that $(e_R)_{f,w',c}$ are such that $(e_{NS})_{f,w',c}$.

In conditionals, the default quantifier is universal. The claim one makes when asserting an afactual conditional then is that every appropriate world that satisfies the antecedent is such that it satisfies the consequent. The lf of an afactual conditional is of the form in [17], where lf_a and lf_q stand for the lfs contributed by the antecedent and the consequent, respectively.

[17] $\forall_{w'}$ $[lf_a]_{w'}$ $[lf_q]_{w'}$

R here, as always, contains an expression that determines the 'cases' that form the domain of quantification, and the NS contains an expression that determines what has to be true in those cases. The crucial difference is that the cases involved are now worlds rather than individuals. For a function *f* to satisfy R it has to satisfy the conditions in lf_a at every appropriate w'; in order for *f* to satisfy the NS, it has to satisfy the conditions in lf_q at the same worlds w'. The satisfaction conditions of [17] are as in [18]:

[18] [17] is satisfied in w wrt *M* and c iff there is a function *f* with the following property: for every $w' \in W$ such that w' is close to w such that $(lf_a)_{f,w',c}$, $(lf_q)_{f,w',c}$.

The condition in [18] is a particular case of [16], which in turn is an elaboration of the schema in [5]; the cases that form the domain of quantification in this instance are worlds that meet the condition contributed by the antecedent.

Note that the main predications of both the antecedent and the consequent are interpreted at the worlds w', rather than the initial world *w*. By the same token, the main predication of a modalized sentence is interpreted at the worlds introduced by the modal. This is indicated in [17] and [15] by the subscripted w' on R and the NS.

---

[6] The details of the closeness relation will not concern us here.

To exemplify, consider [19a], and its simplified lf, [19b].[7] The satisfaction conditions of [19b] are given in [19c].

[19] a. If Martin were sick, he'd be in bed.
b. $\forall_{w'}$ $[sick(m)]_{w'}$ $[(in\text{-}bed(m)]_{w'}$
c. The expression in [19b] is satisfied in *w* wrt *M* and *c* iff there is an assignment function *f* with the following property: for every $w' \in W$ that is close to *w* such that $(sick(m))_{f,w',c}$, $(in\ bed(m))_{f,w',c}$.

Since in order to simplify the representation I am assuming that both the proper name and the pronoun contribute constants, the choice of *f* is irrelevant, and [19b] will be satisfied in *w* iff every world w' that is close to *w* such that $V(m,w') \in V(sick,w')$, is such that $V(m,w') \in V(in\text{-}bed,w')$. Note that one arrives at this complex condition starting from the components of [19b]: the NS constrains the base function *f* to be such that it satisfies lf_q relative to a set of worlds W' and a context *c*. What that set of worlds is is determined by R to be the worlds w' such that $(lf_a)_{f,w',c}$. Just as before, R here defines the set of 'cases' to be considered, only now we have a set of worlds, rather than a set of individuals (given by a set of assignment functions), and the NS predicates something of these cases. With individual quantification, R introduces a set of assignment functions and the NS is evaluated relative to these functions. With quantification over worlds, R introduces a set of worlds W', and the NS is evaluated with respect to the worlds in this set. As a result, the main predications of both e_R and e_{NS} in afactual conditionals are evaluated at the worlds in W', rather than the initial world *w*.

Let us call the world (or set thereof) that has to satisfy the conditions of some lf *e* the base world(s) of *e*. Taking α = [19b], the base world for α is the initial world *w*; the base worlds for lf_a and lf_q are the worlds in W' introduced by R.

Quantification over situations

Quantification over situations is dealt with on a par with quantification over worlds, except that evaluation is done with respect to an extensional model M_w, where S_w, the situations in *w*, play the role of *W* in intensional models. Sentences involving adverbs of quantification are similar to modalized sentences in that they involve quantification over a contextually determined subset of S_w. Factual conditionals are treated on a par with afactual ones: the antecedent contributes the expression in R, and it serves to define the set of situations that form the domain of quantification; the consequent contributes the NS, evaluated with respect to situations that extend the situations in R.[8] Quantifiers now

[7] To keep things simple discourse referents have been ignored.

[8] Following Kratzer 1989, I am assuming that the relation 'part of' is defined for situations, and that one considers minimal situations when evaluating sentences involving quantification over situations.

are subscripted with situation-level variables. The lf of a factual conditional is of the form in [20a], and its satisfaction conditions are as in [20b].

[20] a. $\forall_{s'}$ $[lf_a]_{s'}$ $[lf_q]_{s''}$

b. The expression in [20a] is satisfied in *w* wrt *M* and *c* iff there is an assignment function *f* with the following property: for every $s' \in S_w$ such that $(lf_a)_{f,s',c}$, there is a situation $s'' \in S_w$ such that s' is part of s'' and $(lf_q)_{f,s'',c}$.

The situations s'' depend on the situations s' in the same way that the functions in F'' depend on those in F' in the case of individual quantification. Whether the conditional is factual or afactual is indicated by the verbal morphology in the antecedent and the consequent.

To sum up, quantificational statements involve predication over the 'cases' in the domain, which are determined by the expression in R. The NS expresses the predicate. Morpho-lexical and syntactic information determines (more or less unambiguously) what type of quantification is involved as well as which surface constituent affects which component of the quantificational expression.

Common to all types of quantification is that they involve the introduction of a set of evaluation parameters: assignment functions, worlds or situations, depending on whether the domain of quantification is made up of individuals, worlds or situations. The three types of quantification discussed above fall into two natural classes, *extensional* and *intensional*, depending on whether one stays within the limits of a single world or not. Extensional quantification, in turn, may be *individual* or *situational* depending on whether the domain of quantification is made up of individuals or situations.

2.2 A direct account of scope

2.2.1 Background

I am assuming here a semantic notion of scope defined in [21]:

[21] An expression α is in the semantic scope of an expression β iff the interpretation of α is affected by the interpretation of β.

There are three notions of scope: (a) the scope of a variable, which is a matter of the properties of the function that evaluates it; (b) the scope of a quantifier (with respect to a variable), which is a matter of which variables can be interpreted as co-varying with the variable bound by the Q; (c) the scope of the DC of a noun phrase, which is a matter of which worlds or situations the DC has to be satisfied in.

As will be clear from the discussion below, all three kinds of scope are seen as involving the question of fixing evaluation parameters for particular expressions. The effect of β on α mentioned in [21] above concerns the question of whether or not the evaluation of α is done with respect to parameters introduced by β. A question of particular interest to linguists is that of limits on inverse scope (see Farkas 1981, Fodor and Sag 1982, Abusch 1994, Reinhart 1995, Beghelli and Stowell 1997, Winter 1997). The issue concerns the relation between semantic and syntactic scope. An expression e_1 has *direct scope* over an expression e_2 iff e_2 is in the semantic scope of e_1 and e_1 c-commands e_2 at surface structure.[9] An expression e_1 has *inverse scope* over an expression e_2 iff e_2 is in the semantic scope of e_1 and e_2 c-commands e_1 at surface structure. Taking syntactic scope to be determined by c-command, 'direct scope' describes cases when semantic and syntactic scope are parallel, and 'inverse scope' describes cases when they are not. I turn now to a brief review of the main empirical facts that need to be accounted for.

a. Scope of a variable

Let us first consider the case of a variable introduced by an ordinary indefinite.[10]

[22] a. Every student speaks an Indo-European language.
b. Every critic who had praised a Czech movie from the sixties felt vindicated.
c. If Martin had seen a Czech movie from the sixties, he would have understood the joke.

These sentences are scopally ambiguous: the indefinites in [22a,b] can be interpreted either as co-varying with the variable introduced by the universal noun phrase, in which case the scope relation is direct, or they can be interpreted as not co-varying, in which case the indefinite is said to have inverse scope relative to the universal.[11] The indefinite in [22c] can be interpreted as co-varying with the worlds that form the domain of quantification (direct scope), or it may be interpreted as not so co-varying (inverse scope). Under the former interpretation, the claim one makes is that any appropriately chosen world in which it is the case that there is a Czech movie from the sixties that Martin had seen is a world in which Martin understood the joke. Under the latter interpretation, the claim one makes is that any appropriately chosen world in which it is the case that Martin had seen some particular Czech movie (*Shop on Main Street*, for instance), is a world in which Martin understood the joke. Under this interpretation the choice of movie is fixed relative to the worlds in question.

[9] An expression e_1 c-commands an expression e_2 iff all the branching nodes that dominate e_1 also dominate e_2.

[10] We only deal with ordinary indefinites until Section 2.3, where we examine in detail the case of one extraordinary indefinite.

[11] Note that in this case the universal is not within the semantic scope of the indefinite according to [21]. Semantic scope and syntactic scope are not parallel here in the sense that the indefinite is within the syntactic scope of the universal but outside its semantic scope.

As discussed in Farkas 1981, Fodor and Sag 1982, as well as more recent work, the ambiguity of examples such as [22b,c] falsifies the claim, made initially in Rodman 1976, that inverse scope is sensitive to syntactic islands. Rodman's claim is of particular interest because, if true, it would provide convincing evidence in favor of a movement analysis of scope, as proposed initially in May 1977, where a syntactic rule of Q(uantifier) R(aising) is introduced, whose effect is to obliterate inverse scope at the level of Logical Form. If inverse scope is the result of a syntactic rule that moves noun phrases at Logical Form to a position from which they c-command their scope, inverse scope out of a syntactic island should not be possible, just as surface wh-movement is not possible out of such constructions. The discussion in Farkas 1981 showed that there is no such parallelism between inverse scope of indefinites and overt syntactic movement. The empirical generalization concerning the scopal behavior of ordinary indefinites is given in [23]:

[23] *Generalization A*
A variable introduced by an indefinite may be in an inverse scope relation with any expression that c-commands the indefinite.

This freedom of scope of indefinites is highly unusual. Fodor and Sag 1982 attempt to reduce it to bounded scope by claiming that indefinites are ambiguous between a quantificational and a referential reading. Under the former reading, the inverse scope of indefinites is bounded; under the latter, they are scopeless elements whose interpretation is equivalent to that of widest scope indefinites. This attempt is untenable, however, because of the existence of intermediate readings of examples such as [24]:[12]

[24] Every candidate commented on every essay that mentioned a major 19th century poet.

The reading we are interested in is one where poets co-vary with candidates but not with essays. This is the case when the task of every candidate was to choose some poet and then comment on every essay that mentions that poet. Under this reading the indefinite scopes out of its island and yet it cannot be referential, given that it does not have widest scope. The generalization in [23] is therefore valid and needs to be captured. Since it has been established since Ross 1967 that no movement rule is unbounded, I conclude that the inverse scope of indefinites should not be accounted for by such a rule.

Let us now turn to the case of a variable introduced by a noun phrase whose determiner is *every*. The question here is whether such a variable can be interpreted as co-varying with another variable. Consider the examples in [25]:

[12]Such examples, and their importance to Fodor and Sag's claim were first discussed in Farkas 1981. Kratzer 1998 calls their existence into question by claiming that the problematic intermediate reading arises only in the presence of a bound pronoun in the second universal, but [24], as well as examples discussed in Farkas 1981, show that this is not so.

[25] Every$_1$ child read every$_2$ poem.
Every$_1$ child ate every$_2$ apple.

These sentences are ambiguous between an 'independent' reading, in which the sets of children and poems/apples are established independently, in which case the claim made is that every element of the set of children is in the read/eat relation with every element of the set of poems or apples, and a dependent reading, in which the domain of the second quantifier is dependent on the first. Under the dependent reading, every child is associated with a set of poems/apples and the claim made is that every child is in the read/eat relation with every element of *that* set. Because of the nature of eating and apples, the independent reading is unnatural for the second sentence but since the sentence is not judged as absurd, I conclude that the dependent reading exists and has to be accounted for.

b. Scope of the quantifier
The question I turn to next is that of how far the influence of a quantifier can reach, i.e., the question of when a variable can co-vary with the variable bound by the quantifier. Consider the contrast between the scopally ambiguous [26a], and the scopally unambiguous [26b,c]:

[26] a. A member of our group attended every rally.
b. A member of our group said that every candidate will win.
c. If three relatives of mine die, I will inherit a house. (Ruys 1992)

The ambiguity of [26a] shows that *every* may have scope over a c-commanding clause-mate indefinite. The fact that [26b] lacks a reading in which members of our group co-vary with candidates shows that the inverse scope of *every* is clause-bounded. The fact that [26c] lacks a reading according to which if either one of three relatives of mine die I inherit, shows that the inverse scope of the universal implicit in distributive readings is clause-bounded as well.[13] The relevant empirical generalization is given in [27]:

[27] *Generalization B*
A quantifier can be in an inverse scope relation only with a c-commanding expression in the same clause.[14]

Note that the clause-boundedness of distributive noun phrases follows from the treatment of distributivity as involving universal quantification over the key. Thus, if distributive noun phrases such as *the/three students* in a sentence like

[13]The clause-boundedness of distributive universals was first noted in Farkas 1981, where it is pointed out that neither the scoping freedom of indefinites, nor the scoping boundedness of distributives is sensitive to syntactic islands.

[14]For a discussion of whether the relevant notion is clause-boundedness or semantic co-argumenthood, and of cases where the universal has inverse scope over a non-clausemate, see Farkas and Giannakidou 1996.

The/three students sang are taken to contribute a universal quantifier binding the variable associated with the noun phrase and a Restrictor, the functional parameter introduced by these noun phrases is limited in the same way as that of noun phrases whose determiner is *every*.

c. Scope of the DC

The issue here concerns the world(s) in which the DC condition of a noun phrase is supposed to hold of the referent. In [28], for instance, the italicized condition may be interpreted as holding in *w*, in which case the speaker is committed to it but Professor Talc may not be, or the condition is to be interpreted with respect to the worlds introduced by *believe*, in which case Prof. Talc is committed to it but the speaker need not be. Under the former reading the description has wide scope with respect to *believe*; under the latter, it has narrow scope.

[28] Prof. Talc believes that a/every *remarkable student in History 101* is an idiot.

The fact that [29] exhibits the same ambiguity as [28] with respect to the scope of the description leads to the conclusion in [30].

[29] Prof. Talc believes that the woman who married a *remarkable student in History 101* married an idiot.

[30] *Generalization C*
The DC of a noun phrase may be in an inverse scope relation with any expression that c-commands the noun phrase.

Given [27] and [30] we correctly predict that the scope of the quantifier contributed by a noun phrase whose D is *every* may be different from the scope of its DC. Consider [31]:

[31] A reporter thought that a former government official believes that *every person in this room* has had contact with the enemy.

As predicted by [27], this sentence does not have a reading in which government officials co-vary with persons in this room, i.e., the scope of the variable contributed by the indefinite cannot be within the scope of the universal quantifier contributed by the italicized noun phrase. As predicted by [30], on the other hand, the DC of this noun phrase may be interpreted as being the speaker's description and not the reporter's, in which case the DC has scope over both *think* and *believe*.

An adequate treatment of scope has to account for the generalizations in [23], [27] and [30] in an explanatory way. An approach that relies on syntactic movement fails to achieve this goal. The questions that remain unanswered in such a theory are the following: (i) Why is the movement needed to account for the scope of indefinite noun phrases unbounded? (ii) Why is the movement needed to account for the scope of the quantifier clause-bounded? (iii) Why is the movement needed to account for the scope of the DC unbounded? Moreover, the double scope of the universal in [31] shows that the scopal properties of noun phrases cannot be accounted for by a movement rule that affects the D and the DC together.

2.2.2 Account

In what follows I propose a theory of scope which has the following characteristics: (a) It is not structure-driven in the sense that structure (at all levels) underdetermines the scopal fate of an expression. Consequently, no movement operations have to be resorted to in order to account for inverse scope readings. (b) The theory is indexical in the sense that scopal dependencies between expressions are captured directly as relations between their evaluation indices. (c) The generalizations in [23], [27] and [30] are accounted for. The three types of scope identified above will be treated in turn.

a. Scope of the variable

(i) The scope of a variable with respect to a D-quantifier

Let α be a quantificational expression based on a D-quantifier whose base function is *f*, and let *x* be a variable introduced by an indefinite. The question of the scope of *x* wrt the quantifier reduces to the following possibilities: (a) *x* is 'bound by the quantifier', in which case the value of *x* is fixed by the functions in F', the base functions of the expression in R. In this case *x* is in the variant set of f': for every $f' \in F'$, $f'(f/x)$; (b) *x* is bound by 'NS-level existential closure', which means that the value of *x* is fixed by the functions in F'', the base functions of the expression in the NS. In this case *x* is in the variant set of f'': for every $f'' \in F''$, $f''(f'/x)$; (c) *x* has wide scope with respect to the quantifier, which means that the value of *x* is fixed by *f* or some other assignment function. In this case *x* is not in the variant set of either f' or f''.

In the approach I propose scopal dependencies are represented directly as dependencies between evaluation indices of expressions. In particular, I assume that at lf variables are accompanied by functional indices, which are evaluation parameters specifying which functions assign values to the variable in question. What the functional index of a particular variable is depends on the type of noun phrase introducing the variable, as well as on the properties of the expression the variable is part of. Scope ambiguity arises when there are several possible index choices. Certain indexings result in dependencies and others do not. Morphological and lexical information on the D as well as the head noun may constrain index choices. Thus, a variable introduced by a noun phrase whose D is *every* must be bound by the Q contributed by the D, i.e., it must be in the variant set of f'. Crucially now, (in)definites impose no special condition on the evaluation function of the variables they introduce. As a result, these variables may be indexed by any accessible function, a notion to be discussed shortly. This is what explains why such noun phrases are particularly prone to scopal ambiguity.[15] The choice between several accessible functional indices for a variable is similar in nature to the choice between several potential antecedents for a pronoun.

Before we turn to the discussion of the all-important question of accessibility of indices, let us exemplify with a variable introduced in the NS, where [32b,c] are the two lfs associated to the sentence in [32a]. Note that the only difference is in the index choice for *y*.

[32] a. Every student speaks an Indo-European language.
b. *Narrow scope:*
$\forall_x$ [$x_{f'}$: *student(x)*]$_{f'}$ [$y_{f''}$: *I-E lang.(y) speak(x,y)*]$_{f''}$
c. *Wide scope:*
$\forall_x$ [$x_{f'}$: *student(x)*]$_{f'}$ [y_f: *I-E lang.(y) speak(x, y)*]$_{f''}$

The f' and f'' indices on R and NS respectively indicate that the former are the base functions for the Restrictor, and the latter, for the NS. I assume that the base function for the whole expression in both [32b] and [32c] is *f*. The index f' on *x* indicates that *x* is given values by the functions f', i.e., that *x* is in the variant set of f'. The choice of f' as an index for *x* is forced by the fact that *x* is a variable contributed by a noun phrase whose D is *every*. Such variables must be bound by the quantifier introduced by their noun phrases. The variable *y*, on the other hand, is introduced by an indefinite and therefore its functional index is free. Choosing f'' in [32b] makes *y* be in the variant set of f''. This means that the functions f'' are variants of the functions f' with respect to *y*, and therefore languages will co-vary with students. Because of the relation between f' and f'', a relation imposed by the fact that the former are base functions of R, and the latter, of the NS, this indexing results in the values of *y* being dependent on the values of *x*. Choosing *f* in [32c] makes *y* be evaluated by the initial function *f*, i.e., both functions f' and f'' assign the same value to *y* as f does. As a result, *y* will be independent of *x* and languages will not co-vary with students. The satisfaction conditions for the narrow scope reading are given in [33], and for the wide scope reading in [34]:

[33] [32b] is satisfied in *w* wrt *M* and *c* iff there is a function *f* with the following property: for every function $f'(f/x)$ such that $f'(x) \in$ *V(student,w)*,

[15] As mentioned before, the crucial difference between definites and indefinites has to do with a familiarity/uniqueness condition associated with the referent of the former. As a result, the context must meet a rather special set of conditions in order for a definite to have narrow scope but once these conditions are met, definites exhibit narrow scope readings. Thus, assuming that the context made clear that the subjects in a particular experiment where each faced with a red and a black button, (i) is most naturally understood with the definite having narrow scope with respect to the universal:

(i) Every subject pressed the red button.

there is a variant $f''(f'/y)$ such that $f''(y) \in$ *V(I-E lang.,w)* and $\langle f'(x),\ f''(y)\rangle \in$ *V(speak,w)*.

[34] [32c] is satisfied in *w* wrt *M* and *c* iff there is a function *f* with the following property: for every function $f'(f/x)$ such that $f'(x) \in$ *V(student,w)*, there is a trivial variant f'' such that *f(y)* $\in$ *V(I-E lang.,w)* and $\langle f'(x),\ f(y)\rangle \in$ *V(speak,w)*.

Because the value of *y* co-varies with the value of *x* in [33], *y* will be said to *depend* on *x* and *x* will be said to be the *domain variable* for *y*.

Note that these two conditions are elaborations of the schema in [11]. Thus, the existence of f' and f'' and their relation is a consequence of the fact that [32b] and [32c] contain expressions that quantify over individuals. The difference between them is a matter of whether *y* is in the variant set of f'' or not. The complex conditions in [33] and [34] are determined from the conditions imposed by the components of [32b] and [32c].

The scopal fate of an (in)definite is determined by the fact that this type of noun phrase imposes no special conditions on its evaluation parameters, which obey the condition in [35]:

[35] The evaluation parameters of expressions introduced by (in)definites may be any of the accessible parameters.

Consequently, the functional index of a variable introduced by such a noun phrase is free, and therefore it may be set to any function accessible to that variable. The limits of what is possible are set by the content of the accessibility relation. Recall that I am assuming that expressions at lf have evaluation parameters that specify (minimally) the world(s), situations, context and assignment function(s) relative to which the expression is to be evaluated. Let us call these parameters the *base parameters* of e, and let us assume the simple accessibility relation in [36] below:

[36] *Accessibility relation*
The base parameters of an expression *e* are accessible to any subpart of *e*.

Note that the main use of the level of lf made here involves the structure of expressions at this level, since it is the articulation of expressions at lf that determines index accessibility.

Taking now the special case when the parameter we are interested in is the functional index, and the relevant subpart of *e* is a variable in *e*, the relevant accessibility relation for functional indices on variables is [37].

[37] The base function of an expression *e* is accessible to any variable in *e*.

Let α be a quantificational expression made up of e_R and e_{NS}. A variable in either e_R or e_{NS} is in α; a variable in e_R is not in e_{NS} and vice versa. Let *x* be a variable introduced by an indefinite in α, and let f be the base function of α. The scoping possibilities for x allowed by [37] are the following: (a) x may be indexed by f, since f is accessible to any variable in α. This gives us the *wide scope* reading of x with respect to the quantifier. (b) If x is in e_R, it may be indexed by f' because f' is a base function of e_R. This gives us the reading in which an indefinite in R is 'bound by the quantifier', and accounts for the quantificational force variability of indefinites in R. (c) If x is in e_{NS} it may be indexed by f'' because f'' is a base function of e_{NS}. This gives us the reading in which an indefinite in NS is 'bound by NS-level existential closure'.

Note that if x is introduced in the NS it may not be bound by the Q. For that to happen, it would have to be indexed by f', which is an inaccessible parameter to x. By the same token, if x is introduced in R it may not be bound by 'NS-level existential closure'. For that to happen it would have to be indexed by f'', which is not accessible to variables in R.

The accessibility relation in [36], and its application to functional indices in [37], have precisely the welcome consequences of the Heimean requirement that a variable should be bound by the first c-commanding quantifier. The advantage of the current system is that it does not have to pay the cost of assuming unbounded optional movement of indefinites and arbitrary existential closure rules. The preliminary result achieved so far then, is that we have an account of the unbounded inverse scope of indefinites with respect to nominal quantification without having to posit unbounded movement at any level. The account extends in a straightforward way to give intermediate scope readings.

(ii) The scope of a variable with respect to a modal/situational quantifier

The question here concerns the world/situation parameter of the evaluation function of a variable. Recall that these are part of the evaluation parameters of an expression, and that the evaluation parameters of variables introduced by indefinites are free. Consequently, their value can be set to any modal or situational parameter accessible to the variable in question. The accessiblity relation in [36] gives [38] when applied to modal parameters:

[38] The base world of an expression *e* is accessible to any variable in *e*.

Assume that α is an expression involving quantification over worlds whose base world is w, and x is a variable introduced by an ordinary indefinite in α. Since w is accessible to x, x may have w as its modal index, which results in the wide scope reading of x with respect to the quantifier; x may bear w' as its modal index as well, whether it is introduced in R or NS, since w' is a base world of both R and NS. This choice results in a reading where x has narrow scope with respect to the quantifier. In the narrow scope case the variable will be *dependent* on the world variable bound by the quantifier. To exemplify, consider [39] and its two possible lfs in [40], which determine the two satisfaction conditions in [41].

[39] If a Czech movie from the sixties were available, I'd be happy.

[40] a. *Narrow scope*
$(_{\alpha}\ \forall_{w'}\ [\ x_{w'}\text{: } \textit{Czech movie(x) available(x)}]_{w'}\ [\ \textit{happy(I)}]_{w'}\ )_{w}$
b. *Wide scope*
$(_{\alpha}\ \forall_{w'}\ [\ x_{w}\text{: } \textit{Czech movie(x) available(x)}]_{w'}\ [\ \textit{happy(I)}]_{w'}\ )_{w}$

[41] a. The expression in [40a] is satisfied in *w* wrt *M* and *c* iff there is a function *f* with the following property: for every w' close to *w* such that *f(x)* $\in$ *V(Czech movie,*w'*)* and *f(x)* $\in$ *V(available,*w'*)*, *V(happy(I,*w'*)*.
b. The expression in [40b] is satisfied in *w* wrt *M* and *c* iff there is a function *f* with the following property: for every w' close to *w* such that *f(x)* $\in$ *V(Czech movie,w)* and *f(x)* $\in$ *V(available,*w'*)*, *V(happy(I,*w'*)*.

In the narrow scope case the identity of the movie may change from world to world, while in the wide scope case it may not.[16] The case of quantification over situations will not be treated separately since it works just like modal quantification.

(iii) The scope of a variable with respect to an intensional predicate
The base world of the complement of an intensional predicate is the world (or worlds) introduced by that predicate. The main predication of such a complement must be interpreted with respect to these worlds. Our treatment of scope correctly predicts that a variable introduced within the complement by an ordinary (in)definite may be interpreted either relative to these worlds (narrow scope), or relative to any base world of a superordinate expression (wide scope). The two lfs associated with the complement of [42] are given in [43]:

[42] Susan wants to marry a Norwegian.

[43] a. *Wide scope*
$(y_{w}\text{: } \textit{Norwegian(y) marry(S,y)}\ )_{w'}$
b. *Narrow scope*
$(y_{w'}\text{: } \textit{Norwegian(y) marry(S,y)}\ )_{w'}$

Note that the worlds w' introduced by the main predicate function as base worlds for the expression in the complement of the predicate in question, and therefore will be accessible only to subparts of the complement, and not to elements in the matrix.

[16]Note that in the lfs in [40] the expression *Czech movie(x)* is a restrictive expression on *x* and not a main predication conjoined with *available(x)*, and therefore the satisfaction conditions of these lfs are not automatically met in a world in which there is something which is not a Czech movie.

We have now achieved a significant result: the generalisation in [23] is accounted for without having to posit unbounded movement at any level. Moreover, we have a unitary account of the scope of indefinites over quantifiers of various types as well as predicates. We now turn to the question of dependent/independent universals.

(iv) The scope of a variable introduced by a universal noun phrase[17]
Recall that the crucial requirement for a variable v contributed by a universal noun phrase is that it be in the variant set of a set of functions that are variants of some domain function h. Consequently, we expect the choice of domain function for a variable contributed by a universal to be open to any function accessible to the variable in question. Adopting this assumption leads to the correct predictions for examples like [25], repeated here as [44].

[44] Every_1 child read every_2 poem.

Structurally, $every_2$ is within the NS of $every_1$. At lf we have here a quantificational expression β embedded within the NS of a quantificational expression α as in [45]:

[45] $({}_\alpha\, Q_1\, [x \ldots]_R\, [({}_\beta\, Q_2\, [y \ldots]_{R'}\, [\ldots]_{NS'}\,)]_{NS}\,)$

The first universal noun phrase contributes a variable x in the Restrictor R of α; the second contributes a variable y in the Restrictor R' of β. Note that x occurs in α but not in β, and y occurs in α and β. The base function of α is assumed to be f; the base functions of β are the functions f'', which are the base functions of the expression in NS. There is only one accessible domain function for x, namely f. There are, however, two accessible domain functions for y: f and f''. The choice of the former gives the independent reading; the choice of the latter gives the dependent reading, where the domain over which $every_2$ quantifies co-varies with the values given to x.

Let us assume that the functional index of a variable contributed by a universal noun phrase specifies the choice of domain function. The two readings of [44] are represented at lf as in [46]:

[46] a. *Dependent reading*
$({}_\alpha\, [x_{f'(f/x)} \ldots]_R\, [({}_\beta\, [y_{f'''(f''/y)} \ldots]_{R'}\, [\ldots]_{NS'}\,)]_{NS}\,)$
b. *Independent reading*
$({}_\alpha\, [x_{f'(f/x)} \ldots]_R\, [({}_\beta\, [y_{g(f/y)} \ldots]_{R'}\, [\ldots]_{NS'}\,)]_{NS}\,)$

The satisfaction conditions of these lfs are as in [47] below, where world indices are ignored for the sake of simplicity.

[47] a. *Dependent reading:*
f satisfies the conditions in α iff every $f'(f/x)$ such that

[17] I wish to thank Barry Schein for asking the right questions with respect to the interpretation of universal noun phrases.

$f'(x) \in$ *V(child)* is such that it has a variant f'' that satisfies the conditions in β. f'' satisfies the conditions in β iff every $f'''(f''/y)$ such that $f'''(y) \in$ *V(poem)* is such that $\langle f'(x),\ f'''(y)\rangle \in$ *V(read).*

b. *Independent reading:*
f satisfies α iff every $f'(f/x)$ such that $f'(x) \in$ *V(child)* has a variant f'' that satisfies β. f'' satisfies β iff every *g(f/y)* such that *g(y)* $\in$ *V(poem)* is such that $\langle f'(x), g(y)\rangle \in$ *V(read).*

(v) The intermediate reading

Going back now to the intermediate reading of [24], repeated here as [48], note that just as in the case of [44], we have a universal quantificational structure whose Nuclear Scope is another quantificational structure.

[48] Every candidate commented on every essay that mentioned a major 19th century poet.

The indefinite we are interested in occurs in the Restrictor of the latter, as illustrated in [49].

[49] $\forall_x$ [*x: candidate(x)*]$_R$ [$\forall_y$ [*y z: essay(y) poet(z) mention(y,z)*]$_{R'}$ [*comment(x,y)*]$_{NS'}$]$_{NS}$

Let us assume that the base function for the entire formula is f. Let us first consider the main quantificational structure. The base function of the expression in R is $f'(f/x)$, which is also the functional index of x. The base function of the expression in NS is f''. With respect to the embedded quantificational structure, assuming that the second universal is independent of the first, the base function of R' is $g(f/x)$, which is also the index of y, and the base function of NS$'$ is g', a possibly trivial variant of g. The formula in [50] repeats that in [49] but now with the base functions indexing the constituents.

[50] [$\forall_x$ [x'_f: *candidate(x)*]$_{f'}$ [$\forall_y$ [y_g *z*: *essay(y) poet(z) mention(y,z)*]$_g$ [*comment(x,y)*]$_{g'}$]$_{f''}$]$_f$

Note now that the variable contributed by the indefinite, z, is in R'. Therefore, the functional indices accessible to it are f, f'' and g. The former choice results in the widest scope reading, where z does not co-vary with candidates, the second results in the intermediate reading, where poets co-vary with candidates but not with essays, and the third results in the narrowest scope reading, where poets co-vary with essays.

b. Scope of the quantifier

A variable introduced by an indefinite is within the scope of a universal noun phrase if either (a) the variable is in the Restrictor of *every* and is evaluated by the base functions f' of the Restrictor; the variable is then 'bound by Q', or (b) the variable is in the NS and is evaluated by the base functions f'' of the NS;

the variable then is 'bound by NS existential closure'. In this case there is co-variation between the variable introduced by the indefinite and variables bound by Q. A variable is in the Restrictor iff the indefinite introducing it is within the DC of the universal. A variable is in the NS iff the indefinite introducing it is in the NS of the quantificational expression whose Restrictor is given by the universal. This may happen in the following cases: (i) the indefinite and the universal are co-arguments, in which case the variable is an argument of a relation that distributes over the domain introduced by the universal, (ii) the indefinite occurs as part of a co-argument of the universal. Consequently, a universal noun phrase may have scope over a co-argument (clause-mate) indefinite, as in [26a], repeated here as [51a] but not over a c-commanding non-co-argument indefinite, as in [26b], repeated here as [51b].

[51] a. A member of our group attended every rally.
b. A member of our group said that every candidate will win.

Neither the functions f' nor f'', introduced in the quantificational structure whose R is contributed by *every candidate* in [51b], are accessible to the variable contributed by the indefinite *a member of our group* because this variable is neither in the Restrictor nor the NS of the quantificational expression in question. The variable is obviously not in the Restrictor because it is not part of the DC of the NP whose D is *every*. The variable is not in the NS because it is not part of a relation predicated of the universal noun phrase.

Recall that the distributive readings of plural and coordinate noun phrases are treated as involving universal quantification over the i-parts of their denotations. The clause-bounded nature of the scope of distributive plural and coordinate noun phrases follows: the key/Restrictor introduced by the distributive reading of the noun phrase *three relatives of mine* in [26c], repeated as [52], cannot have the worlds quantified over by the conditional in its scope because the evaluation functions introduced by this noun phrase are not accessible to the modal variable.

[52] If three relatives of mine die, I will inherit a house.

The generalization B in [27], as well as the clause-boundedness of distributivity, are accounted for. Note that we also have an account of the double scope of cardinal, plural or coordinate noun phrases discussed in Winter 1997: the scope of distributivity is clause-bounded but the i-sum variable introduced by such noun phrases scopes freely.

The contrast between the free inverse scope of indefinites and the bound inverse scope of universals is accounted for under the present theory by the fact that the former is a matter of indefinites choosing an accessible index, while the latter is a matter of a quantifier or predicate making its index accessible to an indefinite. The essence of the account of both generalizations is that an evaluation index is accessible to subordinate expressions but not to superordinate ones.

The above discussion gives the limits of what is in principle possible. What is actually possible in particular cases depends, besides pragmatic effects, on the type of noun phrases involved, on discourse coherence considerations, on issues that have to do with the logical subject/predicate or topic/focus articulation, as well as on possibly language specific requirements on the interface between semantics and syntax which may impose further limits on inverse scope. The fact that inverse scope readings tend to be relatively marked cross-linguistically may be connected to a preference for aligning semantic and syntactic hierarchy/priority.

c. Scope of the DC

Recall that at lf the DC of noun phrases are predicative expressions of the form $P(v_1,...,v_n)$ which have modal indices that specify which worlds *P* has to be evaluated at. Such predicative expressions may have either a predicative function (in which case they are called main predications) or a restrictive function (in which case they are called restrictive expressions.) Now the modal index of main predications may be the base modal parameter or any of the accessible modal parameters. Thus, the modal index of main predications in modalized sentences, afactual conditionals or arguments of intensional predicates is bound in the sense that the index has to be that of the worlds introduced by the Restrictor or the predicate. The modal index of main predications of unembedded sentences is free: it can be set to either the base world (which is the default choice), or to any discoursally accessible index, where discourse accessibility involves structural considerations at the discourse level. Thus, the discourse in [53] is ambiguous with respect to whether the main predication of the second sentence is indexed to *w* or to the world of the dream introduced by the immediately preceding sentence:

[53] I had a terrible dream last night.
It was extremely hot and a car alarm kept going off.

The freedom of scope of the DC introduced by (in)definites is accounted for by simply assuming that their modal index, on a par with their other evaluation parameters, is free. Assuming the accessibility condition in [36], the modal index of the italicized DC in [54] may be set to either *w*, the base world of the whole expression, resulting in the wide scope reading of the description relative to *believe*, or to *w(T)*, the base world of the complement, resulting in the narrow scope reading of the description. The speaker is committed to the description under the former indexing, and the professor under the latter.

[54] Prof. Talc believes that a/every [remarkable student in *History 100*]$_{w/w(T)}$ is an idiot.

The account predicts that the inverse scope of the DC is unbounded, and therefore captures the generalization in [30] without relying on syntactic movement. The unbounded nature of the scope of the variable and that of the scope of the DC are accounted for by the same mechanism, that of allowing free evaluation indices to be set to any accessible value. The clause-bounded inverse scope of *every* and the unbounded inverse scope of the DC in [31], repeated below with the intended indexings informally indicated, is accounted for:

[55] A reporter thought that [a former government official]$_{f/*f''}$ believes that every [person in this room]$_w$ has had contact with the enemy.

The functions f'' introduced by the Restrictor contributed by *every person in this room* are not accessible to the variable contributed by *a former government official* because the latter does not occur in an expression whose base function is f''. The initial world *w* on the other hand is accessible to the DC of the universal, and therefore the description may have widest scope, while the quantifier has narrowest scope.

The above account can be extended to discoursal scope, assuming that discourse structure considerations determine accessibility of indices at this level. In [56] we have an example where the modal index of a DC may be inherited from previous discourse:

[56] Ellen thought that there was a [castle]$_{w(E)}$ in the distance.
[The [castle]$_{w(E)}$ turned out to be a huge oaktree]$_w$.

2.2.3 Conclusion

The theory presented here has three main advantages over other existing proposals. (i) It captures the unbounded scope of indefinites without resorting to any special mechanisms. No unbounded syntactic movement rule need be posited. This is an advantage over LF approaches in which scope is determined by c-command at the level of LF. Furthermore, no special mechanism for binding indefinites has to be resorted to. This is an advantage over the 'choice function' theory of indefinites in Reinhart 1995 and Winter 1997, where the scoping properties of indefinites are captured by assuming the application of an existential closure rule that binds choice function variables at any distance. Existential closure rules (whether constrained, as in Heim 1982, Ch.2, or unconstrained, as in the Reinhart/Winter proposal) do not come for free (for discussion, see Heim 1982, Ch.3). Just as in DRT, in the present approach existential closure rules are dispensed with. Recall also that the present proposal accounts for all binding possibilities of indefinites, including the case when they occur in the Restrictor and are bound by the quantifier. This possibility is not accounted for in approaches where the scope of indefinites is captured by assuming free existential binding of choice functional variables. The analysis presented here can be recast in terms of choice functions: assignment functions can be viewed as choice functions that may be differentiated depending on their values. (ii) The mechanism proposed here solves not only the puzzles raised by intrasentential scoping of indefinites, universals, and distributives, but also the issues raised by the scope of the DC, and is extendable to intersentential data. (iii) Finally, the proposed approach makes distinctions that are useful in characterizing noun phrases that turn up in natural language. This point will be illustrated in the following section. For the moment we review the major theoretical distinctions drawn above.

With respect to variables, the theory distinguishes between *dependent* and *domain* variables. Intuitively, a variable v_2 is dependent on a domain variable v_1 iff the values assigned to v_2 co-vary with the values assigned to v_1. In order for co-variation to be possible v_1 must refer non-rigidly, i.e., it must be assigned several potentially different values.

In the proposed approach whether a variable is dependent or not is a matter of the properties of its functional index. The notion of dependent variable is defined in [57]:

[57] A variable v_2 is dependent on a domain variable v_1 iff the functional index of v_2 is a variant of the functional index of v_1.

The variable y in [58] is dependent on x because its functional index is dependent on f', the index of x.

[58] $Q_x\ [x_{f'}\ ...\ ]_R\ \ [y_{f''}\ ...\ ]_{NS}$

The variable y in [59] is dependent on w' because the modal parameter of its functional index is set to w', the variable bound by the quantifier.

[59] $\forall_{w'}\ [\ ...\ y_{w'}\ ...\ ]_{w'}$

Thus, the characteristics of the functional index of a variable determine whether a variable is dependent or not, and if it is dependent, what its domain variable is. A further distinction that can be drawn based on the properties of the functional index of a variable is that between *rigid* and *non-rigid* variables. The former are assigned a single value in the course of the evaluation, i.e., their functional index is a single function with a single modal or situational parameter, while the latter are assigned multiple values, i.e., their functional index is either a set of functions, as in [58] or its modal or situational parameter ranges over a set of worlds, as in [59].

With respect to the coarsest sortal distinction, we distinguished between individual, situational and world variables. The former two form a natural class in that they are extensional, while the latter is intensional:

[60]

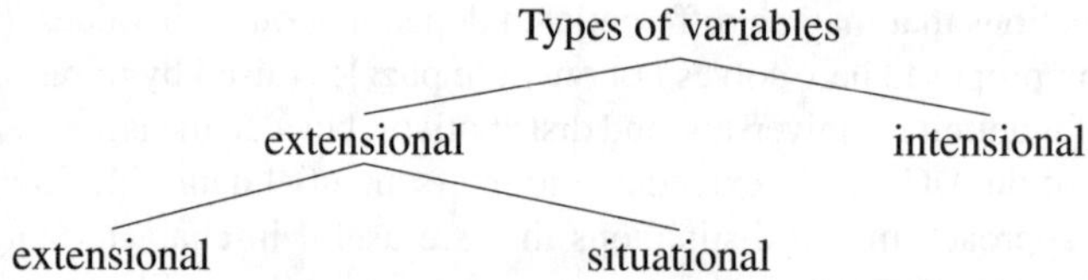

We expect then to find natural language phenomena that are sensitive to these distinctions. In the next section it will be shown that indefinites with reduplicated Ds in Hungarian exemplify just such a phenomenon.

2.3 Dependent Indefinites in Hungarian

I assume that noun phrases fall into several semantic classes defined with respect to the contribution of the noun phrase to semantic structure. The highest-level distinction is that between noun phrases that introduce a variable and those that do not. The latter are either predicative or function as Predicate Operators (see Szabolcsi 1997a). In my terms, Predicate Operators only contribute a DC that restricts an argument position of the predicate. As a consequence, these noun phrases do not scope independently of the predicate, i.e., they take narrowest scope. Existential bare plurals in English, and preverbal bare noun phrases in Hungarian are examples of Predicate Operators.

The distinctions we drew above are relevant to noun phrases that introduce variables. We now turn to a noun phrase type whose distribution can be correctly characterized, I claim, only if one makes reference to the distinction between dependent and domain variables, as well as to the sortal distinctions in [60].

Reduplicated Determiners in Hungarian

Hungarian makes use of morphological reduplication to achieve semantic effects. Here we will concentrate on the reduplication of the indefinite article *egy*, as well as of cardinals, illustrated in [61].[18]

[61] Minden gyerek olvasott egy-egy / hét-hét könyvet.
every child read a-a seven-seven book-ACC
'Every child read a/seven book(s).'

I will call this phenomenon D-reduplication. There are two related questions that arise now: (i) what is the semantic effect of D-reduplication, and (ii) what is its distribution? I will attempt to answer the first question by providing a detailed answer to the second.

[18]Other determiner-like morphemes that may reduplicate are *más* 'different', and *külön* 'separate'. The phenomenon of determiner reduplication is discussed briefly in Moravcsik 1978 and Gil 1995.

The generalization that governs the distribution of D-reduplication in Hungarian is stated in [62]:

[62] *Extensional dependent variable condition*
D-reduplication is possible only in noun phrases that introduce a variable that is dependent on an extensional domain variable.

There are two conditions on D-reduplication then: (i) the variable introduced by the indefinite must be dependent; (ii) the domain variable must be extensional, i.e., individual or situational. I turn now to showing that both restrictions in [62] are necessary.

Dependent variables
Note first that the examples in [61] are scopally unambiguous: the indefinite is necessarily interpreted as being within the scope of (i.e., dependent on) the universal. The non-reduplicated counterparts of [61] (and all other examples to follow) are scopally ambiguous. Second, D-reduplication is not allowed in case the noun phrase introduces the key in a distributive predication:

[63] * Hét-hét gyerek szalad.
seven-seven child runs
'Seven children are running.'

This fact is covered by [62] since the subject here, even though it refers non-rigidly under the distributive interpretation of [63], does not introduce a dependent variable.

Next, note that the restriction to dependent variables together with our treatment of distributivity correctly predict that D-reduplication will be allowed in noun phrases that have narrow scope with respect to a non-quantificational distributive noun phrase, as in the distributive reading of [64]:

[64] A gyerekek hoztak egy-egy könyvet.
the children brought a-a book.ACC
'The children brought a book each.'

Because noun phrases whose D is reduplicated have to introduce dependent variables they will be called *dependent*.

Extensional domain variable
The restriction of extensionality on the domain variable correctly predicts that D-reduplication may occur in case the domain variable is individual-level, as in [61], or situational, as in [65][19]:

[65] (Időnként) egy-egy diák megbukik.
occasionally a-a student fails
'Occasionally a student fails.'

[19] As indicated by the parentheses, the adverb may be omitted. In the absence of an explicit adverb, D-reduplication is understood to involve existential quantification over situations.

As expected, given the condition in [62] and our treatment of conditionals, D-reduplication is possible in factual conditionals:

[66] Ha egy-egy tanár megbetegedik, helyettesíti egy szülő.
if a-a teacher gets sick replaces-him a parent
'If a teacher gets sick, a parent replaces him.'

The exclusion of D-reduplication when the domain variable is intensional is needed to account for the fact that D-reduplication is not allowed in afactual conditionals or modalized sentences:

[67] * Ha a tanár megbetegedne, helyettesítené egy-egy szülő.
if the professor sick.COND.III. replace.COND.III a-a parent
'If the teacher were to get sick, a parent would replace him.'

[68] * Mari kell találkozzon egy-egy párizsi tanárral.
Mari must meet a-a Parisian professor-with
'Mari must meet a professor from Paris.'

The counterparts of [67] and [68] without reduplication are perfectly grammatical and scopally ambiguous. Under the narrow scope reading of the indefinite, the variable it introduces is dependent on an intensional domain variable, and the restriction to extensional domains rules D-reduplication out. Note that, as predicted by [62], D-reduplication is allowed within intensional contexts as long as the relevant variable is dependent on an individual-level domain variable, as in [69]:

[69] Mindenki kell találkozzon egy-egy párizsi tanárral.
Everybody must meet a-a Parisian professor-with
'Everybody must meet a professor from Paris.'

The restriction against intensional domain variables correctly predicts that D-reduplication will not occur in generic noun phrases:

[70] * Ha egy-egy gyerek beteg, lázas.
If a-a child sick feverish
'If a child is sick, she is feverish.'

For a recent discussion of the modal dimension of genericity, see Condoravdi 1994.

Note that the condition in [62] predicts that D-reduplication will not occur when the indefinite has narrow scope with respect to negation, since such indefinites do not introduce dependent variables. We see in [71] that this prediction is correct.

[71] * Mari nem olvasott egy-egy könyvet.
Mari not read a-a book
'Mari didn't read a book.'

Until now we have seen that the dependent/domain variable is relevant to the distribution of D-reduplication in Hungarian, and so is the distinction between extensional and intensional variables. There are two further questions that arise at this point, namely (i) does one have to distinguish between individual and situational domain variables, and (ii) does one have to distinguish between article and cardinal reduplication? Note that the so-called indefinite article *egy* in Hungarian is the same as the cardinal numeral *egy* 'one' and therefore the question of whether one ever needs to distinguish between the two is an important one for Hungarian grammar.

The answer to both these questions is affirmative. In order to account for the full range of facts the condition in [72] is needed as well:

[72] *Condition on cardinal reduplication*
The reduplication of cardinal determiners is not allowed in case of dependence on a situation-level domain variable.

The reduplication of the indefinite article is not sensitive to this condition. The condition in [72] accounts for the contrast below:

[73] Ahányszor egy-egy híres személy meglátogatta a várost,
Whenever a-a famous person visited the town
elvitték a kastélyba.
they-took-him the castle-to
'Whenever a famous person visited the town, they took him to the castle.'

[74] * Ahányszor két-két híres személy meglátogatta a várost,
Whenever two-two famous person visited the town
elvitték a kastélyba.
they-took-him the castle-to
'Whenever two famous persons visited the town, they took them to the castle.'

The indefinite here is dependent on a situation-level variable. D-reduplication is allowed with *egy* but not with other morphemes that are unambiguously cardinals.

We have seen so far that both the distinction between domain and dependent variables, and that between the variable types in [60] are relevant to the account of D-reduplication in Hungarian. Let us also note that there is a reduplicated morpheme in Hungarian, namely *ki-ki* 'who-who', interpreted as a D-linked universal, which must introduce a domain variable, i.e., a variable that must have a co-variant. This is illustrated in the contrast between [75] and [76].

[75] Ki-ki leült a székére / egy-egy székre.
who-who sat-down the chair.their.on a-a chair
'Everybody sat down on their/a chair.'

[76] * Ki-ki leült.
who-who sat-down
'Everybody sat down.'

Example [75] is grammatical even if the indefinite article is not reduplicated, but only if the indefinite is understood as dependent on the universal.[20]

We still have to answer the question of what the semantic effect of D-reduplication is, a question closely connected to the question of why D-reduplication would obey the constraint in [62]. My tentative answer is that D-reduplication signals *iterated plurality*. Variables that are dependent on extensional domain variables, I suggest, are iterated plurals in the sense that they are assigned a multiplicity of values because of their iterative association with the values of the domain variable. Note that Hungarian allows reduplication outside the nominal domain as well, and there the semantic effect of signaling iteration is more obvious. Thus, preverbal particles may reduplicate, as illustrated in [77]:

[77] A gyerek fel-fel ébredt.
The child up-up woke
'The child kept waking up.'

The function of reduplication here is to indicate the iteration of the event denoted by the predicate. Without reduplication, the sentence would refer to a single waking up event; with reduplication, it refers to a series of such events.

Note that the constraint on extensional domain variables is also connected to plurality. Narrow scope indefinites dependent on extensional domains trigger plural discourse anaphora, while those dependent on intensional variables can only license singular anaphors:

[78] Mindenki meglátogatott egy-egy rokont és aztán írt nekik.
everybody visited a-a relative and then wrote them
'Everybody visited a relative and then wrote them.'

[79] Mari kell találkozzon egy tanárral és aztán írjon neki/*nekik.
Mari must meet a professor and then write him/them
'Mari must meet a professor and then write to him/*them.'

I conclude then that D-reduplication signals iterated plurality, which is defined in terms of dependency on an extensional domain variable.

Conclusion

There are several morals to be drawn from the discussion of dependent indefinites in Hungarian. With respect to the grammar of Hungarian, we have

[20] English *each* is claimed to introduce a domain variable as well (Vendler 1967, Beghelli and Stowell 1997). There is a difference between *each* and *ki-ki*, namely that the co-dependent of the former may be the event variable associated with stage-level predicates, while the co-dependent of the latter must be a full-fledged argument variable.

evidence that the indefinite article is distinguished from the cardinal numeral 'one'. With respect to the theoretical constructs we want our semantics to accommodate, we have evidence that both situations and worlds are needed. Finally, with respect to the details of the scope theory we adopt, we have here a class of noun phrases whose distribution can be naturally characterized in terms of the distinctions the approach to scope presented above led to. Note that the class of dependent indefinites is not easily characterizable in either standard structural approaches or in the choice functional view of scope. This observation leads to the final point, namely the questions we are left with. On the empirical side, there is the immediate question of how common dependent indefinites are in the languages of the world. This is a particular aspect of the general issue of the typology of natural language noun phrases. On the theoretical side, we have the task of devising an approach to noun phrase semantics that accounts for the typology we find. In such a theory, actual noun phrase types should be characterized as natural classes, and non-occurring noun phrase types should not.

References

Abusch, D. 1994. The Scope of Indefinites. *Natural Language Semantics* 2, 83–135.

Beghelli F. and T. Stowell. 1997. Distributivity and Negation: The Syntax of *Each* and *Every*. In A. Szabolcsi, ed., 71–107.

Condoravdi, C. 1994. *Descriptions in Context*. Doctoral dissertation, Yale University.

Farkas, D. F. 1981. Quantifier Scope and Syntactic Islands. *CLS 17*, 59–66.

Farkas, D.F. 1993. Modal Anchoring and NP Scope. LRC working paper, UCSC, Santa Cruz.

Farkas, D. F. 1997. Evaluation Indices and Scope. In A. Szabolcsi, ed., 183–215.

Farkas D. F. and A. Giannakidou. 1996. How Clause-Bounded is the Scope of *Every*? *SALT VI*, 35–52.

Fodor, J. and I. Sag 1982. Referential and Quantificational Indefinites. *Linguistics and Philosophy* 5, 355–398.

Gil, D. 1995. Universal Quantifiers and Distributivity. In E. Bach et al., eds., *Quantification in Natural Languages*, 321–362. Dordrecht: Kluwer Academic Publishers.

Groenendjik, J. and M. Stokhof. 1991. Dynamic Predicate Logic. *Linguistics and Philosophy* 14, 683–722.

Heim, I. 1982. *The Semantics of Definite and Indefinite Noun Phrases*. Doctoral dissertation, University of Massachussetts, Amherst.

Kamp, H. and U. Reyle 1993 *From Discourse to Logic*. Dordrecht: Kluwer Academic Publishers.

Kratzer, A. 1980. The Notional Category of Modality. In H.-J. Eikmeyer, and H. Rieser, eds., *Words, Worlds, and Contexts*, 38–74. Berlin: Walter de Gruyter.

Kratzer, A. 1989. An Investigation of the Lumps of Thought. *Linguistics and Philosophy* 12, 607–653.

Kratzer, A. 1998. Scope or Pseudoscope? Are there Wide Scope Indefinites? In Susan Rothstein, ed., *Events and Grammar*, 163–196. Dordrecht: Kluwer Academic Publishers.

McCawley, J. D. 1980. *Everything Linguists Have Always Wanted to Know About Logic*. Chicago: The University of Chicago Press.

Reinhart, T. 1995. *Interface Strategies*. OTS Working Papers.

Roberts, C. 1991. Distributivity as a Mode of Predication. *SALT I*, 209–229.

Rodman, R. 1976. Scope Phenomena, Movement Transformations and Relative Clauses. In B.H. Partee, ed., *Montague Grammar*, 165–177. New York: Academic Press.

Ross, J.R. 1967. *Constraints on Variables in Syntax*. Doctoral dissertation, MIT.

Ruys, E. G. 1992. *The Scope of Indefinites*. Doctoral dissertation, Utrecht University.

May, R. 1977. *The Grammar of Quantification*. Doctoral dissertation, MIT.

Moravcsik, E. 1978. Reduplicative Constructions. In J. H. Greenberg, ed., *Universals of Human Language, Vol. 3: Word Structure*, 297–334. Stanford: Stanford University Press.

Szabolcsi, A. 1997a. Strategies for Scope Taking. In A. Szabolcsi, ed., 109–154.

Szabolcsi, A. (ed.). 1997b. *Ways of Scope Taking*. Dordrecht: Kluwer Academic Publishers.

Vendler, Z. 1967. Each and every, any and all. In Z. Vendler, *Linguistics in Philosophy*, 70–97. Ithaca: Cornell University Press.

Winter, Y. 1997. Choice Functions and the Scopal Semantics of Indefinites. *Linguistics and Philosophy* 20, 399–467.

3

Universal Concessive Conditionals and Alternative NPs in English

JEAN MARK GAWRON

3.1 Introduction

There are many ways in which language can describe the dependency of one occurrence on another and hence many varieties of conditional constructions, including conditionals with *if*, *when*, *since*, and *as*, the absolute conditionals of Stump (1985), and the correlative conditional construction (*the more, the merrier*) discussed in Fillmore (1986). This paper will be concerned with investigating one species illustrated in (1a) and (1b).

(1) a. Whoever John chooses, the committee will approve him.
   b. Whoever John chooses, there will be a loss of confidence.
   c. The committee will be pleased with whoever John chooses.
   d. The committee will approve whoever John chooses.

Sentences (1a) and (1b) are examples of something we will call the Universal Concessive Conditional (UCC).[1] Our first concern will be to argue that (1a) and (1b) are indeed examples of a conditional construction. A second will be to show that the protases of those conditionals are very closely related to English questions; and a third will be with the kind of NP shown in (1c), which is formally identical to the UCC protasis in (1a). These NPs have sometimes been called "free relatives"(for example, in Jacobson 1990). We will call them

[1]The name is due to Ekkehard Koenig, see Koenig (1986) for discussion. Actually, the name is a slight misnomer; as with all conditionals, the quantificational force of UCCs may vary, as we shall see in Section 3.5.2. However, the name captures the core cases. The construction is most often used with universal force, and, when universal, it has its strongest concessive character.

Logical Perspectives on Language and Information.
Cleo Condoravdi and Gerard R. Renardel de Lavalette.

alternative NPs, anticipating the arguments, laid out in Section 3.2.2, that they, too, are related to questions.

I will try to show below that some of the peculiarities of UCCs fall out from natural interactions of the properties of questions and conditionals. In particular, I will argue that UCCs share the presuppositions of questions. Essentially the same properties hold of alternative NPs, which will make certain alternative NPs a species of definite. The end result is that parallel UCC and alternative NP examples like (1a) and (1c) will sometimes end up conveying essentially the same meaning. We will see, however, that, due to the quantificational properties of the conditional construction, UCC sentences in general will have different discourse functions and different meanings from analagous alternative NP sentences.

Sentence (1b) illustrates a key point about the Universal Concessive Conditional (UCC), that there is no anaphoric or binding dependency between the protasis and the apodosis. If *whoever John chooses* were treated simply as a universal quantifier, (1b) would be a case of vacuous binding.

As evidence that (1a) and (1b) are in fact examples of a conditional construction, consider that it appears to occur in all conditional flavors, including counterfactual:

(2) *present generic:*
Whatever John chooses, Mary is pleased with it.
If John chooses something, Mary is pleased with it.

futurate present:
Whatever John chooses, Mary will be pleased with it.
If John chooses something, Mary will be pleased with it.

futurate past:
Whatever John chose, Mary would be pleased with it.
If John chose something, Mary would be pleased with it.

past/past:
Whatever John chose, Mary was pleased with it.
If John chose something, Mary is pleased with it.

past/indeterminate:
Whatever John chose, Mary will be pleased with it.
If John chose something, Mary will be pleased with it.

counterfactual:
Whatever John had chosen, Mary would have been pleased with it.
If John had chosen something, Mary would have been pleased with it.

Although there are analogies between the UCCs and the ordinary conditionals, there are clear differences as well. The kinds of situations (or worlds) quantified over may differ slightly from the analogous ordinary conditional. In the counterfactual case, the understanding seems to be that factual and non-factual alternatives alike are quantified over. The claim made is that it doesn't matter; the consequent holds whether factual or non-factual alternatives are chosen.

We will argue that a central feature of the UCC is a syntactic and semantic connection with questions. As a point of departure we note that there is a class of UCC protases that utilize the question complementizer *whether*. Within this class of cases, the UCC construction makes an interesting distinction:

(3) a. Whether you eat or drink, you (still) get fat.
   b. Whether you drink beer or wine, you (still) get fat.
   c. Whether you think that Tom drinks beer or wine, he will (still) get fat.
   d. Whether Mary hates John or John hates Mary, the fact is that they don't get along.
   e. Whether you eat or not, you (still) get fat.
   f. * Whether you eat, you get fat.

Alongside the constituent question analogues of the first examples, we have a set of questions in *whether*. Although as a question each of the antecedents in (3a) through (3d) is ambiguous between a yes-no question reading and an alternative question reading, in each case it is a reading like the alternative question reading, accompanied by the list-intonation characteristic of alternative questions, which is relevant in the UCC construction. Also note that (3c) has only the interpretation on which *or* takes wider scope than *think*. The scope of the alternative disjunction must be the entire protasis of the conditional.

If, following Bolinger (1978), we take *or not* questions like *whether you eat or not* in (3e) to be alternative questions, the generalization is clear: The UCC construction admits alternative questions or *wh*-questions, but not, as (3f) shows, plain yes/no questions.

Bolinger observes that em or not questions cannot be answered simply *yes* or *no*. As with other alternative questions, some overt indication of which alternative holds is required.[2] Further evidence that *or not* questions should in fact be classified with alternative questions can be found by considering verbs that select for yes/no questions, excluding alternative and constituent questions:

[2]The relevance of Bolinger's observation was pointed out by Manfred Krifka (pc).

(4) a. * John doubted who came.
b. John doubted whether Mary came.
c. John doubted whether Mary or Sue came.
d. ? John doubted whether Mary came or not.

Example (4c), although grammatical, lacks the alternative question reading; and (4d) is anomalous.

An important question about the UCC construction is why yes-no questions are excluded. We will propose an account along the following lines. Where many conditionals serve to describe dependence, the force of UCCs is to assert independence. Suppose we associate with certain questions a propositional function f which defines, in a manner to be made precise below, a set of entities that answers the question. Then, schematically, the UCC construction does the following:

$$\begin{cases} \text{(a)}\ \forall x f(x) \Rightarrow g(x) \\ \text{(b)}\ \forall x f(x) \Rightarrow g \end{cases}$$

The case of (a) corresponds to (1a), where the *wh*-variable occurs in both protasis and apodosis, and (b) corresponds to (1b), where the variable occurs only in the protasis. What the UCC construction asserts is that the truth of g or $g(x)$ is independent of the value of x, that is, of the answer to the question f is related to. In a very clear sense, the UCC is about f; it tells us an important property of f, its irrelevance to g. We return to this point in Section 3.2.1, where we discuss the topic-like character of UCC protases (UCCPs). In the case of *wh-ever* UCCs, f will be a propositional function of the *wh*-variable, systematically related to but not identical with a constituent question denotation. We will argue that alternative questions should be related, in an analogous fashion, to a propositional function of an alternative variable whose domain is restricted to the explicitly supplied alternatives. The account of why UCCs exclude yes-no questions is thus located in the compositional semantics: UCCs assert that the consequent is independent of the propositional function in the antecedent, and yes-no questions are not related to propositional functions.

Although we argue that UCCPs are clearly related to questions, there is ample evidence questions and UCCPs are distinct. Note that other than the above alternative questions in *whether*, no forms may double both as indirect questions and UCC protases. Syntactic constituent questions are not welcome in the UCC construction.

(5) * Which boys Mary danced with, John was displeased.

Nor are *wh*-words with *ever* allowed in indirect questions:

(6) * John wonders whichever boys left.

Moreover, there are cases of UCCPs which are neither questions nor alternative NPs:

(7) a. No matter what John ate, he got sick.
    b. * No matter whatever John ate, he got sick.
    c. * Mary devoured no matter what John ate.
    d. * Mary discovered no matter what John ate.
    e. Either Alice or Simon will win. Either way, the electorate will be swindled.

Examples (7a) and (7b) show that *no matter*, in complementary distribution to *ever*, performs an analogous function; (7c) and (7d) show that it does not thereby create either an NP or a question. Example (7e) shows a special purpose proform that requires a disjunction of alternatives be in the context, showing that UCC-like quantification is by no means limited to clauselike antecedents. We will return to the significance of this proform below.

We see the following properties converging in UCC constructions:

1. Syntactic apparatus connected with questions appears.
2. Elements of the construction can be used with NPs which have a universal-like interpretation.
3. Both constituent questions and alternative question elements appear in the construction.

This is a peculiar configuration of facts. It is thus quite striking to find the same configuration occurring in a language as different as Japanese in a construction whose semantics appear quite similar to the UCC construction. Thus, consider the following examples in Japanese, modified from those in Gawron and Harada (1996):

(8) a. Dono kyoju-wo tazune-te-mo rusu-dat-ta.
    which professor-acc visit-GER-MO absent-be-PAST
    Whichever professor I/you visited, he was absent.
    b. Tazune-ta dono kyoju-mo rusu-dat-ta.
    visit-PAST which professor mo absent-be-PAST.
    Whichever professor I/you visited was absent.
    c. Dono-gakusei-ga kimasita-ka.
    Which of the students came?
    d. Dono-gakusei-mo kimasita.
    All of the students came.

Example (8a) shows a conditional construction in Japanese characterized by use of the particle *mo* following the verb of the protasis, and the use of *dono N* somewhere in the clause. Example (8b) shows a related construction in which the *mo*-particle follows a *dono N* NP with a relative clause, which may receive a universal reading. Example (8c) shows that in Japanese constituent questions *dono N* NPs play a role analogous to *wh*-phrases in English constituent questions. Example (8d) shows that the relative clause of example (8b) is not necessary. The particle *mo* can give a universal reading to an unmodified *dono* NP.

There are analogous examples with other members of the Japanese *wh*-phrase paradigm. Thus three elements of the English construction in (1a) recur in the Japanese construction in (8a): (a) forms that may be questions with the appropriate syntactic marking show up as UCC protases; (b) a new form marks the conditional protasis function (*ever* in English, *mo* in Japanese); (c) closely related forms (still using *ever* or *mo*) may be used as freely occurring NPs, which *may* have universal force.

Finally, there are examples involving alternative question-like elements:

(9) a. Tabete-mo tabenakute-mo futoru.
eat-GER-MO eat-NEG-GER-MO get-fat.
Whether you eat or you don't eat, you get fat.

b. Tabete-mo non-de-mo futoru.
eat-GER-MO drink-GER-MO get-fat.
Whether you eat or you drink, you get fat.

c. Biru-mo wine-mo nomeba futoru.
beer wine drink-COND-MO get-fat.
Whether you drink beer or wine, you get fat.

There are complexities here, such as the use of *mo* to mark NPs in (9c),[3] and differences, such as the lack of any overt disjunction marking, but the basic similarity of a disjunctive conditional construction is striking.

Michaelis (1996) reports some analogous facts for the particle *cũng* in Vietnamese:

(10) a. Cô ãy di dâu, anh ãy cũng muõn du theo.
woman that go where, man that c. want go follow.
Wherever she goes, he wants to follow.

b. Ai cũng có-thê học duọc tiẽng Việt.
who c. can learn language Vietnamese.
Anyone can learn Vietnamese.

c. Caí gì con chó dó cũng ăng.
CLF what CLF dog that c. eat.
That dog will eat anything.

Vietnamese *cũng* shows both a UCC-like function and a universal-NP function, in both cases interacting with words taken from the language's '*wh*-word' paradigm. In both cases, Vietnamese has a somewhat different marking pattern from Japanese. In the conditional construction in (10a), the Vietnamese 'concessive' marker *cũng* goes into preverbal position in the main clause rather than

[3] Japenese *mo* is an NP focus particle as well, in complementary distribution with *wa*.

on the dependent verb; and in non-conditional cases, (10b) shows that *cũng* does not need to be adjacent to the *wh*-word that it 'universalizes.' The analogy between Japanese *mo* and Vietnamese *cũng* goes further than the resemblance to English UCCs and alternative NPs, however. The Japanese and Vietnamese particles also occur in sentence without *wh*-words, where they serve a variety of complex functions that seem to be related to English particles like *even* and *also*, including marking ordinary concessive conditionals that would be translated into English using *even if*.

Here we focus on the two functions illustrated in English. What we have is evidence for the cross-linguistic status of a construction that quantifies over a set of alternatives, conveniently marked through the use of question words. Why should question words and conditionals fall together so naturally? And why should they be linked to NP quantification?

Given the cross-linguistic evidence, it seems particularly important to get clear on the semantic function of *ever* in the English construction, which seems to be the closest analogue to Japanese *mo* and Vietnamese *cũng*. Although UCCPs and alternative NPs are frequently tied up in quantificational effects, we will argue, much as has been argued for *any* since Ladusaw (1980), that *ever* carries no quantificational force of its own. Following a suggestion in Harada and Honda (1999) for Japanese *mo*, we assume that *ever* invokes a pragmatic scale. Quantificational effects will be attributed to an interaction with pragmatic scales and scalar implicatures.

As evidence that *ever* carries no quantificational force of its own, consider the case of UCCPs with multiple *wh*-words:[4]

(11) a. Whoever buys whoever's/whosever property, the town council will still grant a building permit.

b. * Whoever buys whose property, the town council will still grant a building permit.

c. Mary will review whatever property whoever buys.

d. * Mary will review whatever property who buys.

Note that *ever* is required on all the *wh*-words and that there is no double quantification effect in sentence (11c).[5] Thus, *ever* shows behavior characteristic of concord elements rather than of an independent quantificational operator.[6]

[4]The fact that both *whoever's* and *whosever* are both grammatical in alternative NPs may argue that *ever*, like the English possessive marker, is a clitic.

[5]That is, sentence (11c) refers to whatever property anyone buys, not whatever property everyone buys.

[6]For Japanese, in contrast, the corresponding particle *mo* shows up on the verb of the embedded clause and does not require any concord-like copying.

3.2 Descriptive Preliminaries

3.2.1 Topic-like Nature of UCCPs

In Section 3.1 we claimed that the UCC construction was a conditional construction and that the preposed *wh*-clauses were the protases. This amounts to a semantic claim. Since any free-standing clause with appropriate verbal mood can be a conditional with pragmatically supplied antecedent constraints, the burden is to show that UCCs are always conditionals, and that what we have called the protasis must indeed contribute semantically to the antecedent required by the main clause. This shows that the *wh*-clause performs a syntactic and semantic function analogous to the *if*-clause in ordinary conditionals.

We suggest in this section that a somewhat stronger claim may be justified: UCCPs not only contribute to the antecedent of the conditional, but the propositional function they are associated with is the topic. Thus, UCCPs not only constrain what the conditional quantifies over in the antecedent; they also constrain the contexts in which UCCs are appropriate.

The point can be made by contrasting a UCC with an alternative NP in some small discourses. Consider the following question-answer pairs:

(12) a. – Who will win?
{ – Whoever the mayor supports will win.
{ – # Whoever the mayor supports, he will win.

b. Who will the mayor support?
{ – Whoever the mayor supports, he will win.
{ – # Whoever the mayor supports will win.

The first responses in discourses (12a) and (12b) are on point. Although the alternative NP response in (12a) might be viewed as only a partial answer and the UCC response in (12b) as a change of subject, both clearly acknowledge what the current subject is. The second responses in (12a) and (12b), on the other hand, are close to incoherent. We focus here on the UCCs. In the context of asking who will win, asserting that the victory of the mayor's candidate is independent of his identity is irrelevant. In the context of asking who the mayor's candidate is, the UCC in (12b) may function as a way of claiming shared conversational goals can be satisfied without answering that question, but it clearly acknowledges what the question under discussion is.

Next consider the discourses in (13) in the context provided:

(13) – We've got to do everything we can to bring home John's message on jobs in the last week of the campaign.
– What's the difference?
{ a. Whoever the mayor supports will win.
{ b. # Whoever the mayor supports, he will win.

In marked contrast to the alternative NP sentence (13a), the UCC sentence

(13b) is quite odd in this context. The UCC sentence is odd because it is about the efficacy of the mayor's support. It is appropriate if the topic of the discourse is who the mayor might support, or perhaps better, as the discourses in (12) suggest, if the topic is *the question* of who the mayor will support. It is thus irrelevant to the discourse in (13).

It is important to note that the issue here is not really that (13b) is a conditional and (13a) is not. One might still analyze the future tense in (13a) as a modal conditional with a pragmatically supplied antecedent. In that case, the conditional means something like:

(14) (Even) if we do all that, whoever the mayor supports will win.

Under this understanding of the alternative NP sentence, it remains quite relevant to the discourse in (13b), and still contrasts sharply with the UCC variant.

We take examples (12) and (13) to provide evidence that UCCPs are topic-like. This may appear to be an abuse of terminology, because, as the discourses in (12) and (13) suggest, the relevant "topics" are propositional functions, but we assume this simply means there are second-order topics. The main descriptive point is that UCCs require the propositional functions denoted by their protases to be salient in the current discourse. We will not attempt to formalize this idea in the analysis presented here, but we will try to keep the analysis consistent with it. Syntactically, we propose that UCCPs are NPs adjoined to Ss in a topic-like configuration. It is striking in this connection that there are UCCPs which seem to function simply as proforms for previously determined alternatives, as in (7e).

Note that UCCPs can in fact be strongly referential, as one would expect of topics. Consider indicative versions of (13a) and (13b):

(15) a. Whoever the mayor supported won.
  a. Whoever the mayor supported, he won.

Note that while (15a) has a salient universal reading quantifying over different candidates the mayor supported, (15b) strongly prefers a referential reading.[7] We will give *whoever the mayor supported* the same interpretation in (15a) and (15b) and attribute the referentiality in (15b) to facts about the construction. The desire for a uniform analysis of this sort is one reason not to attribute the universal quantification in (15b) to a universal operator internal to *whoever the mayor supported.*

Summing up, we observe that UCCPs are topic-like. Perhaps it is better to say that UCCs are appropriate when the *question associated with the UCCP* is the topic. This seems especially apt for those UCCPs that are inherently non-referential, such as those in (3), which are related to alternative questions.

[7]To be clear, both sentences allow both readings. But there seems to be a clear preference for referentiality in the UCC sentence.

3.2.2 Syntactic Arguments for a Question-source for UCCs and Free Questions

Presenting a number of arguments anticipated in Richardson (1995), we argue that alternative NPs should be related to questions rather than relatives, showing that they pattern with questions in many syntactic properties distinguishing free relatives from questions. The same arguments carry over to UCCPs.

The argument for the question-like syntactic nature of alternative NPs hinges on four syntactic diagnostics:

(16) a. *Else:* The occurrence of *else* (Baker, Richardson)
b. The occurrence of a small class of question epithets alternative NPs (Baker, Richardson)
c. *Wh-paradigm:* The occurrence of *wh*-determiners *what*, *which*, *how + many*, *how + adj*
d. *Clefts:* The occurrence of clefts in alternative NPs

In the examples below, we abbreviate the argument by comparing alternative NPs with free relatives on one hand (which behave differently) and questions on the other (which behave the same). The facts in free relatives always follow those in relatives, showing that they have been correctly related to relative clauses. For a fuller discussion see Richardson (1995).

In contrast to free relatives and like ordinary questions, alternative NPs allow *else*:

(17) a. John will have room for whoever else Mary brings.
b. * John will have room for who else Mary brings.
c. John wondered who else Mary would bring.

In contrast to ordinary free relatives and like ordinary questions, alternative NPs allow epithets like *the hell*:[8]

(18) a. John will do whatever on earth Mary tells him to.
b. * John will do what on earth Mary brings.
c. John wondered what on earth Mary would tell him to do.

Alternative NPs and questions allow the determiners *which* and *what*, and free relatives do not.

(19) a. John bought whichever/whichever books Mary bought.
b. * John bought which/what books Mary bought.
c. John wonders which/what story Mary read.

Note the determiner *which* is not a restrictive relativizer in standard English:[9]

[8] Other examples of such epithets: *on earth*, *in heaven's/God's name*, *the devil*, and *the fuck*.

[9] A determiner *which* as a relativizer does appear to be possible in loosely connected nonrestrictive relatives like *After many years the story finally appeared in printed form in The Times, which*

(20) a. * The story which story John read was reprinted.
b. * The story what story John read was reprinted.

Again, the *wh*-specifier *how* occurs in questions and alternative NPs, but not free relatives:

(21) a. Mary will eat however many cream puffs John eats.
b. Chicago will build however large a stadium New York builds.
c. * Mary will eat how many cream puffs John eats.
d. * Chicago will build how large a stadium New York builds.
e. John wonders how many stadiums New York has built.
f. John wonders how large a stadium New York has built.

In contrast to ordinary free relatives and like ordinary questions, alternative NPs allow the cleft construction:

(22) a. Whatever it was that John chose annoyed Sandra.
b. * What it was that John chose annoyed Sandra.
c. Sandra wondered what it was that John chose.
d. # John, it was the red car car he chose.

It is not entirely clear what constraint rules out clefts in relative clauses, but one possibility is incompatibility of constructions marking focus and topic, illustrated in sentence (22d). If relativized elements are basically topic-like in nature and the cleft construction is a focusing construction, then the sentences in (22) may illustrate a discourse function clash, inherited by the true free relative in (22b). On the other hand, if questioned elements are basically focuslike elements, then no clash of function occurs in (22a).

3.2.3 Question and UCCP Presuppositions

We have examined some syntactic arguments for the close relationship of UCCPs and questions. Strong semantic evidence for the connection of UCCPs to questions can also be found by examing the presuppositional properties of UCCs.

We have characterized UCCs as conditional constructions, but certain UCCs show features strikingly different from other conditionals: Thus while (23a) as a whole entails that John is standing on something, (23b) does not:

(23) a. Whatever John is standing on, it will collapse soon.
b. If John is standing on something, it will collapse soon.
c. If John is standing on the table, it will collapse soon.

---

story was picked up and reprinted and eventually circulated throughout the civilized world. But this non-restrictive relative, if it is active in standard English, does not carry over to free relatives.

One account of the distinction is that the UCCP somehow takes wide scope; but we will see in Section 3.5.2 that there are UCCPs using the adverb *usually*, which means that the quantificational force of a UCC varies like that of other conditionals, making it hard to see how a scope account could be made to work.

An attractive alternative is that UCCPs carry an existential presupposition. The presuppositions of the protasis of a conditional are typically entailed by the conditional as a whole. This is shown in (23c), which as a whole does entail the existence of a table.[10]

Note that the same assumption would explain the anaphora facts illustrated in (24):

(24) a. Whatever John is standing on, it will collapse soon. It's made of cardboard.

b. John read whatever book Susan read. He found it in the kitchen.

If the entities answering to the properties of the *wh*-word in (24a) are presupposed to exist already, then it is natural for a pronoun to be able to refer to them. Example (24b) shows that the same property carries over to alternative NPs. If they share the existence presupposition, the anaphora properties would follow.

But if the UCCP of (23) does carry an existential presupposition, where does it come from? The possibility I want to explore is that this is a property shared with the questions UCCs are related to.[11]

Existential Presupposition of Constituent Questions

The claim that constituent questions carry existential presuppositions is not uncontroversial. Consider the question in (25a).

(25) a. Who shot Mr. Burns?

b. No one.

c. No one. There is no Mr. Burns. It's a cartoon!

The fact that (25b) is a viable continuation would seem to suggest that (25a) has no existential presupposition. Yet, as has often been observed, answers like (25c) are also viable, and (25c) clearly violates a presupposition carried by the name *Mr. Burns,* that the name's bearer exist. Similarly although denying other

[10]Note that alternative NPs show the same existence entailment (as noted also in Jacobson 1990 for the singular case):

Whatever John is standing on will collapse soon—namely, nothing.

[11]The account to be presented also assumes that presuppositions of the protasis of a conditional become presuppositions of the conditional as a whole. The essential observation about the presupposition-projecting properties of conditionals is in Langendoen and Savin (1971), somewhat more fully articulated in Karttunen (1973); and the dynamic account of presupposition in conditionals is due to Heim (1982). The semantics sketched in section 3.6 will show how such presuppositions are projected.

sorts of presuppositions is difficult in positive sentences (Levin 1983), it is less difficult in negative sentences and questions:

(26) a. # John regrets eating bagels, because in fact he never ate any.
b. John doesn't regret eating bagels, because in fact he never ate any.
c. – Did Bill shoot the king of France?
– No, because there never was one.

The facts appear to be that nothing rules out overt contradiction of presuppositions in questions. The question about cases like (25b), then, is, do they count as an answer to the question, or as a contradiction of its presupposition?

There seem to be three possible positions on the question of the existential presupposition of questions:

(27) a. Empty set answers to *wh*-questions are just like all other answers.
b. A *wh*-question doesn't have an existential presupposition. It has an *existential entailment*.[12]
c. A *wh*-question has an existential presupposition. If uttered in a discourse which does not entail the existential claim, it is infelicitous.

One difficulty with (27a) is that it doesn't explain how question words can serve as the antecedents of pronouns. *Wh*-words license pronouns even when their questions go unanswered. Thus (25a) can certainly be answered:

(28) I don't know, but he's insane.

For the reasons noted above, positions (27b) and (27c) solve this problem.

The classic argument that an expression E carries a presupposition p involves embedding E under entailment blocking operators, to see if the embedding expression still implies the truth of p. It is difficult to find embedding contexts for UCCs and matrix questions. But the argument may straightforwardly be made for embedded questions:

(29) a. John wondered who shot Mr. Burns.
b. If John wondered who shot Mr. Burns, then he asked Mary.
c. It is clear who shot Mr. Burns.
d. It is not clear who shot Mr. Burns.
e. It is not clear that there was a crime committed.

As a starting point, (29a), an embedded question verb *wonder*, has an entailment that someone shot Mr. Burns. The entailment persists in (29b), where the clause occurs as the antecedent of a conditional, normally an entailment blocking context ('if p, then q' does not entail p). Examples (29c) and (29d) show

[12] A difficulty with (27b) is that it is not immediately clear what the "entailments" of a question are. There have been proposals in the literature for a similar notion, including one by Groenendijk and Stokhof (1984) (G&S). Briefly, the intuition is this: Whatever is systematically entailed by all possible answers to a question is entailed by the question.

the same pattern for the embedded question adjective *clear*, using negation as the entailment blocking context ($\neg p$ does not entail p). Example (29e) shows that *clear* is not factive, so there is no reason to suspect lexical properties of *clear* as the explanation of the entailments in (29c) and (29d).

There is at least one available entailment-blocking context for embedding UCCs and matrix questions, but there are problems interpreting the data.

(30) a. If Mary isn't here, then who shot Mister Burns?
b. If Mary isn't here, then whoever shot Mister Burns, he can't be the most likely suspect.

As desired, the existence entailment seems to carry. A potential problem with these examples is that they are 'epistemic' conditionals which announce a deduction on the part of the speaker. The entailment properties of these constructions are murky.

It appears that the sentences in (30) may be used as a challenge. That is, when someone has asserted Mary's absence, one may respond with (30a) as a way of refuting the claim. In such a context, Mary's absence really is being hypothetically assumed. It's still not clear, however, that the question is being posed in that hypothetical context, or whether it's even meaningful to talk about posing a question in a hypothetical context.

An independent argument for treating the existential of a question as a presupposition, rather than an entailment, is the suspendability (Horn 1972) of the existential claim. Presupposition, but not entailments, generally can be suspended.

(31) a. Who—if anyone—shot Mr. Burns?
b. John regrets going to grad school—if in fact he did.
c. # John shot Mr. Burns—if indeed a gun was fired.

In the next section other question presuppositions are explored; if a variety of question presuppositions become properties of UCCs, then the case for presupposition projection into UCCs is strengthened, and with it the case for treating the facts in (23) as an example of presupposition projection.

Other Presuppositions of Questions

In a dynamic framework such as that of Heim (1982), sentences are partial functions from contexts to contexts; presuppositions are the restrictions on the domain of that function. In this framework, simple cases of presupposition projection are handled by the simple mechanism of function composition. If the semantics of Node A is computed by composing the semantics of daughter B with the input context, then the felicity conditions of B will be inherited by A. This, for example, is what happens for the simplest conditionals with respect to their protases. The conditional as a whole is validated by just those cases of the input context which, if they can be extended to validate the protasis, can also be extended to validate the apodosis. Testing this condition means evaluating the semantics of the protasis against the input context; therefore the conditional as a whole inherits the presuppositions of the protasis.

Not all conditionals can be handled by these means. Counterfactuals, for example, require revision of the input context; as a result, only the revised context will be required to satisfy the presuppositions of the protasis. There the story about what presuppositions can be projected out of a counterfactual protasis must include a story about what can be revised in a counterfactual.

Nevertheless, the general shape of a dynamic account of presupposition is the following: All things being equal, all presuppositions are equal. If one presupposition is projected, so should they all. Other accounts of presupposition projection share this property. Thus, if our account of the reference properties of UCCs is to be based on the presupposition projection, then all things being equal, it would be best if *all* the presuppositions of questions and UCCs were shared. Otherwise, the story will require additional apparatus.

Fortunately, no such additional apparatus appears to be needed. For example, determiner *which*, used in questions with singular nouns, appears to carry the presupposition that the questioned entity is one of a known set and is *unique* in carrying the question property:

(32) a. Which book did Mary read? # *War and Peace* and *Crime and Punishment.*

b. Whichever book Mary reads, Alice will criticize it. # Since Mary will read *War and Peace* and *Crime and Punishment*, Alice will criticize them.

c. Whatever Mary reads, Alice will criticize it. Since Mary will read *War and Peace* and *Crime and Punishment*, Alice will criticize them.

The UCC in (32b) appears to carry the same presupposition.

Consider next the well-known cases of presuppositions of alternative questions, which as we have already seen, enter into the UCC construction along with constituent questions.

(33) a. Does John drink whiskey or beer?

b. Whether John drinks whiskey or beer, he will get fat.

On the alternative question reading, sentence (33a) carries the presupposition that either John drinks beer or he drinks whiskey, and asks for the matter to be settled. The analogous UCC in (33b) appears to carry the same presupposition.

Finally, consider the felicity condition on questions whose answer is unknown to the speaker. Although, strictly speaking, this ought not to be regarded as a presupposition, because it can be suspended in 'quizmaster-question' and indirect question contexts, it is clearly linked to the discourse function of direct questions. Just as clearly, there is an implicature, discussed in Section

3.2.3, that speakers using descriptive UCCs and alternative NPs do not know the identity of their referents.[13] Again, it is reasonable to suppose that this property is projected directly from a common source for questions, UCCs, and alternative NPs.

3.3 To be Explained

We will call the class of constructions including UCCPs and alternative NPs *free alternative constructions*. Then the previous sections have suggested that there are two important sets of facts to be explained about free alternative constructions.

- Shared syntactic properties of free alternative constructions and questions
- Shared presuppositions of free alternative constructions and questions

There are two kinds of accounts of these shared properties. First, one might propose that free alternative constructions are derived from questions. There is a serious objection to this idea, given all known theories of the semantics of questions. There is no way, given the denotation of a constituent question in standard theories of questions, to get at the property of individuals from which the constituent question semantics was built. But this is what would be required in order to derive alternative NPs from questions.

Consider the Groenendijk and Stokhof semantics for *which boy walks* used in Section 3.6.1:

$$\lambda \dot{i} \lambda \dot{j} [\, \lambda \dot{x}[\text{boy}(\dot{i})(\dot{x}) \wedge \text{walk}(\dot{i})(\dot{x})] = \lambda \dot{x}[\text{boy}(\dot{j})(\dot{x}) \wedge \text{walk}(\dot{j})(\dot{x})]\,]$$

This is what Groendijk and Stokhof call a propositional concept, a function from worlds to propositions, which picks out a different proposition at each world, namely the one specifying who does the walking for that world. The propositional function we want for our alternative NP semantics is the one used in the interior equality:

$$\lambda \dot{x}[\text{boy}(\dot{j})(\dot{x}) \wedge \text{walk}(\dot{j})(\dot{x})]$$

But there is no way to recover the propositional function from the propositional concept. A similar argument can be made for a Kartunnen-style semantics for questions.

A second hypothesis is that free alternative constructions and questions are derived from a common source. This is the account we shall pursue:

> **Hypothesis A**: Free alternative constructions and questions are derived from a common source we call *pre-questions*.

[13] This property of alternative NPs is noted in Jacobson (1990).

To give a uniform treatment of question formation we will allow all questions to have pre-questions, but only constituent questions and alternative pre-questions will be related to free alternative constructions. The exclusion of yes-no questions will be due to the fact that free-alternative constructions are formed only from pre-questions denoting propositional functions; and a *wh*-like operator is required to form a propositional function denotation. In the case of constituent-questions this operator is supplied by the *wh*-phrase; in the case of alternative questions, it is supplied by a special alternative-forming version of disjunction. But nothing relates yes-no questions to a propositional function. Thus we have:

> **Hypothesis B**: Alternative questions and *Wh*-Questions form a natural semantic class.

There are besides a host of finer grained semantic facts to be accounted for:

(34) a. Scopal differences of UCCPs and alternative NPs
b. Quantificational Behavior of Alternative NPs
c. What does the *ever* add semantically?
d. Evocation of Scales by UCCPs

3.4 Alternative NPs

We turn first to the treatment of alternative NPs. The compositional treatment we will propose will build UCCPs up out of a variety of NPs, including alternative NPs, alternative question NPs (*whether John drinks whiskey or beer*), and proforms like *either way*. Thus the preliminary question is what their semantics is.

Consider the following sentences:

(35) a. Whoever the mayor endorsed made a large contribution to his campaign.
b. Every candidate the mayor endorsed made a large contribution to his campaign.
c. The candidates the mayor endorsed made a large contribution to his campaign.

Examples (35a) and (35b) share a reading on which each candidate the mayor endorses contributes a large sum to the mayor's campaign. We will call this the Q (or quantificational) reading. Example (35c) has the Q-reading but it also has another reading on which the endorsed candidates collectively make a large contribution to the mayor's campaign; on this reading, which we will call the G (for group) reading, the portion that each endorsed candidate contributes may be small, as long as the contributions taken together total to a large sum. Neither (35a) nor (35b) has the G-reading. In not showing clear evidence of group readings, alternative NPs are like universally quantified NPs.

Other cases where one might expect to find group readings show a similar pattern:

(36) a. They gathered the candidates Clinton had campaigned for in the vice-president's office.

b. ? They gathered whoever Clinton had campaigned for in the vice-president's office.

c. ? They gathered every candidate Clinton had campaigned for in the vice-president's office.

d. John found the paintings he was looking for in opposite corners of the museum.

e. * John found whatever he was looking for in opposite corners of the museum.

f. * John found every painting he was looking for in opposite corners of the museum.

Some attempts to force G-readings on alternative NPs work better than expected, as in (36b), but in such cases analogous universals are unexpectedly good too. Alternative NPs, in general, seem very reluctant to accept group readings, as well as quantificational apparatus reserved for imposing distributive readings on group arguments:

(37) a. ? John gave whoever the mayor endorsed $100 apiece/each.

b. ? John gave every candidate the mayor endorsed $100 apiece/each.

a. John gave the candidates the mayor endorsed $100 apiece/each.

To explain Q-readings analogous to those in (35a), Jacobson (1990) proposes that free relatives (FRs) are semantically unmarked for number and may denote groups. Given the same kind of distributivity operator usually appealed to to explain the Q-reading of (35c), she then derives Q-readings for free relatives. But the patterns cited here make such an analysis less appealing for alternative NPs.

Are alternative NPs then universally quantified NPs? There are clearly cases for which this seems an unlikely possibility. It turns out that alternative NPs that use the determiners *whichever* are *whatever* are much more reluctant to admit a quantificational reading like that of (35a):

(38) Whatever/Whichever candidate the mayor endorsed made a large contribution to the mayor's campaign.

These facts might be explained, however, by appealing to the uniqueness presuppositions we argued for in Section 31. If alternative NPs built from *whichever* and *whatever* determiners have uniqueness presuppositions, they should only accept quantificational readings in contexts in which some kind of local accommodation is possible. That is, they should basically behave like definites. This leaves open the possibility of analyzing those alternative NPs as referential NPs, with no quantificational force of their own, like definites and indefinites in DRT and File Change Semantics, and analyzing other alternative NPs as universals.

But there is evidence suggesting that no alternative NP should be analyzed as universal. Consider (39):

(39) a. John would accept every salary they offered.

b. John would accept whatever they offered.

Example (39a) is a little odd pragmatically, because it asks us to imagine John being offered an arbitrary number of salaries and accepting each. But given the most natural kind of context, one in which a fixed *they* have placed a fixed job under negotiation, the only way John would be given a second offer was if he rejected the first one, and this is exactly what (39a) rules out.

On the other hand (39b) does not have the pragmatic oddity of (39a). This illustrates one problem with analyzing alternative NPs like *whatever they offered* as quantificational: They do not show the kind of double quantification effects other universally quantified NPs show under external quantification.

On the contrary, the right description of (39b) seems to require analyzing the alternative NP as non-quantificational. Suppose we hypothesize some sort of job-application situation as setting the modal context (satisfying the job-existence presupposition of an offer). In a dynamic framework, this would be represented something like:

(40) $[\exists s \exists x \text{job}(s)(x) \Rightarrow \text{offer}(s)(\textbf{they}, x); \text{accept}(s)(\textbf{j}, x)]$

In this paper, we will work in a non-dynamic framework.[14] Basically, if one wants to keep the distinction between referential NPs and generalized quantifiers, this means one needs to treat definites and indefinites alike as free variables which may be overtly bound by a higher operator, in this case the conditional operator. We will represent the static equivalent of the above as:

(41) $[\text{job}(s)(x) \Rightarrow_{\{s,x\}} \text{offer}(s)(\textbf{they}, x) \wedge \text{accept}(s)(\textbf{j}, x)]$

The subscripts on the conditional arrow indicate the variables that need to be universally quantified over by the conditional operator.

This leaves us with a dilemma. There is much to be said for analyzing alternative NPs as referential, but if they are referential, and not plural, then where do quantificational readings like those in (35) come from?[15]

[14]We present compositional rules in a static framework because there are numerous issues about extending the Groenendijk and Stokhof semantics for questions to a dynamic framework which take us beyond the scope of this paper.

[15]The dilemma here is of course reminsicsent of the problem of free-choice *any*.

The analysis we will propose is the one proposed for the analogous NPs in Japanese in Harada and Honda (1999). Alternative NPs are referential NPs that invoke a pragmatic scale and denote an entity that takes a minimum value on that scale. Quantificational readings arise by scalar implicature. The function of *ever* is to signal invocation of the pragmatic scale.

For example (35a) the account has to be something like the following. Call the set of entities the mayor endorsed S; and let the scale we are interested in for (35a) be an entailment ordering such that x is a mininum if and only if

$$\forall y \in \mathbf{S}\Box[\mathbf{ML}(x) \rightarrow \mathbf{ML}(y)]$$

Here ML denotes the property of making a large contribution to the mayor's campaign. The modality reflects the intuition that the scale measures a likelihood: In all likely worlds, the implication holds. For a scalar implicature account, we want *whoever the mayor endorsed* to denote a minimum x and to presuppose the above implication. Let us define an operator Π that gives the pragmatic scale, and holds of the domain set, the scaling property, and the minimum on the scale.

$$\Pi(\mathbf{P}, \mathbf{Q}, x) \equiv \forall y \in \mathbf{P}\Box[\mathbf{Q}(x) \rightarrow \mathbf{Q}(y)]$$

In the intensional language of Gallin (1975), used in Section 3.6, this becomes:

$$\Pi(\mathbf{P}, \mathbf{Q}, x) \equiv \forall y \in \mathbf{P}\Box_i[\mathbf{Q}(i)(x) \rightarrow \mathbf{Q}(i)(y)]$$

If we assume that *ever* takes the propositional functions associated with *wh*-questions as its arguments, this gives it a determiner-like semantics, something like the following:

$$[\![ever]\!] = \lambda\mathbf{P}\lambda\mathbf{Q}[\mathbf{P}(x) \wedge \mathbf{Q}(x) \wedge \partial(\Pi(\mathbf{P}, \mathbf{Q}, x))]$$

In the framework of Gallin (1975) this becomes:

$$[\![ever]\!] = \lambda\mathbf{P}\lambda\mathbf{Q}\lambda i[\mathbf{P}(i)(x) \wedge \mathbf{Q}(i)(x) \wedge \partial(\Pi(\mathbf{P}, \mathbf{Q}, x))]$$

Here we use the ∂ symbol used in Beaver (1993) to encode presupposed material.[16] So *ever* is basically a referential determiner like *a* or *the* which carries a presupposition that the entity denoted by the NP is a mininum on a scale. This would give a sentence like (35a) a semantics like the following:

$$[\mathbf{endorse}(x)(\mathbf{m}) \wedge \mathbf{ML}(x) \wedge \partial(\Pi(\lambda y[\mathbf{endorse}(y)(\mathbf{m})], \mathbf{ML}, x))]$$

It is worth pointing out that the scalar apparatus we have associated with *ever* resembles the apparatus needed for the focus particle *even*:

(42) JOHN even made a large contribution to the mayor's campaign.

[16]The operator is actually only definable in a dynamic framework. We use it here as a notational device to distinguish presupposed from asserted material, to help make clear how presupposition projection issues interact with the compositional semantics.

Here the NP *John* must denote a person unlikely to make a large contribution, with the implicature that others more likely to did as well. The difference between *even* and *ever* on this analysis is that *ever* makes explicit a set of entities being measured on the scale and occurs inside the NP defining that set. It is suggestive that, as discussed in Harada and Honda (1999), the Japanese particle *mo* may be used to mark referential NPs like proper names and can then have a function very like that of *even*. Beyond this, the tightness of the connection between *even* and *ever* is an intriguing open issue.

The Π-operator provides an account of Q-readings but we have noticed numerous cases of alternative NPs with readings on which a unique referent satisfies the alternative NP description. We will account for these readings simply as cases in which the propositional function defined by the *wh* phrase determines an alternative set with a single member; in such cases, the pragmatic scale can do no work. This will always be the case for singular alternative NPs in *which* or *what*, because the NP presupposition requires that the alternative set have a single member.

Such a scalar account of *ever* makes an interesting prediction concerning the interaction of universal readings with negation:

(43) a. Bill did not campaign for whoever the mayor endorsed.
b. Bill did not campaign for every candidate the mayor endorsed.

Consider how the scalar implicature account works for (43a). First, we try a scale ranking people for their likelihood NOT to be campaigned for, making x a minimum on that scale.

$$\begin{aligned}[\ &\mathbf{endorse}(\mathbf{m})(x) \wedge \neg\mathbf{campaign\text{-}for}(\mathbf{b})(x) \wedge \\ &\partial(\Pi(\mathbf{endorse}(\mathbf{m}), \lambda y \neg\mathbf{campaign\text{-}for}(\mathbf{b})(y), x))]\end{aligned}$$

This asserts that Bill did not campaign for the endorsed x he was least likely not to campaign for (most likely to campaign for) and yields the implicature that for all endorsed y he was more likely not to campaign for, he did not campaign for y. In other words, the implicature cranked out gives the universal wider scope than the negation.

Suppose we next try a scale in which the negation has been left out, in effect, scoping the alternative NP inside the negation:

$$\begin{aligned}\neg[\ &\mathbf{endorse}(\mathbf{m})(x) \wedge \neg\mathbf{campaign\text{-}for}(\mathbf{b})(x) \wedge \\ &\partial(\Pi(\mathbf{endorse}(\mathbf{m}), \lambda y\mathbf{campaign\text{-}for}(\mathbf{b})(y), x))]\end{aligned}$$

In this case, the scale does no work. We are told that the minimum x was not campaigned for, but the presupposition licenses a universal inference only in the case when x *is* campaigned for. Thus, no universal reading can result from this scoping.

The consequence of the scalar account is thus that (43a) should lack a reading consistent with there being some endorsed candidates Clinton did campaign for, the negation-outscoping-universal reading that is quite salient for (43b).[17] This prediction seems to be correct. Discourse (44a), in contrast to (44b), is contradictory.

(44) a. # Clinton did not campaign for whoever the mayor endorsed. But he did campaign for some of the mayor's candidates.
b. Clinton did not campaign for every candidate the mayor endorsed. But he did campaign for some of the mayor's candidates.

Summing up, we have argued for analyzing all alternative NPs as referential NPs, with apparent quantificational effects accounted for by appeal to pragmatic scales.

3.5 UCCs

We have proposed that UCCs are built out of alternative NPs composed with their main clauses in a topic-like construction. We discuss syntactic and semantic issues. What are UCCPs syntactically? We assume they are NPs, although the evidence is admittedly far from decisive. Semantically, we discuss the idea that the situation (or world) variables associated with alternative NPs in UCCs need to function like antecedent clause situation variables in ordinary conditionals, interacting with the modality of the particular conditional type to determine the referentiality of the NPs.

3.5.1 What are UCCPs syntactically?

Constituents like *whoever John chooses* might reasonably be analyzed either as NPs or as clauses. In this section we argue for treating them as NPs. First it is worth pointing out that constituents constraining the antecedents of conditionals are a mixed bag. The following sentences should all probably be analyzed as conditionals with the 'preposed' constituent constraining the antecedent.

(45) a. The classier the paint job, the more you need alloy wheels. (Fillmore 1986)
b. With his red cap and green breeches on, John would look quite dapper.
c. ? Any dish John cooked, Mary would (usually) be pleased.
d. Either way, the electorate will be swindled.

Example (45d) is particularly relevant to the case of UCCs, since it has the semantics of quantifying over a disjunction of alternatives, and what is preposed seems to be an NP.

[17] The facts for *Bill refused to campaign for whoever the mayor endorsed* are quite parallel, but the account is somewhat more problematic. There is a salient reading under which the alternative NP (and the universal force) scopes under *refuse* and over negation. On this reading, the scale property needs to include the negation, as in (43). Short of lexical decomposition, it is not obvious how to give alternative NPs such a scoping.

UCCPs do not allow pied-piped prepositions.

(46) * To whatever city we travel, we will need good locks on our suitcases.

This is true of alternative NPs as well. The simplest account of this coincidence is to have the alternative NPs themselves occurring in the UCC construction. There is some motivation for treating the alternative questions as NPs too:

(47) Whether John ate creampuffs or napoleons is not the issue.

Thus we provisionally adopt the analysis that all UCCPs are NPs.[18] For simplicity, we will assume a single rule combining *ever* with any pre-question denoting a propositional function to yield an NP. We assume that in the case of alternative questions, this has no pronounced effect. That is,

whether + ever = whether.

The semantic idea is that the scalar effects we attribute to *ever* extend to all UCCPs, alternative NPs and alternative questions. On the syntax side, nothing hangs on this except a saved rule.

3.5.2 Quantificational Nature of UCCs

Since Lewis (1975) pointed out sentences like

(48) Most of the time, if a man buys a horse, he pays cash for it.

writers studying the semantics of conditionals have made reference to the quantificational nature of conditionals, identifying the protasis with the restrictor and the apodosis with the scope. The question then arises as to what, exactly, is being quantified over in (48); various writers have made reference to situations, cases, occasions, or events. For ease of exposition we will refer to quantification over situations.

The question we now address is what needs to be counted or quantified over in UCCs.

(49) a. If John cooks, Mary is usually pleased.
b. Whatever dish John cooks, Mary is usually pleased.

The meaning of example (49a) can be paraphrased roughly as follows: In most situations in which John cooks, Mary is pleased. Example (49b) differs crucially in this respect. Consider the following state of affairs:

(50) John cooked twenty dishes on one occasion, pleasing Mary with each; and on eight others John cooked a dish apiece, and on each of those eight occasions Mary was displeased.

[18]A remaining syntactic mystery about all UCCPs, whether alternative questions or alternative NPs, is the exclusion of all infinitival questions. Since this is a restriction shared with free relatives, it may have something to do with NP-hood, although it is not shared by embedded alternative questions in subject position.

In these circumstances, sentence (49a) has a reading on which it is false, but sentence (49b) does not. Crucially, sentence (49b) seems to require that dishes be counted. What this shows is that the variable asssociated with the *wh*-word has a special status in UCC conditionals: It must be one one of the variables quantified away by the selective binding of conditional formation, and one of the variables *counted* when the conditional force is evaluated. This is consistent with what we called the topic-like nature of UCCPs in Section 3.2.1. UCCs are about whatever the UCCP is about; and in a quantificational context, aboutness means quantifying over (see Partee 1991). It was argued in Section 3.5.1 for independent reasons that UCCPs should be NPs. As we will see when we give the semantics of UCCPs, that will be consistent with treating the -variable as special.

Three of the key elements in what Partee (1991) calls the Lewis-Kratzer-Heim analysis of conditionals are collected in (51):

(51) 1. Conditionals involve quantification, with the restrictor of the quantifier identified with the protasis, and the nuclear scope identified with the apodosis.

2. Conditionals can quantify over situations (or something very like them).

3. The exact quantificational force of a conditional is determined by sentence-level operators (such as quantificational adverbs). The conditional construction only determines restrictor and nuclear scope of a quantification; and universal force is only a kind of default invoked when no overt operator is present.

Example (49b) shows that claims (1) and (3) are upheld for UCCs. We next argue for the importance of situations in the account of UCCs.

We return to an example discussed in Section 3.2.3. here reproduced as (52):

(52) Whatever John is standing on, it will collapse soon.

Recall that this sentence as a whole entails that there is something John is standing on. Following the discussion in Section 3.2.3 and abstracting away from numerous details, we propose the following as the semantics for (52):

(53) $[\partial[\exists \dot{z}\ \text{stand-on}(\dot{s_0})(\mathbf{j}, \dot{z})] \wedge \text{stand-on}(\dot{s_0})(\mathbf{j}, \dot{x}) \wedge \partial[\text{present}(\dot{s_0})]\,] \Rightarrow_{\{\dot{s_0}, \dot{x}\}} \text{soon-collapse}(\dot{s_0})(\dot{x}, \dot{y})]$

The antecedent of the conditional breaks into two components, a presupposition derived from the question (within the scope of the operator ∂), and an asserted component, which claims of x that John is standing on it. The presupposition requires that there exists a situation s_0 in which John is standing on something. The conditional further presupposes that it be a situation overlapping with the time of utterance. Thus, the sentence as a whole requires a present situation in which John is standing on something.

Consider in contrast a non-referential example.

(54) Whatever$_i$ John reads, Mary will read it$_i$ next.

Note that this has no entailment of the existence of a book John is presently reading and thus no entailment of a specific book. If both (52) and (54) are conditionals, our problem now is to account for the difference between them. Why does (52) entail the present existence of something John is standing on while (54) does not?

Abstracting away from the details of the question semantics and how it becomes part of the conditional (these details are presented in Section 3.6), the semantics of (54) will be

$$\begin{array}{l}[\,\partial[\exists\dot{z} \wedge \text{book}(y) \wedge \text{read}(\dot{s_0})(\mathbf{j}, \dot{z})] \wedge \\ \;\text{read}(\dot{s_0})(\mathbf{j}, \dot{y}) \wedge \partial[\text{non-present}(\dot{s_0})]\,] \Rightarrow_{\{\dot{s_0},\dot{x}\}} \\ \text{read-next}(\dot{s_0})(\mathbf{m})(\dot{y})]\end{array}$$

Note that the situation variable $\dot{s_0}$ is now constrained to be non-past, which include future situations. In contrast to (53), this semantics as a whole presupposes that there is some present or future event in which John reads something. The existence entailment disappears, but the sentence still imposes an expectation that John will read something.[19] The pastness or non-pastness of the situation variable will roughly correlate with the tense morphology of the conditional in ways that are beyond the scope of this paper to account for. As a check that verbal tense and mood play the key role here, consider the ordinary conditionals corresponding to (52) and (54).

(55) a. If John is standing on something, it will collapse soon.
b. If John reads a book, Mary will read it next.

Example (55a) quantifies over situations overlapping with the time of utterance, (55b) over non-past situations.

An alternative account of (53) would be to make the situation variable s_0 be free. This would make the entire conditional an assertion about some particular discourse-marker s_0 which must already be available in the discourse, with the accompanying presupposition that in that situation $\dot{s_0}$, John be standing on something. This might also be the right account of the strong referentiality of topic-like examples like (15), discussed in Section 3.2.1, which seems to be shared with (52). Such conditionals would no longer quantify over situations.

[19]Both semantics allow for a universal reading, but the pragmatic fact that John can only stand on one thing at a time blocks a universal reading for (53). Conditional quantification thus offers a way of obtaining universal readings which is quite independent of the scalar implicature account in Section 3.4.

They collapse into simple assertions about the referent of the alternative NP. In the semantics of Section 3.6, we always identify the alternative NP situation variable with the situation variable quantified away by the conditional, omitting any treatment of free situations variables.

3.6 Sketch of a Semantic Analysis

The semantics proposed below assumes previous work on questions and conditionals. The novel elements are the analysis of *ever* discussed in Section 3.4 and an attempt to rework the semantics of alternative questions to make them fall into a natural class with *wh*-questions.

3.6.1 Groenendijk and Stokhof Semantics for Questions

We turn first to the re-analysis of alternative questions. For Groenendijk and Stokhof (1984), $[_{\text{S:[wh,+que]}}$Whether Bills walks$]$ translates into Ty2 (Gallin 1975) as:

$$\lambda\dot{i}\lambda\dot{j}[\,[\text{walk}(\dot{i})(\mathbf{b})] = [\text{walk}(\dot{j})(\mathbf{b})]\,]$$

This is what they call a propositional concept, a function from worlds to propositions. For any world i, the question concept takes you to the proposition that answers the given question in i.

For G&S $[_{\text{S:[wh,+que]}}$Which boy walks$]$ translates as:

$$\lambda\dot{i}\lambda\dot{j}[\,\lambda\dot{x}[\text{boy}(\dot{i})(\dot{x}) \wedge \text{walk}(\dot{i})(\dot{x})] = \lambda\dot{x}[\text{boy}(\dot{j})(\dot{x}) \wedge \text{walk}(\dot{j})(\dot{x})]\,]$$

For G&S $[_{\text{S:[wh,+que]}}$Whether Mary drinks whiskey or beer$]$ translates as:

$$\begin{aligned}\lambda\dot{i}\lambda\dot{j}[\,&[\text{drink}(\dot{i})(\text{m})(\text{w})] = [\text{drink}(\dot{j})(\text{m})(\text{w})] \wedge \\ &[\text{drink}(\dot{i})(\text{m})(\text{b})] = [\text{drink}(\dot{j})(\text{m})(\text{b})]\,]\end{aligned}$$

Note the conjunctive translation here, which is the correct translation given the assumptions of G&S. Using disjunction would yield answer propositions that were too weak. For a world in which John drank whiskey and not beer, the propositional concept would yield the proposition that John drinks whiskey or beer or neither.

We modify the translation of *whether Mary drinks whiskey or beer* to:

$$\begin{aligned}&[\![_{\text{S:[wh,+que]}}\text{Whether Mary drinks whiskey or beer}]\!] = \\ &\lambda\dot{i}\lambda\dot{j}[\lambda\dot{x}[(\text{beer} = \dot{x} \vee \text{whiskey} = \dot{x}) \wedge \text{drink}(\dot{i})(\text{m})(\dot{x})] = \\ &\qquad \lambda\dot{x}[(\text{beer} = \dot{x} \vee \text{whiskey} = \dot{x}) \wedge \text{drink}(\dot{j})(\text{m})(\dot{x})]]\end{aligned}$$

Here we have chosen to parallel the constituent question semantics as much as possible, yielding a translation that might be paraphrased *what, whiskey or beer, does John drink*, or *what does John drink, whiskey or beer*. This gives us the same function as G&S's translation, but we have managed to express it with a disjunction. We sketch below how this might be acheived compositionally. A further refinement not shown here would be to capture the associated presupposition that one or ther other of the alternatives holds. We discuss this in Section 3.7.

For G&S $[_{\text{S:[wh,+que]}}$Whether Bills walks or not$]$ translates as:

$$\lambda\dot{i}\lambda\dot{j}[\ [\text{walk}(\dot{i})(\text{b})] = [\text{walk}(\dot{j})(\text{b})] \wedge [\neg\text{walk}(\dot{i})(\text{b})] = [\neg\text{walk}(\dot{j})(\text{b})]\ ]$$

This is completely equivalent to the translation of *whether John walks.*

We modify this to:

$$\lambda\dot{i}\lambda\dot{j}[\lambda\dot{p}[(\dot{p} = \lambda\dot{i}\text{walk}(\dot{i})(\text{b}) \vee \dot{p} = \lambda\dot{i}\neg\text{walk}(\dot{i})(\text{b})) \wedge \dot{p}(\dot{i})] = \lambda\dot{p}[(\dot{p} = \lambda\dot{i}\text{walk}(\dot{i})(\text{b}) \vee \dot{p} = \lambda\dot{i}\neg\text{walk}(\dot{i})(\text{b})) \wedge \dot{p}(\dot{j})]\ ]$$

This is roughly *which proposition holds, that John walks or that John doesn't walk.* This is equivalent to the G&S translation.

3.6.2 Semantics of Pre-Questions

We hypothesize constituents we call pre-questions which we characterize as S:[wh,–que] and which feed a question formation rule. All questions are derived from pre-questions, but only constituent and alternative pre-questions denote propositional functions. Yes-no pre-questions denote propositions. Thus yes-no questions cannot feed the NP formation rules that provide the antecedents for UCCs.

The pre-question $[_{\text{S:[wh,–que]}}$Which boy walks$]$ translates as:

$$\lambda\dot{i}\lambda\dot{x}[\text{boy}(\dot{i})(\dot{x}) \wedge \text{walk}(\dot{i})(\dot{x})]$$

The pre-question *whether Mary drinks whiskey or beer* translates as:

$$[_{\text{S:[wh,–que]}}\text{Whether Mary drinks whiskey or beer}] = \lambda\dot{i}\lambda\dot{x}[(\text{beer} = \dot{x} \vee \text{whiskey} = \dot{x}) \wedge \text{drink}(\dot{i})(\text{m})(\dot{x})]$$

And the pre-question $[_{\text{S:[wh,–que]}}$Whether Bills walks or not$]$ translates as:

$$\lambda\dot{i}\lambda\dot{p}[\ (\dot{p} = \lambda\dot{i}\text{walk}(\dot{i})(\text{b}) \vee \dot{p} = \lambda\dot{i}\neg\text{walk}(\dot{i})(\text{b})) \wedge \dot{p}(\dot{i})]$$

In contrast the pre-question $[_{\text{S:[wh,–que]}}$Whether Bills walks$]$ translates as something of a different type, a proposition.

$$\lambda\dot{i}[\text{walk}(\dot{i})(\text{b})]$$

3.6.3 Rules Consuming Pre-Questions

In the following rules we assume the translation of *ever* given in Section 3.4, written here as ever′.

Let PreQ be an abbreviation for S:[wh,–que]s. Question formation is the same for all PreQs, whether they denote propositional functions or not. Thus $[_{\text{S:[wh,+que]}}\ [_{\text{PreQ}}\alpha]]$, where $\alpha\prime = [\![[_{\text{PreQ}}\alpha]]\!]$:

$$[\![[_{\text{S:[wh,+que]}}\alpha]]\!] = \lambda\dot{i}\lambda\dot{j}[\alpha\prime(\dot{i}) = \alpha\prime(\dot{j})]$$

This just gives the G&S semantics, with the revisions indicated above.

For alternative NPs[20] we simply add *ever*, $[_{\text{np:[ever]}}\ \text{ever}\ [_{\text{PreQ}}\alpha]]$:

$$[\![[_{\text{NP:[ever]}}\ \text{ever}\ \alpha]]\!] = \text{ever}\prime(\alpha\prime)$$

Note that alternative NPs are not *wh*-NPs, because they cannot function as the extracted NP in ordinary questions.

For the semantics of UCCs, we will scope the alternative NPs using a free (pragmatically assigned) property, letting scalar properties be determined by the pragmatics. We assume the conditional operator is supplied by the construction. See Partee (1991) for the intriguing suggestion that such a conditional-like operator might generally be the assertion operator connecting topics and main clauses. Note that capturing the situation variable of the NP works out very cleanly in the Gallin/G&S semantics, because it is the first argument of the intensional NP-denotation. Of course a host of difficulties plaguing a static semantics, involving other variables that may need to be captured, including donkey variables, are not dealt with.

Finally, the topic-like construction that combines alternative NPs with Ss to give fulls UCCs. For $[_{\text{S:[cond]}}\ [_{\text{NP:[ever]}}\ \alpha\ ]_x\ [_{\text{S:[]}}\ \beta\ ]]$, where $\alpha\prime = [\![[_{\text{NP:[ever]}}\ \alpha\ ]_x]\!]$ and $\beta\prime = [\![[_{\text{S:[]}}\ \beta\ ]]\!]$:

$$[\![[_{\text{S:[cond]}}\ \alpha\ ]]\!] = [\alpha\prime(\dot{s})(\text{P}_0) \Rightarrow_{\{\dot{s},\dot{x}\}} \beta\prime(\dot{s})]$$

Note that we have written the rule to apply to alternative NPs, but the semantic operations here may well extend to a wider class of cases.

3.6.4 Special Semantics of Disjunction

We turn now to the question of how to derive the kind of semantics we have assumed for alternative NP pre-questions.

The idea we pursue is that a special meaning of disjunction produces *wh*-phrase-like meanings. We thus begin by recalling the G&S translation of a *wh*-NP like *which boy*:

$$\lambda\dot{i}\lambda\dot{P}\lambda\dot{x}[\text{boy}(\dot{x}) \wedge \dot{P}(\dot{i})(\dot{x})]$$

Note that the denotation of a *wh*-phrase differs from an ordinary NP denotation

---

[20]The rule given will yield the wrong denotations for certain alternative NPs. Our assumption has been that the alternative NP always denotes what the *wh*-variable denotes. But as is often the case, pied-piping makes the facts more complicated:

(i) Mary will eat however many cream puffs John eats.

(ii) Whosever beer this is can have it back. (Richardson)

In (i), the alternative NP denotes cream puffs, not a number. In (ii), an example of Richardson's cited by Jacobson, it denotes what we would expect on our account, the owner of the beer, not the beer. Taken together these examples show that the formation of alternative NPs need to keep track of two different variables, much as gap and *wh*-variable dependencies need to be kept separate in the semantics of questions and relative clauses.

only in that scoping it in yields a propositional function instead of a proposition.

The scheme is to define a family of special disjunction rules creating alternative pre-questions. For example, the rule for an alternative question disjunction of two NPs with meanings α_1 and α_2 is:

(56) $$\lambda\dot{i}\lambda\dot{P}\lambda\dot{x}[\,[\alpha_1(\dot{i})(\lambda\dot{z}[\dot{z}=\dot{x}]) \vee \alpha_2(\dot{i})(\lambda\dot{z}[\dot{z}=\dot{x}])] \wedge \dot{P}(\dot{i})(\dot{x})]$$

This rule would yield the following simplified result for the alternative question NP *whiskey or beer*:

(57) $$\lambda\dot{i}\lambda\dot{P}\lambda\dot{x}[(\text{whiskey} = \dot{x} \vee \text{beer} = \dot{x}) \wedge \dot{P}(\dot{i})(\dot{x})]$$

Compare this to the *wh*-phrase denotation above. This, too, is an operator which can be scoped in to create a propositional function.

Analogous rules can be formulated for disjunctions of Ss and VPs. For a disjunction of S's with meanings $\dot{p}_1$ and $\dot{p}_2$, we have:

(58) $$\lambda\dot{i}\lambda\dot{p}[(\dot{p}_1 = \dot{p} \vee \dot{p}_2 = \dot{p}) \wedge \dot{p}(\dot{i})]$$

For a disjunction of VPs with meanings $\dot{P}_1$ and $\dot{P}_2$:

(59) $$\lambda\dot{i}\lambda\wp\lambda\dot{P}[(\dot{P}_1 = \dot{P} \vee \dot{P}_2 = \dot{P}) \wedge \wp(\dot{i})(\dot{P})]$$

A single rule now covers "quantifying in" of *wh* and alternative disjunction NPs, where $[\![\text{NP}]\!] = \alpha$ and $[\![\text{S}]\!] = \beta$:

(60) $$\lambda\dot{i}[\alpha(\dot{i})\lambda\dot{y}[\beta(\dot{i})]\,]$$

An analogous rule will account for "quantifying in" VPs, where $[\![\text{VP}]\!] = \alpha$ and $[\![\text{S}]\!] = \beta$:

(61) $$\lambda\dot{i}[\alpha(\dot{i})\lambda\dot{P}[\beta(\dot{i})]\,]$$

Obviously, polymorphous rules are possible here. The main goal of this section is simply to show what the general semantics of *wh*-type alternative constituents would look like. Although a general approach along these line would require quantifying in rules for various types, there is some evidence that this is required for disjunction independently of alternative questions: Parallel to our examples (3a) through (3c) for *whether*, we have the following cases for *either*, including VP disjunction.

(62) a. Either you eat or drink.
b. Either you drink beer or wine.
c. Either you think that Tom drinks or smokes.
d. Either you drank or not.

As in (3c), the only available interpretation for (62c) appears to be a disjunction wider than *think*. Thus, the two co-conjunctions *either* and *whether* appear to act as *scope-markers* for the disjunction. Example (62d) shows the extremely restricted *or not* construction with *either*, suggesting that *either* and alternative question *whether* form a small paradigm of co-conjunctions that occur in co-construction with *or*.

3.7 Conclusion

In this paper we have proposed a very close relationship between UCCPs and questions. All three constructions are derived from a common source, pre-questions that denote propositional functions. In turn, UCCPs enter into a topic-like construction with main clauses to yield the UCC construction.

The semantics given in Section 3.6 left open the treatment of presuppositions. The general form of the account is quite clear. For a pre-question with translation ϕ, the presupposition is:

(63) $$\lambda \dot{i}[\phi(\dot{i}) \neq \emptyset]$$

This is the proposition that the extension of the propositional function not be empty. For alternative pre-questions, this is the presupposition that one of the disjuncts must be true; for constituent pre-questions this is the existential presupposition that the question have a non-empty answer.

Pre-questions with determiners *which* and *what* need the stronger presupposition that effectively makes the derived alternative NPs definite. For the pre-question *Which boy walks*, for example:

(64) $$\lambda \dot{i}[\mathbf{Card}(\lambda \dot{x}[\text{boy}(\dot{x}) \wedge \text{walk}(\dot{i})(\dot{x})]) = 1]$$

None of this makes very clear why the alternative questions and constituent questions should share an important presuppositional property. On the kind of account sketched here, disjunction and *wh*-words would have to carry along these properties independently. Nor is there yet anything to be said about possible connections with focus constructions, which, like alternative questions, show intonational peculiarities, though different ones, and also seem to exploit alternatives, although in a different way, and which also may carry existential presuppositions. It may be that pre-questions, focus constructions, and negative polarity constructions all need to be accounted for using something like alternatives and that the deeper roots of the presuppositional properties of these constructions lie there. This is suggested by the kind of treatment of negative polarity items pursued in Krifka (1995), but there is a great deal of work to be done in fleshing such a thought out.

The other connection that seems to have deeper roots is the connection between questions and a pragmatic scale operator. We have offered no particular reason why an operator like *ever* should enter into the formation of conditionals with elements of questions. And yet, the facts of three languages suggest that there ought to be one. There is clearly more to be said here.

We close with a remark on one aspect of the treatment proposed here, the suggestion that there is a deep connection between alternative questions and constituent questions. In particular, we have gone so far as to give disjunctions in alternative questions *wh*-phrase-like denotations, making a syntactic claim about a special class of disjunction constituents.

There is independent evidence of a close relationship between *wh*-phrases and disjunctions in alternative questions, Both constituents, in contrast to yes-no questions, have list-pair readings:

(65) a. What does everyone drink?
b. Does everyone drink light beer or dark?
c. Does everyone drink beer?
d. Who drinks everything?
e. Does John or Mary like everyone?

Thus (65a) has a reading which can be answered as a list, pairing drinkers with drinks, and so can (65b). In contrast, (65c) cannot be answered with a list pairing domain members with yes and no. Example (65d) illustrates the C-command or weak-crossover like restriction on such readings (see Chierchia 1992) for a constituent question, and (65e) shows it for an alternative question.[21]

Neither sentence has pair-list readings.

References

Beaver, David. 1993. What Comes First in Natural Language Semantics: A Compositional, Non-Representational Account of Natural Language. ILLC Prepublication Series for Logic, Semantics, and the Philosophy of Language. LP-93-15. University of Amsterdam.

Bolinger, Dwight. 1978. Yes/No Questions are not Alternative Questions. In Henry Hiz, ed., *Questions*, 87–105. Dordrecht: Reidel.

Bresnan, Joan. 1972. *Theory of Complementation in English Syntax*. Doctoral dissertation, MIT, Cambridge, Massachusetts.

Chierchia, Gennaro. 1992. Questions with Quantifiers. *Natural Language Semantics* 1, 181–234.

Fillmore, Charles J. 1986. Varieties of Conditional Construction. *ESCOL III*.

Gallin, Daniel. 1975. *Intensional and Higher-Order Modal Logic*. Amsterdam: North-Holland.

[21]There are differences between NP disjunctions in alternative questions and *wh*-phrases as well. In particular, the two cannot be freely mixed to yield multiple *wh*-questions:

(i) Who drinks what?
(ii) Who drinks whiskey or beer?
(iii) What do Sam or Bill drink?
(iv) Who swims or fishes?

(i) has a multiple-*wh* reading but (ii), (iii) and (iv) do not. Indeed, it is difficult to even utter these preserving the list intonation of alternative questions.

Ginzburg, Jonathan. 1996. Interrogatives: Questions, Facts and Dialogue. In Shalom Lappin, ed., *The Handbook of Contemporary Semantic Theory*, 385–422. Oxford: Blackwell.

Gawron, Jean Mark, and Yasunari Harada. 1996 . Indefinites, Conditionals, and Quantification in Japanese and English. In H. Nakagawa, ed., *A Cognitive Study of Situatedness in English and Japanese*. Ministry of Education, Science and Culture Research Report, Yokohama, Japan.

Groenendijk, Jeroen, and Martin Stokhof. 1984. *Studies on the Semantics of Questions and the Pragmatics of Answers*. Doctoral dissertation, University of Amsterdam, Amsterdam.

Hamblin, Charles L. 1973. Questions in Montague English. *Foundations of Language* 10, 159–168.

Harada, Yasunari, and Honda, Kumiko. 1999. Indefinites and Covariation in Quantification in Japanese: Interpreting *dono*. Manuscript, Waseda University, Tokyo.

Harada, Yasunari, and Noguchi, Naohiko. 1992. On the Semantics and Pragmatics of *dake* (and *only*). In Chris Barker and David Dowty, eds., *Proceedings of Semantics and Linguistic Theory II*, 125–144. The Ohio State University, Columbus, Ohio.

Heim, Irene. 1982. *The Semantics of Definite and Indefinite Noun Phrases*. Doctoral dissertation, University of Massachussetts, Amherst.

Horn, Lawrence R. 1972. *On the Semantic Properties of Logical Operators in English*. Indiana University Linguistics Club.

Jacobson, Pauline. 1995. On the Quantificational Force of English Free Relatives. In Emmon Bach, Eloise Jelinek, Angelika Kratzer and Barbara H. Partee, eds., *Quantification in Natural Languages*, 451–486. Dordrecht: Kluwer Academic Publishers.

Jacobs, Joachim. 1991. Focus Ambiguities. *Journal of Semantics*. 8, 1–36.

Kadmon, Nirit and Fred Landman. 1990. Polarity Sensitive *Any* and Free-Choice *Any*. In Martin Stokhof and Leen Torenvliet, eds., *Proceedings of the Seventh Amsterdam Colloquium, Part I*, 227–251. University of Amsterdam, Amsterdam.

Kamp, Hans. 1981. A Theory of Truth and Semantic Representation. In Jeroen Groenendijk, Theo Janssen, and Martin Stokhof, eds., *Formal Methods in the Study of Language*, 277–322. Mathematisch Centrum, Amsterdam.

Kartunnen, Lauri. 1973. Presuppositions of Compound Sentences. *Linguistic Inquiry* 4, 169–93.

Kartunnen, Lauri. 1977. Syntax and Semantics of Questions. *Linguistics and Philosophy* 1, 3–44.

Koenig, Ekkehard. 1986. Conditional, Concessive Conditionals, and Concessives: Areas of contrast, overlap, and neutralization. In Elizabeth Traugott, ed., *On Conditionals*, 229–246. Cambridge: Cambridge University Press.

Kratzer, Angelika. 1986. Conditionals. *CLS 22: Papers from the Parasession on Pragmatics and Grammatical Theory*, 1–15.

Kratzer, Angelika. 1989. An Investigation of the Lumps of Thought. *Linguistics and Philosophy* 12, 607–653.

Kratzer, Angelika. 1995. Stage-Level and Individual-Level Predicates. In Gregory N. Carlson and Francis Jeffry Pelletier, eds., *The Generic Book*, 125–175. Chicago: Chicago University Press.

Krifka, Manfred. 1995. The Semantics and Pragmatics of Polarity Items. *Linguistic Analysis* 25, 209–257.

Ladusaw, William. 1980. *Polarity Sensitivity as Inherent Scope Relations*. Indiana University Linguistics Club.

Langendoen, D. Terence and Savin, Harris B. 1971. The Projection Problem for Presuppositions. In Charles J. Fillmore and D. Terence Langendoen, eds., *Studies in Linguistic Semantics*, 55–60. New York: Holt, Rinehart and Winston, Inc.

Lahiri, Utpal. 1991. *Embedded Interrogatives and the Predicates that embed them*. Doctoral dissertation, MIT, Cambridge, Massachusetts.

Levinson, Stephen C. 1983. *Pragmatics*. Cambridge: Cambridge University Press.

Lewis, David. 1975. Adverbs of Quantification. In Edward L. Keenan, ed., *Formal Semantics of Natural Language*, 3–15. Cambridge: Cambridge University Press.

Michaelis, Laura A. 1996. Expectation Contravention and Use Ambiguity: The Vietnamese connective *cũng*. *Journal of Pragmatics* 21, 1–36.

Partee, Barbara. 1991. Topic, Focus and Quantification. In Steven Moore and Adam Wyner, eds., *Proceedings of the First Semantics and Linguistic Theory Conference (SALT I)*, 159–187. Cornell Working Papers in Linguistics, Ithaca, New York.

Richardson, John F. 1995. The Interrogative Nature of *Wh-ever* Presentations. New Orleans, LSA Presentation.

Stump, Gregory. 1985. *The Semantic Variability of Absolute Constructions*. Dordrecht: Reidel.

4

Information Articulation and Truth Conditions of Existential Sentences

YOOKYUNG KIM

4.1 Introduction

This paper presents a new formal semantic analysis which reflects the information articulation of a statement. Information articulation refers to the way that the information conveyed by a statement is packaged in order to facilitate the addition of information to the hearer's knowledge store (Vallduví 1990). Information articulation at the statement level is concerned with the topic-comment structure and the focus-background structure. Since Rooth (1985), the effect of focus to the interpretation of a statement, in particular its truth-conditional effect has been much discussed in the literature. While the topic-comment structure has been the main concern of discourse analyses or syntactic analyses from the point of view of functional grammar, its truth-conditional effect has not been seriously considered in formal semantic studies.

The purpose of this paper is two-fold. First, I propose that statements which differ in information articulation with respect to the topic-comment structure should be analyzed as having different propositional contents based on the fine-grained analysis of propositions in Situation Semantics (Barwise and Perry 1983). Second, I present cases in which truth-conditional differences arise due to different topic-comment structures, and give an account of them by the proposed analysis.

As a case study, I will consider the interpretation of a *there* existential sentence in comparison to that of the corresponding subject-predicate sentence without *there*. After showing that they are distinguished in terms of their topic-comment structure, I will analyze existential sentences as expressing Aus-

Logical Perspectives on Language and Information.
Cleo Condoravdi and Gerard R. Renardel de Lavalette.

tinian propositions about some situation, capturing their theticity. Categorical subject-predicate statements, by contrast, will be analyzed as expressing Russellian propositions about their topic.

My analysis will explain why the same cardinal quantifier admits of different readings in (1).[1]

(1) a. There were 26 bumble-bees busily feeding.
(cardinal reading only)
b. 26 bumble-bees were busily feeding.
(partitive and cardinal readings both possible)

I will also account for the fact that indefinite subjects can constitute the restriction of an adverb of quantification, but post-copular NPs of existential sentences cannot. (2)c has a reading in common with (2)d but (2)a does not have a reading in common with (2)b.

(2) a. There are usually pigeons twittering in a basket.
b. Most pigeons are twittering in a basket.
c. Sales usually suffer in hot weather.
d. Most sales suffer in hot weather.

4.2 Comparison between Existential Sentences and Subject-Predicate Sentences

Let us compare an existential sentence such as (3)a with the corresponding subject-predicate sentence in (3)b.

(3) a. There was a car hanging off the edge.
b. A car was hanging off the edge.

Except for the expletive element *there*, the two sentences in (3) are composed of the same parts. From the tradition of compositional truth-conditional semantics, their propositional contents would be calculated to be the same. The two sentences would have the same truth conditions. However, truth conditions do not exhaust the meaning of a sentence. Considering the two statements in terms of the information they convey in an appropriate context, we find some difference between them. They differ in the way information is conveyed, in particular, in the topic-comment structure: While (3)b can be used to give information about a certain car, (3)a is not used that way but rather it is used to describe a state of affairs as a whole without singling out an entity denoted by *a car*.

Due to their different information articulation, (3)a and (3)b are used appropriately in different utterance contexts. For instance, when one intends to contrast a car's condition to some bus' condition, only (3)b is appropriate, as seen in (4).

[1] Most examples in this paper are obtained from the New York Times and the Hector Corpus.

(4) In that accident, a bus managed to stay on the road, but

a. a car went off and was hanging off the edge.

b. # there was a car hanging off the edge.

As we will see later, only a categorical statement about a car is felicitous in this case since contrasting two entities presupposes naming those entities.[2]

4.2.1 Sentence Topic

Topics of sentences are one of the means available in the language to organize or classify the information exchanged in linguistic communication. In the literature, the notion of *topic* has been used in various senses. Among those, "the sentence topic" in Reinhart (1981) is the most relevant notion to differentiate existential sentences and subject-predicate sentences. A sentence topic corresponds to an expression whose denotation is what the sentence is about.[3]

Identification of the sentence topic is based on the following two principles proposed in Strawson (1964). First, "the principle of the presumption of knowledge" requires that assertions depend for their effect upon knowledge assumed to be already in the audience's possession. Second, "the principle of relevance" requires that discourse relates itself to and makes use of what is presumed to be known and it intends to give or add information about what is a matter of standing or current interest or concern. The first principle leads us to expect that the sentence is about what is already in our presumed knowledge, and accordingly the sentence topic is more or less old information. But more importantly, the second principle guides us to understand an expression as representing the topic if the assertion is understood as intending to expand our knowledge of the entity denoted by that expression.

In addition to these principles, verification of statements is also a criterion to identify the sentence topic. Assessments of statements as true or false are commonly, though not only, topic-centered. The selection of a topic for a given assertion in a given context may be viewed as a selection among the various ways to assess it—it will be verified by checking what we know about the topic.

Consider the following two statements which contain a definite description whose presupposition is not satisfied. Note that they are assessed differently. (5)a tends to be assessed as false but (5)b as truth-valueless.

(5) a. The exhibition was visited yesterday by the king of France.

b. The king of France visited the exhibition yesterday.

[2] If a contrast is made between two situations instead of the two entities, two thetic statements can be made using existential sentences.

[3] This pragmatic definition of "sentence topic" is distinguished from the definition of "link" in Vallduvi (1990), which is designated by b-accent and characterized as introducing a new file card.

The NP *the exhibition* tends to be selected as the topic of (5)a, and thus the statement can be verified by checking the list of people who visited the exhibition. Since we will not find the king of France in the list because there is no king of France, the statement is assessed as false. The offending definite description *the king of France* is absorbed in the predicate and does not cause a truth-value gap. On the other hand, (5)b is assessed as truth-valueless because *the king of France* is most easily selected as the topic and its presupposition is not satisfied. Even if the identification of the topic is determined by pragmatic aboutness, independently of truth conditions, it may affect the actual verification strategies.

Reinhart's (1995) survey shows that the sentences in (6)a and (6)b are assessed differently.

(6) a. There were two American kings in New York. (False)
    b. Two American kings lived in New York. (False or truth-valueless)

Given no context, half of the class-participants judged (6)b as false and the others judged it as truth-valueless. Because there is no individual satisfying the description *American kings*, when it is selected as the sentence topic, the sentence is judged as truth-valueless. But there was no variation in judgments of (6)a and all participants judged (6)a as false. This fact indicates that the NP *two American kings* is not selected as the sentence topic in (6)a. While (6)b can be a statement about two American kings, (6)a is not so interpreted but interpreted as a simple (false) description of a state of affairs without topic or a statement about New York.

From the assessment pattern illustrated in (6), we can argue that the post-copular NP of an existential sentence cannot be the sentence topic, in contrast to the subject NP of a subject-predicate sentence. Another piece of supporting evidence for this claim can be found in relativization facts. Compared to ordinary subject-predicate sentences of which any part can be freely selected as the sentence topic in an appropriate context, it is well-known that the topic and focus of a locative inversion sentence is determined constructionally: the locative phrase is the topic and the theme argument is the presented focused element. Aissen (1975) and Langendoen(1979) observed that in locative inversion sentences only the locative but not the theme argument can be relativized, as in (7).

(7) a. I expect that on these trails can be found many kinds of mushrooms.
    b. ... these trails, on which I expect — can be found many kinds of mushrooms.
    c. ?*...many kinds of mushrooms, which I expect on these trails can be found —.

The unacceptability of (7)c can be explained from the assumption that the relativized element is the grammaticalized topic of the sentence (Bresnan 1994). Because the theme argument is what is presented by the construction, it cannot be the topic, and thus it cannot be relativized.

(8) shows that the post-copular NP cannot be relativized, while the adjunct locative phrase can. Therefore, we can conclude that the post-copular NP cannot be the sentence topic while the adjunct can.

(8) a. I expect that there are many kinds of mushrooms on these trails.

b. ... these trails, on which I expect there are many kinds of mushrooms —.

c. ?*... many kinds of mushrooms, which I expect there are — on these trails.

The following tables represent the contrast in the topic/comment structures of existential sentences and subject-predicate sentences.

(9) a.

There be Post-copular NP Coda Predicate Adjunct
No Topic

b.

There be Post-copular NP Coda Predicate	Adjunct
Comment	Topic

(10) a.

Subject Predicate
No Topic

b.

Subject	Predicate
Topic	Comment

In most cases, an existential sentence contains no sentence topic, as in (9)a, but sometimes an adjunct phrase may be selected as the topic, as in (9)b. Crucially, neither the post-copular NP nor the coda predicate can be the sentence topic in any case. The existential sentence in (5)a illustrates that only the adjunct *New York* but not the post-copular NP *two American kings* can be the sentence topic. In contrast, the subject[4] of a subject-predicate sentence can be selected as the topic, as in (10)b, while the sentence may also be regarded as having no sentence topic, as in (10)a. For instance, the sentence in (5)b can have either of the topic-comment structures in (10): when it has (10)a, it is judged false because there is no situation described that way, and when it has (10)b with *two American kings* as the topic, it is judged as truth-valueless because the topic fails to refer to anything.

4.2.2 Thetic vs. Categorical Statements

We compared existential sentences with subject-predicate sentences regarding the question whether they can contain a sentence topic and which part can be

[4] NPs other than the subject NP can be the sentence topic, too. For the relation between subject and topic, see Li (1976).

the topic. The difference found in these respects is related to another interesting distinction identified by Brentano (1973), namely the distinction between categorical and thetic statements, which has received attention in the linguistics literature including Kuroda (1992), Sasse (1987), Ladusaw (1994) and McNally (1995).

The two statements in (11), from Schmerling (1976), exemplify a categorical statement and thetic statement, respectively. They illustrate how a different type of statement is chosen in a different context. In English, different intonation patterns are used for the two types of statement. A thetic statement is made by accenting only the subject, whereas a categorical statement is made by accenting the predicate as well as the subject.

(11) a. TRUman's DIED. (categorical)
     b. JOHNson's died. (thetic)

Although an event of death is described in both (11)a and (11)b, the information expected by the hearer is different in each case. The whole nation has been concerned with Truman's condition because he has been ill. For this reason, the event of death in (11)a is used to characterize his condition, and Truman constitutes an independent entity outside the event. In contrast, Johnson's death came entirely unexpectedly and thus the addressees were not prepared to hear about Johnson's condition; in such a case it is necessary to present the involved entity as part of the described event.

Due to the different information available prior to the statements, (11)a and (11)b are uttered with different intonational patterns so as to signal the informational packaging appropriate in each case. We could characterize the different contexts for (11)a and (11)b using different salient questions, as in (12)a and (12)b, respectively.

(12) a. What happened to Truman?
     b. What's new?

As these questions show, in (11)b the information of Johnson's death is significant as a whole. Both parts, the event and the individual involved, are of equal communicative value. In (11)a the question is put in such a way as to require information about Truman. Hence, it is assumed that Truman and the event of his death are of different communicative value.

As illustrated above, categorical statements are utterances which are analyzed into two successive, mutually related judgments, one naming an individual and one naming an event. Together they make a "predication". The term "predication" is reserved for a relation holding between an element denoting an entity and an element used to say something about that entity: "ascribing a property to and thereby adding information about an autonomous, independently established individual" (Sasse 1987). An entity serving as a predication base is always autonomous, that is, independent of and *outside* the predicated event.

The choice of the predication base of categorical statements is determined, by and large, by the topic. Not just any given 'situationally present' or 'generally known' element, but only those elements about which information is expected to be added can qualify as a predication base. Therefore, the sentence topic, as defined in the previous section, can be said to serve the predication base of a categorical statement. Hence, a sentence which lacks a sentence topic cannot be used to make a categorical statement.

Existential sentences usually do not contain a sentence topic. This means that they make a thetic statement without making a predication. A state of affairs is simply posited (hence 'thetic', from Greek *thetikós* 'positive'). An entity that may happen to be involved in the state of affairs so asserted is not picked out as the predication base but is presented as part of the event. An entity involved in a simple 'recognition' is *inside* the event and may not be conceived as an entity at all. Statements made by existential sentences are thetic statements in which the logical relations between the various parts of the communicated state of affairs remain unanalyzed.

Strictly speaking, it is wrong to say that existential sentences are used only as thetic statements, as claimed in Ladusaw (1994). In case an existential sentence has an adjunct and which is selected as the sentence topic, the sentence is used as a categorical statement about the entity denoted by that adjunct. From now on, if some existential sentence is claimed to be used only as a thetic statement, that will be because the sentence does not have a topic adjunct.

In sum, the difference between subject-predicate sentences and existential sentences can be stated in the following way: a subject-predicate sentence can be used as a categorical statement whose predication base comes from the subject NP, but an existential sentence cannot be used to make a categorical statement about the entity denoted by the post-copular NP.

4.3 Formal Analysis in Situation Semantics

We have shown that existential sentences and the corresponding subject-predicate sentences can be distinguished in terms of the articulation of information conveyed by their utterance. When one tries to incorporate this aspect of interpretation in a formal analysis, the kind of tools that one needs have to be more fine-grained than those provided by the classical view of propositions as sets of possible worlds. In Situation Semantics (Barwise and Perry 1983), a finer-grained classification of information is achieved by adopting a structured universe of situation theoretic objects, in which various things such as individuals, properties, relations, types, situations, propositions and units of information are objects on their own right.

A semantic analysis of a natural language involves quite complicated situation theoretic objects. To represent them in a way that is perspicuous, Barwise & Cooper (1993) developed EKN (Extended Kamp Notation), which I will use in this paper. EKN is a sorted notation system which contains only terms, not sentences. The sorts of EKN form the smallest set containing the basic sorts such as *Situation, Infon, Proposition, Relation, Type, Assignment,* and *Object* that is closed under the relevant recursive rules. For each sort v there is also a sort v-abstract. The terms of sort v-abstract denote objects obtained by abstracting parameters from objects denoted by terms of sort v. The terms of EKN are defined inductively. Atomic terms are constants and parameter symbols. The set of terms consists of atomic terms plus boxes constructed from them. We assume that we have a denotation function $\mathcal{D}$ which assigns denotations to the basic constant and parameter symbols. For instance, if R is an relation symbol, then $\mathcal{D}(\mathcal{R})$ is a relation.

The basic notions of situation theory are that of a situation and information. The notion of *information* that Devlin (1991) adopts is "objects $a_1, \ldots, a_n$ do/do not stand in the relation P." Such a unit of information is called an infon. For instance, an infon that Claire is reading *War and Peace* is represented as (13). It denotes the information that the individual named Claire and the book named *War and Peace* stand in the relation of reading.

(13) | reading(Claire,WP) |

To represent basic *propositions*, we need to represent the fact that some infon holds in some situation. Propositions rather than infons are what can be true or false. The following box in (14), which is constituted of situation s and the supported infon, represents a proposition that situation s *supports* the information that Claire is reading *War and Peace*. Because only a small part of the world is needed to verify such a fact, a situation, i.e., a part of the world, rather than the whole world is used to constitute a proposition.

(14) | s / reading(Claire,WP) |

In general, a proposition is a predication that some arguments are of a certain type, as represented in (15).

(15) | A / T | ,

where A is an assignment term and T is a type term.

(15) denotes the proposition that $[\![A]\!]$ is of type $[\![T]\!]$.

(14) is a special case where the type is an infon and the argument is a situation, and such propositions are called *Austinian* propositions, contrasted to *Russellian* propositions (Barwise and Etchemendy 1987).

A parameter term instead of a constant term can be used in any situation-theoretic object. For instance, when a parameter X occupies an argument position of a relation, as in (16), we call such a proposition a parametric proposition. We can abstract over the parameter to form a proposition-abstract, which is called a type. In this case, we obtain a type of individuals reading WP in s, as represented as (17).

(16)

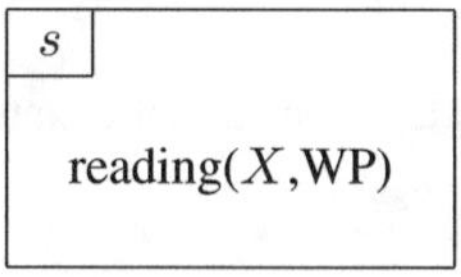

(17)

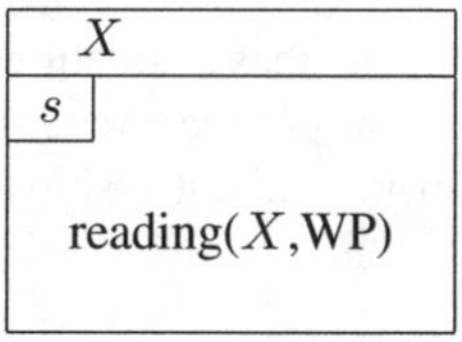

If we predicate the type in (17) of an assignment term which assigns the individual constant Claire to the parameter symbol X, we obtain another proposition in (18).

(18)

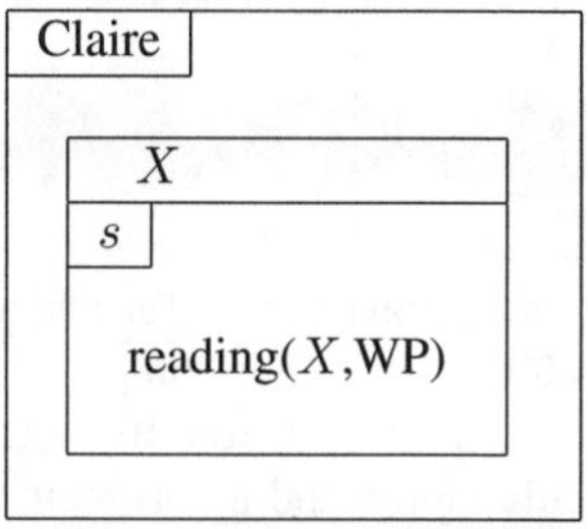

The two propositions in (15) and (18) are logically equivalent but distinct from each other. (15) asserts that the situation s is of the type corresponding to the infon that Claire is reading War and Peace, while (18) asserts that Claire is of the type of individuals reading War and Peace in s. Because many distinct but logically equivalent objects are available, Situation Semantics can readily accommodate different information articulations of a statement. Note that an assignment term which assigns Claire to X, or simply speaking the individual term Claire, is an immediate constituent of the proposition in (18), but not of that in (15). This difference will be crucially used in differentiating the interpretation of a categorical statement from that of a thetic statement.

According to Gawron & Peters (1990), the meaning of any expression is a relation of circumstances in which the expression is uttered and the content that the utterance of it expresses in those situations. In the case of a sentence, its content would be a proposition. In current Situation Semantics, all utterances of declarative sentences are taken to be about situations, but I propose that the propositional content of a sentence should reflect its information articulation in a given utterance situation. Therefore, in my proposal, a sentence may have two different propositional contents: the propositional content of a thetic statement is an Austinian proposition about a certain situation, whereas that of a categorical statement is a Russellian one about an individual which its sentence topic denotes.

For instance, the sentence in (19) can be used as either a thetic statement or a categorical statement.

(19) A car was hanging off the edge.

When (19) is used to make a thetic statement, it describes a situation without singling out any part of the sentence as a predication base. Accordingly, its content will be analyzed as an Austinian proposition about a situation s, chosen by the speaker, as follows.

(20)
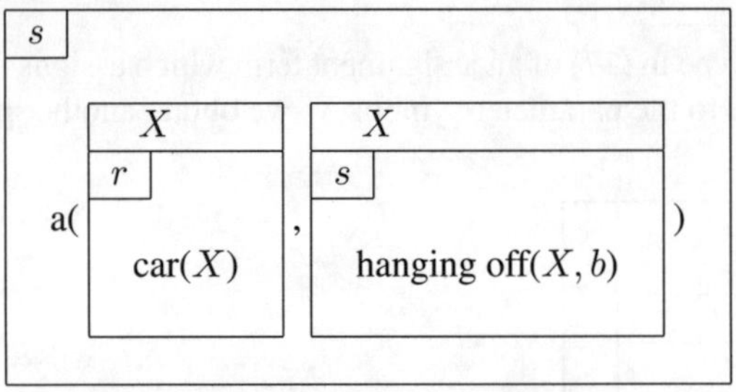

The proposition in (20) is constituted of some situation and an infon and asserts that the situation s supports a quantificational infon, which is composed of the determiner a and its restriction and nuclear scope.[5] (20) is true iff there is an object in s which is a car in some resource situation r and it was hanging off an edge b referred to by the utterance of "the edge". The fact that a situation instead of an entity expressed by a part of the sentence is the predication base of the proposition captures the theticity of the statement.

The same sentence (19) is analyzed to express the following Russellian proposition when it is used as a categorical statement about some specific car

[5]Following Generalized Quantifier theory (Barwise and Cooper 1981), I assume that a determiner relates two types. The restriction type of the quantifier exploits a resource situation r which may be different from the described situation s.

c referred to by the speaker by utterance of "a car". I assume that indefinite NPs should be interpreted referentially (Fodor and Sag 1982) to be a sentence topic.[6]

(21)

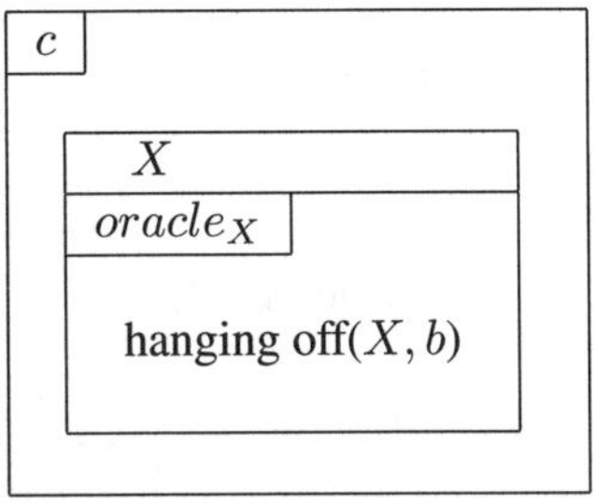

The proposition (21) says that a car c is of the type of individuals which were hanging off the edge. The argument of the predication of this proposition comes from the subject NP *a car* and the remainder of the sentence contributes the type predicated of that argument, which nicely reflects the information articulation of the categorical statement: the NP *a car* is the sentence topic and the rest of the sentence is a comment about it.

Another thing to note in this proposition is the use of an oracle situation. The oracle of an individual a, notated as $oracle_a$, is the situation comprising that part of the world and the entire "body of knowledge" that concerns a (Devlin 1991). The use of the oracle situation is intended to make sure that the utterance of a categorical statement expands the information about an individual instead of an arbitrary situation.

(21) is logically equivalent to the following proposition in (22).

(22)

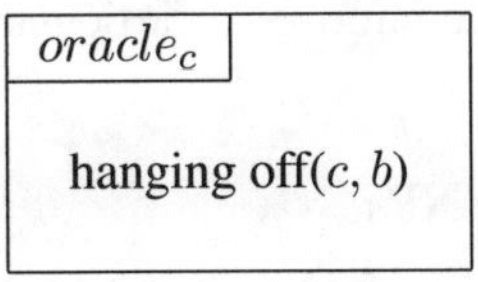

Let us compare (20) and (22). The truth of (22) depends on the object denoted by c and on whether the object denoted by c was hanging off the object denoted by b, whereas the truth of (20) depends on the situation denoted by s and the fact it supports. Even if the fact that a car was hanging off the

[6]An anonymous reviewer pointed out that in the following conditional sentence, the non-referential indefinite NP *a car* is non-comment and non-focus.

(i) A car on the dock doesn't mean trouble, but if a car is hanging off the edge one should try to have it removed as soon as possible.

I think this kind of sentence can be dealt with along the line with the proposal for adverbial quantification in this paper. A conditional involves an implicit adverbial quantification. The indefinite is non-referential because it is part of the restriction of an adverb of quantification, but that very fact explains the intuition why it does not count as comment or focus. As it will be shown later, the restriction of a quantification is formed from the topical element of the modified proposition.

edge holds in the world, (20) could be false, if some inappropriate situation is chosen for s. But, (22) is true as long as there is a situation which supports the fact that a car c was hanging off the edge because the oracle of c includes all the facts about it.[7]

Now, let us consider an existential sentence such as (23).

(23) There was a car hanging off the edge.

Because (23) can only make a statement about a situation, its propositional content will be analyzed only as (24), which is the same as (20).[8]

(24)

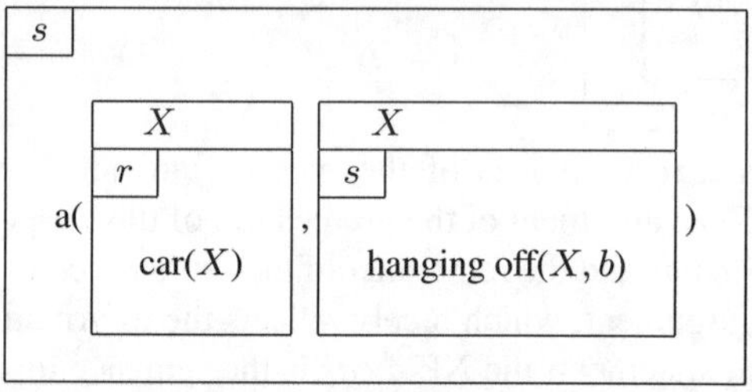

As in the thetic interpretation of a subject-predicate sentence, the truth of (24) depends on the choice of s: (24) is about a certain situation, not about the whole world nor about a certain car.

To sum up this section, adopting the fine-grained analysis of a proposition in Situation Semantics, we can formalize the interpretations of an existential sentence and a subject-predicate sentence in different ways incorporating their different information articulation. In the following two sections, we will discuss two cases where the two types of sentence even have different truth conditions. We will see how useful it is to incorporate information articulation in the semantic analysis in dealing with such cases.

4.4 No Partitive Reading in Post-copular NPs

It is well-known that weak quantifiers have a partitive reading as well as a simple cardinal reading (Diesing 1992, de Hoop 1992). For instance, the quantifier *twenty six bumble-bees* can be interpreted as 'twenty six out of a certain set of bumble-bees' in addition to simply indicate that the cardinality of bumble-bees is twenty six.

In order for a weak quantifier to have a partitive reading, there must be some particular set in the context on which the partition is applied. The set serving for the domain of weak quantifiers in the partitive reading must be a

[7] $oracle_X \models \sigma(X)$ iff
$w \models \sigma(X)$ iff
$s \models \sigma(X)$ for some $s \leq w$.

[8] In Kim (1997), the propositional content of an existential sentence is analyzed as more complicated than the one presented here to incorporate the presentative function of the sentence.

"familiar" one, which the addressee is able to uniquely identify because he already has a representation of it (Gundel et al. 1993, Büring 1994).

Consider the following discourse in (25).[9]

(25) Although in the garden at present there are around 70 species of plants in bloom, on some sunny days recently it became apparent that only two of these were attracting mass attention from insects, and that the latter were demonstrating marked specific preferences. Thus on a patch of a deep purple thyme, about a square yard in extent,

a. Twenty six bumble-bees were busily feeding.

b. There were twenty six bumble-bees busily feeding.

In this context, there is no familiar set of bumble-bees which would serve as the domain of the quantifier *twenty six bumble-bees* in (25)a or (25)b. Because the condition for the partitive reading is not met, the quantifier gets the cardinal reading in both (25)a and (25)b.

To distinguish an existential sentence from a subject-predicate sentence in terms of the availability of a partitive reading, we need a discourse in which the domain for the partition is established and a clear truth conditional difference between the two readings is manifested. Consider the following simple discourse.

(26) We planted twenty species of plants in our garden in the spring.

a. Unfortunately, at most five species are in bloom now.

b. Unfortunately, there are at most five species in bloom now.

c. (OK after a.; # after b.) But, the ten species we had planted last year are all again in bloom, so the garden is beautiful.

First of all, note that the cardinal reading of (26)a entails its partitive reading but not vice versa.[10] In the cardinal reading, (26)a means that the number of species of plants in bloom now is at most five. This contradicts the following sentence in (26)c. However, in the partitive reading, (26)a only means that at most five out of the twenty species planted in the spring are in bloom now, without any commitment as to the total number. The fact that (26)c is infelicitous after (26)b indicates that the existential sentence has only the cardinal interpretation, in contrast to the subject-predicate sentence which could have a partitive reading. The truth conditions for (26)a and (26)b are clearly different. (26)a can be true even if a total of fifteen species are in bloom now as long as at most five of them were planted in the spring. (26)b is certainly false in such a case. It is true just in case the total number of species in bloom now is at most five.

---

[9]The original discourse has (25)b. But (25)a also makes a perfect discourse with the same interpretation.

[10]For a monotone increasing quantifier, the entailment is reversed.

We can explain this contrast in terms of the different information articulation of the two sentences. Recall that a subject-predicate sentence can make not only a thetic statement but also a categorical statement. In the previous section, we considered a case where an indefinite subject refers to a specific object and provides the predication base of a categorical statement. When the subject NP is not referential but quantificational, as in (26)a, we can assume that the type which is the restriction of the quantification is the predication base of the categorical statement.

(26)a can be interpreted as giving information about a certain set of plants such that at most five species of the set are in bloom now. In this information articulation, its propositional content can be represented as follows.

(27)

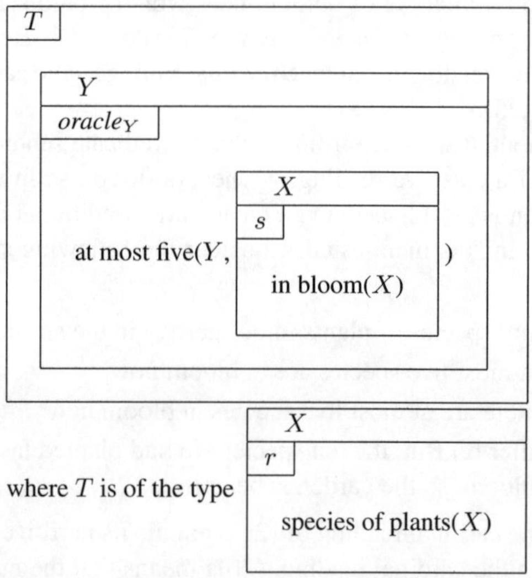

The type T, which is a type of species of plants in r, is not only the restriction of the quantifier *at most five* but also the predication base, i.e., the topic of the categorical statement. Hence, T should not be any arbitrary type of plants but a type of plants familiar in the preceding discourse which is appropriate to be the topic of the sentence. Only a certain set of plants salient in the context, such as something in the score-board (Lewis 1979), can be the appropriate object for T.

The resource situation r in T mediates the interpretation. In the given circumstances of the discourse, the situation in the spring where the speaker planted twenty species of plants is salient. Hence, it can be chosen for the resource situation r in the type. In that case, the extension of the type T can be the set of twenty species planted in the spring. The proposition in (27) is true iff at most five members out of this set are in bloom now. Because it is a proposition about a certain type of plants instead of any arbitrary plants, it renders the partitive reading.

On the other hand, the proposed interpretation of an existential sentence is incompatible with the partitive reading of its weak post-copular NP. An existential sentence describes a situation without a topic status given to the post-copular NP. The post-copular NP combines with the coda predicate to form an infon supported by the described situation. The propositional content of the existential sentence (26)b can be represented as (28).

(28)

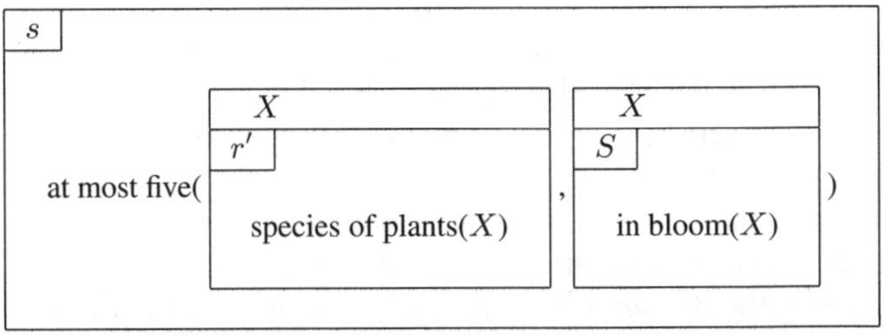

A certain type of plants is the restriction of the quantifier *at most five* both in (27) and (28), but it has a different status in the information articulation in the two cases: in (27) it is the predication base (topic), but in (28) it is merely part of the information characterizing the described situation. Because the type is not the topic in (28), it does not need to refer to a pre-established set in the score-board, but any relevant set of people can be the extension of it.[11] Any set of plants qualifies as the domain of the quantification, as far as it is a relevant set of plants at the workshop. There is no reason for the domain to be restricted to the plants planted in the spring excluding those planted last year. This renders the simple cardinal reading.[12] The proposition in (28) is true iff the described situation s supports the infon that the number of the species of plants which are in bloom is at most five.

An essential point of this account lies in the different possibility of information articulation of the two sentences. The subject-predicate sentence in (26)a can be analyzed as expressing a proposition asserted of a certain type of plants, hence the domain of the cardinal quantifier is restricted to a pre-established type of plants, rendering the partitive interpretation. In contrast, as the existential sentence in (26)b is interpreted as a proposition asserted of a situation, the domain of the same quantifier is not restricted to a pre-established type but any appropriate type available in the context, which renders the cardinal

[11] Although the cardinal reading of *at most five species of plants* does not quantify over a pre-established set about which the sentence is intended to give information, the domain of the quantifier need not be the set of plants in the whole world. Generally, a quantifier quantifies over objects in some restricted domain relevant to the context. The use of resource situation r' is intended to capture this fact.

[12] It seems that the restriction type tends to pick the biggest set available in the context compatible with the description. Why this must be the case needs further research.

reading. Crucially, existential sentences cannot be interpreted as giving information about a certain pre-established type of individual, hence the partitive interpretation of a weak quantifier in the post-copular position is impossible.

Consider (29), which seems to be a counter-example of this claim.

(29) a. Mary: We need some students to prepare the orientation. My students are all out of town. What about your students?

b. John: There are three students available.

It seems that (29)b gives information about John's students and the quantifier *three students* is interpreted as 'three of John's students'. But this apparent partitive interpretation is simply inferred due to the conversational maxim of relevance (Grice 1975). Although Mary's question seeks information about John's students, John's answer using the existential sentence does not give information about his students but about a situation in which three students are available. While the domain of the quantifier can be restricted to the set of John's students to make the statement a relevant answer, it is only a pragmatically inferred interpretation. The addition of (30) does not make the discourse incoherent.

(30) They are Bill's students.

In this case, John's statement would not be a direct answer to Mary's question but it can still be regarded as a relevant answer for it provides information relevant for the purpose of the conversation. This means that the utterance of the existential sentence in (29)b is still thetic describing a situation in which the number of students available is three. The quantifier has a simple cardinal reading and its apparent partitive interpretation is a pragmatically inferred one.

In this section, we have seen that the different information articulations of an existential sentence and a subject-predicate sentence can give rise to different interpretation of the same cardinal quantifier contained there. The proposed analysis that the subject NP but not the post-copular NP can provide the predication base of the proposition explains the fact that the partitive reading is possible in subject-predicate sentences but absent in existential sentences.

4.5 Adverbs of quantification

Another interesting truth-conditional contrast can be found between subject-predicate sentences and existential sentences when they contain adverbs of quantification. The following subject-predicate sentences in (31) and existential sentences in (32) illustrate that indefinite subjects can constitute the restriction of an adverb of quantification, whereas post-copular NPs cannot be so interpreted and keep their existential force.

(31) a. Sales usually suffer in hot weather.
b. Milk is usually marketed in the republic through co-ops whose farmer members own #1 shares.
c. Industrialists are always coming along to him claiming that even if their mergers are anti-competitive in the UK, this will be offset by gains in efficiency or international competitiveness.
d. Rights issues are always bad news for the City—except for the institutions making money out of managing them.

(32) a. There has always been a problem in the relationship between Mel, who's a smashing lad, and the supporters.
b. There's always a really lively atmosphere day and night.
c. There's always a great atmosphere among the players.
d. And always, in the museum, there is music playing.
e. There is never a sense of lives and reigns being at stake.
f. There is usually a live human being to take information or answer questions.
g. There is usually a breakdown in communications between mothers and their teenagers who become pregnant.

(31)a means that 'most sales suffer in hot weather'. But (32)a does not mean that 'every problem has been in the relationship between Mel and the supporters', but means that 'in every relevant situation or all the time, some problem or other has existed between Mel and the supporters'.

The correlation between information articulation and adverbial quantification has been noted in the literature. Rooth (1985, 1995) shows focus can affect the interpretation of sentences with adverbs of quantification. The sentences in (33)a and (33)b have different truth conditions.

(33) a. Mary usually took John_F to the movies.
'When Mary took someone to the movies, she usually took John.'
b. Mary_F usually took John to the movies.
'When someone took John to the movies, Mary usually took him.'

If Mary took John to the movies five times and Bill did so ten times, (33)a can be true, but (33)b is certainly false. These examples show that when everything else remains the same the different placement of focus can change truth conditions.

Assuming that the logical form of a sentence with an adverb of quantification has a tripartite structure with a quantifier, its restriction and nuclear scope, Rooth (1985) obtains the restriction of an adverb of quantification from the focus closure of the main sentence, i.e., the union of the set of events where the focused position is replaced with an alternative object. This has the effect of existentially quantifying the focused position. In the case of (33)a, the union set is the set of events at which Mary takes someone to the movies. Thus, (33)a is interpreted as meaning that most events of Mary taking someone to the movies are events of Mary taking John to the movies. In contrast, (33)b is interpreted as meaning that most events of someone taking John to the movies are events of Mary taking John to the movies.

In his analysis, adverbs of quantification can quantify over not only events (de Swart 1991) but also variables introduced by indefinites, as illustrated in (34).

(34) a. A dog is usually intelligent$_F$.

b. USUALLY ([dog(x) $\wedge$ x has some property], [x is intelligent])

c. When something is a dog, it is usually intelligent.
(Most dogs are intelligent.)

Similarly, (35) is interpreted like (36)b via the logical form in (36)a.

(35) Gangs always fight$_F$ in the park.

(36) a. ALWAYS ([gang(x) $\wedge$ x has some property in the park], [x fight in the park])

b. All gangs fight in the park.

However, the corresponding existential sentence in (37) never gets such an interpretation even when some heavy accent is put on the coda predicate *fighting*.

(37) There are always gangs FIGHTING in the park.

If we assume that the post-copular indefinite NP is existentially quantified over instead of introducing free variables, we can avoid the interpretation in (36). However, if the focus is still assumed to be only on the coda predicate, (37) would have the logical form in (38)a, where the adverbial quantifier quantifies over situations, and would be interpreted as (38)b.

(38) a. ALWAYS ([s is a situation in the park and some gangs have some property in s], [the gangs have the property of fighting in s])

b. Whenever there are some gangs in the park, they are fighting there.
(Every situation in the park where there are some gangs is a situation in which the gangs are fighting.)

While this interpretation does not involve quantification over gangs, it quantifies over situations in the park in which there are some gangs. This is still not the correct interpretation of the existential sentence in (37).

Suppose that gangs come to the park only on weekends and they fight whenever they are in the park. In this case, (37) is false, but it is incorrectly judged true according to the interpretation in (38). This means that (37) is interpreted as (39), the quantifier simply quantifying over situations in the park whether it has gangs or not.

(39) a. ALWAYS ([s is a situation in the park and some fact holds in s], [some gangs are fighting in s])

b. Every situation in the park is a situation in which some gangs are fighting.

This interpretation is obtained if the whole part composed of the post-copular NP and the coda predicate is regarded as being in focus in (37), as in (40).

(40) There are always [gangs FIGHTING]$_F$ in the park.

Presumably, the accented coda predicate *fighting* gets some contrastive focus, but what is relevant to the adverbial quantification is presentational focus. Because (37) describes a situation in the park as one supporting the infon that some gangs are fighting, the post copular NP *gangs* should be taken in the focus as well as the accented coda predicate *fighting*. The automatic application of alternative semantics to existential sentences ignoring this fact cannot work.

Apart from the effect of focus, it has been noted that there is some correlation between the topic (background) and the restriction on the one hand, and the comment (focus) and the nuclear scope on the other hand (Partee 1991, von Fintel 1994). However, this interesting kind of approach is not at the stage of a full-fledged formal analysis. This is partly because there has not been available a theory to formalize the notion of topic. The proposed analysis of the propositional content of a statement which incorporates the topic-comment structure can be regarded as a way to formally accommodate this correlation between the topic and the restriction of adverbial quantification.

In syntax, an adverb of quantification Qadv is a one-place operator modifying a sentence ϕ, as in (41)a. If ϕ has the propositional content in (41)b and Qadv denotes a quantifier relation Q, then the quantificational sentence Qadv(ϕ) is interpreted as (41)c, where a' and b' are relevant types formed from a and b.

(41) a. Qadv(ϕ)

b. 

c. 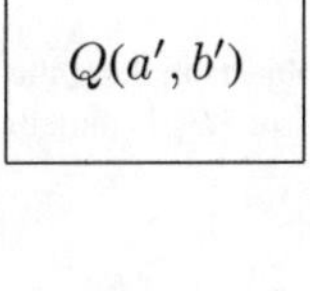

There arises no partition problem for an adverbial quantification in our analysis, because the propositional content of ϕ is already given some kind of partition reflecting its information articulation. A sentence ϕ is interpreted as a proposition which involves predication of some argument a—a situation or an individual which is expressed by the sentence topic). We can form the restriction of Q out of the predication base a, and the nuclear scope from the predicating part b. An adverb of quantification relates types like other generalized quantifiers. Depending on the predication base, an adverb of quantification quantifies over situation types or individual types.

Now, we can account for the different interpretation of the two sentences in (35) and (37). According to the proposed semantics of existential sentences, the post-copular NP and the coda predicate are not separated into a and b but they together form b, an infon characterizing a, a situation. The non-quantificational existential sentence (42)a is analyzed as expressing the proposition (42)b. The PP adjunct *in the park* restricts the spatial location of the described situation s, and provides the background information for the proposition that some gangs are fighting in s.[13] The proposition in (42)b is not asserted of an arbitrary situation, but a situation whose location is in the park.

(42) a. There are gangs fighting in the park.

b. 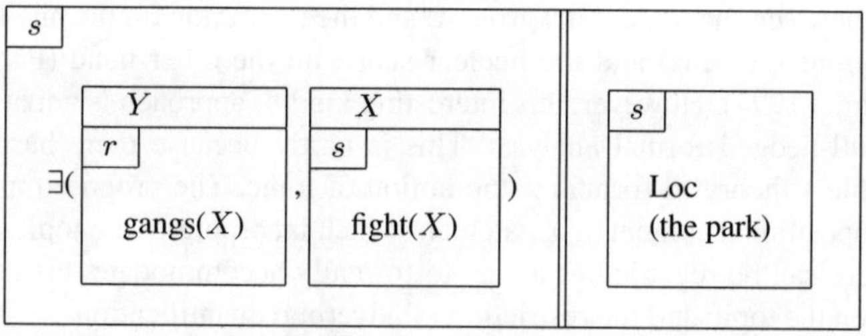

When the adverb of quantification *always* combines with (42)a, the propositional content of the quantificational existential sentence (43)a (=(37)) can be

13 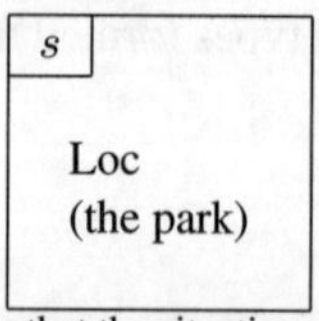

means that the situation s's location is in the park.

Whenever we have a situation theoretic object represented by some box B, we indicate the result of the *restriction* of the object by a proposition P as follows.

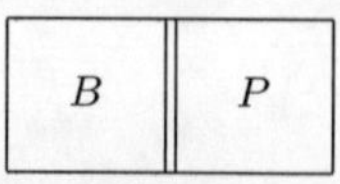

The effect of this is to restrict any parameters in $[\![B]\!]$ to range over objects making the proposition $[\![P]\!]$ true. The restriction is undefined if $[\![P]\!]$ is false or either of $[\![B]\!]$ or $[\![P]\!]$ is undefined.

represented as (43)b.

(43) a. There are always gangs fighting in the park.

b. 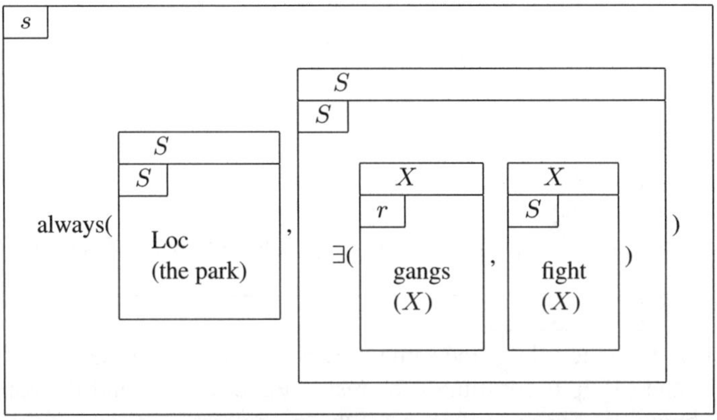

The restriction of the quantifier *always* in (43)b is obtained from the predication base of (42)b. As (42)b is asserted of a situation whose location is in the park, the type of such a situation serves the restriction of the adverbial quantification in (43)b. The proposition (43)b correctly captures the interpretation of (43)a: every situation in the park is of the type of situation supporting the infon that some gangs are fighting.[14]

On the other hand, the subject-predicate sentence in (44)a can be analyzed to have the propositional content in (44)b, because it is possible for the subject NP to be the topic and for the remainder to be its comment.

(44) a. Gangs fight in the park.

b. 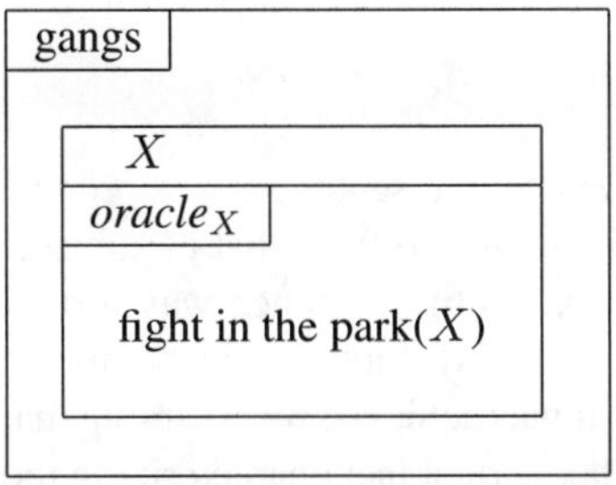

Accordingly, when it is modified by the adverb of quantification *always*, as in (45)a (=(35)), it can be interpreted as (45)b. Since (44)b's predication

[14]If the locative phrase *in the park* is syntactically analyzed as part of the coda predicate rather than as an adjunct, it would belong to the information supported by the described situation S, hence part of the focus. Under this information articulation, the quantificational existential sentence is analyzed to mean that every (relevant) situation supports the infon that some gangs are fighting in the park.

base is an individual constant *gangs*,[15] the type of individuals who are gangs constitutes the restriction of the quantifier *always* in (45)b. Therefore, it means that all gangs fight in the park.

(45) a. Gangs always fight in the park.

b. 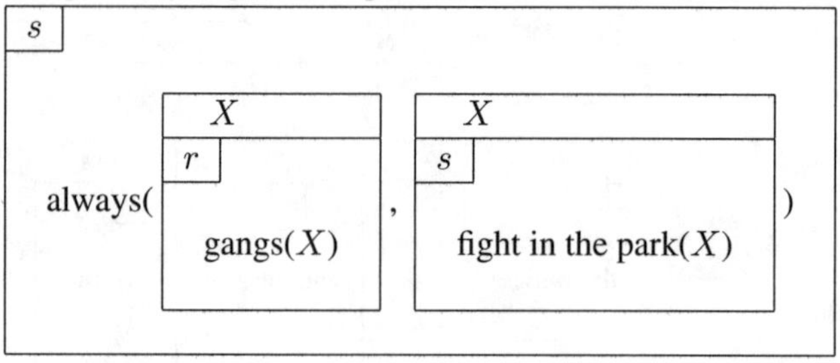

Compare the role of the same type box representing the type of gangs in (43)b and (45)b. It constitutes the restriction of *always* and the parameter in it is bound by the quantifier in (45)b. In contrast, it belongs to the nuclear scope of *always* and the parameter in it is bound by an existential quantifier in (43)b. Hence, the two propositions have different truth conditions. If there is no gang at all in the park, (43)b is false, but (45)b is still true. If there are gangs who never fight in the park, (45)b is false, but (43)b still can be true as long as fightings of some gangs always happen in the park. Such truth-conditional differences are due to the fact that the indefinite NP *gangs* has a different role in the information articulation of the two sentences: it is part of the comment in (42) but of the topic in (44). To sum up this section, considerations of the topic-comment structure is essential to account for the different truth conditions of existential sentences and subject-predicate sentences modified by an adverb of quantification.

4.6 Conclusion

In this paper, a semantic analysis of existential sentences was proposed to capture their information articulation distinguished from that of subject-predicate sentences. The interpretation of an existential sentence was formalized in a way reflecting the fact that its post-copular NP can never be the topic but rather must always be part of the comment. It was achieved by assuming that the post-copular NP and coda predicate together form a fact characterizing the situation described by the utterance of the existential sentence. In contrast, a subject-predicate sentence, which can be readily interpreted as a statement about the subject NP, was formalized as asserting that the individual denoted by the subject NP is of a certain type.

---

[15]In this case, the bare plural names a kind (Carlson 1977). It is beyond the scope of this paper to propose a way to handle bare plurals in Situation Semantics. A relevant discussion is found in Glasbey (1995).

By analyzing the propositional contents of the two types of sentence in a way fine-grained enough to distinguish their different information articulation, we could account for the different interpretation of cardinal quantifiers and adverbial quantification in the two types of sentence: the partitive interpretation is absent in the post-copular NP but possible in the subject NP, and only the subject NP but not the post-copular NP can constitute the restriction of an adverb of quantification. The fact that even such truth-conditional differences arise due to information articulation strongly supports the proposed position that the propositional content of a statement should be analyzed in such a way as to accommodate not only its truth conditions but also its information articulation.

References

Aissen, Judith. 1975. Presentational-*there* insertion: A cyclic root transformation. In *Proceedings of CLS 11.1*, 1–14.

Barwise, Jon, and Robin Cooper. 1981. Generalized Quantifiers and Natural Language. *Linguistics and Philosophy* 4:159–219.

Barwise, Jon, and Robin Cooper. 1993. Extended Kamp Notation: A Graphical Notation for Situation Theory. In *Situation Theory and its Applications*, ed. P. Aczel, D. Israel, Y. Katagari, and S. Peters. 29–54. Stanford: CSLI.

Barwise, Jon, and John Etchemendy. 1987. *The Liar: An Essay on Truth and Circularity*. New York: Oxford University Press.

Barwise, Jon, and John Perry. 1983. *Situations and Attitudes*. Cambridge, MA: MIT Press.

Brentano, Franz. 1973. Psychology from an Empirical Standpoint. Translated by Antos C. Rancurello, D. B. Terrell, and Linda L. McAlister from Psychologie vom empirischen Standpunkt (1874).

Bresnan, Joan. 1994. Locative Inversion and the Architecture of Universal Grammar. *Language* 70:72–131.

Büring, Daniel. 1994. Topic. In *Proceedings of the IBM/Journal of Semantics Conference on Focus*, ed. Peter Bosch and Rob van der Sandt. 271–280. Heidelberg.

Carlson, Gregory N. 1977. *Reference to Kinds in English*. Bloomington: Indiana University Linguistics Club.

de Hoop, Helen. 1992. *Case configuration and Noun phrase interpretation*. Doctoral dissertation, Groningen University.

de Swart, Henriëtte. 1991. *Adverbs of Quantification: a Generalized Quantifier approach*. Doctoral dissertation, Groningen University.

Devlin, Keith. 1991. *Logic and Information, Volume 1: Infons and Situations*. Cambridge, England: Cambridge University Press.

Diesing, Molly. 1992. *Indefinites*. Cambridge, MA: MIT Press.

Fodor, Janet, and Ivan Sag. 1982. Referential and Quantificational Indefinites. *Linguistics and Philosophy* 5:355–398.

Gawron, Jean Mark, and Stanley Peters. 1990. *Anaphora and quantification in Situation Semantics*. Stanford: CSLI.

Glasbey, Sheila. 1995. A Situation-Theoretic Interpretation of Bare Plurals. Ms. Center for Cognitive Science, University of Edinburgh.

Grice, H. Paul. 1975. Logic and Conversation. In *Syntax and Semantics 3: Speech Acts*, ed. Peter Cole and Jerry L. Morgan. Academic Press.

Gundel, Jeanette, Nancy Hedberg, and Ron Zacharski. 1993. Cognitive Status and the form of referring expressions in discourse. *Language* 69(2):274–307.

Kim, Yookyung. 1997. *A Situation Semantic Account of Existential Sentences*. Doctoral dissertation, Stanford University.

Krifka, Manfred. 1992. A Framework for Focus-Sensitive Quantification. In *Proceedings of SALT II*, 215–234. Ithaca, NY. Cornell University.

Kuroda, S.-Y. 1992. *Japanese Syntax and Semantics*. Dordrecht: Kluwer.

Ladusaw, William. 1982. Semantic Constraints on the English Partitive Construction. In *Proceedings of WCCFL 1*, 231–242. Stanford, CA. CSLI.

Ladusaw, William. 1994. Thetic and Categorical, Stage and Individual, Weak and Strong. In *Proceedings of SALT IV*, 220–229. Ithaca, NY. Cornell University.

Langendoen, Terence D. 1979. More on Locative Inversion Sentences and the structure-preserving hypothesis. *Linguistic Analysis* 5:421–437.

Lewis, David. 1979. Score-keeping in a language game. In *Semantics from Different Points of View*, ed. R. Bäuerle, U. Egli, and A. von Stechow. Berlin: Springer.

Li, Charles N., and Sandra A. Thompson. 1976. Subject and Topic: A New Typology of Language. In *Subject and Topic*, ed. Charles N. Li. 457–589. New York: Academic Press.

McNally, Louise. 1995. Stativity and theticity. In *Proceedings of Bar-Ilan conference on Event and Grammar*.

Partee, Barbara H. 1991. Topic, Focus and Quantification. In *Proceedings of SALT I*, 159–187. Ithaca, NY. Cornell University.

Reinhart, Tanya. 1981. Pragmatics and Linguistics: An Analysis of Sentence Topics. *Philosophica* 27:53–94.

Reinhart, Tanya. 1995. Topics and the Conceptual Interface. Part IV of Interface Strategies, Ms.

Rooth, Mats E. 1985. *Association with Focus*. Doctoral dissertation, University of Massachusetts at Amherst.

Rooth, Mats E. 1995. Indefinites, Adverbs of Quantification, and Focus Semantics. In *The Generic Book*, ed. Greg Carlson and Jeff Pelletier. University of Chicago Press.

Sasse, Hans Jürgen. 1987. The Thetic/Categorical distinction revisited. *Linguistics* 25:511–580.

Schmerling, Susan F. 1976. *Aspects of English Sentence Stress*. Austin: University of Texas Press.

Strawson, P. F. 1964. Identifying reference and truth-values. In *Semantics*, ed. D. Steinberg and L. Jacobovits. 86–99. Cambridge University Press.

Vallduví, Enric. 1990. *The Informational Component*. Doctoral dissertation, University of Pennsylvania.

von Fintel, Kai. 1994. *Restrictions on Quantifier Domains*. Doctoral dissertation, University of Massachusetts at Amherst.

5

Cofinal Circumscription

TOM COSTELLO

5.1 Introduction

Circumscription is a form of non-monotonic reasoning. It allows the default conclusions of a theory to be expressed in second order logic. It was introduced by McCarthy (1977, 1980, 1986). Classical logic has the property of monotonicity, if a conclusion is warranted by a set of premises, then it is warranted by every superset of those premises. It is precisely this property that non-monotonic logics deny.

In reasoning about common sense phenomena humans often make judgments that are not certain. These conclusions later may have to be withdrawn in the light of new evidence. If we want computers and robots to function in the world they too will have to make speculative jumps that are not classically warranted. In Section 5.1.2 we give some examples of how a computer or robot could use non-monotonicity—or this ability to make leaps of judgment.

Circumscription is a formalism that allows us to make cognitive leaps of faith. It is based around the idea that a predicate or formula is *minimized*, or made true of as few things as possible. The consequences of this minimization can be defined in terms of the minimal models of a partial order on models. A model $\mathfrak{A}$ is considered minimal if no other model has an extension for that predicate that is a proper subset of the model $\mathfrak{A}$'s extension. This class of minimal models are the models of the circumscribed theory. This circumscribed theory contains conclusions that the original theory did not. Should new infor-

Logical Perspectives on Language and Information.
Cleo Condoravdi and Gerard R. Renardel de Lavalette.

mation be added however, these conclusions can be withdrawn.

The idea of using minimal models as a paradigm for non-monotonic reasoning was further considered by (Bossu and Siegel 1984) and later (Shoham 1986). Each of these took a different direction. Bossu and Siegel restricted the class of policy, or minimality criterion, but overcame the problem of presupposing that minimal models existed. They minimized all predicates, while circumscription classically only minimizes some predicates. They, following Lewis (1973), rejected the assumption that there were minimal models, and instead took as the resulting theory, all sentences true in sufficiently minimal models. Lewis called the assumption that there were minimal models or in his terminology, closest worlds, the Limit Assumption. Many orderings do not have the property that every subset of the ordering has a least element; ordering that have this property have been called well-founded by Lifschitz (1985), smooth by Kraus et al. (1990), and stoppered by Makinson(1989). Bossu and Siegel definition was in terms of all sufficiently minimal models, again following Lewis's sufficiently close worlds. Removing the assumption that there was always a minimal model overcame the problem that circumscription could sometimes map a consistent theory onto the inconsistent theory.

Shoham took another path—he expanded the class of preferences between models to allow any preferences. Whereas in circumscription preferences must be expressible as set inclusion on the extension of a predicate or formula, Shoham considered all possible preferences. An advantage of this proposal is that new preferences are allowed, (however no new preferences are gained in the finite propositional case (Costello 1996b)) a disadvantage is that he did not supply a new language for describing these new preferences.

The formal system for circumscription, expressed in classical second order logic,[1] was one of the strengths of circumscription. The benefits of a more expressive semantics are not as obvious if we lose the ability to represent the new semantics in a formal logical system.

5.1.1 Problems

Meanwhile, the formalization of circumscription itself was running into problems. Etherington et al. (1985) claimed that circumscription could never infer a new positive ground instance of a predicate. McCarthy attempted to answer this criticism in his 1986 paper (McCarthy 1986), explicating how predicates could be varied.

The varying of predicates allowed models that differed in some of their predicates to be compared. A set of predicates—called fixed predicates—that all comparable models must agree upon was specified. This allowed circumscription to infer new positive instances of varied predicates.

[1]This formalism was introduced by Lifschitz (1985), the original formalism was in terms of an axiom schema of first order logic.

More seriously Etherington et al. following Davis (1980), show that circumscription could sometimes make theories inconsistent. This was not surprising in the light of the semantics being defined in terms of minimal models that did not necessarily exist. The set of minimal models always exists, it is, however, sometimes empty.

5.1.2 Uses of Circumscription

Circumscription has been used for formalizing many different domains. We introduce a sample of these domains, where circumscription becomes inconsistent.

The assumption that a property is sufficiently or arbitrarily close to a certain value has many applications. In mathematics it is closely connected with the theory of limits. We say that a function $f(x)$ has a value c in the limit as x approaches e, if for an arbitrarily small, non zero value δ we can always find a nonzero ϵ such that $|x - e| < \epsilon \rightarrow |f(x) - c| < \delta$.

It is also used as a simplifying assumption in many common sense problems. If we are told that the price of a plane ticket is less than one hundred dollars, then for planning reasons it is wise to assume that it is only just less. To assume that it is $100 is inconsistent with what we have been told, so we cannot easily make that our assumption. On the other hand to assume that it was, say $40, is not in general wise.

We also use the notion of sufficiently or arbitrarily close to specify behaviors. This differs from making a simplifying assumption. When we make an assumption we give a different value to a particular property. When we ask what a person would buy for their birthday if money were no object, we implicitly ask them to imagine that they had an arbitrarily large amount of money. This differs from assuming that whatever one does one will have sufficient money. When we want to characterize behaviors, we want to describe the results not for just some finite set, but for as large an area of inputs as possible. When the range of inputs is openended we need to talk about arbitrarily large or small values.

We now look at some cases in particular. The first example concerns a group of MBA students who discover that they can intercept satellite transmissions of the new prices from the Tokyo Stock Exchange. They see an opportunity for profit if they can buy or sell before the rest of the stock exchange gets the information. They ask a mathematically inclined friend to calculate whether this is possible. She naturally asks how fast a computer they will use to do the necessary computation—perhaps there is a small amount of encryption. They tell her to assume that she can use any computer—money is no object. The question is how we characterize the last assumption, that there is unlimited financial resources to be spent on computers.

Example 1. We have a theory of the stock market T which includes time information. The time between the satellite transmission and the publication of the information is t, the time for transmission by the MBAs is a, the time for one transaction is b and the computer time t_c is characterized by the following rules.

$$money < \$2000 \rightarrow c = pentium \wedge t_c = 10$$
$$\$2000 \leq money < \$1,000,000 \rightarrow c = sparcstation \wedge t_c = 5$$
$$\$1,000,000 \leq money \rightarrow c = cray \wedge t_c = 1$$

The question is whether $a+b+t_c < t$. We wish to minimize $\lambda x.money < x$. That is we prefer models where interpretation of $\lambda x.money < x$ is smaller. This is equivalent to preferring models where $money$ is larger. We can write this in the notation of circumscription as,

$$Circ(T; \lambda x.money < x).$$

There are no minimal models in this order, minimal entailment entails falsity.

The intuitive answer is that $t_c = 1$. However, because the amount of money available can grow without bound, we have no minimal model.

Our next example concerns an old favorite of logical AI, the blocks world. We wish to say that we can move a block through a space, as long it has some space on either side. The question arises, 'how much space is needed'? A natural assumption is that there is no particular amount of space needed, there just has to be some.

Example 2. We have one unit cube C, positioned at $(0,0,0)$, at time 0 in our blocks world. We also have a predicate $empty(p, x, y, z)$, that states that a rectangular region x by y by z, centered at p, is empty. We consider the notation of the situation calculus, a formalism for reasoning about action introduced in (McCarthy and Hayes 1969). A recent presentation is found in (Gelfond et al. 1991). We have the axioms,

$$\forall t.empty((0,0,0), 1, 1+\epsilon, 1+\epsilon) \rightarrow$$
$$at(C, (1,0,0), result(move(C, (1,0,0), 0), t)),$$
$$\epsilon > 0.$$

In this case we know that the entire space is empty, save for our one block. We would like to infer that we can move the block one unit in the x direction.

Now, as before, we wish to minimize ϵ, that is our preference on modes prefers models with smaller interpretation of ϵ. There are no minimal models in this order.

Thus we see that there are common sense examples where our assumptions lead to situations where we do not have minimal models.

These two examples share a feature that does not exist in general. The models were totally ordered, rather than partially ordered. The intuitive answer is much easier to grasp in these totally ordered situations. For this reason we give a third example, where we do not have this totality.

Example 3. This example concerns ice-cream. Rather than consider what we minimize, we draw out order directly, as this is easier to visualize. For simplicity there are two flavors of ice-cream, chocolate and vanilla. Ice-creams can also be compared in smoothness. Ice-cream with smaller ice crystals is smoother. Our subject likes smoother vanilla ice-cream. That is, for any two vanilla ice-creams, he prefers the smoother.

He does not have a preference among chocolate ice-cream, "no chocolate ice-cream is better than any other, nor can chocolate ice-creams be compared to other flavors".

Ice-cream is totally ordered with respect to smoothness. Thus, we can represent his preferences by the following diagram.

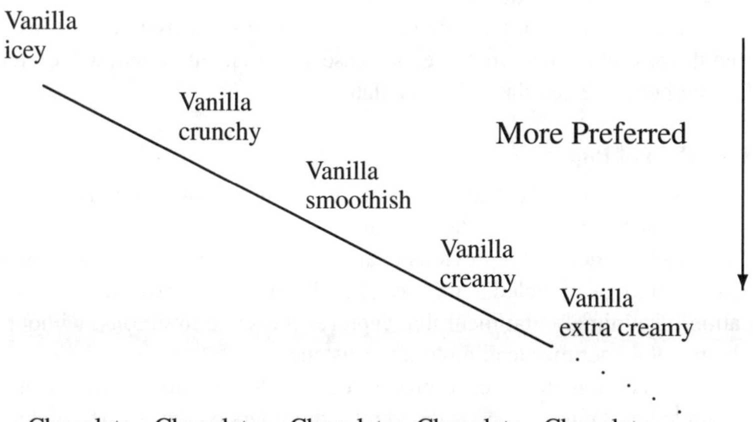

It is worth noting that we have not decided whether or not there is a smoothest ice-cream. We might imagine that it is always possible to make a smoother ice-cream, in which case, his favorite ice-cream would be chocolate, despite the fact that he considers chocolate ice-cream incomparable to vanilla ice-cream.

Our second character shares this preference for smoother vanilla ice-cream, but for a given smoothness of ice-cream she prefers chocolate to vanilla. Thus her preferences can be drawn as,

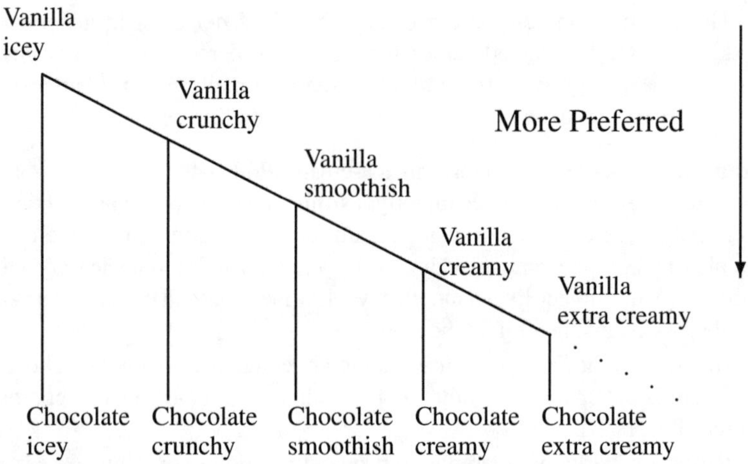

The important point her example raises is that her favorite flavor is chocolate. This is despite the fact that for any given ice-cream there is a vanilla ice-cream that she considers incomparable.

In the first case, minimal entailment will incorrectly assume that his preferred flavor is chocolate. In the second case, minimal entailment will correctly infer that her preferred flavor is chocolate.

5.1.3 Plan of Paper

We have now discussed circumscription, and the notion of minimal entailment, that is considering the formulas true in the minimal models of a certain partial order on models. The previous examples have shown that certain natural defaults cannot be modeled in this way. For this reason we now look for a modification of minimal entailment that captures the same intuitions, without the problems of sometimes leading to inconsistency.

As we mentioned earlier, a proposal to modify minimal entailment was propounded by Lewis. He considered total preorders on worlds. He said a formula was true in all sufficiently close possible worlds, if there was some world w, such that the formula was true in all worlds less than or equal w.

We consider partial orders, rather than total preorders. For this reason, Lewis's proposal does not agree with minimal entailment, even for partial orders over finite domains. In general, there will be incomparable minimal models. Each minimal model can be taken as the world w, considered above. If one minimal model entails ϕ and the other $\neg\phi$, then Lewis's notion of true in sufficiently close possible worlds will lead to inconsistency.

For this reason we reexamine the intuition behind minimal entailment, by looking at what are the reasonable states of belief, given an partial order on likliehood of states of the world. This leads us to a notion of reasonable beliefs that has certain consistency properties. We show that it agrees with minimal entailment, when enough minimal models exist. Finally, we show how this gives rise to a new form of circumscription that can be captured in second order logic.

5.2 Reasonable States of Belief

We now look at the question of what are the *reasonable* epistemic states, given that we have some facts we consider true, and some ordering on states of the world that represents likelihood. We consider several conditions that we claim any *reasonable* epistemic state should obey. We first formally define epistemic state, and state of the world to avoid misunderstandings.

Definition 1 We assume a fixed underlying first order language L. An epistemic state is a class of L-structures. A state of the world is an L-structure.

The first possible criterion we consider is that any belief we have should not exclude a state of the world, if we believe that it is possible, and there is no other state that is more likely. Thus the structures that are minimal in our ordering should always be included in *reasonable* states of belief. The following propositions will all delimit the reasonable beliefs with respect to a partial ordering $\leq$, and a class of possible states of the world/models A.

Criterion 1 Minimal *Given a notion of $\leq$ on states of the world, and a class of states of the world A that are possible, the reasonable epistemic states include all minimal states of A with respect to $\leq$.*

It also seems reasonable that, given a particular model $\mathfrak{M}$ there should be at least one model in our final class, that is as likely as $\mathfrak{M}$. This is not implied by our previous consideration, as if we have an infinite descending chain, without a limit, then there is no minimal element. This new consideration would say that, in this case, we would include some model, below each particular model in the chain.

These two principles can be expressed formally by saying that the set of models we select out, should be a *dense*.

Definition 2 A class of objects M, is *dense*, with respect to a partial order $\leq$, over a class of objects, N, exactly when for each object x in N, there is an object y in M less than or equal to x.

$$\forall x \in N \exists y \in M . y \leq x$$

Given a class of models, A, and a partial order $\leq$ on A, then the class of models we select should be dense with respect to $\leq$. This is the second criterion on states of belief that we propose. However, it subsumes the first criterion.

Criterion 2 Dense *Given a notion of $\leq$ on states of the world, and a class of states of the world A that are possible, the reasonable epistemic states should be dense in A with respect to $\leq$.*

Proposition 1 *Criterion 2 implies Criterion 1.*

Proof: Consider the minimal objects in the partial order. By density, there are objects less than or equal to them in the dense class. But the only elements less than or equal to a minimal element is itself. Therefore every dense class contains every minimal element. ∎

Another principle that has some justification is that our class of models should be downwards closed. If a model $\mathfrak{A}$ is in our selected class, then every more likely model should also be in our class. This property can be stated as every acceptable class is a ideal, or downwards closed class. As we are considering partial orders not lattices an ideal is just a downwards closed class—there is not requirement that it be closed under meets. Ideals of partial orders are sometimes called order ideals or lower sets.

Definition 3 A class M is an ideal of a partial order $\leq$, over a class N, exactly when M is downwards closed.

$$\forall x \in M, y \in N. y \leq x \rightarrow y \in M$$

Definition 4 The restriction of a partial order $\leq$ to a class A, is the partial order $\leq_{\downarrow A}$ defined by,

$$\forall x, y. x \leq y \wedge x \in A \wedge y \in A \equiv x \leq_{\downarrow A} y.$$

Criterion 3 Ideal *Given a notion of $\leq$ on states of the world, and a class of states of the world A that are possible, the reasonable epistemic states should be an ideal of $\leq$ restricted to A.*

Having looked at these principles, we now consider what the *reasonable beliefs* of reasoner should be. The characterization we consider is that a reasoner should believe ϕ, if ϕ is true in some reasonable state of belief.

Because of the ambiguity of English we define the set of sentences true in some dense ideal of a partial order on models more formally.

Definition 5 The set of sentences Φ true in some dense ideal of a partial order $\leq$ on a class of models A is defined to be the set:

$$\left\{ \phi \;\middle|\; \begin{array}{l} \exists N. \forall x \in A \forall y \in N. x \leq y \rightarrow x \in N \wedge \\ \forall x \in A \exists y \in N. y \leq x \wedge N \models \phi \end{array} \right\}$$

We call Φ the *reasonable beliefs*, given a class of models A and a partial order $\leq$ on A.

Theorem 2 *The class of models of the reasonable beliefs given a class of models A and a partial order $\leq$ need not be a reasonable epistemic state.*

Proof: We imagine that our partial order on beliefs is an infinite descending chain, with no least element. For simplicity we imagine each structure interprets a constant c as a natural number, where $\mathfrak{M} \leq \mathfrak{N}$ if and only if $c^{\mathfrak{M}} \geq c^{\mathfrak{N}}$, where $\geq$ is greater than or equal on the naturals. Here the class of models of the reasonable beliefs is not dense. Its only models have a nonstandard interpretation of c, and no model in A has a nonstandard interpretation of c. ∎

This theorem may seem damning, but things are not as bad as they may now seem. The notion of reasonable beliefs still has nice properties.

We now question whether this notion of *reasonable beliefs* has certain consistency properties. We note (theorem 4) that as our logic is first order then the set of sentences true in some dense ideal of a partial order is guaranteed to be logically closed, and consistent.

We first show that the intersection of two dense ideals is a dense ideal.

Lemma 3 *The intersection of two dense ideals is a dense ideal.*

Proof: We need to show that the intersection of two dense ideals, I_1 and I_2, is dense, and an ideal. The intersection of two downwards closed classes is downwards closed. Finally, the intersection of two dense ideals is a dense ideal by the following argument. For each object y, there is an object x in I_1 below y by density. Also by density there is an object z in the ideal I_2 below x. This z is in the first ideal I_1, as the ideal is downwards closed. Thus z is in the intersection of I_1 and I_2. We have thus shown that there is an object in the intersection below every object, as needed. ∎

Theorem 4 *For a first order language L and a nonempty class of L-structures A, and a partial order on A, $\leq$, the set of sentences true in some dense ideal of a $\leq$ is a consistent theory.*

Proof: We first show that the set of sentences true in some dense ideal is logically closed. Let Γ be the set of sentences true in some dense ideal. Let ϕ be a logical consequence of Γ. Then, by the compactness of first order logic, there is a finite subset $\Gamma' = \{\gamma_1, \ldots, \gamma_n\}$, of Γ such that $\Gamma' \models \phi$. Let a dense ideal that entails γ_i be denoted I_i. These exist as every element of Γ was true in some dense ideal. Then, by the above Lemma, the intersection $I' = \bigcap_{i \leq n} I_i$ is a dense ideal. Further, every $\gamma_i \in \Gamma'$ is true in I'. This follows, as truth in a class of models is preserved by intersection. Thus, ϕ is true in I', and thus it is in Γ, as Γ is the set of all sentences true in some dense ideal. Thus the set Γ is closed under logical consequence.

We now show that Γ is consistent. Suppose that Γ was not consistent, then, as it is logically closed, it would contain $\perp$. Then there would be a dense ideal that entailed $\perp$. But the only ideal that entails $\perp$ is the empty ideal, which is not dense. Thus Γ is consistent, and hence its class of models is nonempty, as required. ∎

Definition 6 A consequence relation $\mid\!\sim$ is a binary relation on sets of formula and formulas.

We say that a consequence relation is consistency preserving if every satisfiable theory is mapped to a satisfiable theory.

Definition 7 A consequence relation $\Gamma \mid\!\sim \gamma$ is consistency preserving exactly when, if Γ is consistent, then the set of γ, such that $\Gamma \mid\!\sim \gamma$, is consistent.

Definition 8 Let $\leq$ be a partial order on L-structures. We say a set of sentences Γ in L ideally entails, under $\leq$, a sentence α if α is in the reasonable beliefs of the models of Γ under $\leq$.

This defines a consequence relation. That is, a binary relation between sets of sentences in L and sentences in L.

Theorem 5 *Ideal entailment is consistency preserving.*

Proof: This follows the analysis of Theorem 4. ∎

We have now shown that our notion of reasonable beliefs does not map satisfiable sets of first order sentences to contradiction.

As next consideration we ask does the derived entailment relation obey the structural rules suggested by Gabbay(1985), and the rule **Or** suggested by Kraus, Lehmann and Magidor(1990). Kraus et al. considered compact consequence relations, and thus considered a binary relation on sentences, $\alpha \mid\!\sim \beta$. We generalize their rules so that $\mid\!\sim$ takes a set of formulas and a formula as arguments. In the following $\models$ denotes first order entailment, Γ and Δ sets of first order formulas, and $\gamma, \delta, \alpha, \beta$ first order formulas.

Definition 9 A consequence relation $\mid\!\sim$ over a language L is said to be *preferential* if and only if it contains all instances of the following Reflexivity axiom **ID** and is closed under the inference rules of Left Logical Equivalence **LLE**, Right Weakening **RW**, Cut **Cut**, Cautious Monotonicity **CM**, and **Or**.

$$\textbf{(ID)} \quad \Gamma, \alpha \mid\!\sim \alpha$$

$$\textbf{(LLE)} \quad \frac{\Gamma \models \delta | \delta \in \Delta, \Delta \models \gamma | \gamma \in \Gamma,\ \Gamma \mid\!\sim \alpha}{\Delta \mid\!\sim \alpha}$$

$$\textbf{(RW)} \quad \frac{\models \alpha \to \beta, \Gamma \mid\!\sim \alpha}{\Gamma \mid\!\sim \beta}$$

$$\textbf{(Cut)} \quad \frac{\Gamma, \delta \mid\!\sim \gamma, \Gamma \mid\!\sim \delta}{\Gamma \mid\!\sim \gamma}$$

$$\textbf{(CM)} \quad \frac{\Gamma \mid\!\sim \delta, \Gamma \mid\!\sim \gamma}{\Gamma, \delta \mid\!\sim \gamma}$$

$$\textbf{(Or)} \quad \frac{\Delta \mid\!\sim \alpha,\ \gamma \mid\!\sim \alpha}{\{\delta \vee \gamma | \delta \in \Delta\} \mid\!\sim \alpha}$$

We call this system **P** for preferential.

The rule **Or** differs from the rule proposed by Kraus et al. in that they insisted that both Δ and γ be formulas, while we allow Δ, though not γ to be a set of formulas.

Theorem 6 *Ideal entailment, over a first order language, is a preferential consequence relation.*

Proof: We need to check each rule. Let $||\Gamma||$ denote the models of Γ. Let a dense ideal of $||\Gamma||$ be understood to be a dense ideal of $||\Gamma||$ relative to some fixed order $\leq$.

ID is immediate, as every model in $||\Gamma, \alpha||$ satisfies α, and hence $||\Gamma, \alpha||$ is a dense ideal of $||\Gamma, \alpha||$ that models α.

LLE is immediate as if Γ and Δ satisfy the same formulas then the $||\Delta|| = ||\Gamma||$.

RW is true as satisfaction on a set of states is defined classically.

Cut We need to show that if a dense ideal I of $||\Gamma, \delta||$ models γ, and a dense ideal I' of $||\Gamma||$ models δ, then there is a dense ideal I_1 of $||\Gamma||$ that models γ. We can choose $I' \cap I$ as density and ideality are preserved under intersection. We claim that $I \cap I'$ is the necessary dense ideal of $||\Gamma||$. It is an ideal, as intersection preserves downwards closedness. We need to show that it is a dense ideal of $||\Gamma||$. We consider a model $\mathfrak{A}$ of Γ, we show that there is a model below it in $I \cap I'$. As I' is dense in $||\Gamma||$ there is a model $\mathfrak{B} \in I'$. Further, as $\Gamma \mid\!\sim \delta$, $\mathfrak{B} \models \delta$. Thus $\mathfrak{B} \in ||\Gamma, \delta||$. But as I is a dense ideal of $||\Gamma, \delta||$, there is a model $\mathfrak{C} \in I$ below $\mathfrak{B}$ that models γ. This is also in I' as I' is downwards closed, and $\mathfrak{C} \leq \mathfrak{B}$ $\mathfrak{C} \models \Gamma$ and $\mathfrak{B} \in I'$. Therefore $\mathfrak{C}$ is our needed witness of the density of $I \cap I'$ in $||\Gamma||$.

Finally we need to show that $I \cap I' \models \gamma$. This follows as I models γ.

CM We need to show that if a dense ideal I of $||\Gamma||$ models γ, and a dense ideal I' of $||\Gamma||$ models δ, then there is a dense ideal I_1 of $||\Gamma, \delta||$ that models γ.

We consider the intersection of the two ideals I and I'. $I \cap I'$ models γ. Furthermore, $I \cap I'$ is a dense ideal of $||\Gamma||$. We need to show that $I \cap I'$ is a dense ideal of $||\Gamma, \delta||$. It is downwards closed, as it is the intersection of two downwards closed sets. Thus we have to show that it is contained in $||\Gamma, \delta||$, and that it is dense in $||\Gamma, \delta||$. It is contained in $||\Gamma||$ as I is contained in $||\Gamma||$ and $I \cap I' \subset I$. It is contained in $||\delta||$ as I' models δ. As $||\Gamma, \delta|| = ||\Gamma|| \cap ||\delta||$, $I \cap I'$ is in $||\Gamma, \delta||$. Finally we need to show that $I \cap I'$ is dense in $||\Gamma, \delta||$.

Let $\mathfrak{A}$ be a model in $||\Gamma, \delta||$. There is a model $\mathfrak{B}$ in I' that is less that $\mathfrak{A}$. This model $\mathfrak{B}$ models δ, as all elements of I' model δ. There is a model $\mathfrak{C}$ below $\mathfrak{B}$ that models γ, as I is a dense ideal, and I models γ. But this $\mathfrak{C}$ must model δ, as I' is downwards closed, and models δ. Thus we have found a model below $\mathfrak{A}$ in $I \cap I'$ that models Γ and δ, and thus is in $||\Gamma, \delta||$, proving that $I \cap I'$ is a dense ideal of $||\Gamma, \delta||$.

Or We need to show that if a dense ideal I' of $||\Delta||$ models α, and a dense ideal I of $||\gamma||$ models α, then there is a dense ideal I_1 of $||\{\delta \vee \gamma | \delta \in \Delta\}||$ that models α.

We consider the union of the two dense ideals. This set $I \cup I'$ is downwards closed, and models α. Thus we need just show that $I \cup I'$ is dense in $\|\{\delta \vee \gamma | \delta \in \Delta\}\|$. Consider a model of $\{\delta \vee \gamma | \delta \in \Delta\}$, call it $\mathfrak{A}$. Either $\mathfrak{A}$ is a model of γ, in which case, as I is dense in $\|\gamma\|$, we can find a $\mathfrak{B} \leq \mathfrak{A}$ in the set I and hence in $I \cup I'$, or $\mathfrak{A}$ is a model of Δ, in which case, as I' is dense in $\|\Delta\|$, we can find a $\mathfrak{B} \leq \mathfrak{A}$ in the set I' and hence in $I \cup I'$. Thus in both cases, $I \cup I'$ is dense in $\|\{\delta \vee \gamma | \delta \in \Delta\}\|$, as required. ∎

We now show that when enough minimal models exist, our new semantics agrees with minimal entailment.

Proposition 7 *For a given class of models A, and a partial order $\leq$ on A, if for every model $\mathfrak{A}$ there is a minimal model $\mathfrak{B}$ such that $\mathfrak{B} \leq \mathfrak{A}$, then the theory of the minimal models of A is the reasonable beliefs of A under $\leq$.*

Proof:

$\Rightarrow$: By the assumption, there is a minimal model below every model, therefore the minimal models are a dense ideal. Therefore, each sentence ϕ in the theory of the minimal models is a reasonable belief, as the models of ϕ contain a dense ideal, as the models of ϕ are a superset of the models of the theory of the minimal models of A.

$\Leftarrow$: Consider any reasonable belief ϕ, we show that it is true in all minimal models. ϕ is true in a dense ideal, therefore it is true in every minimal model, as every dense ideal contains all minimal elements. ∎

Thus we have an entailment relation that is consistency preserving, and obeys the rules of preferential entailment. We now ask whether is correctly models the examples we considered earlier.

5.2.1 Examples

In our first example, the models of $t_c = 1$, that is, the models where the computer time is one unit, contains a dense ideal. In fact, the models of our theory of the stock market, that satisfy $t_c = 1$ are a dense ideal in the order generated by preferring models where $money$ is larger. Furthermore, we have avoided the inconsistency, as ideal entailment is consistency preserving.

In our second example we tried to move a block, but minimal entailment led to inconsistency. In this example, the models of our domain that model the statement that we can move the block one unit in the x direction contain a dense ideal. In fact, these models are all the models of our theory, and thus the improper dense ideal.

The third example, rather than presume, as minimal entailment does that the preferred flavor is chocolate, ideal entailment denies this, as the models where chocolate is true do not contain a dense ideal, in particular there is no chocolate model below any given vanilla model.

The second part of the third example would have us infer chocolate. In this case the chocolate models are a dense ideal. The clause that requires us to find a chocolate model below or equal to every given model is supplied by choosing the model with equal smoothness and with chocolate flavor.

It is worth noting that there are linearizations of the partial order from the second part of the third example that do not contain a dense ideal where Chocolate is valid. Consider the linearization that orders all flavors by smoothness. This has alternating chocolate and vanilla models, and thus does not contain a dense ideal.

5.3 Second Order Characterizations

Now that we have chosen to use ideal entailment as our basis for reformulating circumscription, we recapitulate the changes that we make to the semantics, and then look at possible second order characterizations of these notions.

5.3.1 Semantics

Our semantics differ from classical circumscription in one important way. We shall consider our final theory to be the sentences that are true in some dense ideal, rather than those true in all (possible nonexistent) minimal models.

The justification for the difference from classical circumscription is simple. In the case where there are enough minimal models so that every non-minimal model has a minimal model below it, the two semantics agree, as we showed in proposition 7. Lifschitz (1985) calls this condition wellfoundedness, Kraus et al, (1990) call this smoothness. When there is a model that has no minimal model below it then the original semantics are defined in terms of something nonexistent, that is, the class of minimal models is the empty class.

We call our new version Cofinal Circumscription. The entailment relation generated by Cofinal Circumscription is the syntactic analogue of ideal entailment. We use ideal entailment for arbitrary preferences on models, and Cofinal entailment etc. for preferences defined by circumscription policies.

Semantics of Cofinal Circumscription

We will define the semantics so that they do not assume minimal models exist. We notice that this formalism has some advantages over regular circumscription, namely it never makes a satisfiable first order theory unsatisfiable.

Let L be a first order language. The objects under consideration, referred to as (circumscriptive) theories, are finite sets of sentences stated in L. We will often view this as a first order sentence (the conjunction of all sentences in the set).

Let $A(\overline{P})$ be a theory in L, all of whose predicate constants are among $\overline{P} = \{P_1, \ldots, P_n\}$ and whose functions are $f_1 \ldots, f_m$ $n, m \in \omega$, and whose constants are all the constants in some set C. Let $\Phi = \{\phi_1, \ldots, \phi_l\}$ be the minimized formulas, and $\Psi = \{\psi_1, \ldots, \psi_o\}$ $l, o \in \omega$, be the maximized formulas.

Definition 10 Let $\mathfrak{A}$ and $\mathfrak{B}$ be models of A. We say that $\mathfrak{A}$ is preferred to $\mathfrak{B}$ written $\mathfrak{A} \leq^{\text{Cofinal}}_{\Phi,\Psi} \mathfrak{B}$, if and only if

1. $\mathfrak{A}[\phi] \subseteq \mathfrak{B}[\phi]$ for every minimized formula $\phi \in \Phi$.
2. $\mathfrak{A}[\psi] \supseteq \mathfrak{B}[\psi]$ for every maximized formula $\psi \in \Psi$.

We write $\mathfrak{A} <^{\text{Cofinal}}_{\Phi,\Psi} \mathfrak{B}$ if $\mathfrak{A} \leq^{\text{Cofinal}}_{\Phi,\Psi} \mathfrak{B}$ and $\mathfrak{B} \not\leq^{\text{Cofinal}}_{\Phi,\Psi} \mathfrak{A}$.

Note that this is exactly how preferences are defined in domain formula circumscription (Costello 1996a). The semantics differ on the definition of entailment $\models_{\leq^{\text{Cofinal}}_{\Phi,\Psi}}$.

Definition 11 [$\models_{\leq^{\text{Cofinal}}_{\Phi,\Psi}}$] We say a sentence ϕ is entailed by A in this semantics if every model $\mathfrak{A}$ has a model $\mathfrak{B}$, that is smaller or equal to $\mathfrak{A}$, that satisfies ϕ, and all smaller models than $\mathfrak{B}$ satisfy ϕ.

$$A \models_{\leq^{\text{Cofinal}}_{\Phi,\Psi}} \phi \stackrel{def}{=} \tag{5.1}$$

$$\begin{aligned}&\forall \mathfrak{A}.(\mathfrak{A} \models A) \rightarrow\\ &\quad \exists \mathfrak{B}.((\mathfrak{B} <^{\text{Cofinal}}_{\Phi,\Psi} \mathfrak{A}) \vee (\mathfrak{B} = \mathfrak{A})) \wedge (\mathfrak{B} \models A) \wedge (\mathfrak{B} \models \phi) \wedge\\ &\quad \forall \mathfrak{C}.((\mathfrak{C} <^{\text{Cofinal}}_{\Phi,\Psi} \mathfrak{B}) \wedge (\mathfrak{C} \models A)) \rightarrow (\mathfrak{C} \models \phi)\end{aligned}$$

This states that ϕ is entailed only if every model has a model below it, such that it and everything below it entails ϕ, or the model itself entails ϕ as does every model below it. Thus this can be thought of as saying that if we go sufficiently far down the preference relation, then all the models will entail ϕ.

Lemma 8 *The set of first order sentences ϕ such that $A \models_{\leq^{\text{Cofinal}}_{\Phi,\Psi}} \phi$ is the theory of a class of models.*

We call these sentences the Cofinal sentences.

Proof: The theory of a class of models is a set of sentences closed under logical consequence. This follows as if two sentences are Cofinally entailed, then their conjunction is. Therefore if a set of sentences are Cofinally entailed, then their consequences will be Cofinally entailed. ∎

5.3.2 Formal System

Motivations

We have given a new semantics to circumscription. Classically circumscription had both a simple semantics and a simple formal system, expressed in second order logic. We here develop a formal system for our new semantics.

We use the language of sorted second order logic in this section.

Definition 12 The relativization of a formula γ with respect to a unary predicate variable ϕ, written γ^{ϕ}, is the result of a syntactic replacement applied to γ which we define inductively as follows.

- If $\gamma = P(t_1, \ldots, t_n)$ then $\gamma^\phi = P(t_1, \ldots, t_n)$.
- If $\gamma = \alpha \wedge \beta$ then $\gamma^\phi = \alpha^\phi \wedge \beta^\phi$.
- If $\gamma = \neg\alpha$ then $\gamma^\phi = \neg\alpha^\phi$.
- If $\gamma = \exists x.\alpha$ then $\gamma^\phi = \exists x.\phi(x) \wedge \alpha^\phi$.
- If $\gamma = \forall x.\alpha$ then $\gamma^\phi = \forall x.\phi(x) \rightarrow \alpha^\phi$.

If ϕ_1, ϕ_2 is a sequence of predicate variables, then γ^{ϕ_1,ϕ_2} denotes the iterated relativization of γ, that is, $(\gamma^{\phi_1})^{\phi_2}$.

Definition 13 $[(Z,S) <_{\Phi,\Psi} (Z',S')]$ Given a sorted second order language L, and two finite sets of formulas in L, $\Phi = \{\phi_1, \ldots, \phi_n\}$, $\Psi = \{\psi_1, \ldots, \psi_m\}$, we define the following notation:

$$
\begin{gathered}
(Z,S) \leq_{\Phi,\Psi} (Z',S') \equiv \\
\bigwedge_{i=1\ldots n} \forall \overline{x_i}.\phi_i^S(\overline{x_i}) \rightarrow \phi_i[Z/Z']^{S'}(\overline{x_i}) \\
\wedge \bigwedge_{j=1\ldots m} \forall \overline{x_j}.\psi_j^S(\overline{x_j}) \leftarrow \psi_j[Z/Z']^{S'}(\overline{x_j})
\end{gathered}
$$

where Z and Z' are tuples of second and first order variables, of equal length, sort and type, $\alpha[Z/Z']$ denotes the simultaneous replacement of all occurrences of Zs by Z's in α, S and S' are formulas of L with one free variable, and $\overline{x_i}$ is a tuple of variables equal in number and sort to the free object variables of ϕ_i while $\overline{y_i}$ is a tuple of variables equal in number and sort to the free object variables of ψ_i.

We define:

$$
\begin{aligned}
&(Z,S) <_{\Phi,\Psi} (Z',S') \stackrel{def}{=} \\
&(Z,S) \leq_{\Phi,\Psi} (Z',S') \wedge \neg[(Z',S') \leq_{\Phi,\Psi} (Z,S)]
\end{aligned}
$$

Definition 14 $[Closed_L(\phi)]$ If ϕ is a unary predicate variable, then $Closed_L(\phi)$ stands for the conjunction of $\phi(c)$ for every constant c in the language L, conjoined with $\forall x_1 \ldots, x_n.\phi(x_1) \wedge \ldots \phi(x_n) \rightarrow \phi(f(x_1, \ldots, x_n))$, for each n-ary function constant f in L.

Definition 15 [inf] We define $inf(L)$ to be the sentence that states that there are a countable number of objects not in any of these sorts.

If the sorts of L are S_1, S_2, then this is the second order sentence,

$$
\begin{aligned}
\exists\zeta, x.\ &\forall y.\zeta(y) \neq x \wedge \forall y, z.\zeta(y) = \zeta(z) \rightarrow y = z \\
&\wedge \neg(S_1(x) \vee S_2(x)) \wedge \forall y.\neg(S_1(y) \vee S_2(y)) \rightarrow \\
&\quad \neg(S_1(\zeta(y)) \vee S_2(\zeta(y)))
\end{aligned}
$$

Definition 16 $[Circ_L(A;\Psi;\Phi)]$ Given a language L, the circumscription of A minimizing Φ, a finite set of formulas in L, and maximizing, Ψ, a finite set of formulas in L, denoted $Circ_L(A;\Phi;\Psi)$, is defined to be the following schema with schematic variable ϕ which ranges over first order formulas from L:

$$\begin{aligned}
&\inf(L) \wedge A^U \wedge [(\forall Z\ S.A^S[Z] \wedge Closed(S,Z) \rightarrow \\
&\quad \exists Z'S'.(A^{S'}[Z'] \wedge Closed(S',Z') \wedge \phi^{S'}[Z'] \wedge \\
&\quad\quad (Z',S') <_{\Phi,\Psi} (Z,S) \vee Z,S = Z',S' \\
&\quad\quad \wedge(\forall Z''S''.A^{S''}[Z''] \wedge Closed(S'',Z'') \wedge \\
&\quad\quad\quad (Z''S'') <_{\Phi,\Psi} (Z'S') \rightarrow \phi^{S''}[Z'']))) \\
&\rightarrow \phi^U]
\end{aligned}$$

Here $Z, S = Z', S'$ represents $\forall 0\overline{x}.P(\overline{x}) \equiv P'(\overline{x})$, for each pair of predicate P and P' from Z, S and Z', S'.

Lemma 9 *If $L = \langle \overline{P}, \overline{F}, C\rangle$ is a sorted first order language, and $\mathfrak{A}$ and $\mathfrak{B}$ are L-structures, and $\mathbf{A}$ is the set of domains of $\mathfrak{A}$, and $\mathfrak{A}[P]$ is the interpretation of P in $\mathfrak{A}$ then*

$$\mathfrak{A} \leq^{Cofinal}_{\Phi,\Psi} \mathfrak{B} \equiv$$

$$(\mathfrak{A}[\overline{P}], \mathfrak{A}[\overline{F}], \mathfrak{A}[C], \mathbf{A}) \leq_{\Phi,\Psi} (\mathfrak{B}[\overline{P}], \mathfrak{B}[\overline{F}], \mathfrak{B}[C], \mathbf{B}).$$

Proof: We first note that a sequence of domains can be read as a set of sorts, and the interpretations of predicates, functions and objects can be read as an instantiation of a sequence of variables. Thus the second part of the above formula is well formed.

We expand the definitions of $\leq^{\text{Cofinal}}_{\Phi,\Psi}$ and $\leq_{\Phi,\Psi}$ and see that the two notions are equivalent. ∎

Lemma 10 *If $L = \langle \overline{P}, \overline{F}, C\rangle$ is a sorted first order language, and $\mathfrak{A}$ and $\mathfrak{B}$ are L-structures, then if $\mathfrak{A}$ is less than $\mathfrak{B}$ in some partial order on L-structures $\leq_{\Phi,\Psi}$, then there is an L-structure $\mathfrak{C}$ elementarily equivalent to $\mathfrak{A}$, whose domain is contained in $B \cup X$, where X is a countable new set of objects.*

Proof:

We denote the domain of $\mathfrak{A}$ as A etc. We consider the objects $B \cap A$. We construct a model $\mathfrak{C}$, such that $C \subseteq (B \cap A) \cup X$, that agrees with $\mathfrak{A}$ over the objects $B \cap A$, and is elementarily equivalent to $\mathfrak{A}$. This exists, as every substructure of a first order model can be extended to an elementarily embedding by adding a countable number of objects(Chang and Keisler 1990) proposition 2.2.17.

We now notice that this model $\mathfrak{C}$ is $\leq_{\Phi,\Psi} \mathfrak{B}$, as $\mathfrak{A} \leq_{\Phi,\Psi} \mathfrak{B}$, and $\mathfrak{C}$ agrees with $\mathfrak{A}$ on all objects in the intersection of $\mathfrak{A}$ and $\mathfrak{B}$, and the fact that the $\leq_{\Phi,\Psi}$ relation is defined in terms of subset inclusion on the objects common to both models. ∎

The author is grateful to Johan van Benthem for suggesting this key Lemma.

Theorem 11 *If ϕ is a sentence in a first order language L, and Φ and Ψ are finite sets of formulas in L, and A is a finitely axiomatizable theory in L, then*

$$\textit{if } A \models_{\leq^{\textit{Cofinal}}_{\Phi,\Psi}} \phi \textit{ then } Circ_L(A;\Phi;\Psi) \models \phi$$

Proof:

We assume the opposite and show a contradiction. We know that ϕ is a Cofinal sentence under the partial order $\leq^{\text{Cofinal}}_{\Phi,\Psi}$, but ϕ is not a result of the circumscription of A minimizing Φ and maximizing Ψ.

We instantiate ϕ for the schematic variable ϕ in the circumscription schema. We know that the left-hand side of the last implication is not valid, as our assumption is that the circumscription does not entail ϕ.

As before we see we can safely interpret tuples of predicates and a unary predicate as a model. This is because we are only interested in first order properties, from Lemma 10, we need only consider the models whose universe is a subset of the the domain of the current model and some countable set, in this case the set induced by $inf(L)$.

We choose a model that makes this sub-formula false. But this sub-formula says that there is a model below every model, with the property that ϕ is true in this model and in all smaller models. If this is not the case, then there is a model, such that every model below it has a model below it that does not satisfy ϕ. But then ϕ is not a Cofinal sentence, a contradiction ∎

Theorem 12 *If ϕ is a sentence in a first order language L, and Φ and Ψ are finite sets of formulas in L, and A is a finitely axiomatizable theory in L, then*

$$\textit{if } Circ_L(A;\Phi;\Psi) \models \phi \textit{ then } A \models_{\leq^{\textit{Cofinal}}_{\Phi,\Psi}} \phi.$$

Proof:

We need to show that is ϕ is entailed by the circumscription, then it is a Cofinal sentence. To show it is a Cofinal sentence is suffices to show that its models contain a dense ideal. This dense ideal is witnessed by the circumscription formula. Strictly speaking the circumscription formula only gives us a dense ideal of the partial order restricted to models whose universes differ only on a countable number of objects. However, by Lemma 10 this suffices. The circumscription formula, which implies ϕ states that there is an ideal, that entails ϕ below every model. The union of these ideals is the necessary dense ideal. The union of ideals is an ideal, and by construction is it dense. Thus the models of ϕ contain a dense ideal, and thus ϕ is Cofinally entailed. ∎

We again stress that it is necessary that the circumscription be a schema. If we rewrote it as with a universal second order quantified variable rather than a schematic variable ϕ, we would allow instantiations that were not first order definable. However, second order logic is not compact, and thus Lemma 8 does not apply. In fact cofinal circumscription redefined using second order quantification maps satisfiable theories to unsatisfiable theories.

5.3.3 Conclusions

We have introduced a new semantics for circumscription. It has one new principal feature—it does not consider the sentences true in the minimal models, rather it looks for sentences whose models contain a dense ideal. This feature is desirable, as it ensures circumscription is *consistent*.

In summary, the problem that circumscription had—mapping satisfiable theories to unsatisfiable theories—can be seen as a byproduct of defining the semantics in terms of nonexistent minimal models.

The notion of Cofinal sentences is not tied to circumscription. All semantics based on a notion of truth in the most preferred models have natural variants where we consider Cofinal sentences rather than truth in minimal models. It is worth noting that this approach is not immediately applicable to approaches that consider orderings on sets of models rather than models. As assuming minimal models exist is a strong and unnecessary assumption we claim that moving to variants defined in terms of Cofinal sentences is the correct choice.

References

Bossu, G., and P. Siegel. 1984. Saturation, nonmonotonic reasoning, and the closed world assum ption. *Artificial Intelligence* 25(1):13–64.

Chang, C., and H. Keisler. 1990. *Model Theory*. Studies in Logic and the foundations of mathematics, Vol. 73. North Holland. Third edition.

Costello, T. 1996a. Domain Formula Circumscription. under review.

Costello, T. 1996b. The Expressive Power of Circumscription. accepted to *Artificial Intelligence*.

Davis, M. 1980. The mathematics of nonmonotonic reasoning. *Articficial Intelligence* 13(1-2):73 – 80.

Etherington, D.W., R.E. Mercer, and R. Reiter. 1985. On the Adequacy of Predicate Circumscription for Closed World Reasoning. *Computational Intelligence* 1.

Gabbay, D. 1985. Theoretical foundations for non-monotonic reasoning in expert systems. In *Logics and Models of Concurrent Systems*, ed. K.R. Apt. Springer Verlag.

Gelfond, M., V. Lifschitz, and A. Rabinov. 1991. Wat are the limitations of situation calculus. In *Working Notes: AAAI Spring Symposium Series on the Logical f ormalization of Commonsense Reasoning*, 59–69.

Kraus, S., D. Lehmann, and M. Magidor. 1990. Nonmonotonic Reasoning, Preferential Models and Cumulative Log ics. *Artificial Intelligence* 44(1):167–207.

Lewis, D.K. 1973. *Counterfactuals*. Cambridge, MA: Harvard University Press.

Lifschitz, V. 1985. Computing Circumscription. In *Proc. Ninth International Joint Conference on Artificial Intel ligence (IJCAI '85)*, 121–127.

Makinson, D. 1989. General Theory of Cumulative Inference. In *Non-Monotonic Reasoning*, ed. Reinfrank, de Kleer, Ginsberg, and Sandewall. Lecture Notes in Artificial Intelligence, Vol. 346. Springer-Verlag, jan.

McCarthy, J. 1977. Epistemological Problems of Artificial Intelligence. In *Proc. Fifth International Conference on Artificial Intelligenc e (IJCAI '77)*, 223–227. Cambridge, MA.

McCarthy, J. 1980. Circumscription - a Form of Non-Monotonic Reasoning. *Arificial Intelligence* 13(1 and 2):27–39.

McCarthy, J. 1986. Applications of Circumscription to Formalising Commonsense Kno wledge. *Artificial Intelligence* 28:89–116.

McCarthy, J., and P. Hayes. 1969. Some Philosophical Problems From the Standpoint of Artificial Intelligence. In *Machine Intelligence*, ed. D. Michie. 463–502. Edinburgh, UK: Edinburgh University Press.

Shoham, Y. 1986. *Reasoning about Change: Time and Causation from the Standpoint of Artificial Intelligence*. Doctoral dissertation, Yale University.

6

A Logic of Vision: Preliminaries

MICHIEL VAN LAMBALGEN AND JAAP VAN DER DOES

Our mistake lies in supposing that things present themselves as they really are, names as they are written, people as photography and psychology give an unalterable picture of them. But in reality this is not at all what we ordinarily perceive. We see, we hear, we conceive the world in a lopsided fashion.

Marcel Proust, *La Fugitive*

6.1 Introduction

It often happens in life that we perceive a person (or an object) only partially, but are nonetheless able to reason about this person and to incorporate him or her in our schemes. Such a situation has been eloquently described by Marcel Proust in *La Fugitive*:

> Had I been obliged to draw from memory a portrait of Mlle d'Eporcheville, to furnish a description of her, or even to recognise her in the street, I should have found it impossible. I had glimpsed her in profile, on the move, and she had struck me as being simple, pretty, tall and fair; I could not have said more. But all the reflexes of desire, of anxiety, of the mortal blow struck by the fear of not seeing her if my father took me away, all these things,

*We are grateful for the comments and suggestions of Johan van Benthem, Ulrich Felgner, Rosalie Iemhoff, Dick Oehrle, Frank Veltman, Marco Vervoort, and Frans Voorbraak. Special thanks to the Research group on nominalisation and perception reports and the Semantics colloquium (Seminar für Sprachwissenschaft, Universität Tübingen) led by Uwe Mönnich and Fritz Hamm. This research is part of the PIONIER-project 'Reasoning with Uncertainty' sponsored bt the Netherlands Organization for Scientific Research (NWO) under grantPGS 22–262.

Logical Perspectives on Language and Information.
Cleo Condoravdi and Gerard R. Renardel de Lavalette.

> associated with an image of which on the whole I knew nothing, and as to which it was enough that I knew it to be agreeable, already constituted a state of love. (Penguin Classics ed., p. 577-8)

At the other extreme we may have a situation in which we perceive an object in its entirety, but nonetheless misidentify it. Again Proust furnishes an example:

> I opened the Figaro. What a bore! The main article had the same title as the article which I had sent to the paper and which had not appeared. But not merely the same title... why, here were several words that were absolutely identical. This was really too bad. I must write and complain. But it wasn't merely a few words, it was the whole thing, and there was my signature... It was my article that had appeared at last! But my brain which, even at that period, had begin to show signs of age and to tire easily, continued for a moment longer to reason as though it had not understood that this was my article, like an old man who is obliged to complete a movement that he has begun even if it has become unnecessary, even if an unforeseen obstacle, in the face of which he ought at once to draw back, makes it dangerous. (*ibidem*, p. 579)

In this article, we aim to give a semantics for direct perception reports which is sufficiently flexible to accomodate these examples, as well as the more common cases in which we correctly infer the identity of objects on the basis of partial information. Our methodology is akin to that of Barwise's work on naked infinitive perception reports. He maintains that our intuitions about the semantics of perception are fairly clear, 'but to square with these intuitions, the model-theoretic machinery [of possible worlds semantics] became quite bizarre' ((Barwise 1989, p. 7)). For this reason, he rather prefers a semantics which 'fits nicely with a realist philosophical-psychological account of perception to be found in the writings of Dretske, R.J. Hirst, and J.J. Gibson' (*ibidem*, p. 9). In the same vein, we strive to develop a logical model of vision along the lines of (Marr 1982), and show how it complies with the semantical data. This in contrast to a more instrumentalist approach, which would allow us to explain the semantic facts in purely abstract terms ((van der Does 1991) is an example).

There is another methodological aspect of our approach worth mentioning. The dynamic turn in logical semantics for natural language was an eye-opener for all people working in the field. Yet, other areas of research, such as probability theory, have been 'dynamic' for a long time. The semantics of perception reports developed in this paper is based on conditional quantification, which resulted from a logical analysis of conditional expectation. As a consequence, the dynamics of this probabilistic notion is imported naturally into the semantics. Indeed, we shall make heavy use of it, since retraction of information is crucial to perception. But before we show how this can be, let us first review some basic facts and received opinions concerning the perception of objects and scenes.

6.2 Direct perception

This article is mainly concerned with description of direct perception. Linguistically, this can take several forms; e.g., the 'simple' perception in (1), the naked infinitive form in (2), the gerundive form in (3), and the complementised form in (4).

(1) Jack saw Sharon.

(2) Jack saw Sharon wash her face.

(3) Jack saw Sharon washing her face.

(4) Jack saw that Sharon washed her face.

There are subtle semantic differences between the perception reports, which have to do with the kinds of object perceived. Sentence (1) describes the perception of objects, (2) and (3) that of scenes, while (4) gives the content of what is seen. Also, (1-3) report on what is seen directly, whereas (4) may state a conclusion inferred from what is actually perceived. The difference between (2) and (3) is aspectual; (2) concerns a finished action, (3) an ongoing one.

These differences also manifests themselves in the restrictions placed on the semantic ingredients of perception reports: (i) the part of objective reality perceived, (ii) the perceiver's field of vision, and (iii) the semantic content of the perceptual description. Direct perception reports require an immediate link between fields of vision and semantical content. Since fields of vision normally represent part of objective reality, this link often gives a close connection between reality and semantic content. But of course, such a connection is not necessary. This is shown by misperceptions and hallucinations.

(5) Macbeth saw a dagger move in front of his eyes.

In case (5) is true, Macbeth's immediate perceptions should truly involve a dagger moving in front of his eyes, even though this is fysically impossible. In what follows we concentrate on the perception of objects, as in (1), and on naked infinitive perception reports, as in (2).

6.2.1 Perceiving objects

Simple expression does not mean simplicity of semantics. Although 'Snow is white' is well-suited to explain one's theory of truth, the semantics of a mass term as 'snow' is still in many ways open. Analogously, sentences like (6a) are used in textbooks to show that transitive verbs can be interpreted as two-place relations; here 'to see' as 'S'.

(6) a. Jack saw Sharon.
b. $S(j, s)$.

But to do so one has to idealise from considerable semantic facts. The introduction has already made clear that Jack need not see much of Sharon to make (6) true. To perceive an object it is often sufficient to see one of its (prototypical) parts. In fact, the truth conditions are even weaker, in that parts of representations may go proxy for the objects themselves. Most people will only have seen enlivened celluloid or electro-magnetic representations of famous Sharon, rather than Sharon herself. The important point is that the weak conditions of truth make simple descriptions of perception highly fallible, as the following example from Miller and Johnson-Laird 1976 shows.

(7) He saw an extraordinary rock formation and too great pains to avoid it; later he found out that it was an effect created by trees in the mist.

The example nicely illustrates another crucial aspect of perceiving objects. Perceptions and representations not only concern parts of objects, they also come with a certain granularity. In fact, different parts of a single field of vision may have varying grades of precision:

(8) While focussing on Sharon, Jack saw Maria vaguely out of the corner of his eye.

Change of granularity could induce change of truth value. We sometimes have to retract our descriptions if we come to see more of an object, or if the accuracy of the relevant representations and perceptions alter. In the next section we shall see that similar adjustments are typical of more complex perception reports. But even at this point we observe that a psychologically realistic semantics should contain two ingredients. Firstly, it should use models which refine each other in several ways (with infinite precision in the limit). Secondly, the semantics should formalise retractability of descriptions relative to a certain degree of precision. These ingredients are developed in section 6.3, combined in section 6.3.5, and applied in section 6.4. Section 6.5, finally, is on laws of vision, which are here delimited by means of preservation theorems.

6.2.2 Naked infinitive perception reports

Ideally, naked infinitive reports (whence: 'NI reports') are used to report on the perception of reality. Indeed, in most semantics an NI report such as 'Jack saw Sharon walk' is true iff Jack stands in the 'see'-relation with a part of the world in which Sharon walks.[1] However, this approach makes perception highly factual, which can only be sustained under the perfect circumstance

[1] See (Barwise 1981) and (Kamp 1984), among other people; also for a discussion of the logical principles. A detailed discussion of our position and further references can be found in Van der Does and Van Lambalgen 1997.

where our perceptual field truly represents reality. *Normally* a perfect match between language and perception is often assumed, if only by default, but there are situations in which the connection between reality and a field of vision are less certain. Such looseness between reality on the one hand, and vision and semantics on the other makes NI reports retractable over time; cf. (9) which is perfectly in order.

(9) From a distance, Jack saw a dime fall on Main Street, but on coming closer he saw it was a dollar.

The intimate relationship between semantic content and reality is often used to explain the logical transparancy of NI reports. As soon as we take the uncertainty in this relation seriously, as in the present semantics, most of this transparancy is lost. To see this, let us revisit some well-known logical principles which have been considered to hold for NI reports.

Partial perception

One of the most basic non-inferences concerns the interplay between perception of objects and NI reports; (11) does not follow from (10).

(10) Jack saw Sharon, and Sharon winked.

(11) Jack saw Sharon wink.

There is a twofold explanation of this fact: either Sharon's action is not within Jack's perceptual field, or it is too subtle to be discerned by him. The two possibilities combined identify a field of vision with a coarsened part of reality.

Veridicality

Veridicality is the principle which allows us to conclude (13) from (12).

(12) Jack saw Sharon was her face.

(13) Sharon washed her face.

Since (13) describes 'the world' rather than Jack's field of vision, veridicality does not comply with the acceptability of (9). In general, we shall argue that the principle of veridicality can only be sustained in idealised situations, which makes it a default rule rather than a logical inference.

Quantifiers

Along similar lines the validity of other logical principles can be questioned, e.g., those concerning quantificational behaviour. Apart from scope phenomena *pur sang*, there is the question to what extent NI reports are epistemically neutral; i.e, whether a perceptual field alters the interpretation of quantifiers within the scope of 'to see'. If this is not so, someone's visual field will determine the extent in which quantifiers may be imported into or exported out of the scope of a perception verb.

It seems we have to following situation. If NI reports are epistemically neutral, quantifiers may be moved freely into and out of the scope of 'to see'. Then, (14) is equivalent with (15), (16) with (17), and (18) with (19).

(14) Jack saw a girl swim.

(15) A girl is such that Jack saw her swim.

(16) Jack saw no girl swim.

(17) No girl is such that Jack saw her swim.

(18) Jack saw every girl leave his party.

(19) Every girl is such that Jack saw her leave his party.

But if NI reports are not neutral in this sense, the pairs may well be independent of each other. Whether or not this is so, is contingent on the accuracy of Jack's visual information. Jack may be too confused to perceive a 'real' girl as a girl, and what he perceives to be a girl need not be one.

This ends our discussion of naked infinitive perception reports. We now give an informal sketch of the semantics developed in the remainder of our paper.

6.2.3 Sketch of the formal semantics

Logics for perception reports are often based on the assumption that the perceived objects are 'points' which cannot be refined any further; all partiality comes from their properties. However, in the previous sections we have seen many cases where it is more natural to assume that these objects are underdetermined. We therefore favour an approach where the infinitely precise points arise in the limit of increasingly refined stages. In the formalisation each stage is a first order model; and the properties of an object may vary with the stages, although we normally expect they do not. Despite such instability, it is possible to define an *inverse limit*, which we take to represent reality.

Reality is but one side of perception's coin, we also need linguistic means to describe it. Given the evidence that the dynamics of retraction is crucial to the semantics of perception reports, this cannot be just a 'static' logic. Instead, we shall use so-called *conditional quantification* which is rather different from the generalisation of quantifiers in (Mostowski 1957) and (Lindström 1966). Conditional quantification singles out the logical core of conditional expectation in probability theory. It offers a natural way to relativise quantification to varying measures of accuracy, and is hence well-suited for our purposes.

To be more precise, we model a field of vision as a stage in the above limit construction, and show that quantification local to a visual field can be mimicked in the inverse limit. Within this framework, perception can be analysed as consisting of a non-veridical, approximative core, which becomes veridical by our expectation that what is perceived will remain the case.

As we have said before, David Marr's theory of vision is the heuristic backdrop against which the formal theory is developed (Marr 1982). The next section starts with the essentials of his theory.

6.3 Vision, and a blurred view on logic

We have seen that the principle of veridicality is an idealisation which does not allow for the retraction of perception reports. We believe that retraction is a very real phenomenon, and that any semantics for perception reports should account for this. Moreover, a semantics should also allow for partially perceived objects. This could possibly be achieved by introducing partial objects in the domain, but we favour a principled solution in which, roughly speaking, partial perception is the rule not the exception.

The semantics for perceptual expressions introduced here is characterised by the following features:

1) it is completely model theoretic in nature;
2) it tries to stay close to psychological models of perception;
3) it takes veridicality to be a defeasible principle which allows for the possibility to retract a perception report.

The reader might think there is a certain tension between 1) and 2), since typically the psychological models involve mathematical constructs such as Gaussians, Laplace operators etc., which one would not like to have in one's semantics. Indeed, it is incumbent on us to show that these psychological theories contain a model theoretic 'core' that is relevant to a semantics of perception. We believe that the two central notions here are 'inverse limit' and 'conditional quantification'; whether these indeed capture the semantically significant part of psychological modelling we must leave for the reader to judge. In any case, whatever the fate of this proposal, we are in agreement with Marr when he writes, criticising Gibson's 'realistic' approach

> The underlying point is that visual information processing is actually very complicated, and Gibson was not the only thinker who was misled by the apparent simplicity of the act of seeing. The whole tradition of philosophical inquiry seems not to have taken seriously enough the complexity of the information processing involved (Marr 1982, 30)

We maintain that, in order to explain the logic of perception, some of these complications have to be imported in the model theoretic machinery.

Inevitably, this section will be rather technical. We have tried to organise the presentation in such a manner that the main thrust of the argument can be followed also by those not willing to delve into the technicalities. Section 6.3.1 gives a rapid introduction to David Marr's theory of vision in so far as it is relevant to our concerns. In section 6.3.2 we extract from his work two model theoretic notions, that of a refining inverse system of models, and the inverse limit thereof. A model theoretic correlate of a third notion, that of a filter (in the sense of, say, an UV- or a Dolby-filter, not in the familiar logical sense), is studied in section 6.3.3. The three notions are linked in section 6.3.5.

6.3.1 David Marr on vision

We start by explaining the psychological motivation underlying the model theory. Here, we base ourselves on an abstract account of Marr's theory of vision (Marr 1982). Of course, basing one's semantics on an empirical theory brings with it the danger that the empirical theory is wrong; indeed, it has been claimed that Marr's views are 'almost completely wrong' (Mayhew, as quoted in (Boden 1988, p. 74)). Nevertheless, we hope to convince the reader that Marr's theory is extremely suggestive from a model theoretic point of view. In particular Marr's idea of a hierarchy of three dimensional models has a good model theoretic correlate; 'good' in the sense that the associated preservation and non-preservation theorems may shed some light on the logic of perception. The model theory is sufficiently abstract to be compatible with other approaches based on the idea of a hierarchy of perceptual models, such as Jackendoff's work on what he calls 'conceptual semantics' (1983, 1987, 1990), which also takes (Marr 1982) as point of departure, or (Biederman 1987).[2]

Marr's fundamental idea is that vision is in many ways approximate. Filtering takes place at many of the earlier levels of visual processing, leading up to the so called primal sketch; and, at the other end, the perception of 3-D objects and scenes takes place by means of a hierarchy of ever more refined, but never completely accurate models. Here we shall concentrate on the last stage of the visual process.

Seeing a 3-D object involves two processes: constructing an image from visual data, and matching the image to a catalogue of 3-D models, where the matching is based on some salient features derived from the image. At this point we can do no better than discuss the illustration in Figure 1 from (Marr 1982, p. 306).

What is depicted is an increasingly detailed series of models of an arm. Obviously, this series can be extended further by detailing the shape of the fingers, by replacing the cylinders by less rigid shapes etc. Marr's point is that we recognise an object in the real world in terms of these 3-D models, and that we may often use a rather rough approximation to correctly identify the object.[3]

---

[2](van der Does and van Lambalgen 1997) has a comparison of Jackendoff's work and the logic of vision.

[3]This is strikingly clear in case of neurological deficit. Thus, Dr. P., the man who mistook his wive for a hat, could come no closer than a circumscription of a glove: " 'A continuous surface,' he

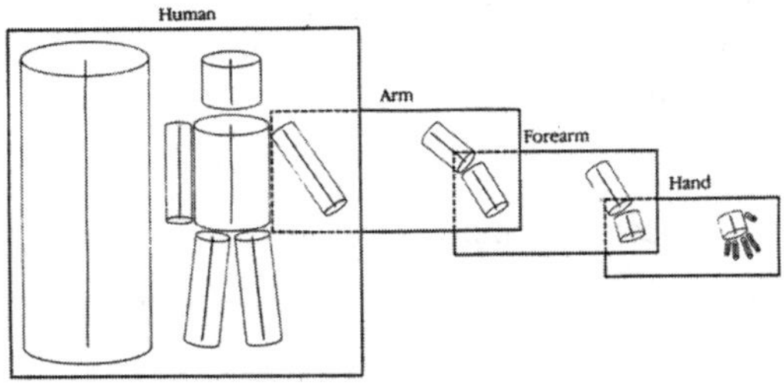

FIGURE 1 *Refinement of an arm*

> Modularity [...] allows the representation to be used more flexibly in response to the needs of the moment. For example, it is easy to construct a 3-D model description of just the arm of a human shape that could later be included in a new 3-D model description of the whole human shape. Conversely, a rough but usable description of the human shape need not include an elaborate arm description. Finally, this form of modular organisation allows one to trade off scope against detail. This simplifies the computational processes that derive and use the representation, because even though a complete 3-D model may be very elaborate, only one 3-D model has to be dealt with at any time, and individual 3-D models have a limited and manageable complexity ((Marr 1982, p. 307)).

There exists an interplay between the clues derived from an image and the matching process, cf. (Marr 1982, p. 321): after a 3-D model has been selected (guided by the image), it can be used to search for additional clues in the image; in turn, these can be used (when necessary) to match the image to a more detailed 3-D model. However, it may turn out to be impossible to find a more detailed 3-D model *of the kind we expected*. Indeed, like all computationally efficient heuristics, the use of such approximate models brings with it the possibility of error: what is identified as a real arm with respect to a given approximation may turn out to be something else (e.g., a wooden arm) when 'looking closer', i.e. with respect to a more refined approximation. (This point is not much emphasised in (Marr 1982) though.) In any case a theory such as Marr's is well-suited to account for partial perception of an object: this is simply the matching of an object to a 3-D model without an expectation as to the

announced at last, 'infolded on itself. It appears to have'—he hesitated–'five outpouchings, if this is the word. (...) It could be a change-purse, for example, for coins of five sizes.' " ((Sacks 1985), chapter 1).

direction in which the model can be refined. These observations suggest a formal semantics for visual reports in terms of approximate models and a stability condition. For instance, informally still, the expression

(20) I see an arm

can be taken to mean the conjuction of (i) and (ii).

i) with the present approximation the object that I focus on is identified as an arm;

ii) I expect this to be the case for every more refined approximation.

That is, the arm reported on in (20) is viewed as a (possibly infinite) series of ever more accurate approximations; recognising something as an arm means finding a matching 3-D model somewhere in this series. The stability condition says that we could also find less approximate models in this series, if we would care to submit the image to more elaborate processing. By contrast, if we say: 'What I see *looks like* an arm' we imply only condition (i), not (ii).

6.3.2 Inverse limits

Consider again Marr's suggestive example of 3-D models of an arm. Viewed abstractly, what we see is a series of first order models, composed of objects and relations between them, together with a mapping specifying how an object occurring at one level is decomposed at the next. This situation can be represented abstractly by means of an *refining system* of first order models. The basic ingredient is the following:

Definition 17 Let T be a set directed by a partial order $\geq$; i.e., $\geq$ is reflexive, transitive, anti-symmetric, and for $s, t \in T$ there is $r \in T$ such that $r \geq s, t$. A *refining inverse system* (indexed by T) is a complex $\langle \mathcal{M}_s, h_{st} \rangle_{s,t \in T}$ with

i) for each $s \in T$, $\mathcal{M}_s$ is a model for signature $\mathcal{S}_s$;

ii) for any R in the union of the signatures there is $t \in T$ such that R is in $\mathcal{S}_s$ if $s \geq t$.

iii) for each $s, t \in T$ with $s \geq t$ there is $h_{st} : |\mathcal{M}_s| \longrightarrow |\mathcal{M}_t|$ with for each R in $\mathcal{S}_t$ and in $\mathcal{S}_s$

  (ρ) $\{\langle h_{st}(d_1), \ldots, h_{st}(d_n) \rangle : \langle d_1, \ldots, d_n \rangle \in [\![R]\!]_s\} \subseteq [\![R]\!]_t$;

iv) $h_{rr} = id_r$, and for $s \geq t \geq r$, $h_{sr} = h_{st} \circ h_{tr}$.

Here $|\mathcal{M}|$ denotes the domain of $\mathcal{M}$, and $[\![R]\!]_i$ the interpretation of R in $\mathcal{M}_i$. If no confusion is likely, we omit $[\![-]\!]$ and write, say, R_s instead of $[\![R]\!]_s$. The mappings h_{st} will be called *bonding* mappings. A refining inverse system is *total* if in addition the bonding mappings are surjective; we then have the usual concept of homomorphism between models. In the following, we shall often use 'refining system' instead of: refining inverse system.

Condition (ρ) is the reason for using the adjective 'refining'. Further, it is mainly for conceptual reasons that we allow the signatures of the models to vary; we may wish to say that a predicate is not yet applicable at a certain stage. For instance, in a rough approximation of 'human being' given by six appropriately positioned cylinders, representing torso, arms, legs and head, the predicate 'hand' is not applicable. Yet, once introduced a predicate should remain applicable. The above definitions can be simplified somewhat by working with a fixed signature for all models, and assuming that intuitively non-applicable predicates trivially apply to all objects in an approximation. But for present purposes we think this is an artifact which is better circumvented.

We now show that the set of 3-D models (in the sense of Marr) can be given the structure of a refining system of models (in our sense): the condition of directedness then says that two refinements will themselves have a common refinement, as in the Arm-Forearm-Hand part of Figure 1.

Indeed, Marr's hierarchy of 3-D models can be obtained if we restrict ourselves to refining systems of *finite* models of a special kind. In the example, let $\mathcal{M}_t$ be a model $\langle D_t; A, \ldots \rangle$ with A a unary predicate for 'arm'. An arm $a \in A$ may become a composite $\{e, f\}$ in a more refined version $\mathcal{M}_s$ of $\mathcal{M}_t$ ($s \geq t$), with e an upperarm joined to a forearm f. On this view, unanalysed objects and composite objects have different types, but this difference can be eliminated by identifying an unanalysed object d with the singleton $\{d\}$.

Definition 18 A *Marr model* is a finite first order model with domain $\wp^+(E) := \wp(E) - \{\emptyset\}$ and a 'part-of'-relation $\subseteq$, among other relations.

Inverse systems of Marr models allow for bondings between complexes which preserve $\subseteq$.

Definition 19 An *refining inverse system of Marr models* is a refining inverse system $\langle \mathcal{M}_s, h_{st} \rangle_{s,t \in T}$ such that

i) each $\mathcal{M}_s$ is a Marr model;

ii) each h_{st} is a bonding mapping with

  a) $|X| \geq |h_{st}(X)|$;

  b) $h_{st}(Y) \subseteq h_{st}(X)$ if $Y \subseteq X$ (*monotonicity*).

Condition (iia) ensures that the bonding mappings never assign a more refined object to a coarser one, while condition (iib) says that parts of more refined complexes are mapped onto parts of the corresponding coarser object. Write d° for the singleton $\{d\}$. To continue the example, $\mathcal{M}_s$ could be a model $\langle D; A, U, F, J, \ldots \rangle$, in which $\{e, j\}$ is an arm ($\{e, j\} \in A_s$) with e° an upperarm ($e^\circ \in U$) and f° a forearm ($f^\circ \in F$) joined to each other $\langle e^\circ, f^\circ \rangle \in J$. Clearly $\mathcal{M}_s$ represents the same situation in more detail than $\mathcal{M}_t$ via the bonding mapping h_{st} with $h_{st}(e^\circ) = h_{st}(j^\circ) = h_{st}(\{e, j\}) = a^\circ \in A_t$. But creating structure as in $h_{st}(e^\circ) = \{a, b\} \in D_t$ is disallowed.

A model in a refining system approximates reality, but reality itself is assumed to be infinitely precise. This means, e.g., that for a sequence of models

$$\ldots \mathcal{M}_{n+1} \xrightarrow{h_n} \mathcal{M}_n \longrightarrow \ldots \mathcal{M}_1 \xrightarrow{h_0} \mathcal{M}_0$$

with h_n the bonding mapping $h_{n+1,n}$, reality arises as an inverse limit $\mathcal{M}$ refining all models in this sequence

$$\mathcal{M} \xrightarrow{\pi_i} \mathcal{M}_i$$

via projections $\pi_i : |\mathcal{M}| \longrightarrow |\mathcal{M}_i|$. Topological results can be used to show that such inverse limits exist for *any* refining inverse systems of 'sufficiently rich' models (not just the linearly ordered systems).

Definition 20 Let $\langle \mathcal{M}_s, h_{st} \rangle_{s,t \in T}$ be a refining inverse system. Its *inverse limit*

$$\mathcal{M} := \varprojlim{}_{t \in T} \mathcal{M}_t$$

is defined as follows

i) the domain $|\mathcal{M}|$ consist of the *threads* in the product $\Pi_{t \in T} |\mathcal{M}_t|$; i.e., functions $\xi : T \longrightarrow \bigcup_{t \in T} |\mathcal{M}_t|$ satisfying: $\xi_t \in |\mathcal{M}_t|$, and $h_{st}(\xi_s) = \xi_t$ for $s \geq t$.

ii) the interpretation function $[\![-]\!]$ is given by: for each R there exists $t \in T$ such that

$$[\![R]\!](\xi^1, \ldots, \xi^n) \Leftrightarrow_{\text{def}} \forall s \geq t : [\![R]\!]_s(\xi^1_s, \ldots, \xi^n_s)$$

Again, when no confusion is likely, we omit $[\![-]\!]$.

The inverse limit $\mathcal{M}$ is a submodel of the direct product $\Pi_{t \in T} \mathcal{M}_t$ (Chang and Keisler 1990, 224); however, the domain of this submodel might be empty. Under the additional assumption that the $\mathcal{M}_s$ are finite this cannot be so.

Theorem 13 *Suppose* $\langle \mathcal{M}_s, h_{st} \rangle_{s,t \in T}$ *is a refining inverse system of finite models. Then* $|\mathcal{M}|$ *is non-empty.*

Before giving the more general topological proof, we first give a 'selfcontained' algebraic argument (Graetzer 1979, 132).

PROOF. The argument uses an ultrafilter version of compactness to obtain the thread desired from finite approximations.

The sets $[J] \subseteq \prod_{t \in T} |\mathcal{M}_t|$ of finite approximations to threads are defined as follows:

$$[J] := \{f \in \prod_{t \in T} |\mathcal{M}_t| : \forall t, s \in J[s \geq t \Rightarrow h_{st}(f_s) = f_t]\}$$

Each set $[J]$ is nonempty. By directedness, there is $k \in T$ with $k \geq j$ for all $j \in J$. Take $g \in \prod_{t \in T} |\mathcal{M}_t|$ and define $g^* \in \prod_{t \in T} |\mathcal{M}_t|$ by

$$g_i^* := \begin{cases} h_{ki}(g_k) & \textit{if } i \leq k, \\ g_i & \textit{otherwise.} \end{cases}$$

Then $g^* \in [J]$, since $h_{st}(g_s^*) = h_{st}(h_{ks}(g_k)) = h_{kt}(g_k) = g_t^*$ for $s, t \in J$ with $s \geq t$. Compactness shows that the set of threads

$$\bigcap_{J \in \wp_\omega(T)} [J]$$

is nonempty as well.[4]

The set $A = \{[J] : J \in \wp_\omega(T)\}$ has the finite intersection property. Indeed, $[J] \supseteq [I]$ if $J \subseteq I$, so:

$$\emptyset \neq [J_1 \cup \ldots \cup J_n] \subseteq [J_1] \cap \ldots \cap [J_n].$$

By the ultrafilter theorem, there is an ultrafilter $F \supseteq A$. This filter can be 'projected' into $|\mathcal{M}_t|$ by first defining for each $X \in F$: $X_t := \bigcup_{f \in X} \{f_t\}$, and next: $F_t := \{X_t : X \in F\}$.

Let $\mathrm{pr}_t : \prod_{t \in T} |\mathcal{M}_t| \longrightarrow |\mathcal{M}_t|$ be the projection onto the t-th coordinate. That F_t is an ultrafilter, too, follows from the fact that $\mathrm{pr}_t^{-1}(-)$ preserves Boolean structure, in combination with:

(*) $X \in F_t$ iff $\mathrm{pr}_t^{-1}(X) \in F$,

for all $t \in T$. To prove (*) first note that $\mathrm{pr}_t^{-1}(X)_t = X$. As to the other direction, let $X \in F_t$. Then there is $Y \in F$ with $X = Y_t$. But for each $Z \in F$: $\mathrm{pr}_t^{-1}(Z_t) \in F$, because $Z \subseteq \mathrm{pr}_t^{-1}(Z_t)$. In particular, $\mathrm{pr}_t^{-1}(X) \in F$.

Notice that F_t is a *finite* ultrafilter, because $|\mathcal{M}_t|$ is finite. Therefore $\{a_t\} = \bigcap F_t \in F_t$ for some $a_t \in |\mathcal{M}_t|$. Define $\xi \in \prod_{t \in T} |\mathcal{M}_t|$ by $t \mapsto a_t$. This is a thread! For let $s, t \in T$ be such that $s \geq t$. Clearly, $\{\xi_s\} \in F_s$ and $\{\xi_t\} \in F_t$. So

$$\mathrm{pr}_s^{-1}(\{\xi_s\}) \cap [\{s, t\}] \cap \mathrm{pr}_t^{-1}(\{\xi_t\}) \in F.$$

Choose a g in this nonempty intersection. Then:

$$h_{st}(\xi_s) = h_{st}(g_s) = g_t = \xi_t$$

as required. □

It is worthwhile to observe that the inverse limit comes with (homomorphic) projections

$$\pi_t : \mathcal{M} \longrightarrow \mathcal{M}_t$$

for $t \in T$ defined by $\xi \mapsto \xi_t$. For $s \geq t$ in T one has:

$$h_{st}(\pi_s(\xi)) = h_{st}(\xi_s) = \xi_t = \pi_t(\xi).$$

So the projections satisfy $h_{st}(\pi_s(\xi)) = \pi_t(\xi)$; cf. the relevant part of the diagram in Figure 5.

[4]The set $\wp_\omega(T)$ consists of all *finite* subsets of T.

Proposition 14 *If the bonding mappings h_{ij} are surjective, π_t is surjective as well.*

PROOF. Choose $d \in |\mathcal{M}_t|$. One has to find $\xi \in |\mathcal{M}|$ so that $\pi_t(\xi) = d$. Such a ξ can be found as corollary to theorem 13. To see this, define

$$|\mathcal{M}_k^*| := \begin{cases} h_{kt}^{-1}(\{d\}) & \text{if } k > t, \\ \{d\} & \text{if } k = t, \\ h_{tk}(\{d\}) & \text{if } k < t, \\ |\mathcal{M}_k| & \text{otherwise.} \end{cases}$$

By surjectivity of h_{kt}, $h_{kt}^{-1}(\{d\}) \neq \emptyset$ for $k > t$. So each $|\mathcal{M}_i^*|$ is a finite nonempty subset of $|\mathcal{M}_i|$. Next, define h_{ij}^* as h_{ij} restricted to $|\mathcal{M}_i^*|$. Then, $h_{ij}^* : |\mathcal{M}_i^*| \longrightarrow |\mathcal{M}_j^*|$ if $i \geq j$. Consequently, $\langle |\mathcal{M}_t^*|, h_{st}^* \rangle_{s,t \in T}$ is an inverse system of nonempty finite sets. Theorem 13 says that its inverse limit contains a ξ. Clearly $\xi \in |\mathcal{M}|$, too, and $\pi_t(\xi) = d$. □

As a result of proposition 14 one sees that the inverse limit $\mathcal{M}$ of a total refining inverse system is a subdirect product of the $\mathcal{M}_s$; i.e., it is a submodel $\mathcal{N}$ of the direct product $\prod_T \mathcal{M}_t$ such that $\pi_t(|\mathcal{N}|) = |\mathcal{M}_t|$ (Chang and Keisler 1990, 419).

Theorem 13 does not generalise to the infinite case; the inverse limit of a system of infinite sets *may* be empty. For example, let $\langle \omega^+, \leq \rangle$ be the set $\omega \backslash \{0\}$ of positive integers with its natural ordering; $A_n := \omega^+$ and $h_{nm} : A_n \longrightarrow A_m$, $n \geq n$, such that $k \mapsto 2^{n-m}k$. An element ξ of the inverse limit of the system $\langle A_n, h_{nm} \rangle_{n,m \in \omega^+}$ would satisfy

$$\xi_1 = 2^n \xi_{i+1}$$

which is impossible (the example is from (Graetzer 1979, 132)). For the infinite case more structure on the sets is required. This is one of the reasons why the logic of vision lives more naturally in topology (other reasons will be encountered shortly).[5] For completeness sake, we now give a topological proof of Theorem 13. It uses the *discrete topology* $\mathbf{T}_s^d$ on $|\mathcal{M}_s|$ (all subsets of $|\mathcal{M}_s|$ are open; $s \in T$), for which the bonding mappings h_{st}, $s \geq t$, are continuous.

TOPOLOGICAL PROOF OF THEOREM 13. For finite $J \subseteq T$, let the sets $[J]$ be defined as before, but now as subsets of the product topology $\mathbf{P} := \Pi_T \mathbf{T}_s^d$. It suffices to show that the $[J]$ are closed. Indeed, since each $|\mathcal{M}_s|$ is finite, the $\mathbf{T}_s^d$ are compact Hausdorff. So by Tychonoff's theorem (i.e., an equivalent of the ultrafilter theorem) $\mathbf{P}$ is compact. This means that the intersection of a

[5] The reader who is not familiar with topology will notice that the concepts used in this article do not go beyond the elementary facts of compact Hausdorff spaces; see, e.g., (Engelking 1989): §1.1, pp. 11–14; §1.5, pp. 36–37; §2.3, pp. 77–78; §3.1, pp. 123–125; §3.2, pp. 138-139; or any other introduction to the subject. However, the body of the article should be comprehensible without being familiar with these notions.

set of closed subsets of **P** with the finite intersection property is non-empty. In particular, if the $[J]$ are closed, then

$$\bigcap_{J \in \wp_\omega}(T)[J] \neq \emptyset,$$

which gives the thread desired.

To show that $[J]$ is closed, we prove that its complement is open. Choose a point $p \in \mathbf{P}$ not in $[J]$. There are $i, j \in J$ so that $h_{ij}(p_i) \neq p_j$. Since $\mathbf{T}^d_j$ is Hausdorff, there are disjoint open sets U_j, V_j with $h_{ij}(p_i) \in U_j$ and $p_j \in V_j$. Define $V_i := h^{-1}_{ij}(U_j)$. By continuity of h_{ij}, V_i is open, and $p_i \in V_i$. Choose an (open) base element B_p for **P** with $p \in B_p$ and V_i, V_j as coordinates. Since U_j, V_j are disjoint, B_p and $[J]$ are also disjoint; for $r \in B_p \cap [J]$ would have $r_j \in U_j \cap V_j$, which is impossible. So, the complement of $[J]$ is the open set $\bigcup_{p \notin [J]} B_p$, whence $[J]$ is closed. □

As in the algebraic case the inverse limit comes with projections

$$\pi_t : \mathcal{M} \longrightarrow \mathcal{M}_t$$

for $t \in T$ defined by $\xi \mapsto \xi_t$ such that $\pi_t = h_{st} \circ \pi_s$ $(s \geq t)$. And it can be proved that if the bonding mappings h_{ij} are surjective, π_t is surjective as well (Engelking 1989, 142). This is used to define the topologies relevant for the following.

We work with assignment spaces $\mathcal{F}_s := |\mathcal{M}_s|^{\mathrm{Var}}$ and $\mathcal{F} := |\mathcal{M}|^{\mathrm{Var}}$ on the models $\mathcal{M}_s$ and $\mathcal{M}$. The *formula topology* $\mathbf{T}^f_s$ on $\mathcal{F}_s$ is the topology generated by the clopen sets $[\varphi]_{\mathcal{M}_s} := \{g \in \mathcal{F}_s : \mathcal{M}_s, g \models \varphi\}$. The discrete topologies $\mathbf{T}^d_s$ introduced earlier are compact Hausdorff. Hence the product topology on $\mathcal{F}_s$ is compact Hausdorff as well, so that formula topology $\mathbf{T}^f_s$ on $\mathcal{F}_s$, as a subtopology of the product topology, is compact.

Define a projection $\mathbf{p}_s : \mathcal{F} \longrightarrow \mathcal{F}_s$ by: $\mathbf{p}_s(f)(x) := f(x)_s$. Sometimes we write '$f_s$' instead of: $\mathbf{p}_s(f)$. The projections $\mathbf{p}_s$ are surjective: Let $g \in \mathcal{F}_s$. For each x, choose ξ^x such that $g(x) = \pi_s(\xi^x)$. This is possible, because the projections $\pi_s : \mathcal{M} \longrightarrow \mathcal{M}_s$ are surjective. Define: $f(x) := \xi^x$, then $\mathbf{p}_s(f) = g$.

Let **T** be the smallest topology on $\mathcal{F}$ which makes all the $\mathbf{p}_s$ continuous, when the $\mathcal{F}_s$ are given the formula topology. **T** is a subtopology of the product topology on $\mathcal{F}$. Since $|\mathcal{M}|$ is compact Hausdorff in the topology induced by the $\pi_s : \mathcal{M} \longrightarrow \mathcal{M}_s$ and the discrete $\mathbf{T}^d_s$ (Engelking 1989, p. 141), so is $\mathcal{F}$; whence **T** is compact.[6] Whenever we use the phrase 'by compactness', we tacitly refer to **T**.

It will appear that the use of topology is fruitful in the following respects. Firstly, it allows one to reason with sets that may not be definable by means of a formula. Secondly, it makes the use of inverse limits less dependent on the

[6]There exists another topology on $\mathcal{F}$ determined by first order definable subsets of assignments on $\mathcal{M}$. This topology will not be used.

size of the approximating models. Thirdly, it gives a uniform method of proof. Nevertheless, we have tried to keep this article accessible to readers who are not familiar with topological notions and techniques.

Back to reality. Reality is taken to be an inverse limit of a refining inverse system. Inherent in this approach is a certain claim concerning the relationship between partial objects (the elements in an $|\mathcal{M}_s|$) and the material objects (the threads in the inverse limit). In particular, if the inverse limit is obtained from a total refining system (all bonding mappings are surjective), then each partial object is real in the sense that it is an approximation of a real object. But if a partial object may disappear under closer scrutiny, such as Macbeth's dagger, the inverse limit should be constructed from a refining system *simpliciter*.[7]

6.3.3 Conditional quantification

Consider clause (i) of the proposed semantics for 'I see an arm': with the present approximation the object that I focus on is identified as an arm. The logical form of this statement is some kind of existential quantification, namely 'there exists an arm in my (filtered) perceptual field', the filter corresponding to the degree of approximation. (The meaning of the word 'filter' here has nothing to do with its logical meaning; one should think rather of, say, a UV filter in photography, or the Dolby filter on a cassette deck.) However, this notion of quantification is *nonstable*: with respect to a finer filter, the existential statement may become false. The technical problem is, how to incorporate the filter into the existential quantifier. We first discuss a way of doing this. In section 6.3.5 we return to the question of formally representing Marr's hierarchy of 3-D models.

The notion of a 'conditional quantifier' originated from an attempt to extract the logical content of conditional expectation in probability theory.[8] Since this heuristic motivation is directly relevant to our theme, vision, we reproduce it here, apologising to those readers who are not familiar with probability. In any case we shall first give a simple example which hopefully succeeds in illustrating the main idea.

Example 1: Suppose we have a variable X on a sample space Ω which takes values 0 and 1 both with probability $\frac{1}{2}$. Let A_i be the subset of Ω on which X takes value i, then $P(A_i) = \frac{1}{2}$. Suppose furthermore that we cannot measure X directly, but can only measure $X + Y$, where Y is some small perturbation. Let $B_i \subseteq A_i$ be such that $P(B_0) = \epsilon \neq P(B_1) = \delta$, where $\epsilon, \delta \ll 1$; Y takes value $\frac{1}{2}$ on B_0 and value $-\frac{1}{2}$ on B_1. Then $X + Y$ takes value 0 on $A_0 - B_0$, value 1 on $A_1 - B_1$ and value $\frac{1}{2}$ on $B_0 \cup B_1$. The smallest Boolean algebra B

[7] For a similar construction in the logic of time, see (Thomason 1989).

[8] There does exist a (largely forgotten) body of work studying quantifiers over Boolean algebras in a probabilistic context; cf. (Wright 1963) and references given therein.

which contains $A_0 - B_0$, $A_1 - B_1$ and $B_0 \cup B_1$ does not contain A_0 and A_1. If we can measure only $X + Y$, not X, this implies that we cannot determine the expectation $\mathbf{E}(X)$ of X, which would equal $\frac{1}{2}$, but only its expectation $\mathbf{E}(X|\mathcal{B})$ with respect to $\mathcal{B}$, which equals $\frac{1}{2} + \frac{1}{2}\epsilon - \frac{1}{2}\delta \neq \frac{1}{2}$. What we are after is a logical analogue of the expression '$\mathbf{E}(X|\mathcal{B})$'. [•][9]

Example 2: A more realistic example is furnished by a typical instance of filtering. As in (Marr 1982, pp. 54–61), we may think of a filter as a blurring operation (in his case applied to an image), usually by means of a Gaussian. Formally, we have a random variable X on a sample space Ω (measurable with respect to an algebra $\mathcal{B}$) which we want to measure; however, due to, for example, noise, we can only observe $X + c.\xi$, where ξ is a Gaussian with mean 0 and standard deviation 1. $X + c.\xi$ is measurable with respect to an algebra $\mathcal{G}$, which need not be the same as $\mathcal{B}$ (when both $\mathcal{B}$ and $\mathcal{G}$ are taken to be minimal). Hence we can only determine properties of X as filtered through $\mathcal{G}$; this is represented by the conditional expectation $\mathbf{E}(X|\mathcal{G})$. $\mathbf{E}(X|\mathcal{G})(\omega)$ is a $\mathcal{G}$-measurable random variable on Ω, representing the questions that can be asked about X from the point of view of $\mathcal{G}$. Suppose an experiment has been performed. The only information available to us regarding which sample point ω has been chosen is the value of $Z(\omega)$, for each $\mathcal{G}$-measurable random variable Z. This determines a measurable set $A \in \mathcal{G}$. Then the expected value of X given this information, $\int_A XdP$, equals $\int_A \mathbf{E}(X|\mathcal{G})dP$; from the point of view of $\mathcal{G}$, no other questions about X can be answered. The Radon-Nikodym theorem is used to show that a function $\mathbf{E}(X|\mathcal{G})(\omega)$ with these properties exists. It can be shown to satisfy (equalities are understood to hold almost everywhere)

1) $\mathbf{E}(1_\emptyset|\mathcal{G}) = 0$, $\mathbf{E}(1_\Omega|\mathcal{G}) = 1$;
2) $X \subseteq Y$ implies $\mathbf{E}(1_X|\mathcal{G}) \leq \mathbf{E}(1_Y|\mathcal{G})$; and
3) $\mathbf{E}(f \bullet \mathbf{E}(g|\mathcal{G})|\mathcal{G}) = \mathbf{E}(f|\mathcal{G}) \bullet \mathbf{E}(g|\mathcal{G})$.

Here, f, g vary over functions, and 1_Z is a characteristic function. [•]

We shall take conditional expectation as our heuristic model; the form of quantification we are interested in will be called *conditional quantification*. It is helpful to think of the conditioning algebras as filters (in the sense of blurring operations). That such a notion of quantification is feasible is suggested by the algebraic treatment of existential quantification in (Halmos 1952). Let $\mathcal{M}$ be a model $\langle D, \ldots \rangle$; $\mathcal{B}$ the algebra of first order definable subsets of $\mathcal{F}$ ($\mathcal{F}$ is the set of assignments on $\mathcal{M}$); and $\mathcal{G}_x$ the subalgebra of $\mathcal{B}$ generated by formulas with free variables in Var $- \{x\}$. Then $\exists x$ is the unique surjective mapping $\mathcal{B} \longrightarrow \mathcal{G}_x$ with properties (1–5).

[9]The sign '[•]' indicates the end of an example.

1) $\exists x \mathbf{0} = \mathbf{0}$, $\exists x \mathbf{1} = \mathbf{1}$;
2) $\varphi \leq \psi$ implies $\exists x\varphi \leq \exists x\psi$;
3) $\exists x(\varphi \vee \psi) = \exists x\varphi \vee \exists x\psi$;
4) $\exists x(\varphi \wedge \exists x\psi) = \exists x\varphi \wedge \exists x\psi$; and
5) $\varphi \leq \exists x\varphi$.

It worthwhile to observe that $\exists x$ does not share all properties with conditional expectation; in particular, conditional expectation may lack property 5.[10]

Intuitively speaking, $\mathcal{G}_x$ represents the situation that we have precise information about variables other than x, and no information about x. Indeed, we may view $\mathcal{G}_x$ as the set of questions about variables (of the type 'does y satisfy ψ?') that can be asked and answered in this situation. We assume that all questions can be formulated in a first order language; since $\mathcal{G}_x$ contains all formulas in free variables other than x, it represents maximal information about those variables. Note that this way of analysing the existential quantifier is very different from the Fregean one which led to Mostowski-Lindström generalised quantifiers: there, $\exists$ is interpreted as the set of nonempty subsets of the domain, and the truth condition reads

$$\mathcal{M} \models \exists x\varphi(x) \text{ iff } \{d \in D : \mathcal{M} \models \varphi(d/x)\} \in \exists$$

The difference is that in Frege-Mostowski-Lindström quantification variables are analysed away (they are just place holders, whereas here quantification is defined with respect to a given variable.

To continue the analogy between conditional expectation and quantification, we think of both variables and formulas as random variables on a space, namely the set of assignments. Let $\mathcal{M}$ be a model with set of assignments D^{Var}. If x is a variable, it corresponds to a function $X : D^{\mathrm{Var}} \longrightarrow D$ with

$$X(f) = f(x)$$

for all $f \in D^{\mathrm{Var}}$. Similarly a formula $\varphi(x_1, \ldots, x_n)$ corresponds to a function Φ which maps the 'random variables' $X_1, \ldots, X_n$ to the 'random variable' $\Phi(X_1, \ldots, X_n) : D^{\mathrm{Var}} \longrightarrow \{0, 1\}$ by

$$\Phi(X_1, \ldots, X_n)(f) = 1 \text{ iff } \mathcal{M}, f \models \varphi(x_1, \ldots, x_n)$$

The meaning of this move is that variables acquire individuality, instead of being 'explained away' as Quine would have it. This is suggestive when we seek to apply probabilistic concepts to logic.

Example 3: A common situation in probability theory is that one wants to refine a sample space Ω' into a sample space Ω. This means that points of Ω' correspond to *sets* of points of Ω; intuitively, elementary events of Ω' are

[10]The Boolean averages in (Wright 1963)—which satisfy (1–4),—capture a common core of existential quantification and conditional expectation in an algebraic fashion.

further subdivided in Ω. Let $\mathcal{G}$ be a σ-algebra on Ω and $\mathcal{G}'$ a σ-algebra on Ω'. The refinement is then given by a surjective map $\eta : \Omega \longrightarrow \Omega'$ such that $\eta^{-1}(\mathcal{G}')$ is a subalgebra of $\mathcal{G}$. If X is a random variable on Ω, it can be 'blurred' to a random variable on Ω' by taking the conditional expectation $\mathbf{E}(X|\eta^{-1}(\mathcal{G}'))$. [•]

The analogy between this example and the logical notion we are after is the following. Let h be a homomorphism from $\mathcal{M}$ to $\mathcal{M}'$; e.g., $\mathcal{M}$ is an inverse limit and $\mathcal{M}'$ one of its approximations. As in the probabilistic case, we want to compare a formula on D^{Var} with its 'blurred' version on ${D'}^{\mathrm{Var}}$; given the analogy between formulas and random variables, conditional quantification seems suited to play the role of conditional expectation here. Conditional quantification uses the notion of a *frame* where conditional expectation uses a σ-algebra.

Definition 21 *A* lattice *L is a partially ordered set in which meets and joins of finite sets exist. A lattice L is an* $\vee, \bigwedge$-frame *if it is closed under arbitrary meets, such that the following distributive law holds:*

$$a \vee \bigwedge_I b_i = \bigwedge_I (a \vee b_i).$$

The customary notion of frame, the complete Heyting algebra or $\wedge, \bigvee$-frame, is dual to our notion. However, since we shall be concerned with $\vee, \bigwedge$-frames only, we refer to these structures simply as frames. The collection of closed sets of a topology is the prime example of a $\vee, \bigwedge$-frame. So, if a frame is generated from clopen sets, as in the case of $\mathbf{T}_s^f$, all its elements are closed; in particular, $\exists(\varphi|\mathcal{G})$ is.

In the present framework information has to form a frame $\mathcal{G}$ over the set $\mathcal{F}$ of assignments for a first order model $\mathcal{M}$. Much as a random variable, each piece of information $X \in \mathcal{G}$ gives partial information on the value of (sequences of) variables. For example, the set

$$\{f(x) : f \in X\}$$

need not be a singleton. Often, but not always, the frames are generated from sets of assignments defined by formulas φ:

$$[\varphi]_{\mathcal{M}} := \{f \in \mathcal{F} : \mathcal{M}, f \models \varphi\}.$$

Conditional quantifiers filter information using frames over sets of assignments. If $\mathcal{G}$ is a proper subframe of $\mathcal{G}_x$, this means that for some variable y, not all possible questions about y can actually be asked (e.g., for lack of a sufficiently accurate measurement device). Below we shall give several examples illustrating this possibility. The definition of quantification with respect to a subframe is as follows.

Definition 22 Let **Form** be the frame generated by the first order definable sets of assignments, and let $\mathcal{G}$ be a subframe of **Form**. $\exists(\bullet|G)$, the *existential quantifier conditional on* $\mathcal{G}$, is the unique mapping **Form** $\longrightarrow \mathcal{G}$ satisfying

(*) For all $C \in \mathcal{G}$ $[[\varphi]_{\mathcal{M}} \subseteq C$ iff $\exists([\varphi]_{\mathcal{M}}|\mathcal{G}) \subseteq C]$

In the following we often write just φ for $[\varphi]_{\mathcal{M}}$, when the model is clear from context.

Roughly speaking, $\exists(\varphi|\mathcal{G})$ represents the best estimate of φ on the basis of the information available in $\mathcal{G}$; hence we require $\exists(\varphi|\mathcal{G}) \in \mathcal{G}$. Note that a quantifier with these properties, when it exists, is unique. In particular, from left to right the Galois correspondence (*) says that each approximation to $[\varphi]_{\mathcal{M}}$ in $\mathcal{G}$ is an approximation of $\exists([\varphi]_{\mathcal{M}}|\mathcal{G})$, while (*) from right to left implies that $\exists([\varphi]_{\mathcal{M}}|\mathcal{G})$ itself approximates $[\varphi]_{\mathcal{M}}$. So (*) implies that $\exists(\varphi|\mathcal{G})$ must be defined as the least upper bound

$$\bigwedge\{C \in \mathcal{G} | \varphi \subseteq C\}.$$

Since $\mathcal{G}$ is a frame, this meet exists in $\mathcal{G}$, hence indeed

$$\exists(\bullet|\mathcal{G}) : \textbf{Form} \longrightarrow \mathcal{G}.$$

From this we also see that $\exists(\bullet|\mathcal{G})$ has the following properties (here it is essential that the frame is generated by an algebra)

1) $\exists(\mathbf{0}|\mathcal{G}) = \mathbf{0}, \exists(\mathbf{1}|\mathcal{G}) = \mathbf{1}$;
2) $\varphi \subseteq \psi$ implies $\exists(\varphi|\mathcal{G}) \subseteq \exists(\psi|\mathcal{G})$ (monotonicity);
3) $\exists(\varphi \vee \psi|\mathcal{G}) = \exists(\varphi|\mathcal{G}) \vee \exists(\psi|\mathcal{G})$ (additivity);
4) $\exists(\varphi \wedge \psi|\mathcal{G}) = \exists(\varphi|\mathcal{G}) \wedge \psi$ where $\psi \in \mathcal{G}$ ('taking out what is known');
5) $\varphi \subseteq \exists(\varphi|\mathcal{G})$ (coarsening).

All properties are trivial except (4). The inclusion from left to right follows by (*) and the fact that $\psi \in \mathcal{G}$. Conversely, without loss of generality choose $\theta \in \mathcal{B}$ such that $\theta \geq \varphi \wedge \psi$. We have $\varphi \leq (\psi \rightarrow \theta)$, with $\psi \rightarrow \theta$ in the algebra $\mathcal{B}$; whence also $\exists(\varphi|\mathcal{G}) \leq \psi \rightarrow \theta$ by (*). Further, (*) clearly implies that $\exists(\bullet|\mathcal{G})$ is the identity on $\mathcal{G}$. Thus, (4) is the analogue of the Frobenius property in logic

$$\exists(\varphi \wedge \exists(\psi|\mathcal{G})|\mathcal{G}) = \exists(\varphi|\mathcal{G}) \wedge \exists(\psi|\mathcal{G}).$$

We adopt the following convention concerning *free variables*:

$$\text{FV}(\exists(\varphi|\mathcal{G})) = \text{FV}(\varphi) \cap \bigcup\{\text{FV}(\psi)|\psi \in \mathcal{G}\}.$$

Notice that the number of free variables need not be reduced by conditional quantification! In the formula $\exists(\varphi(x,y)|\mathcal{G})$ x is neither fully bound nor fully free; whereas ordinary existential quantification $\exists x$ has the effect of abolishing all restrictions on x, a conditional quantifier need only liberalise restrictions on x to some extent, without fully abolishing them (cf. coarsening). This may seem strange on the usual view of variables, but it becomes less strange when variables are taken as observable quantities, measured by means of some device with finite accuracy. If the variable is real-valued, this could mean, for instance, that a measurement only constrains the variable to lie in an interval. To put this in currently fashionable terms: we wish to introduce a resource-bounded form of quantification, where the resource is the degree of accuracy with which one can 'measure' variables. As indicated above, ordinary predicate logic has unbounded resources in this respect.

We give some examples, showing that $\exists(\bullet|\mathcal{G})$ is truly a generalised quantifier.

Example 4: *Generalised quantification.* We show that the existential quantifier is the same as the quantifier $\exists(\bullet|\mathcal{G}_x)$ with $\mathcal{G}_x$ the frame generated by sets $[\varphi]_{\mathcal{M}}$ where x does not occur free in φ. The inclusion

$$\exists(\varphi|\mathcal{G}_x) \subseteq \exists x\varphi$$

is immediate from the Galois correspondence for $\exists(\bullet|\mathcal{G}_x)$. As to the converse inclusion, $\varphi \subseteq \exists(\varphi|\mathcal{G}_x)$ because $\exists(\varphi|\mathcal{G}_x) \in \mathcal{G}_x$. But all sets in $\mathcal{G}_x$ are closed under the relation $=_x$ between assignments differing at most at x. This is true in particular of $\exists(\varphi|\mathcal{G}_x)$, so $\exists x\varphi \subseteq \exists(\varphi|\mathcal{G}_x)$. [•]

Example 5: *Blurring of individuals. In nuce*, the following example describes our approach to a semantics of perception. A statement like 'y sees φ' is rendered formally as: '$\exists x[\varphi(x) \wedge S(y,x)]$', where φ defines a unique x. Symbol S gives the denotation of the transitive verb 'to see', and it delimits the set of objects $\{d : Sad\}$ seen by a. The quantifier $\exists x$ ranges over completely accurate objects; in formal terms, the elements of the inverse limits constructed in the previous section. To accomodate actual perception, which always has finite precision, we replace the quantifier $\exists x$ by a conditional quantifier $\exists(\bullet|\mathcal{G})$, where $\mathcal{G}$ represents the degree of blurring. Here we present only a simple case.

Let $\mathcal{M} = \langle\{1,2,3,4,5\}, S, W, U\rangle$, with '$S(a,b)$' for: a sees b, 'W' for: West, and 'U' for: up. In particular, $S = \{\langle 2,1\rangle, \langle 2,3\rangle, \langle 4,5\rangle\}$, $W = \{1,5\}$, $U = \{1,2,3\}$. Put $\varphi(x,y) = S(y,x) \wedge W(x) \wedge U(y)$, then for f such that

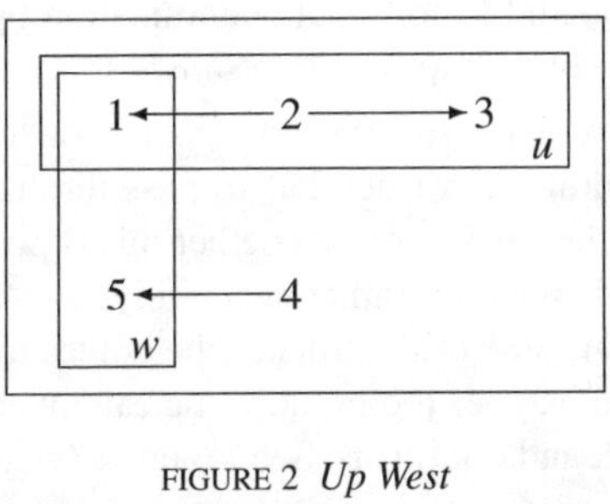

FIGURE 2 *Up West*

$f(y) = 2$: $\mathcal{M}, f \models \exists! x\varphi(x,y)$ ('y occupies the 'up' position and, y sees exactly one object looking to the West'); in fact:

$$\begin{aligned} & \{f : \mathcal{M}, f \models \exists x\varphi(x,y)\} \\ = & \{f : \mathcal{M}, f \models \exists(\varphi(x,y)|\mathcal{G}_x)\} \\ = & \{f : f(y) = 2\} \end{aligned}$$

The algebra $\mathcal{G}_x$ represents the case that the viewer y has complete information, both about its own position ('up') and the direction in which it is looking ('west'). Let us now vary this situation, for instance by depriving the viewer of the information that he is in the 'up' position. The (finite) algebra $\mathcal{G}$ on the set of assignments, corresponding to this state of affairs, is determined by the formula algebra generated by the set $\{S(y,x), W(x)\}$. We now have:

$$\begin{aligned} & \{f : \mathcal{M}, f \models \exists(\varphi(x,y)|\mathcal{G})\} \\ = & \bigwedge\{\psi \in \mathcal{G} : \varphi \leq \psi\} \\ = & \{f : \mathcal{M}, f \models S(y,x) \wedge W(x)\} \\ = & \{f : (f(y) = 2 \wedge f(x) = 1) \vee (f(y) = 4 \wedge f(x) = 5)\} \end{aligned}$$

Similarly, if y is so disoriented that he does not know whether he is looking East or West, we may describe his predicament by the algebra $\mathcal{H}$ generated by $\{S(y,x), U(y)\}$. In this case:

$$\begin{aligned} & \{f : \mathcal{M}, f \models \exists(\varphi(x,y)|\mathcal{H})\} \\ = & \bigwedge\{\psi \in \mathcal{H} : \varphi \leq \psi\} \\ = & \{f : \mathcal{M}, f \models S(y,x) \wedge U(x)\} \\ = & \{f : f(y) = 2 \vee (f(x) = 1 \wedge f(x) = 3)\} \end{aligned}$$

We trust the reader can subject y to a still more savage experiment. [•]

In the above examples we have: $\exists(\varphi(x,y)|\mathcal{G}) \in \mathcal{G}$, as required by the definition. The next example shows that if one were to tighten the analogy between conditional expectation and conditional quantification by replacing frames by Boolean *algebras*, it may be impossible to satisfy this condition.

Example 6: *Truck through door?* We now replace the dichotomy up-down by a continuum of possibilities. A truck has to pass through a narrow door in a wall; a person behind the truck checks whether this is possible. In this case the viewer must choose his position rather accurately: too far left or right means that he will see only one side of the truck, if he comes too close the truck will occlude the door, but if he goes too far down he cannot accurately estimate the distance between truck and doorposts. See Figure 3 (where $n \geq m$).

Let $O(x)$ be the predicate 'x is a (sufficiently large) opening', $S(y,x)$ the relation 'y sees x' (where the viewer y is identified by the coordinates of his position in the plane) and let $A_n(y)$ be a countable collection of predicates

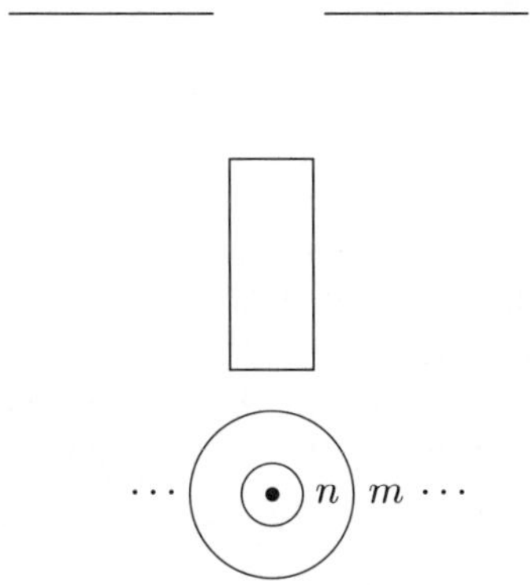

FIGURE 3 *Truck through door?*

denoting sets in the plane. We assume the following logical relations between these predicates:

1) $\forall n \forall x \forall y (O(x) \wedge S(y,x) \rightarrow A_n(y))$;
2) $\forall n \forall y (A_{n+1}(y) \rightarrow A_n(y))$;
3) $\forall n \exists y (\neg A_{n+1}(y) \wedge A_n(y))$.

Let $\mathcal{M}$ be a model for (1)-(3), and suppose $\mathcal{G}$ is the Boolean algebra of subsets of $\mathcal{F}$, the set of assignments for $\mathcal{M}$, generated by

$$\{A_n(y) : n \in \omega\}$$

This algebra represents the situation that the viewer has no precise information about his location y; the only available information is in the form of the sets $A_n(y)$. This has a twofold consequence:

a) $\exists(O(x) \wedge S(y,x)|\mathcal{G}) \notin \mathcal{G}$,
b) $\exists(O(x) \wedge S(y,x)|\mathcal{G})$ is not first order definable.

For (a) and (b), we observe that on $\mathcal{M}$,

$$\exists(O(x) \wedge S(y,x)|\mathcal{G}) \equiv \bigwedge_{n \in \omega} A_n(y)$$

To see this, first note that for all $\varphi \in \mathcal{G}$

(*) $O(x) \wedge S(y,x) \subseteq \varphi \Leftrightarrow$ *there is* $k \in \omega[\varphi \equiv A_k(y)]$

From right to left this is immediate from (1). Conversely, assume $O(x) \wedge S(y,x) \subseteq \varphi$ for $\varphi \in \mathcal{G}$. Since φ is a Boolean combination of the A_n, it can be written in disjunctive normal form. By (1) conjunctions with negative occurrences of the A_n cancel out, so it follows from (2) that ψ is equal to some $A_k(y)$.

It is immediate from (*) and (1) that

$$\begin{array}{rl} & \exists(O(x) \wedge S(y,x)|\mathcal{G}) \\ \equiv_{(*)} & \bigwedge\{A_n(y) : O(x) \wedge S(y,x) \subseteq A_n(y)\} \\ \equiv_{(1)} & \bigwedge_{n\in\omega} A_n(y) \end{array}$$

As to a), assume for a contradiction $\exists(O(x) \wedge S(y,x)|\mathcal{G}) \in \mathcal{G}$. Then also $\bigwedge_{n\in\omega} A_n(y) \in \mathcal{G}$. Since $O(x) \wedge S(y,x) \subseteq \bigwedge_{n\in\omega} A_n(y)$, (*) implies $\bigwedge_{n\in\omega} A_n(y) \equiv A_k(y)$ for some k; contradicting (3).

As to b), assume $\exists(O(x) \wedge S(y,x)|\mathcal{G})$ is first order definable, say by $\chi(x,y)$. Let $\mathcal{M}$ be a ω-saturated model for (1)–(3).[11] On $\mathcal{M}$

$$\exists(O(x) \wedge S(y,x)|\mathcal{G}) \equiv \bigwedge_{n\in\omega} A_n(y),$$

as before. So the theory Γ given by

$$\mathrm{Th}(\mathcal{M}) \cup \{A_n(y) : n \in \omega\} \cup \{\neg\chi(x,y)\}$$

must be consistent; for otherwise

$$\mathrm{Th}(\mathcal{M}) \cup \{A_n(y) : n \in \omega\} \models \chi(x,y)$$

which by compactness of $\models$ and the previous observations implies

$$\mathrm{Th}(\mathcal{M}) \models A_k(y) \leftrightarrow \bigwedge_{n\in\omega} A_n(y)$$

for some $k \in \omega$. With (2) $\in \mathrm{Th}(\mathcal{M})$ this implies

$$\mathrm{Th}(\mathcal{M}) \models A_k(y) \leftrightarrow A_{k+1}(y)$$

contradicting (3) $\in \mathrm{Th}(\mathcal{M})$. Due to ω-saturation

$$\{A_n(y) : n \in \omega\} \cup \{\neg\chi(x,y)\}$$

is realisable in $\mathcal{M}$: there are $c, d \in |\mathcal{M}|$ such that $\mathcal{M} \models \bigwedge_{n\in\omega} A_n(c) \wedge \neg\chi(c,d)$. This conflicts with $\chi(c,d) \equiv \bigwedge_{n\in\omega} A_n(c)$. We conclude that $\exists(O(x) \wedge S(y,x)|\mathcal{G})$ is not first order; in particular it is not equivalent to $\exists x(O(x) \wedge S(y,x))$.

We have seen that (a) and (b) are true. Clearly the trouble is that $\exists(\bullet|\mathcal{G})$ need not be in the *algebra* $\mathcal{G}$ because the required infima do not exist in $\mathcal{G}$. Of course, for conditional quantification on frames this situation cannot arise. It should be noticed, though, that a slight variation of the argument still allows us to prove (b) in terms of frames. Due to the distributive law, each $X \in \mathcal{G}$ has the form $\bigwedge_{j\in I} \bigvee_{1\le k\le n} A_{jk}$. Using (2) this reduces to $\bigwedge_{j\in I} A_j(y)$. So we still have:

$$\exists(O(x) \wedge S(y,x)|\mathcal{G}) \equiv \bigwedge_{n\in\omega} A_n(y),$$

[11] Recall that $\mathcal{M}$ is *ω-saturated* iff for each each type $\Gamma(x_1,\ldots,x_n)$ in the language for $\langle\mathcal{M}, c\rangle_{c\in C}$ with finitely many constants C added: if $\mathrm{Th}(\langle\mathcal{M}, c\rangle_{c\in C}) \cup \Gamma(x_1,\ldots,x_n)$ is consistent, then $\Gamma(x_1,\ldots,x_n)$ is realisable in $\mathcal{M}$. The notion of *ω_1-saturation* is defined similarly with 'at most countably many constants added' instead of: finitely many constants added.

which suffices to prove (b) for frames. Combined with example 4 this observation shows that conditional quantification is truly *generalised* quantification. [•]

Readers familiar with Halmos' algebraic treatment of quantification will recall that quantifiers taking values in an algebra and satisfying properties 1–5 above can be represented by means of an equivalence relation, in a sense to be made precise below. Let us reformulate Halmos' theorem in our context.

Theorem 15 *Let $\mathcal{M}$ be an ω_1-saturated model, $\mathcal{B}$ an algebra of assignments on $\mathcal{M}$, $\mathcal{G}$ the frame generated by $\mathcal{B}$. Then there exists an equivalence relation R on assignments such that for first order formulas φ*

$$f \in \exists(\varphi|\mathcal{G}) \Longleftrightarrow \exists g(R(f,g) \wedge g \in \varphi).$$

PROOF. Define $R(f,g)$ to mean: for all $\psi \in \mathcal{B}$, $f \in \psi$ iff $g \in \psi$. Observe that we would have obtained the same relation had we substituted $\mathcal{G}$ for $\mathcal{B}$. With this definition of R, the direction from right to left is easy, since elements of $\mathcal{G}$ are R-invariant. For the converse direction, suppose that $\forall g(R(f,g) \rightarrow g \notin \varphi)$. Since $\mathcal{B}$ is an algebra, this is equivalent to

$$\forall g(g \in \varphi \rightarrow \exists \psi \in \mathcal{B}(f \notin \psi \wedge g \in \psi)).$$

Hence there exists a cover $\bigcup\{\psi_g \in \mathcal{B}|g \in \varphi\} \supseteq \varphi$, not containing f. By compactness, there exists a finite subcover, i.e., an element of $\mathcal{B}$, with the same property. It follows that $f \notin \exists(\varphi|\mathcal{G})$. □

The question may arise: why not take this representation as a defining condition, instead of the more elaborate formulation we have chosen? The reason is that equivalence relations represent only one particular type of bounded resource, and that various forms of partiality naturally occurring in language impose further bounds on the resource which can be expressed by restrictions on the frames, but not by means of equivalence relations.

6.3.4 Other forms of partiality relevant for vision

So far we have treated only one form of partiality, induced by the approximative nature of all perception. This is not the only form of interest, however. Partiality may occur because of a restricted perceptual field (in the sense that not all potentially visible objects actually are visible), or because the chosen perspective does not permit one to verify whether a certain predicate holds of a perceived object. These forms of partiality are also studied in situation semantics, but receive a somewhat different formal treatment here, due to their combination with the approximative nature of vision. We shall illustrate this for the case of perspective. First, however, we consider a delicate issue: the interaction of knowledge and vision. Since a conditional quantifier, the formal analogue of a perception report, expresses a consistency statement, (implicit) knowledge about what is consistent and what is not will influence the judgements we make. Hence problems of onmiscience are likely to rear their head here.

Knowledge and visual experience

A logic of vision should allow for the possibility of seeing something which is incompatible with the facts. In *La Fugitive*, the narrator, who has accustomed himself to Albertine's death, receives a telegram

> I opened it as soon as I was in my room, and, glancing throught the message which was filled with inaccurately transmitted words, managed nevertheless to make out: 'My dear friend, you think me dead, forgive me, I am quite alive, I long to see you, talk about marriage, when do you return? Affectionately, Albertine.' (Penquin ed., p. 656)

Suppose I know, at a certain stage of approximation s that if some person x is dead, then y is not a recent telegram from x:

$$\forall xy(\psi(x) \rightarrow \neg\varphi(x,y)),$$

where $\psi \in \mathcal{G}_s$. Does it follow that $\forall xy(\psi(x) \rightarrow \neg\exists(\varphi(x,y)|\mathcal{G}_s))$, i.e. that, even when given accurate information about death, I can't see a a recent telegram from someone believed dead? Not necessarily, it seems. Knowledge does not always guide perception in this way, and hallucinations do occur.

Interestingly, however, to accomodate this situation, we have to give up one of our principles, *viz.* Frobenius. This is a consequence of the following result:

Lemma 16 Wright 1963 *The following are equivalent:*

1. $\exists(\varphi \wedge \exists(\psi|\mathcal{G})) = \exists(\psi|\mathcal{G}) \wedge \exists(\varphi|\mathcal{G})$
2. (i) $\varphi \subseteq \exists(\psi|\mathcal{G})$ implies $\exists(\varphi|\mathcal{G}) \subseteq \exists(\psi|\mathcal{G})$
   (ii) $\varphi \wedge \exists(\psi|\mathcal{G}) = \mathbf{0}$ implies $\exists(\varphi|\mathcal{G}) \wedge \exists(\psi|\mathcal{G}) = \mathbf{0}$.

Since 2(ii) is precisely the connection between knowledge and perception that we judged too stringent, in some cases we must be content with property 2(i) only. But Frobenius is a consequence of the fact that our frames were generated by *algebras* of definable sets of assignments, hence a major adaptation of the definition of conditional quantifier is necessary. Reflecting on the example, one sees that one does not always allow negative information to influence one's perceptions. This suggests a restriction to positive information:

Definition 23 A first order formula is *positive* if it is constructed using only $\wedge, \vee, \exists, \forall, \top$ and $\bot$. Henceforth, **Pos** denotes the frame generated by sets of assignments defined by positive formulas.

The following counterexample shows that $\exists(\bullet|\mathcal{G})$, with $\mathcal{G}$ the frame obtained from **Pos**, need not satisfy Frobenius. Consider the models $\mathcal{M}_1$ and

$\mathcal{M}_2$ in figure 4, homomorphically related by the identity map.

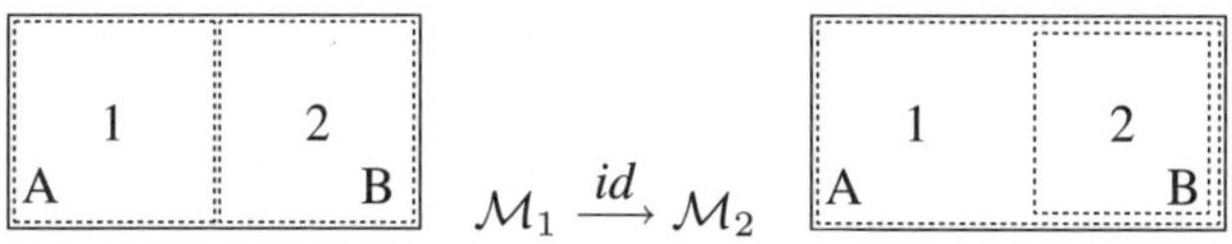

FIGURE 4 *Not Frobenius*

Let $\mathcal{G}$ be the frame over assignments for $\mathcal{M}_1$ generated by sets $\mathbf{p}^{-1}(\varphi)$, φ positive in the language $\{A, B\}$; and let P vary over the predicates A and B. Since the language is monadic, each positive formula can be written as a disjunction of conjunctions of the form $P(x)$, $\exists x P(x)$, or $\forall x P(x)$, where the latter two are equivalent to either $\top$ or $\bot$. Thus we have

$$\exists(A(x)|\mathcal{G}) \cap B(x) = \top \cap B(x) = B(x) \neq \bot = \exists(A(x) \cap B(x)|\mathcal{G}).$$

However, it can be shown that in our framework a much weaker form of property 2(ii) holds, saying roughly that knowledge influences perception in the limit. More precisely, suppose the conditional quantifiers $\exists(\bullet|\mathcal{G}_s)$ derive from an inverse system $\langle \mathcal{M}_s \rangle$, such that $\mathcal{G}_s) = \mathbf{Pos}(\mathcal{M}_s))$. In the next section it will be shown that $\bigcap_t \exists(\varphi|\mathcal{G}_t) = \varphi$ (for φ positive). By means of a compactness argument it then follows that for φ, ψ positive, ψ in some $\mathcal{G}_s)$ such that $\mathcal{M} \models \forall \overline{x}(\psi \rightarrow \neg\varphi)$, there will be $t \geq s$ such that ψ and $\exists(\varphi|\mathcal{G}_t)$ are disjoint.

And indeed, a closer look at the telegram a few days later showed that it was sent by Gilberte ('As for her capital *G*, it resembled a Gothic *A*.').

Perspective and occlusion

When defining inverse systems we allowed that predicates need not be defined on all models of the system. A concrete example where this is useful, is given by perspective: in a model which develops only the hind parts of a human, the predicate 'face' should not be applicable. In terms of perception reports, this means that a phrase like 'I can't see his face' should be construed as *denial*; the phrase is true when 'seeing his face' is 'undefined' because it is evaluated in the wrong perspective. Now it seems that our set up cannot model this, because $\exists(F|\mathcal{G}_s)$ is defined even when the predicate F is not interpreted on $\mathcal{M}_s$. Note, however, that in such a case, $\exists(F|\mathcal{G}_s)$ will typically equal $\mathbf{1}$: there is no non-trivial formula φ such that $F \subseteq \mathbf{p}_s^{-1}(\varphi_s)$. Since clearly one cannot consider the situation where $F \neq \mathbf{1}$ and $\exists(F|\mathcal{G}_s) = \mathbf{1}$ a situation of seeing F, it seems best to leave $\exists(A|\mathcal{G}_s)$ undefined in such cases.

A related phenomenon is that of occlusion, as when someone's face is hidden behind a newspaper. Again, one would say 'I can't see his face' in this case, meaning that 'seeing his face' is undefined. However, in this case the model may have a predicate for 'face', but now the filter should be such that the predicate F_s is not available for estimating F. Here also one would like to leave $\exists(A|\mathcal{G}_s)$ undefined.

To achieve this, the frames which determine the conditional quantifiers must be redefined so that they may lack a top element.

Definition 24 A *pseudolattice* L is a partially ordered set in which meets and joins of finite *non-empty* sets exists. A pseudolattice L is an evidential $\vee, \bigwedge -frame$ if it is closed under arbitrary non-empty meets such that the following distributive law holds

$$a \vee \bigwedge_I b_i = \bigwedge_I (a \vee b_i).$$

(Note that in lattices in which arbitrary finite meets and joins exists, top and bottom can be defined by $\top = \bigwedge \emptyset$ and $\bot = \bigvee \emptyset$; but a pseudolattice may lack top and/or bottom.)

A typical example of an evidential frame can be obtained from a model $\mathcal{M}_s$ by taking the collection of sets of assignments definable by a positive formula, this time however *not* including top or bottom. If there exist disjoint predicates on $\mathcal{M}_s$, then **0** will be in the evidential frame, but if the universe of the model is not covered by non-trivial positive formulas, then **1** will not be in the frame.

6.3.5 Combining inverse limits and conditional quantification

Now that both inverse limits and conditional quantifiers are introduced an obvious question arises: how do they relate? More specifically, is it possible to mimick the 'coarse' information given by a formula relative to an approximation $\mathcal{M}_s$ by means of conditionally quantification? This question is studied in section 6.3.5. But we begin with showing how inverse limits arise as soon as a sufficiently structured supply of 'filters' is available.

Refining systems from filtering

To motivate the following theorem, we return to the beginning of this section, where it was argued that perception should be viewed as applying a 'filter' to reality. Here we show that 'filtering' is in a sense inverse to taking limits of refining systems. Of necessity, the formulation of the result is somewhat sloppy; a full formulation and proof will be published elsewhere.

Definition 25 Let T be a directed set. A collection of algebras $\{\mathcal{B}_s : s \in T\}$ is a *net* if $s \leq t$ implies $\mathcal{B}_s \subseteq \mathcal{B}_t$.

Theorem 17 *Let $\mathcal{M}$ be an ω_1-saturated model, $\mathcal{B}$ an algebra of assignments on $\mathcal{M}$ containing the sets definable by atomic formulas. Let $\{\mathcal{B}_s : s \in T\}$ be a net of algebras such that $\bigcup \mathcal{B}_s = \mathcal{B}$. Then there exists an inverse system $\langle \mathcal{M}_s, h_{st} \rangle_{s,t \in T}$ such that*

1. *$\mathcal{M}$ is the inverse limit of $\langle \mathcal{M}_s, h_{st}\rangle_{s,t\in T}$;*
2. *$\mathcal{M}_s, \mathbf{p}_s(f) \models R(x_1,\ldots,x_n)$ iff $f \in \exists(R(x_1,\ldots,x_n)|\mathcal{B}_s)$, for all relations $R(x_1,\ldots,x_n)$.*

Condition (2) says that the interpretation of predicates on $\mathcal{M}_s$ is given by $\exists(\bullet|\mathcal{B}_s)$; i.e. $\mathcal{M}_s$ is the model that corresponds to the filter $\exists(\bullet|\mathcal{B}_s)$. This result is parallel to a result in situation semantics, which says that a first order model can always be viewed as a direct limit of a directed set of partial submodels, but note the difference: the models $\mathcal{M}_s$ are not submodels of $\mathcal{M}$ but approximations to $\mathcal{M}$. This reflects the subtly different concept of partiality employed here.

From refining systems to conditional quantifiers and back

This section justifies the logical form of perception reports adopted in the next section.

Given the material of the previous section, an obvious question arises. Let $\mathcal{B}_s$ be the following lattice:

$$\mathcal{B}_s := \{C \subseteq \mathcal{F} : C = \mathbf{p}_s^{-1}(\{g \in \mathcal{F}_s : \mathcal{M}_s, g \models \varphi\}) \text{ for some } \textit{positive } \varphi\}$$

with $\mathbf{p}_s$ the projection defined in section 6.3.2. Let $\mathcal{G}_s$ be the frame generated by $\mathcal{B}_s$. If A is any predicate, do we have:

$$\mathcal{M}_s, \mathbf{p}_s(f) \models A \Leftrightarrow f \in \exists(A|\mathcal{G}_s)?$$

This is almost true, as the next results show.

Theorem 18 *If φ is positive, $\varphi \subseteq \mathbf{p}_s^{-1}(\varphi_s)$.*

PROOF. If φ is atomic, this is the truth definition of φ on $\mathcal{M}$. The cases $\vee$, $\wedge$ are trivial. Suppose $f \in \exists x\psi$, then there exists $g =_x f$ such that $g \in \psi$. By the inductive hypothesis, $g_s \in \psi_s$. But $g =_x f$ implies $g_s =_x f_s$, whence $f_s \in \exists x\psi$. For the case $f = \forall x\psi$ we need the surjectivity of the projection mappings. Indeed, let $f \in \forall x\psi$; we have to show that $f_s \in (\forall x\psi)_s$. Let $h \in \mathcal{F}_s$ be such that $h =_x f_s$. By surjectivity, there is $g \in \mathcal{F}$ such that for all $t \in T : g_t(y) = f_t(y)$ $(y \neq x)$ and $g_s(x) = h(x)$; then $g_s = h$ and $g \in \psi$, whence $h = g_s \in \psi_s$. □

Corollary 19 *If φ is positive, $\exists(\varphi|\mathcal{G}_s) \subseteq \mathbf{p}_s^{-1}(\varphi_s)$.*

PROOF. Since $\mathbf{p}_s^{-1}(\varphi_s) \in \mathcal{G}_s$, the statement follows from the Galois correspondence for $\exists(\bullet|\mathcal{G}_s)$. □

This result is best possible in the sense that we cannot expect it to hold even for negations of atomic formulas: $\neg A$ may be false on $\mathcal{M}$ because it fails on a coordinate $t > s$, and in that case $\exists(\neg A|\mathcal{G}_s)$ will not be contained in $\mathbf{p}_s^{-1}(\neg A_s)$. However, the corollary can be strengthened in the sense that under an additional, harmless, condition, we have equality when φ is a predicate.

Definition 26 The pair $\pi_s : \mathcal{M} \longrightarrow \mathcal{M}_s$ is *proper refining* with respect to a predicate A, if there does not exist a formula τ such that $A \subseteq \mathbf{p}_s^{-1}(\tau_s)$ and $\emptyset \neq \tau_s \subset A_s$.

As the next proposition shows, if the pair $\pi_s : \mathcal{M} \longrightarrow \mathcal{M}_s$ is proper refining with respect to a predicate A, then $A_s = \{g \in \mathcal{F}_s | \mathcal{M}_s, g \models A\}$ represents our best estimate of A at stage s.

Corollary 20 *If the pair $\pi_s : \mathcal{M} \longrightarrow \mathcal{M}_s$ is proper refining with respect to a non-empty predicate A, then $\exists(A|\mathcal{G}_s) = \mathbf{p}_s^{-1}(A_s)$.*

PROOF. First observe that (i) and (ii) are equivalent.

i) $\mathbf{p}_s^{-1}(A_s) \subseteq \exists(A|\mathcal{G}_s)$;

ii) $\forall C \in \mathcal{G}_s[A \subseteq C \Rightarrow \mathbf{p}_s^{-1}(A_s) \subseteq C]$.

So if (i) is false, there is $C \in \mathcal{G}_s$ with

(*) $A \subseteq C$ and $\mathbf{p}_s^{-1}(A_s) \setminus C \neq \emptyset$.

Since the frame $\mathcal{G}_s$ is generated from elements $\mathbf{p}_s^{-1}(\tau_s)$, C is of the form $\bigcap_I \mathbf{p}_s^{-1}(\tau_s^i)$ for some index set I. Now (*) gives

$$A \subseteq \mathbf{p}_s^{-1}(\tau_s^i) \text{ and } \mathbf{p}_s^{-1}(A_s) \setminus \mathbf{p}_s^{-1}(\tau_s^i) \neq \emptyset$$

for some $i \in I$. By theorem 18, $A \subseteq \mathbf{p}_s^{-1}(A_s)$, and hence $A \subseteq \mathbf{p}_s^{-1}(A_s \wedge \tau^i)$. But also $\mathbf{p}_s^{-1}(A_s \wedge \tau^i) \subset \mathbf{p}_s^{-1}(A_s)$, contradicting that $\pi_s : \mathcal{M} \longrightarrow \mathcal{M}_s$ is proper refining with respect to A. □

If the bonding mappings, hence the projections, are surjective, we can always modify the interpretation of the predicates A in such a way that we will have $\exists(A|\mathcal{G}_s) = \mathbf{p}_s^{-1}(A_s)$.

Let A be an n-ary predicate. Write $h_{st}^{-1}[\varphi(\vec{a})]$ for $\{h_{st}^{-1}(\vec{a}) : \mathcal{M}_t \models \varphi(\vec{a})\}$, and $\pi_t^{-1}[\varphi(\vec{a})]$ for $\{\pi_t^{-1}(\vec{a}) : \mathcal{M}_t \models \varphi(\vec{a})\}$. Modify $\mathcal{M}_s$ by replacing A_s by $A_s^\dagger$, defined as follows

$$A_s^\dagger := A_s \cap \bigcap_{t \leq s} \bigcap_{\varphi} \{h_{st}^{-1}[\varphi(\vec{a})] : A \subseteq \pi_t^{-1}[\varphi(\vec{a})]\}.$$

Here, φ should be a formula in the original language, not containing E. We have to show that the indexed set of models thus obtained forms an inverse system with respect to the original bonding mappings, with inverse limit $\mathcal{M}$.

Assume for simplicity that A is monadic, then we have to prove

$$a \in A_s^\dagger \textit{ implies } h_{st}(a) \in A_t^\dagger.$$

Choose B such that for some $\varphi(x)$ and some $r \leq t$, $B = \{a : \mathcal{M}_r \models \varphi(a)\}$ and $A \subseteq \pi^{-1}{}_r(B)$. We have to show that $h_{st}(a) \in h_{tr}^{-1}(B)$. But by construction $A_s^\dagger \subseteq h_{sr}^{-1}(B)$, whence $h_{tr}(h_{st}(a)) = h_{sr}^{-1}(a) \in B$.

Lastly, we have to show that for all threads ξ in $\mathcal{M}$, $A^\dagger(\xi)$ iff $A(\xi)$. By construction one has: $A(\xi)$ implies $A_s^\dagger(\xi_s)$, for all s; whence $A(\xi)$ implies $A^\dagger(\xi)$.

Conversely, for all s: $A^\dagger_s \subseteq A_s$; whence one has the following implications

$$\begin{array}{ll} & A^\dagger(\xi) \\ \Rightarrow & \forall s A^\dagger_s(\xi_s) \\ \Rightarrow & \forall s A_s(\xi_s) \\ \Rightarrow & A(\xi). \end{array}$$

Now redefine the frames $\mathcal{G}_s$ by means of the predicates $A^\dagger$. We then have $\exists(A|\mathcal{G}_s) = \mathbf{p}_s^{-1}(A^\dagger_s)$. The inclusion from left to right holds because the $\mathcal{G}_s$ were redefined. To see that the other inclusion holds, it suffices to show that for $B \in \mathcal{G}_s$: if $A \subseteq B$, then $\mathbf{p}_s^{-1}(A^\dagger_s) \subseteq B$. By definition of $\mathcal{G}_s$, B is of the form $\{f : \mathcal{M}_s, f_s \models \varphi\}$ for some formula φ. Since the projections are surjective, one may universally quantify the variables, say $\vec{y}$, occurring in φ but not in A; whence $A \subseteq \{f : \mathcal{M}_s, f_s \models \forall\vec{y}\varphi\}$. By definition of $A^\dagger_s$, $\mathbf{p}_s^{-1}(A^\dagger_s) \subseteq \{f : \mathcal{M}_s, f_s \models \forall\vec{y}\varphi\} \subseteq \{f : \mathcal{M}_s, f_s \models \varphi\}$, and we are done.

Note that we cannot expect this in the case of non-surjective projections, because filtering operates on the elements of $\mathcal{M}$ that is, the set of real objects, whereas now a model $\mathcal{M}_s$ may also contain imaginary objects.

Lastly, we extend Corollary 20 to formulas of the form $\exists x_1 \ldots \exists x_n \theta$, θ a conjunction of predicates.

Theorem 21 *Let φ be a formula of the form $\exists x\theta$, where θ is a conjuntion of atomic formulas; we assume θ is non-empty on $\mathcal{M}$. Assume furthermore that $\pi_s : \mathcal{M} \longrightarrow \mathcal{M}_s$ is proper refining w.r.t. θ.*[12] *If x is a variable, let $\mathcal{B}_{s,x}$ be the subalgebra of $\mathcal{B}_s$ determined by formulas in which x does not occur free, and let $\mathcal{G}_{s,x}$ be the frame generated by $\mathcal{B}_{s,x}$. Then we have*

$$\mathcal{M}_s, g \models \exists x\theta \Leftrightarrow \forall f \in \mathcal{F}[f_s = g \Rightarrow \mathcal{M}, f \models \exists(\theta|\mathcal{G}_{s,x})]$$

PROOF. Suppose $\mathcal{M}_s, g \models \exists x\theta$, and let f satisfy $f_s = g$; we have to show $f \in \exists(\theta|\mathcal{G}_{s,x})$. There exists $g' =_x g$ such that $\mathcal{M}_s, g' \models \theta$. By surjectivity of $\mathbf{p}_s$ there exists f' such that $f' =_x f$. By corollary 20, we must have $f' \in \exists(\theta|\mathcal{G}_s)$, hence $f' \in \exists(\theta|\mathcal{G}_{s,x})$. A little reflection shows that $\exists(\theta|\mathcal{G}_{s,x})$ is $=_x$-invariant, whence $f \in \exists(\theta|\mathcal{G}_{s,x})$. Conversely, suppose that for f with $f_s = g$ we have $\mathcal{M}, f \models \exists(\theta|\mathcal{G}_s, x)$. By theorem 18, $\theta \subseteq \exists x\theta \subseteq \mathbf{p}_s^{-1}((\exists x\theta)_s)$. Since $\mathbf{p}_s^{-1}((\exists x\theta)_s) \in \mathcal{G}_{s,x}$, by the Galois property $\exists(\theta|\mathcal{G}_{s,x}) \subseteq \mathbf{p}_s^{-1}((\exists x\theta)_s)$, in particular $\mathcal{M}_s, g \models \exists x\theta$. □

Corollary 22 *Assuming the conditions of the theorem, we also have*

$$\mathcal{M}_s, g \models \exists x\theta \Leftrightarrow \forall f \in \mathcal{F}[f_s = g \Rightarrow \mathcal{M}, f \models \exists x \exists(\theta|\mathcal{G}_s)]$$

The extension to formulas of the form $\exists x_1 \ldots \exists x_n \theta$ is straightforward. This result explains the particular formalisation of perception reports adopted in the next section.

[12] Note that this may be different from assuming that π_s is proper refining w.r.t. the conjuncts of θ. In general, proper refinement is *not* preserved under conjunction.

To conclude, we conceive of the relationship between approximating models and filters in the following manner. The basic idea is that perception must be viewed as some form of filtering of reality $\mathcal{M}$. Part of the filtering consists of the inevitable blurring imposed upon us by our perceptual apparatus; this is formally captured by the homomorphic images $\mathcal{M}_w$. (In the paper, part of a system $\langle \mathcal{M}_s, h_{st} \rangle_{s,t \in T}$ of first order models which has $\mathcal{M}$ as inverse limit.) Additional filtering occurs because of restricted perceptual fields and the effect of perspective. This is not part of the perceptual apparatus, neither is it a property of reality; it arises as a consequence of 'being in the world', hence it is put in the filters only. Very roughly speaking, $\mathcal{M}_w$ is concerned with the possible structuring of experience, i.e., concepts, whereas the filters $\exists(\bullet|\mathcal{G}_w)$ relate to actual experience, i.e., perception.

6.4 Perception, or: non-monotonicity, the hard way

Now that the formal apparatus is in place, we shall develop a logical semantics for direct perception reports in two steps. First, we discuss the logical form of perception reports using conditional quantification. We discuss some of the inferences of section 6.2 in terms of this semantics. However, it only gives perception relative to an approximation, which is non-veridical. The important veridical part expects that what is perceived will remain the case for more refined approximations. Such expectations are defeasible, and should therefore be given in terms of non-monotonic rules. This is what we shall do in section 6.4.2.

6.4.1 The logical form of perception reports

The logic of vision sustains a natural distinction between directly and indirectly perceived objects. A *directly* perceived object is represented by a free variable, which can only be 'measured' with finite precision; the degrees of precision being given by conditional quantifiers $\exists(\bullet|\mathcal{G})$. Instead, '*indirectly*' perceived objects are represented by means of bound variables. Some examples should clarify the distinction. In the formalisations x corresponds with the object perceived directly, and the frame $\mathcal{G}_I$ with the filter of the speaker's perceptual field.

(21) 'I see this arm' becomes: $\exists(A(x)|\mathcal{G}_I)$.

Here, the demonstrative 'this' is interpreted as the variable x, which receives its value from a contextually given assignment.

There are two ways to interpret proper names. Firstly, one may interpret (22) with a demonstrative element as: 'this object I see is Sharon'. Formally this corresponds to having a free variable in the representation, as in (22).

(22) 'I see Sharon' becomes: $\exists(x = s|\mathcal{G}_I)$.

The constant s, for Sharon, denotes an object in reality. Secondly, one may read (22) indefinitely as: 'an object I see is Sharon', as in (23).

(23) $\exists x \exists (x = s|\mathcal{G}_I)$.

In what follows, we shall often use the open form. Here are some further examples:

(24) 'I see a boy' becomes: $\exists x \exists (B(x)|\mathcal{G}_I)$; and

(25) 'I see a boy swim' becomes: $\exists (B(x) \wedge S(x)|\mathcal{G}_I)$ or
$\exists x \exists (B(x) \wedge S(x)|\mathcal{G}_I)$

An example of a report with an indirectly perceived object is (26).

(26) 'I saw Jack consult a doctor' becomes:
$\exists (x = j \wedge \exists y[D(y) \wedge C(x,y)]|\mathcal{G}_I)$.

The examples indicate that the semantics for perception reports describing objects is similar to those describing scenes; mainly the descriptive content within the scope of 'to see' varies, cf. (Hintikka 1969).

It should be noticed that in all the examples the perception operator has an open statement within its scope; some of the objects described must be seen directly. This is crucial, for a frame $\mathcal{G}$ acts trivially on 'closed' truths or falsities; $\exists(\mathbf{1}|\mathcal{G}) = \mathbf{1}$ and $\exists(\mathbf{0}|\mathcal{G}) = \mathbf{0}$. From this we also see that substitution may fail

$$x = t \;\&\; \exists(\varphi(x)|\mathcal{G}) \not\Rightarrow \exists(\varphi(t)|\mathcal{G}),$$

with t a constant or a variable. Similar effects occur in case of the non-veridical principles discussed in section 6.2.[13]

Retract of perception

Let us start with a simple case based on (7) from Miller and Johnson-Laird. In the formalisation, the first sentence gives $f \in \exists(R(x)|\mathcal{G}_s)$; $f(x)$ is perceived as a rock formation at stage s, and not as the effect of trees in the mist ($E(x)$). However, $f \in \exists(R(x)|\mathcal{G}_s)$ need not imply $f \in R(x)$. Therefore, $f \in \exists(R(x)|\mathcal{G}_s)$ can be retracted to give $f \in \exists(E(x)|\mathcal{G}_t)$ for some stage $t \geq s$, i.e. the *perception* of the effect created by trees in the mist.

Partial perception

Perhaps the first requirement for an analysis of 'see' is that it should be able to cope with reports of the following kind, employing NPs, infinite VPs, and PPs:

$$\frac{\text{Whitehead saw Russell} \quad \text{Russell winked}}{\text{Whitehead saw a winking man}}$$

$$\frac{\text{Whitehead saw Russell} \quad \text{Russell winked}}{\text{Whitehead saw Russell wink}}$$

$$\frac{\text{Whitehead saw Russell} \quad \text{Russell had his shirt unbuttoned}}{\text{Whitehead saw Russell with his shirt unbuttoned}}$$

[13] We use 'non-veridical' as short for: not necessarily veridical (instead of: always not veridical).

The common feature of these examples of invalid inferences is that the sentence 'Whitehead saw Russell' refers to a stage of approximation s, whereas the factual statements are true in an approximation t possibly different from s. In particular, t may be incomparable to s—e.g., if Whitehead saw Russell from behind—or t may be a refinement of s but still the distance between Whitehead and Russell could have been too large for Whitehead to actually see, e.g., that Russell had his shirt unbuttoned.

Observe that formalising the possibly non-veridical semantics of 'w *saw* φ', φ positive, as the conditional quantification $\exists(\varphi|\mathcal{H})$, with $\mathcal{H}$ a suitable frame assigned to perceiver w, would be too crude.. It forces us to declare the above inferences valid; by monotonicity we must have

$$\exists(x = r|\mathcal{G}_s) \wedge \forall x(x = r \rightarrow W(x)) \rightarrow \exists(x = r \wedge W(x)|\mathcal{G}_s),$$

and analogously for the other examples. However, we have seen in section 6.3.4 that taking perspective into account dictates the use of quantifiers conditional on evidential frames; and for such quantifiers

$$\exists(x = r \wedge W(x)|\mathcal{G}_s)$$

may be undefined, making the inference invalid.

Quantifiers

Recall the following pair of sentences, illustrating in- and exportation of $\exists$

(14) Jack saw a girl swim.

(15) A girl is such that Jack saw her swim.

We remarked that neither of these sentences seems to imply the other, if one drops veridicality. On the other hand, the usual translation into first order logic, or even generalised quantifier logic, does give equivalence, cf. (van der Does 1991). We shall now translate these sentences in the framework of conditional quantification; it is then easily seen under what conditions one or both of the two implications fail.[14]

Let V be the set of assignments corresponding to Jack's restricted perceptual field, and let $\mathcal{H}$ be an algebra on V, given by Σ, filtering his field of vision. Whenever this is convenient, we shall assume that V is determined by the formula $D(x) \equiv S(j, x)$ ('D' for 'domain'). Disregarding $D(x)$ for a moment, (14) has interpretation (14'), and (15) has interpretation (15').

(14') $\exists x \exists(G(x) \wedge S(x)|\mathcal{H})$

(15') $\exists x(G(x) \wedge \exists(S(x)|\mathcal{H}))$

In studying some of the relationships between (14') and (15'), we distinguish several cases.

[14]For simplicity we assume Frobenius ('taking out what is known'); for the general case see (van der Does and van Lambalgen 1997).

Case (a) $G(x) \in \mathcal{H}$: 'Jack recognises a girl when he sees one, and he can see all girls'. Then (14) and (15) are equivalent. By 'taking out what is known' we have

$$\exists(G(x) \wedge S(x)|\mathcal{H}) = G(x) \wedge \exists(S(x)|\mathcal{H})$$

whence also

$$\exists x \exists(G(x) \wedge S(x)|\mathcal{H}) = \exists x(G(x) \wedge \exists(S(x)|\mathcal{H})).$$

Case (b) $G(x) \wedge D(x) \in \mathcal{H}$: 'Jack recognises a girl when he sees one, but he might not see all girls'. Now (14') can be derived from (15') by 'taking out what is known' and monotonicity. We have

$$\begin{aligned} & D(x) \wedge G(x) \wedge \exists(S(x)|\mathcal{H}) \\ = \quad & \exists(G(x) \wedge D(x) \wedge S(x)|\mathcal{H}) \\ \subseteq \quad & \exists(G(x) \wedge D(x)|\mathcal{H}) \end{aligned}$$

Now notice that $\exists(S(x)|\mathcal{H})$ should be a subset of $D(x)$, since $\mathcal{H}$ represents Jack's perceptual field. Then actually

$$G(x) \wedge \exists(S(x)|\mathcal{H}) \subseteq \exists(G(x) \wedge D(x)|\mathcal{H})$$

whence $\exists x(G(x) \wedge \exists(S(x)|\mathcal{H})) \models \exists x \exists(G(x) \wedge D(x)|\mathcal{H})$.

This result may seem surprising; couldn't it be the case that there is a girl whom Jack perceives as swimming, without actually being aware that it is *she* who swims? No, because the anaphor 'her' in the scope of 'see' in (15) is taken to imply that the girl is imported in Jack's visual field; since he correctly identifies girls, (14) follows. Of course, we have just restated the above proof in plain English.

Case (c) $G(x) \notin \mathcal{H}$: 'Jack can see all girls, but he cannot identify them correctly'. In this case the derivation of (14') from (15') fails by an argument similar to example 4 in section 6.3.3. That is , let $\mathcal{M}$ be an ω-saturated model, and $\mathcal{H}$ a frame on the set of assignments of $\mathcal{M}$ such that

$$G(x) \wedge S(x) = \mathbf{0} \in \mathcal{H}$$

but for every $A \in \mathcal{H}$ with $\forall x(S(x) \rightarrow A(x))$:

$$\exists x(A(x) \wedge G(x))$$

This is only possible when $G(x) \notin \mathcal{H}$! Then $\neg \exists x \exists(G(x) \wedge S(x)|\mathcal{H})$, but $\exists x(G(x) \wedge \exists(S(x)|\mathcal{H}))$. Notice that in this situation, (15) could be formulated more accurately as 'A girl is such that Jack sees *it* swim'.

The direction from (14) to (15) along with many other inferences will be treated in (van der Does and van Lambalgen 1997).

This section has shown that the non-veridical aspects of perception reports already uses much of the intricacies of the logic of vision, but the situation becomes even more interesting in case of their veridical uses.

6.4.2 Veridical perception

Recall that we took the expression 'I see an arm' to mean the conjunction of (i) and (ii).

i) 'with the present approximation the object that I focus on is identified as an arm',

ii) 'I expect this to be the case for every more refined approximation'.

The second condition is evidently non-monotonic: more precise information may contradict the expectation expressed in (ii).

The expectation that a percept is stable under an increasing series of ever finer approximations can be captured by means of a non-monotonic rule governing the conditional quantifiers. We assume the reader is familiar with default logic in the sense of Reiter. For the following discussion an inverse system $\langle \mathcal{M}_s, h_{st} \rangle_{s,t \in T}$ with inverse limit $\mathcal{M}$ and a corresponding system of quantifiers $\exists(\bullet|\mathcal{G}_s)$ is given. If 's' stands for the present approximation, the statement (i)

> with the present approximation, x, the object that I focus on, is identified as an arm

is formalised as $\exists(A(x)|\mathcal{G}_s)$. In Reiter's format, statement (ii) would then be expressed by the default rule

$$\exists(A(x)|\mathcal{G}_s) : \exists(A(x)|\mathcal{G}_t)/\exists(A(x)|\mathcal{G}_t) \text{ (for } t > s),$$

which says that if evidence at stage s supports $A(x)$, and if it is still consistent to assume $A(x)$ at stage t, then assume $A(x)$ at stage t.

However, a different, 'evidential', interpretation better fits the perceptual situation. The discussion of Marr's theory of object recognition in 3.5 strongly suggests that the stage s, given by (i), should represent the *maximal available information*: we move downward in the hierarchy of 3-D models until the finite resolution of the image leads to a branching. First assume that the frames $\mathcal{G}_s$ are generated by algebras. Let f be an assignment. Suppose $f \in \exists(\varphi|\mathcal{G}_s)$ and that at stage s we know that it is inconsistent that $f \in \exists(\varphi|\mathcal{G}_t)$. Then there is an element $C \in \mathcal{G}_s$ such that $f \in C$ but $C \cap \exists(\varphi|\mathcal{G}_t) = \mathbf{0}$. We then have $\exists(C \cap \exists(\varphi|\mathcal{G}_t)|\mathcal{G}_s) = \mathbf{0}$, whence by Frobenius $C \cap \exists(\exists(\varphi|\mathcal{G}_s)|\mathcal{G}_t) = C \cap \exists(\varphi|\mathcal{G}_s) = \mathbf{0}$. But this contradicts our assumption that $f \in \exists(\varphi|\mathcal{G}_s)$. Hence at stage s we may assume it is consistent that $f \in \exists(\varphi|\mathcal{G}_t)$.

Note that we essentially used the fact that stage s is maximal, in choosing the separating element C in $\mathcal{G}_s$. This argument works nicely when Frobenius is available, but if it is not, e.g. when the frames are generated by positive formulas, we must use a result mentioned earlier, namely that for a positive formula φ and family of frames $\mathcal{G}_s$, there exists s such that for all $t \geq s$, for all positive ψ,

$$\exists(\varphi \wedge \exists(\psi|\mathcal{G}_t)) = \exists(\varphi|\mathcal{G}_t) \wedge \exists(\psi|\mathcal{G}_t).$$

Hence in this case, *maximal available information* should include the requirement that Frobenius holds for φ. This is of course no surprise, since the formulation of the default rule entails that we should be able to consider negative information.

Motivated by these considerations we shall take a default to be a rule of the form

$$\exists(\varphi|\mathcal{G}_s)/\exists(\varphi|\mathcal{G}_t)$$

with φ a *positive* formula. This rule should be interpreted as: 'if I have observed φ at stage s, and s represents the maximum available accuracy, then I may assume that I will observe φ at stage t.[15]

Having introduced the expectation inherent in every perceptual experience in the form of a default rule, we return to the principle of veridicality, which would sanction inferences of the form

$$\frac{\text{I see an arm}}{\text{There is an arm}}$$

or formally

$$\frac{\exists x \exists(A(x)|\mathcal{G}_s)}{\exists x A(x)}$$

To see the connection between the default rules and veridicality, assume that we have an assignment f such that some maximal information state s, $f \in$
$E(A(x)|\mathcal{G}_s)$. By the default rule VER, for all $t \geq s$ (hence for all t) $f \in \exists(A(x)|\mathcal{G}_t)$. Does it follow that $\mathcal{M}, f \models A(x)$? For positive formulas, the answer is 'yes'.

Proposition 23 *Assume the bonding mappings are surjective. For* positive φ,

$$\bigcap_{s\in T}\exists(\varphi|\mathcal{G}_s) = \varphi.$$

This result fails already for negations of atomic formulas! □

A related result, with 'positive' replaced by 'positive primitive', holds if the bonding mappings are not necessarily surjective. Proposition 23 is a consequence of Theorem 30, which characterises the formulas φ with $\bigcap_{s\in T}\exists(\varphi|\mathcal{G}_s) = \varphi$. The theorem is proved in the next section, which is on different kinds of stable information in vision. A compactness argument gives

Corollary 24 *Let the bonding mappings be surjective and φ be positive. If for all $s \in T$, $\mathcal{M} \models \exists x_1 \ldots \exists x_n \exists(\varphi|\mathcal{G}_s)$, then $\mathcal{M} \models \exists x_1 \ldots \exists x_n \varphi$.* □

[15]The difference between Reiter's interpretation and ours is that we take the consistency of the justification to be relative to a stage s, whereas in Reiter's case it refers to an extension of the default theory. Here, we shall forego a discussion of the possible notions of extensions applicable in this context; see (Voorbraak 1997).

From these insights we get veridicality for existential quantifiers in the following sense

$$\frac{\exists x[\exists(\varphi(x)|\mathcal{G}_s)]}{\exists x\varphi(x)}\ \exists$$

To see this, assume $\mathcal{M}, f \models \exists x\exists(\varphi(x)|\mathcal{G}_s)]$. Then there is $g =_x f$ such that $\mathcal{M}, g \models \exists(\varphi(x)|\mathcal{G}_s)$. Choose such a g. Veridicality gives: $\mathcal{M}, g \models \exists(\varphi(x)|\mathcal{G}_t)$, for all stages t. Whence, for all stages t: $\mathcal{M}, f \models \exists x\exists(\varphi(x)|\mathcal{G}_t)$. By Corollary 24: $\mathcal{M}, f \models \exists x\varphi(x)$, as required.

In this way the logic of vision predicts that direct perception is essentially limited to positive information. This corresponds well to the special rôle given to positive information in situation semantics (Barwise 1981), (Kamp 1984), and event semantics ((Higginbotham 1983)).

6.5 Stability in vision

In vision two kinds of stable information play an important rôle. The first is *constraints* holding of perceptual information, the second is *stability of percepts* under refinement of information. In both cases one would like to know how stability is related to truth-in-reality; this is the topic of the present section. For constraints the answers take the shape of preservation theorems concerning refining systems and inverse limits. A convergence theorem for conditional quantifiers provides the answer for stable percepts.

6.5.1 Preservation

To motivate the material in this section, consider a typical constraint on approximations such as: 'human beings have a left and a right arm'. This constraint is expressed by means of a sentence of the form $\forall x(\varphi \rightarrow \exists y\exists z\psi)$, where φ, ψ are quantifier free. Suppose the constraint is true in all sufficiently refined approximations. Does this imply that it is true in reality, i.e. on the inverse limit $\mathcal{M}$ of a refining system $\langle \mathcal{M}_s, h_{st}\rangle_{s,t\in T}$? More generally, what is the logical form of the constraints which ensure truth? This is an abstract version of one of Marr's main questions, namely, what can one derive from available information? We now give a complete answer in terms of several preservation theorems.

Recall that an inverse system is *total and refining* if the bonding mappings are homomorphisms (hence by definition surjective), and *refining* if the bonding mappings h_{st} just satisfy condition (ρ) of section 6.3.2. The first concept reflects the case where all objects in an approximation are supposed to correspond to real objects, whereas the second concept allows for purported objects to vanish under closer scrutiny. A formula is *positive* if it is equivalent to a formula containing only $\exists, \forall, \wedge, \vee$ and $\perp$; a formula is *positive primitive* if it is equivalent to a formula containing only $\exists, \wedge, \vee$ and $\perp$.

A sentence θ is *preserved* by an inverse system $\langle \mathcal{M}_s, h_{st}\rangle_{s,t\in T}$ if whenever

$\mathcal{M}_s \models \theta$ and the inverse limit $\mathcal{M}$ is nonempty, then $\mathcal{M} \models \theta$. To simplify the fomulation of definitions and theorems we assume that all structures involved are models for the same signature. The results easily transfer to the case where for any predicate A, there is $t \in T$ such that for $s \geq t$, A is interpreted on $\mathcal{M}_s$.

Definition 27 A *(primitive) vision formula* is a conjunction of sentences of the form

$$\forall \vec{x}(\varphi \rightarrow \psi),$$

where φ and ψ are positive (primitive) formulas.[16]

Theorem 25 (1) *Each vision formula is preserved by any total and refining inverse system $\langle \mathcal{M}_s, h_{st}\rangle_{s,t\in T}$ of finite models.*

(2) *Each primitive vision formula is preserved by any refining inverse system $\langle \mathcal{M}_s, h_{st}\rangle_{s,t\in T}$ of finite models.*

Theorem 25 follows easily from the following lemma.

Lemma 26 *For positive formulas φ the following are equivalent*

i) *$\mathcal{M}$ is isomorphic to the inverse limit of a total refining system $\langle \mathcal{M}_s, h_{st}\rangle_{s,t\in T}$ with $\mathcal{M}_s, f_s \models \varphi$, for all $s \in T$;*

ii) $\mathcal{M}, f \models \varphi$.

Analogously for refining inverse systems and positive primitive formulas.

PROOF. That (ii) implies (i) is immediate from the fact that the projections $\pi_s : \mathcal{M} \longrightarrow \mathcal{M}_s$ are homomorphism, and that homomorphisms preserve positive formula's (see, e.g., Chang and Keisler 1990, p. 151).

As to the direction from (i) to (ii), let $\mathcal{M}$ be isomorphic to the inverse limit of a system $\langle \mathcal{M}_s, h_{st}\rangle_{s,t\in T}$ with $\mathcal{M}_s, f_s \models \varphi$, for all $s \in T$. The cases were φ is atomic, conjunctive, and universal formulas are trivial. So assume that φ is the disjunction $\varphi_0 \vee \varphi_1$. Then there is a cofinal $T' \subseteq T$ such that $\mathcal{M}_t, f_t \models \varphi_i$ ($i = 0$ or $i = 1$, $t \in T'$).[17] By the induction hypothesis: $\mathcal{M}', f|_{T'} \models \varphi_i$ with $\mathcal{M}'$ the inverse limit of $\langle \mathcal{M}_{s'}, h_{s't'}\rangle_{s',t'\in T'}$, and $f|_{T'}$ the restriction to T'. It is not difficult to show that $\mathcal{M}$ is isomorphic to $\mathcal{M}'$. Therefore, $\mathcal{M}, f \models \varphi_i$, and $\mathcal{M}, f \models \varphi$ as required.

Finally, let φ be an existential formula $\exists x\psi$, and let

$$\widehat{x}.\psi_s := \mathbf{p}_s^{-1}(\{g \in \mathcal{F}_s : g =_x f_s \ \&\ \mathcal{M}_s, f_s \models \psi\}).$$

The set $\widehat{x}.\psi_s$ is closed, being the intersection of the closed sets

$$\mathbf{p}_s^{-1}(\{g \in \mathcal{F}_s : g =_x f_s\}) \text{ and } \mathbf{p}_s^{-1}(\psi_s).$$

By assumption $\widehat{x}.\psi_s \neq \emptyset$, and by preservation of positive formulas under homomorphisms $\widehat{x}.\psi_s \subseteq \widehat{x}.\psi_t$ if $s \geq t$. Since T is directed, $\{\widehat{x}.\psi_s : s \in T\}$ has

[16] The notation '$\vec{x}$' denotes a finite sequence of variables; similarly, '$f(\vec{a})$' as used below, denotes a finite sequence of function values.

[17] T' is *cofinal* in T iff: $\forall t \in T \exists t' \in T' : t' > t$.

the finite intersection property. Compactness of the topology **T** gives a g with

$$g \in \bigcap_{t \in T} \widehat{x}.\psi_s.$$

For this g: $g =_x f$ and $\mathcal{M}, g \models \psi$, whence $\mathcal{M}, f \models \varphi$.[18] □

The proof of the lemma tells us something about *negations of positive formulas* as well: not only $\mathcal{M} \not\models \varphi(\xi)$ iff for some t, $\mathcal{M}_t \not\models \varphi(\xi_t)$, but actually if $\mathcal{M}_t \not\models \varphi(\xi_t)$ then for $s \geq t$, $\mathcal{M}_s \not\models \varphi(\xi_s)$. Here are some examples of vision formulas.

Example A: The class of vision formulas, although defined by means of positive formulas, includes sentences involving negation: e.g., $\forall\vec{x}(\neg\varphi \rightarrow \psi)$ is equivalent to $\forall\vec{x}(\varphi \vee \psi)$; $\forall\vec{x}(\varphi \rightarrow \neg\psi)$ is equivalent to $\forall\vec{x}\varphi \wedge \psi \rightarrow \bot$; and $\exists\vec{x}\neg\varphi$ is equivalent to $\forall\vec{x}(\varphi \rightarrow \bot)$. Here, φ and ψ are positive. On the other hand, a simple formula such as $\exists x(A(x) \wedge \neg B(x))$ is not a vision formula. At any particular stage we can be uncertain whether an A is in fact also a B, even though in the limit there is no longer uncertainty. [•]

Example B: Universal Horn formulas: $\forall\vec{x}(\varphi \rightarrow \psi)$, where φ is a conjunction of predicates, and ψ is a predicate; these formulas express the presence of a law. [•]

Example C: Formulas which express 'there are at most n x such that φ', where φ is positive, since these formulas are of the form

$$\forall x, x_1, \ldots, x_n(\varphi \rightarrow x = x_1 \vee \ldots \vee x = x_n). \qquad [\bullet]$$

A conspicuous example of a formula which is not a vision formula, is the one which expresses 'there are at least n x such that φ', i.e.,

$$\exists x, x_1, \ldots, x_n(\neg(x = x_1) \wedge \ldots \wedge \neg(x = x_n) \wedge \varphi(x)),$$

and indeed it can be shown that such formulas need not be preserved. This is why statements such as 'a human being has two arms', in order to be preserved, have to be formulated positively, for example as 'a human being has a left and a right arm'. That this is no accident is shown by the next theorem.

Theorem 27 (1) *Suppose θ is preserved by all total and refining inverse systems. Then θ is equivalent to a vision formula.*

(2) *Suppose θ is preserved by all refining inverse systems. Then θ is equivalent to a primitive vision formula.*

The proof of (1) combines two ingredients. Firstly, it uses the fact that in a sense the inverse limit is the least refinement of an inverse system.

---

[18] Algebraically one combines the nonemptyness of

$$\lambda x.\psi_s := \{d_t \in |\mathcal{M}_t| : \mathcal{M}_t, f t^{x}_{d_t} \models \psi\},$$

for each $s \in T$, with the fact that the homomorphism h_{st} preserve positive formulas. Thus Theorem 13 can be applied to the system $\langle \lambda x.\varphi_s, h'_{st}\rangle_{s,t \in T}$, with h'_{st} the restriction of h_{st} to $\lambda x.\psi_s$.

Proposition 28 *Let* **S** *be the inverse system* $\langle \mathcal{M}_s, h_{st} \rangle_{s,t \in T}$. *A model* $\mathcal{N}$ refines **S**, *iff there are homomorphisms* $g_s : \mathcal{N} \longrightarrow \mathcal{M}_s$ *satisfying*

$$h_{st} \circ g_s = g_t,$$

for all $s, t \in T$. *The inverse limit* $\mathcal{M}$ *of* **S** *is* least *among these refinements in the sense that for all refinements* $\mathcal{N}$ *of* **S** *there is a homomorphism* $n : \mathcal{N} \longrightarrow \mathcal{M}$ *such that* $g_s = n \circ \pi_s$, *for all* $s \in T$. *In a commuting diagram*

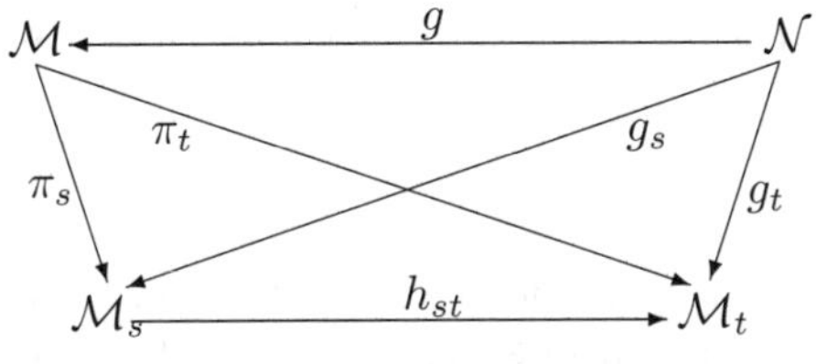

FIGURE 5 *Refinement*

Secondly, the proof of Theorem 27(1) uses Keisler's refinement of Lyndon's Theorem.

Theorem 29 **Lyndon's Theorem** *For special models* $\mathcal{M}$ *and* $\mathcal{N}$ *of the same cardinality (i) and (ii) are equivalent.*

i) *Each positive* φ *true in* $\mathcal{M}$ *is true in* $\mathcal{N}$;
ii) *There is a homomorphism* $h : \mathcal{M} \longrightarrow \mathcal{N}$.

PROOFSKETCH OF THEOREM 27(1) Let θ be preserved under inverse limits. Consider

$$\Sigma := \{\psi : \psi \textit{ is a vision formula} \ \& \ \theta \models \psi\}.$$

Due to compactness, θ is shown to be equivalent to a vision formula, if it can be proved that $\Sigma \models \theta$. Here we restrict ourselves to special models of infinite cardinality λ (for appropriate λ this suffices, since each countable model has a special elementary extension of that size; cf. Chang and Keisler 1990, 5.1.8).

Let $\mathcal{M}$ be a special model of cardinality λ such that $\mathcal{M} \models \Sigma$. To conclude $\mathcal{M} \models \theta$ one tries to view $\mathcal{M}$ as the inverse limit of a sequence $\langle M_n, h_{nm} \rangle_{n,m \in \omega}$ with $\mathcal{M}_n \models \theta$.

Consider $\Gamma := \{\varphi : \varphi \textit{ positive} \ \& \ \mathcal{M} \models \varphi\}$ and an enumeration $\psi_0, \ldots, \psi_n, \ldots$ of the set $\{\psi : \psi \textit{ positive} \ \& \ \mathcal{M} \not\models \psi\}$. Suppose $\mathcal{N}_n$ has been constructed. By compactness and the fact that $\mathcal{M} \models \Sigma$ one find a special model $\mathcal{N}_{n+1}$ with

$$\mathcal{N}_{n+1} \models \Gamma \cup \Phi_n \cup \{\theta\} \cup \{\neg\psi_{n+1}\} \text{ and } |\mathcal{N}_{n+1}| = \lambda.$$

Here $\Phi_0 = \emptyset$ and $\Phi_{n+1} := \{\neg\chi : \chi \textit{ positive} \ \& \ \mathcal{N}_n \models \neg\chi\}$. The homomorphisms $h_{n+1,n}$ and π_n are now provided by Lyndon's theorem. This means that $\mathcal{M}$ refines $\langle \mathcal{N}_n, h_{n+1,n} \rangle_{n\in\omega}$. But $\mathcal{N}_n \not\models \psi_n$ also implies that $\mathcal{M}$ is the least refinement of this system. By Proposition 28, $\mathcal{M}$ is the inverse limit of $\langle \mathcal{N}_n, h_{n+1,n} \rangle_{n\in\omega}$, as required. □

To prove Theorem 27(2), one uses a variant of Theorem 29 for bonding mappings which need not be surjective.

The theorems taken together show that the essence of preservation on inverse limits is given by Lemma 26; namely that positive (primitive) formulas are preserved upward. This is also the core fact for convergence of conditional quantifiers.

6.5.2 Convergence

We now return to the question, for which formulas φ we can reasonably posit the default rule, in the sense that f $\in \exists(\varphi(x)|\mathcal{G}_s)$ for all s implies f $\in \varphi(x)$. Formally, this translates into the question, for which φ one has $\bigcap_{s\in T} \exists(\varphi(x)|\mathcal{G}_s)$ $= \varphi(x)$.

This question has a parallel in probability theory. Let $\{\mathcal{B}_s | s \in T\}$ be a *net* of σ-algebras, in the sense that $s \geq t$ implies $\mathcal{B}_s \supseteq \mathcal{B}_t$. Let X be a random variable measurable with respect to the union $\mathcal{B}$ of the $\mathcal{B}_s$. Then the conditional expectations $\mathbf{E}(X|\mathcal{B}_s)$ form a *martingale*, i.e. for $s \geq t$, $\mathbf{E}(\mathbf{E}(X|\mathcal{B}_s)|\mathcal{B}_t) = \mathbf{E}(X|\mathcal{B}_t)$ (a.e.). A fundamental result is the martingale convergence theorem, which says that $\mathbf{E}(X|\mathcal{B}_s)$ converges to X a.e..

Observe that conditional quantifiers $\exists(\varphi(x)|\mathcal{G}_s)$ form a martingale in the following sense (cf. Wright 1962):

$$s \geq t \text{ implies } \exists(\exists(\varphi(x)|\mathcal{G}_s)|\mathcal{G}_t) = \exists(\varphi(x)|\mathcal{G}_t).$$

The inclusion from right to left is trivial and the other inclusion follows from the observation that for $s \geq t$, $\exists(\varphi(x)|\mathcal{G}_s) \subseteq \exists(\varphi(x)|\mathcal{G}_t)$. Indeed, although in general we do not have $s \geq t$ implies $\mathcal{G}_t \subseteq \mathcal{G}_s$, the inclusion between the conditionally quantified formulas holds because positive formulas are preserved by the homomorphism from $\mathcal{M}_s$ to $\mathcal{M}_t$. Using these facts one easily shows that for a set of assignments C, $\exists(C|\mathcal{G}_s)$ converges to C if and only if C is closed. This suggests that convergence is guaranteed only for positive formulas, but upon closer scrutiny we see that we need a slight generalisation of 'positive'.

Definition 28 A formula $\varphi(\vec{x})$ is called *positive up to disjunction* if there are positive formulas $\psi_1(\vec{x}), \ldots, \psi_n(\vec{x})$ such that

$$\models \forall \vec{x}(\varphi(\vec{x}) \leftrightarrow \psi^1(\vec{x})) \vee \cdots \vee \forall \vec{x}(\varphi(\vec{x}) \leftrightarrow \psi^n(\vec{x})).$$

Here $\vec{x}$ contains all variables free in φ, ψ^i $(1 \leq i \leq n)$.

Theorem 30 *The following two statements are equivalent:*[19]

i) *For each $\mathcal{M}$ isomorphic to the inverse limit of a total refining system $\langle \mathcal{M}_s, h_{st}\rangle_{s,t\in T}$:*

$$\bigcap_{s\in T} \exists(\varphi|\mathcal{G}_s) = \varphi,$$

with $\mathcal{G}_s$ generated from the sets $\mathbf{p}_s^{-1}(\psi_s)$, ψ positive.

ii) *φ is positive up to disjunction.*

PROOF We first prove (ii) from (i). Let $\mathcal{M}$ be a model as described. By assumption φ is equivalent in $\mathcal{M}$ to a positive ψ^i $(1 \leq i \leq n)$. Corollary 19 gives $\exists(\psi^i|\mathcal{G}_s) \subseteq \mathbf{p}_s^{-1}(\psi_s^i)$, whence

$$\bigcap_{s\in T} \exists(\psi_i|\mathcal{G}_s) \subseteq \bigcap_{s\in T} \mathbf{p}_s^{-1}(\psi_s^i).$$

It now suffices to show that $\bigcap_{s\in T} \mathbf{p}_s^{-1}(\psi_s^i) \subseteq \psi^i$. For this implies

$$\psi^i \subseteq \bigcap_{s\in T} \exists(\psi^i|\mathcal{G}_s) \subseteq \bigcap_{s\in T} \mathbf{p}_s^{-1}(\psi_s^i) \subseteq \psi^i,$$

which together with $\mathcal{M} \models \forall\vec{x}(\varphi(\vec{x}) \leftrightarrow \psi^i(\vec{x}))$ gives

$$\bigcap_{s\in T} \exists(\varphi|\mathcal{G}_s) = \bigcap_{s\in T} \exists(\psi^i|\mathcal{G}_s) = \psi^i = \varphi.$$

Notice that $\bigcap_{s\in T} \mathbf{p}_s^{-1}(\psi_s^i) \subseteq \psi^i$ is equivalent to saying that

$$\forall s \in T(\mathcal{M}_s, f_s \models \psi^i) \Rightarrow \mathcal{M}, f \models \psi^i;$$

i.e., that ψ^i is *preserved* by inverse systems of our particular form. For positive ψ^i this is true by Lemma 26.

To prove (i) from (ii), it suffices to consider inverse systems consisting of a single element, say $\mathcal{M}$. By hypothesis, $\varphi(\vec{x})$ can be written as an intersection of positive formulas in $\vec{x}$ on $\mathcal{M}$ (since trivially $\mathbf{p}^{-1}(\psi) = \psi$ in this case). Enumerate the positive formulas in $\vec{x}$ as $\psi_1, \ldots, \psi_n, \ldots$, and let Ω be the function space $\omega \longrightarrow \omega$. For each model $\mathcal{M}$ there exists a function $f \in \Omega$ such that on $\mathcal{M}$, $\varphi(\vec{x})$ equals $\bigwedge_{i\in\omega} \psi_{f(i)}(\vec{x})$. Hence we have

(*) $\models \bigvee_{f\in\Omega} \forall\vec{x}(\varphi(\vec{x}) \leftrightarrow \bigwedge_{i\in\omega} \psi_{f(i)}(\vec{x}))$.

It remains to show that (*) is equivalent to φ being positive up to disjunction. It is clear φ being positive up to disjunction implies (*). So assume that φ is *not* positive up to disjunction. This means that for each $f \in \Omega$ and for each $n \in \omega$

$$\not\models \forall\vec{x}(\varphi(\vec{x}) \leftrightarrow \bigwedge_{i\leq n} \psi_{f(i)}(\vec{x})).$$

Compactness gives that the set

$$\{\exists\vec{x}(\varphi(\vec{x}) \wedge \bigvee_{i\in\omega} \neg\psi_{f(i)}(\vec{x})) \vee \exists\vec{x}(\bigwedge_{i\in\omega} \psi_{f(i)}(\vec{x}) \wedge \neg\varphi(\vec{x})) : f \in \Omega\}$$

is satisfiable, whence (*) is false. □

Related results, with 'positive' replaced by 'positive primitive', hold if the bonding mappings are not necessarily surjective.

[19] Results of this type were first obtained by F.B. Wright (1962).

To see that Theorem 30 already fails for $\neg A(x)$, A a predicate, consider the full binary tree conceived of as an inverse system of first order models $\mathcal{M}_n$. Each $\mathcal{M}_n$ has 2^n elements (the elements of level n), with the obvious homomorphism $\mathcal{M}_k \longrightarrow \mathcal{M}_n$ $(k \geq n)$. Only the rightmost elements have property A.

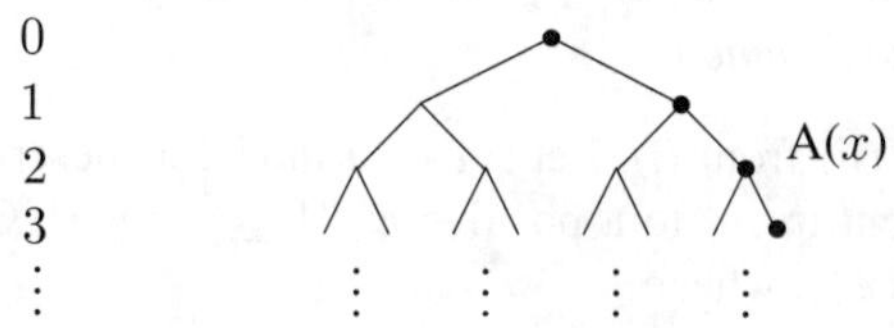

Let $\mathcal{G}_n$ be generated by $\mathbf{p}_n^{-1}(\varphi_n)$, φ positive in the language $\{A\}$. Then $\mathbf{p}_n^{-1}(\top) = \top$, $n \in \omega$, is the only $C \in \mathcal{G}_n$ with $\neg A(x) \subseteq C$. So $\bigcap_{n\in\omega} \exists(\neg A(x)|\mathcal{G}_n)$ is the full set of assignments, whereas $\neg A(x)$ is not.

It is worthwhile to observe that $\bigcap_{n\in\omega} \exists(\neg A(x)|\mathcal{G}_n)$ would still be the full set of assignments if all subsets of $|M_n|$ were definable by means of a (positive) formula; i.e., the (positive) formula topology on $\mathcal{M}_n$ is discrete. Then the $\mathcal{G}_n$ should be defined accordingly. □

The last observation suggests a less trivial version of Theorem 30. Suppose $\mathcal{G}_s$ now stands for the frame generated by the *algebras* $\mathcal{B}_s$ of formulas on $\mathcal{M}_s$. We conjecture that Theorem 30 is still true with this modification, but we were unable to obtain a proof.

*

This concludes the preliminaries of the logic of vision. A detailed discussion of its linguistic, psychological, and philosophical ramifications can be found in (van der Does and van Lambalgen 1997).

References

Barwise, J. 1981. Scenes and other Situations. *Journal of Philosophy* LXXVIII:369–397.

Barwise, J. 1989. *The Situation in Logic*. Lecture Notes, Vol. 17. Stanford, California: CSLI Publications. Distributed by Cambridge University Press.

Biederman, I. 1987. Recognition-by-Components: A Theory of Human Image Understanding. *Psychological Review* 94(a):115–147.

Boden, M. A. 1988. *Computer Models of Mind*. Problems in Behavioural Sciences, Vol. 4. Cambridge: Cambridge University Press.

Chang, C. C., and H. J. Keisler. 1990. *Model Theory*. Studies in Logic and the Foundations of Mathematics, Vol. 73. Amsterdam: North-Holland. Third edition. First edition: 1973, second edition 1977.

Engelking, R. 1989. *General Topology*. Sigma Series in Pure Mathematics, Vol. 6. Berlin: Heldermann. Revised and completed edition.

Graetzer, G. 1979. *Universal Algebra*. New York: Springer-Verlag. 2nd edition.

Halmos, P. R. 1952. Algebraic Logic, I: Monadic Boolean Algebras. *Compositio Mathematica* 12:217–249.

Higginbotham, J. 1983. The Logic of Perceptual Reports: An Extensional Alternative to Situation Semantics. *Journal of Philosophy* LXXX:100–127.

Hintikka, K. J. J. 1969. On the logic of perception. In *Models for Modalities*. Synthese Library, Vol. 23. Dordrecht: D. Reidel Publishing Company.

Jackendoff, R. 1983. *Semantics and Cognition*. MIT Press.

Jackendoff, R. 1987. *Consciousness and the Computational Mind*. MIT Press.

Jackendoff, R. 1990. *Semantic Structures*. MIT Press.

Kamp, H. 1984. A Scenic Tour through the Land of Naked Infinitives. Unpublished manuscript, Univeristy of Texas, Austin.

Lindström, P. 1966. First-order Predicate Logic with Generalized Quantifiers. *Theoria* 32:186–195.

Marr, D. 1982. *Vision: A Computational Investigation into the Human Representation and Processing of Visual Information*. San Fransisco: W.H. Freeman.

Miller, G.A., and P.N. Johnson-Laird. 1976. *Language and Perception*. Harvard: Harvard University Press.

Mostowski, A. 1957. On a Generalization of Quantifiers. *Fundamenta Mathematicae* 44:12–36.

Sacks, O. 1985. *The Man who Mistook his Wive for a Hat*. London: Pan Books Ltd. Picador edition.

Thomason, S. K. 1989. Free Construction of Time from Events. *Journal of Philosophical Logic* 18:43–67.

van der Does, J. 1991. A Generalized Quantifier Logic for Naked Infinitives. *Linguistics and Philosophy* 14:241–294.

van der Does, J., and M. van Lambalgen. 1997. A Logic of Vision. research report LP–97–07. University of Amsterdam: ILLC. Submitted.

Voorbraak, F. 1997. A nonmonotonic observation logic. research report LP–97–09. University of Amsterdam: ILLC.

Wright, F. B. 1962. Convergence of Quantifiers and Martingales. *Pacific Journal of Mathematics* 6:296–307.

Wright, F. B. 1963. Boolean Averages. *Canadian Journal of Mathematics* 15:440–455.

7

A Logic of Modification and Creation

GERARD R. RENARDEL DE LAVALETTE

7.1 Introduction

The purpose of this paper is to present the logic MCL (modification and creation logic) in the context of other dynamic logics and related formalisms. It is intended for any reader who is interested in the logical description of dynamic aspects in natural language, programming languages or theories of action. I will therefore concentrate on the main features and properties of MCL, not on proof details (they are intended to appear elsewhere).

Like QDL, MCL is a multimodal extension of first-order logic, where the modal operator $[\alpha]$ is parametrised with action expressions α. The key feature of MCL is its rich action language, which allows for the definition of actions that act on arbitrary (first-order) structures, not only on simple memory structures like variable assignments (mappings from variables to values). This makes MCL well suited for use in contexts with rich structures. See (Fensel et al. 1998), where MCL provides the unifying semantical framework for specification of reasoning in knowledge-based systems.

The rest of this section is an introduction to the main features of MCL, starting with the syntax definition:

*Department of Computing Science, University of Groningen, P.O. Box 800, 9700 AV Groningen, The Netherlands. E-mail: grl@cs.rug.nl. The author wishes to thank an anonymous referee for constructive criticism and suggestions for making this paper better readable.

Logical Perspectives on Language and Information.
Cleo Condoravdi and Gerard R. Renardel de Lavalette.

terms	$t ::=$	$x \mid \uparrow \mid f(t) \mid \mathsf{new}$
formulae	$\varphi ::=$	$(t = t) \mid p(t) \mid \varphi \wedge \varphi \mid \neg\varphi \mid \forall x \varphi \mid [\alpha]\varphi$
actions	$\alpha ::=$	$\mathsf{Create} \mid f := \lambda x.t \mid p := \lambda x.\varphi$ $\varphi? \mid \alpha;\alpha \mid \alpha + \alpha \mid \alpha^* \mid \cup x.\alpha$

For simplicity, we wrote unary functions and predicates where arbitrary arity is intended, and we shall do so in the sequel. So MCL also has, for example, term $g(t, t')$, formula $q(s, t)$, and the actions $q := \lambda x_1 x_2 x_3.\psi$ and $a := t$. The last action assigns the value of t to nullary function a. Usually, nullary functions are called constants, but that term is not very appropriate in this context, and we call a a *programming variable*, in contrast with the logical variables $x, y, \ldots$ used for quantification. We shall assume that the signature of MCL contains a quaternary function for definition by cases, written in mixfix notation:

$$\lambda xyzw.\mathsf{if}\ x = y\ \mathsf{then}\ z\ \mathsf{else}\ w$$

The basis of MCL is first order logic with partial functions, so terms may fail to refer to a defined value. ($\uparrow$ is such a term; see 7.3.1 for more about this.) Beside terms and formulae, we have *actions* in MCL. They refer to a broad category: not only specific actions (like 'put the block on the table'), but also more general descriptions (or, if you want, specifications) of actions: they may involve sequential composition ('put the chair on the table and then the block on the chair'), choice ('put the block on the table or on the chair'), and they may be impossible to perform ('put the block on the ceiling'). Every action α gives rise to the modal operator $[\alpha]$ and its dual $\langle\alpha\rangle$, with the intended meaning

$[\alpha]\varphi$: whenever α is performed successfully, φ holds;
$\langle\alpha\rangle\varphi$: it is possible to do α in such a way that φ holds.

So, in MCL we can reason about the *effect* of actions *after (successful) termination*. Observe that there are no other ways in MCL to construct formulae from actions, so other aspects of actions are swept under the carpet, such as effects of unsuccessful attempts and effects during the performance of an action (these aspects are treated in process theories and temporal logic). As a consequence, all impossible actions and all nonterminating actions are identified in MCL, since they have no effect. Another consequence is that actions without effect are not an alternative in cases of choice: so 'put the block on the table or on the ceiling' gets the same meaning as 'put the block on the table'.

What is to be changed by the actions? Answer: the universe, and the signature elements (predicates and functions). We have the following atomic actions

Create: add a fresh element to the universe
$f := \lambda x.t$: let function symbol f refer to $\lambda x.t$
$p := \lambda x.\varphi$: let predicate symbol p refer to $\lambda x.\varphi$.

In order to manipulate the newly added element after Create, MCL has the atomic term new, with the following dynamic interpretation: after Create, new refers to the fresh element just added to the universe. So we then can handle the new element, giving it the name a by $a := \mathsf{new}$, a specific property p by $p := \lambda x.(px \vee x = \mathsf{new})$, or sending it to some other value b via function f by $f := \lambda x.\mathsf{if}\ x = \mathsf{new}\ \mathsf{then}\ b\ \mathsf{else}\ fx$.

The atomic actions in MCL have the following properties:

- they are local, i.e. they only change a specified part of the state;
- they are deterministic, i.e. they can be performed in at most one way;
- they are terminating, i.e. they can be performed in at least one way.

Making actions local is the natural way to deal with the frame problem (first formulated in (McCarthy and Hayes 1969)): What changes when there is change, and what remains unchanged? Determinism and termination lead to predictability of atomic actions, which is an attractive property when constructing complex actions (or programs) since it localises all impredictability in the choice operators $+,^*$ and $\cup$. We indicate briefly how these properties of the atomic actions are realised, referring to Section 7.3 for a full treatment.

Modification. For modifications $f := \lambda x.t$, locality is straightforward: only the interpretation of the signature element that is modified (f in the example) may change, the universe and the interpretation of the other signature elements remain the same. Modifications can be read as explicit definitions, which are deterministic by their very nature. What about termination? One may attempt a counterexample like $p := \lambda x.\neg p(x)$, but this is completely unproblematic, for the new extension of p is the complement of the old extension of p. Compare this with the assignment $a := a + 1$, which is a perfectly normal action (assuming that a is a number) and only looks weird if $:=$ is misread as $=$.

Creation. For creation, locality is somewhat more subtle. The universe is extended with a new element, so we have to do something to adapt the interpretation of the functions and predicates. We choose for the general rule: *new elements behave like undefined.* The interpretation of signature elements, when applied to old elements in the universe, remains unchanged. As a consequence, Create is deterministic. Termination presupposes that fresh objects are always available: in the semantics this is realised with a store of countably many fresh objects. See 7.3.3 for the details.

There are also actions that do not change anything (hence are deterministic): tests $\varphi?$, succeeding when φ holds, failing otherwise. Moreover, new actions can be built from others with the following action operators:

$\alpha;\beta$	do first α, then β;
$\alpha+\beta$	do either α or β;
α^*	do α zero or more times;
$\cup x.\alpha$	do α for some value of x (choice quantification).

Observe that $+,^*$ and $\cup$ have a choice character. Some well-known programming constructions can be expressed:

$$\begin{array}{lcl} \textsf{if } \varphi \textsf{ then } \alpha \textsf{ else } \beta \textsf{ fi} & = & (\varphi?;\alpha)+(\neg\varphi?;\beta) \\ \textsf{while } \varphi \textsf{ do } \alpha & = & (\varphi?;\alpha)^*;\neg\varphi? \\ \textsf{do } \alpha \textsf{ until } \varphi & = & (\alpha;\neg\varphi?)^*;\varphi? \end{array}$$

Observe that these defined operators all preserve determinism, although they contain choice operators. Some other possibilities are

$$\begin{array}{rl} \text{do } \alpha \text{ such that } \varphi: & \alpha;\varphi? \\ \text{do } \alpha \text{ provided that it terminates:} & ((\langle\alpha\rangle\top)?;\alpha)+(\neg\langle\alpha\rangle\top)? \end{array}$$

The expressiveness of MCL is demonstrated by the following definition of the natural numbers (modulo isomorphism, provided there is a zero 0 and a successor function s):

$$N := \lambda x.\langle a := 0; (a := s(a))^*\rangle x = a$$

As a consequence, Peano arithmetic can be embedded in MCL. Moreover, many inductive definitions can be expressed in MCL, for example the transitive closure T of a binary relation S:

$$T := \lambda xy.\langle Q := \lambda xy.\bot; (Q := \lambda xy.(Sxy \vee Txy))^*\rangle Qxy$$

7.1.1 Survey of the rest of this paper

After this general introduction, we turn to the ancestors and relatives of MCL in the next section. Then, in section 7.3, we present the semantics and axiomatisation in three stages: first the static part, then modification and finally creation. Section 7.4 contains some properties of MCL: completeness, failure of compactness and interpolation, elimination of Create. Most proofs are only sketched. In section 7.5 possible extensions of MCL are discussed, such as parallel modifications, logic programming and removing objects. We conclude with some suggestions for further work.

7.2 Ancestors and Relatives of MCL

MCL is the first nor the only reasoning system about the effect of actions. In this section, we discuss several ancestors (sources of inspiration for MCL) and relatives of MCL.

7.2.1 Quantified Dynamic Logic

Pratt's dynamic logic (Pratt 1976) is the first modal logic extension of first order logic intended to model and reason about actions (usually called programs).

Like MCL, it has modal operators $[\alpha]$ and the program operators $?, ;, +$ and $\star$. Unlike MCL, QDL has only total functions, and its programs change the assignment of variables to objects, not the interpretation of functions and predicates. Atomic actions in QDL are of the form $x := t$, with the effect that x refers to the value of t. Moreover, $\cup x.\alpha$ is not available in QDL (but can be added easily). (Harel 1984) is an extensive survey of propositional dynamic logic PDL and quantified dynamic logic QDL; an excellent introduction can be found in (Goldblatt 1992).

We sketch the semantics and axiomatisation of QDL: much of it applies to MCL, too. Let M be a model for the first-order part of QDL. In order to interpret the variables, assignments are used which map variables to values in the universe U of M. Now M is extended to a model for full QDL by taking $\mathsf{Var} \to U$, the collection of all variable assignments, as its state space (i.e. collection of possible worlds). The accessibility relations R_α on $\mathsf{Var} \to U$ are defined inductively by

$$\begin{array}{lll} R_{x:=t} & =_{\text{def}} & \{(A, A[x \mapsto [\![t]\!]_{A[x \mapsto u]}]) \mid A \in \mathsf{VA}\} \\ R_{\varphi?} & =_{\text{def}} & \{(A, A) \mid A \models \varphi\} \\ R_{\alpha;\beta} & =_{\text{def}} & R_\alpha \circ R_\beta \\ R_{\alpha+\beta} & =_{\text{def}} & R_\alpha \cup R_\beta \\ R_{\alpha^*} & =_{\text{def}} & R_\alpha^* \end{array}$$

$R_{x:=t}$ is a total functional relation which changes as assignment on its value for x. $R_{\varphi?}$ is a partial identity function, i.e. a subset of the identity relation. Furthermore, sequential composition ';' corresponds to relation composition, nondeterministic choice corresponds to relation union, and repetition * is modeled by transitive closure

$$R^* = \{(A, A') \mid A = A' \vee \exists A_1 \ldots A_n((A, A_1) \in R \wedge \ldots \wedge (A_n, A') \in R)\}.$$

The interpretation of modal formulae reads

$$M, A \models [\alpha]\varphi = \forall A'((A, A') \in R_\alpha \to M, A' \models \varphi).$$

As a consequence, the following principles are valid:

$$\begin{array}{lll} [x := t]\varphi(x) & \leftrightarrow & \varphi(t) \\ [\varphi?]\psi & \leftrightarrow & (\varphi \to \psi) \\ [\alpha;\beta]\varphi & \leftrightarrow & [\alpha][\beta]\varphi \\ [\alpha+\beta]\varphi & \leftrightarrow & ([\alpha]\varphi \wedge [\beta]\varphi) \\ [\alpha^*]\varphi & \leftrightarrow & (\varphi \wedge [\alpha][\alpha^*]\varphi) \end{array}$$

We see that actions change variable assignments, and they do so locally in a controlled way: an action can only change assignments w.r.t. the variables that are explicitly mentioned. So, whatever may happen when $\varphi? + (x := s; y := t)^*$ is performed, we know that at most the values of x and y will be changed, not of any other variable.

Variables play a double role in QDL, being at the same time vehicle for quantification and for assignment. (These roles correspond to the distinction made in programming practice between logical variables and programming variables.) Consider $\forall x[x := x+1]p(x)$: the x in $x+1$ is bound by $\forall x$, the x in $p(x)$ by $[x := \ldots]$. An equivalent and less confusing variant is $\forall x[y := x+1]p(y)$.

A closer look at $\forall x$ and $[x := \ldots]$ reveals that it is possible to reconcile their apparently diverse meanings, viz. by reading $\forall x$ as $[x :=?]$ (and, dually, $\exists x$ as $\langle x :=?\rangle$), where the question mark ? refers to an arbitrary object. More formally, we have

$$R_{x:=?} = \{(s, s[x \mapsto u]) \mid s \in S, u \in U\}$$

which immediately yields $[x :=?]\varphi \leftrightarrow \forall x\varphi$ and $\langle x :=?\rangle\varphi \leftrightarrow \exists x\varphi$. This idea (as old as dynamic logic itself, see (Pratt 1976)) reduces quantification to modality: see (van Benthem 1996, Ch.9) for a deconstruction of first-order logic along these lines, yielding a plethora of (sometimes decidable) subsystems.

We close this subsection with the observation that QDL can be embedded straightforwardly in MCL by systematically replacing variables x involved in assignment by nullary functions a: so $[x := f(y)]p(x, y)$ becomes $[a := f(y)]p(a, y)$, for example. (There are some subtle details, however: consider $\forall x[(x := f(x))^*]p(x)$, which translates to $\forall x[a := x; (a := f(a))^*]p(a)$.)

7.2.2 Two Software Specification Formalisms: COLD and ASM

Software specification, a subdiscipline of Software Engineering, intends to provide high-level, abstract descriptions of the intrinsic properties of software systems to be developed. Algebraic specification is one of the paradigms for attaining the required level of abstraction, which has as a distinctive feature that it concentrates on a purely functional description of input-output behaviour, abstracting away from the notion of state. It is a fruitful area of research and development, see (Wirsing 1990), but the gap between sound but abstract theory and the more traditional state-based practice remains to be considered as a hindrance.

In the '80s, several attempts were proposed to bridge this gap by extending the algebraic paradigm with a notion of state and state change. Two of these attempts, under the acronyms COLD (Common Object-oriented Language for Design) and ASM (Abstract State Machines, formerly known as Evolving Algebra), will be presented here.

COLD was developed at Philips Research, mainly by Hans Jonkers, see (Feijs et al. 1987b), (Feijs et al. 1987a), (Feijs and Jonkers 1992). ASM is proposed and developed by Yuri Gurevich, see (Gurevich 1988), (Gurevich 1991), (Gurevich 1995), and widely applied and extended by Egon Börger and others (see (Börger and Huggins 1998) for an extensive bibliography). The central idea behind both is the generalisation of the machine models in automata theory. An automaton (or machine) is an abstract entity with a number of possible states and transitions from states to states (and often some notion of input and output). The Turing machine is the oldest and most famous example, where the state consists of the internal state of the machine and the sequence of symbols on its tape. There are also simpler machines (finite automata, for example, with only a finite number of states) and more complex machines (register machines, random access machines, etc., see (Hopcroft and Ullman 1979) for a survey).

Now the new idea of COLD and ASM is the following: instead of some specific structure for the state of a machine (a one-way infinite tape, a collection of registers for numbers, etc.), take an arbitrary structure, described with logico-algebraical means (sorts, functions, predicates, equations, axioms), and change that state by changing the sorts, functions and predicates. Primitive state-changing actions in COLD and ASM are: extend a sort with a fresh object; change a function or predicate for some specific value of its argument(s). The usual program operators of PDL apply, and others (parallel composition) have been investigated in the context of ASM.

MCL is a generalisation of other logics based on COLD and ASM. MLCM (Groenboom and Renardel de Lavalette 1994) was the first such attempt and can be characterised as MCL without choice quantification of programs (i.e. the construct $\cup x.\alpha$) and with only *pointwise* modifications $f(t) := s$ and $p(t) :\leftrightarrow \varphi$. An attempt to formalise evolving algebras based on MLCM is given in (Groenboom and Renardel de Lavalette 1995). MLPM (Fensel and Groenboom 1996) is a variant of MLCM with two kinds of bulk (i.e. non-pointwise) updates for predicates, viz. $p := \lambda x.\varphi$ (as in MCL) and $p := \varepsilon x.\varphi$. The intended meaning of the latter is: p becomes a singleton predicate that holds only for one nondeterministically chosen object x satisfying φ. This can be expressed in MCL as follows:

$$p := \varepsilon x.\varphi \;=\; \cup x.(\varphi?; p := \lambda y.(x = y))$$

Related work is in (Tonino 1997), where a theory of many-sorted evolving algebras is developed comparable with MLCM, but extended with contraction updates that remove an object form a sort (see also 7.5.3).

7.2.3 Dynamic Database Logic

The contents of a (relational) database can be described straightforwardly in first-order logic: relations become predicates, attributes become functions. Extending this to database *updates* leads in (Spruit et al. 1995) to the development of the logics PDDL and DDL, (propositional) database dynamic logic. In PDDL, the atomic actions are Ip (passive insertion), Dp (passive deletion), $I^H p$ (active insertion) and $D^H p$ (active deletion). Passive actions only affect the truth value of p; active actions, moreover, perform the logic program H. With help of the notation introduced in Section 7.5, we can formulate this in MCL:

$$\begin{array}{lcl} Ip & \mapsto & p := \top \\ Dp & \mapsto & p := \bot \\ I^H p & \mapsto & (p := \top); \alpha^H \\ D^H p & \mapsto & (p := \bot); \alpha^H \end{array}$$

Here α_H is the least fixpoint of the predicate operator associated with H. In the predicate logic DDL, the atomic actions are:

$\&x\, Ip\, t$ where φ	(insertion) make p true for all instances of t with values of x for which φ holds;
$\&x\, Dp\, t$ where φ	(deletion) make p false for all instances of t with values of x for which φ holds;
$\&x\, Up\, t \to t'$ where φ	(update) make, for all values of x for which φ holds, p false for the corresponding instance of t and true for the corresponding instance of t';
$fs := t$	(assignment) make $f(s)$ equal to t.

Moreover, DDL has the conditional choice construct

$+x\,\alpha$ where φ: do α for one of the values of x for which φ holds.

All these constructions can be expressed in MCL:

$$\begin{array}{lcl} \&x\, Ip\, t \text{ where } \varphi & \mapsto & p := \lambda y.(py \vee \exists x(\varphi \wedge y = t)) \\ \&x\, Dp\, t \text{ where } \varphi & \mapsto & p := \lambda y.(py \wedge \neg\exists x(\varphi \wedge y = t)) \\ \&x\, Up\, t \to t' \text{ where } \varphi & \mapsto & p := \lambda y.((py \wedge \neg\exists x(\varphi \wedge y = t)) \\ & & \qquad \vee\exists x(p(t) \wedge \varphi \wedge y = t')) \\ fs := t & \mapsto & f := \lambda x.\text{if } x = s \text{ then } t \text{ else } fx \text{ fi} \\ +x\,\alpha \text{ where } \varphi & \mapsto & \cup x.(\varphi?; \alpha) \end{array}$$

7.2.4 Tarskian Variations

In (van Benthem and Cepparello 1994), the process of dynamification of logics is considered from the perspective of Tarski's truth definition

$$D, I, A \models \varphi$$

stating that formula φ holds in model $M = \langle D, I, A \rangle$ with domain D, interpretation I and variable assignment A. Now dynamification comes down to 'Tarskian variation', where one or more of the parameters D, I, A are varied.

Variation of A is studied extensively, leading to a variety of logics: QDL, DPL (dynamic predicate logic, (Groenendijk and Stokhof 1991)), UL (update logic, (Veltman 1996)) and DEL (dynamic epistemic logic, (Gerbrandy 1999, Gerbrandy and Groeneveld 1997)). Unlike the others, DPL and UL have no category of action expressions, but their formulae have a dynamic meaning expressing *change potential*, i.e. the ability to change anaphoric references or information states, respectively.

The logic TV formulated in (van Benthem and Cepparello 1994) involves modification of all three parameters D, I, A via the following actions:

ηx (change the value of A at x)
μ (change the interpretation I of the signature elements)
δ (change the domain D)

Observe that ηx yields local change, while μ involves global change; furthermore, all three atomic actions are highly nondeterministic. Compare this with QDL and MCL, where all atomic actions are local and deterministic.

Local versions of μ are straightforward: μp, 'change I at p'. Observe that $[\mu p]$ has the same meaning as the second-order quantifier $\forall p$. Furthermore, there are the variants $\delta\downarrow$ ('shrink the domain'), $\delta\uparrow$ ('extend the domain').

TV is interpreted in collections W of worlds $w = \langle D_w, I_w, A_w\rangle$. The accessibility relations of the atomic actions $\eta x, \mu p, \mu, \delta$ are the so-called shift relations $=_x, =_p, =_I, =_D$, respectively, defined by

$$\begin{array}{lcl} w =_x w' & : & D_w = D_{w'}, I_w = I_{w'}, A_w(y) = A_{w'}(y) \ \text{ for all } y \neq x \\ w =_p w' & : & D_w = D_{w'}, A_w = A_{w'}, I_w(q) = I_{w'}(q) \ \text{ for all } q \in \S - \{p\} \\ w =_I w' & : & D_w = D_{w'}, A_w = A_{w'} \\ w =_D w' & : & I_w = I_{w'}, A_w = A_{w'} \end{array}$$

Deterministic change of A is realisable in TV via $\eta x; x = t?$, provided that x does not occur in t. But that variable condition is restrictive: sometimes we want to define something new in terms of something old (the paradigmatic example is $x := x + 1$). In QDL and MCL this can be expressed directly, but in the case of TV, we have to do something like $\eta y; y = x?; \eta x; x = t[y/x]?$ with y a fresh variable.

7.3 Semantics and Axiomatisation

We present the semantics and the axioms of MCL in three steps: first the static part, then the modification part, finally the creation part. We assume that the signature $\S$ of MCL is divided in a static part Σ_s and a dynamic part Σ_d: only the elements of Σ_d are allowed in the left hand side of modification actions.

7.3.1 The static part

We assume that $\S_d = \emptyset$, i.e. all signature elements are static. The static part of MCL is just first-order logic with partial functions. Its semantics is given in terms of models $M = \langle U, \star, I\rangle$ consisting of universe U, undefined object $\star \notin U$ and interpretation I of the elements of $\S = \S_s$. $\star$ is used to interpret partial functions as total functions on $U \cup \{\star\}$.

We follow the tradition that quantifiers only range over existing objects, whereas free variables may also refer to nonexisting objects (see (Scott 1979) and (Troelstra and van Dalen 1988, 2.2); in (Beeson 1985), both free and bound variables refer to existing objects only). So $\forall x(x = x)$ is valid, whereas $x = x$ is not. The convention w.r.t. free variables enables us to formulate axiom schemata involving arbitrary terms that may be undefined: for if $\varphi(x)$ is valid, then so is $\varphi(t)$ for every term t. It also allows for empty domains: $\exists x(x = x)$ is not valid (but, of course, $[\mathsf{Create}]\exists x(x = x)$ is valid, see below). The existence predicate E, defined by

$$\mathsf{E}t := \exists x(x = t)$$

is used in the instantiation axiom and the principle of universal generalisation:

Inst $(\forall x\varphi \wedge \mathsf{E}x) \rightarrow \varphi$

UG if $\Gamma, \mathsf{E}x \vdash \varphi$ and x does not occur free in Γ, then $\Gamma \vdash \forall x\varphi$

Here (and in the sequel) Γ is some collection of formulae.

In this standard setup for the semantics for partial functions, there is some design freedom in what to do when $\star$ acts as an argument. One option is to work with *strict* functions, which yield undefined whenever one of their arguments is undefined, so we have $\mathsf{E}f(s,t) \rightarrow \mathsf{E}s \wedge \mathsf{E}t$. This leads to proliferation of undefinedness: every term containing an undefined subterm will be undefined. However, there are realistic examples of nonstrict functions: constant functions, multiplication ($x \cdot 0$ is always 0), projection ($\lambda xy.x$), definition by cases (if φ then s else t). We take a permissive stance here and allow nonstrict functions in the semantics of MCL. So $I(f)(\star) \in U$ is allowed.

Another design choice concerns the evaluation of equality (and other predicates) for terms containing partial functions. Several logics exist that have a third truth value *undefined*, interpreting equality as a strict predicate. This opens many options for the definition of the logical connectives, leading to a proliferation of alternative partial logics. The first such logics by Łukasiewicz and Post date from the '20s, and were followed by proposals by Kleene and Bochvar; see the survey papers (Urquhart 1986, Blamey 1986). The alternative is to stay within classical logic with two truth values, roughly by identifying the undefined truth value with false: so $t = t$ is true only when t has a defined value, and false otherwise. This is the approach in (Scott 1967, Scott 1979), also adopted in COLD (see (Koymans and Renardel de Lavalette 1989) for the logic underlying COLD).

Here we choose to stay close to classical logic and to work with the traditional truth values, interpreting equality as a nonstrict predicate satisfying

Eq $\forall x(x = x) \wedge (x = y \rightarrow y = x) \wedge (x = y \wedge y = z \rightarrow x = z)$

So we sacrificed full reflexivity, but that property is met by *weak equality* $\simeq$:

$$(s \simeq t) := (Es \vee Et) \rightarrow s = t$$

which is to satisfy the congruence properties:

Congr $x \simeq y \rightarrow fx \simeq fy$ (for all functions f)
$(x \simeq y \wedge px) \rightarrow py$ (for all predicates p)

Finally, there is an axiom for undefined:

Undef $\neg(x = \uparrow)$

7.3.2 The modification part

We turn to the modification part, so we forget about Create for the time being. The fundamental idea is: modification is realised by transition from some *world* $w = \langle U, \star, I\rangle$ to another world. So, for the semantics we need a collection W of worlds, and accessibility relations $R \subseteq W^2$ for the interpretation of actions. Neither the universe nor the static part of the interpretation will change under the modifications, so $U, \star, I_s$ are the same for all elements of W. As a consequence, we may identify W with a collection of interpretations I_d of the dynamic signature elements, and we have models of the form $M = \langle U, \star, I_s, W\rangle$. M is called a *natural model* when W is the collection of all possible interpretations of $\S_d$ in $U \cup \{\star\}$. In the sequel, we mainly work with natural models.

A consequence of having constant universes is the so-called Barcan formula for atomic modifications μ (not containing x free):

Barcan $\forall x[\mu]\varphi \leftrightarrow [\mu]\forall x\varphi$

Atomic modifications are to be local, so if $p := \lambda x.\varphi$ brings us from I to J then I, J should behave the same on $\S_d - \{p\}$, i.e. $I =_p J$ (with $=_p$ as defined in 7.2.4). Analogously for $f := \lambda x.t$. So the following frame conditions are satisfied:

FrC $\varphi \leftrightarrow [f := \lambda x.t]\varphi$ (f not in φ)
$\varphi \leftrightarrow [p := \lambda x.\psi]\varphi$ (p not in φ)

The desired behaviour of atomic modifications is captured as follows:

Mod $[f := \lambda x.t](fx = y) \leftrightarrow t = y$
$[p := \lambda x.\varphi]px \leftrightarrow \varphi$

for all f, p, all φ and all y, t with y not free in t. Observe that it is not reasonable to expect

$$[a := t]a = t,$$
$$[p := \lambda x.\varphi]\forall x(px \leftrightarrow \varphi)$$

in case a occurs in t and p in φ. To see this, take $a + 1$ for t, $\neg p(x)$ for φ and we get

$$[a := a + 1]a = a + 1,$$
$$[p := \lambda x.\neg px]\forall x(px \leftrightarrow \neg px)$$

which is very undesired indeed.

7.3.3 The creation part

Finally we deal with Create and expanding universes. We distinguish between the static and the dynamic part of the universe. The static part $U \cup \{\star\}$ is there *ab initio*, being the habitat of the interpretations of the static signature elements. The dynamic part consists of the newly created elements. They are provided by a store $V = \{v_1, v_2, v_3, \dots\}$: a Create action adds the first fresh store element to the universe. So the dynamic part of the universe is an initial segment V_n of V, where n corresponds with the number of applications of Create.

As a consequence, a world w has a universe $U_n = U \cup \{\star\} \cup V_n$ for some n, and an interpretation I_d of the dynamic signature elements in that universe. So any world can be represented as $w = \langle n, I_d\rangle$, and a model is a tuple $\langle U, \star, V, I_s, W\rangle$ where W is a collection of worlds. I_s is extended to an interpretation of the static signature in world w by the principle *a new element behaves like undefined*, so $I_s(f)(v_n) = I_s(f)(\star)$ for all n. A model is natural when W is maximal, i.e. contains all pairs $\langle n, I_d\rangle$ with $n \in N$ and I_d an interpretation of $\S_d$ into U_n.

Now that we have models with expanding universes, what to do with variable assignments? The local solution of TV, see 7.2.4 (each world has its own variable assignment) does not work well here, and we choose for the global option: assignments map the variables into the global universe $U \cup \{\star\} \cup V$, and they are relativised to A_w w.r.t. world w by treating not yet created elements as undefined:

$$\begin{aligned} A_w(x) &= A(x) \quad \text{if } A(x) \in U_w \\ &= \star \qquad\;\; \text{if } A(x) \notin U_w \end{aligned}$$

The interpretation of new in world $\langle n, I_d\rangle$ is simply v_n, and Create is interpreted by

$$\{(\langle n, I_d\rangle, \langle n{+}1, I'_d\rangle) \in W^2 \mid I_d = I'_d \upharpoonright U_n, \forall\sigma \in \S_d I'_d(\sigma)(v_{n+1}) = I'_d(\sigma)(\star)\}$$

Observe that the last part of this definition indeed reads *the new element behaves like undefined*, and that $I_d = I'_d \upharpoonright U_n$ implies that v_{n+1} is not in the range of $I'_d(f)$ for any $f \in \S_d$. This leads to the following axioms **C1-5**:

C1 $x = y \leftrightarrow [\mathsf{Create}](x = y \neq \mathsf{new})$

C2 $px \leftrightarrow [\mathsf{Create}]px$

C3 $[\mathsf{Create}]\mathsf{E}(\mathsf{new})$

C4 $[\mathsf{Create}](f(x) \neq \mathsf{new} \wedge f(\mathsf{new}) \simeq f(\uparrow))$

C5 $[\mathsf{Create}](p(\mathsf{new}) \leftrightarrow p(\uparrow))$

C1-2 say: Create does not affect any predicate, except equality w.r.t. new. **C3** says that, after Create, new refers to an existing object (which differs from all old objects, by **C1**). Finally **C4-5** say that, after Create, new does not occur in the range of a function, and behaves like undefined w.r.t. predicates and functions.

As explained in Section 7.1, we want all atomic actions π (i.e. modifications and creations) to be deterministic and terminating. This is axiomatised by

Det $\langle\pi\rangle\varphi \rightarrow [\pi]\varphi$

Term $\langle\pi\rangle\top$

In natural models, these are valid.

7.3.4 Interpretation of MCL

For completeness' sake, we give the interpretation of terms, formulae and programs in world $w = \langle n_w, I_w\rangle$ from model $M = \langle U, \star, V, I_s, W\rangle$, and M-assignment A. For brevity, we shall write σ_w for $I_w(\sigma)$ (if $\sigma \in \S_d$) or $I_s(\sigma)$ (if $\sigma \in \S_s$).

$$\begin{array}{lcl}
[\![x]\!]_{w,A} & = & A_w(x) \\
[\![\uparrow]\!]_{w,A} & = & \star \\
[\![\mathsf{new}]\!]_{w,A} & = & v_{n_w} \\
[\![ft]\!]_{w,A} & = & f_w([\![t]\!]_{w,A})
\end{array}$$

$$\begin{array}{lcl}
w, A \models (s = t) & =_{\text{def}} & [\![s]\!]_{w,A} = [\![t]\!]_{w,A} \neq \star \\
w, A \models pt & =_{\text{def}} & p_w([\![t]\!]_{w,A}) = \textbf{true} \\
w, A \models \neg\varphi & =_{\text{def}} & \textbf{not}\ (w, A \models \varphi) \\
w, A \models \varphi \wedge \psi & =_{\text{def}} & w, A \models \varphi \textbf{ and } w, A \models \psi \\
w, A \models \forall x\varphi & =_{\text{def}} & \textbf{forall}\ u \in (U_w \setminus \{\star\})(w, A[x \mapsto u] \models \varphi) \\
w, A \models [\alpha]\varphi & =_{\text{def}} & \textbf{forall}\ w' \in W(wR_{\alpha,A}w' \Rightarrow w', A \models \varphi)
\end{array}$$

$$
\begin{array}{lll}
R_{\mathsf{Create},A} & =_{\text{def}} & \{(w,w') \in W^2 \mid I_w = I_{w'} \restriction U_{w_n}, \\
& & \quad \forall \sigma \in \S_d I_{w'}(\sigma)(v_{n+1}) = I_{w'}(\sigma)(\star)\} \\
R_{f:=\lambda x.t,A} & =_{\text{def}} & \{(w,w') \in W^2 \mid w =_f w', \\
& & \quad \forall u \in U_{w'}(I_{w'}(f)(u) = [\![t]\!]_{w,A[x\mapsto u]})\} \\
R_{p:=\lambda x.\varphi,A} & =_{\text{def}} & \{(w,w') \in W^2 \mid w =_p w', \\
& & \quad \forall u \in U_{w'}(I_{w'}(p)(u) \Leftrightarrow w, A[x \mapsto u] \models \varphi)\} \\
R_{\varphi ?,A} & =_{\text{def}} & \{(w,w) \mid w, A \models \varphi\} \\
R_{\alpha;\beta,A} & =_{\text{def}} & R_{\alpha,A} \circ R_{\beta,A} \\
R_{\alpha+\beta,A} & =_{\text{def}} & R_{\alpha,A} \cup R_{\beta,A} \\
R_{\alpha^*,A} & =_{\text{def}} & R^*_{\alpha,A} \\
R_{\bigcup x.\alpha,A} & =_{\text{def}} & \{(w,w') \mid \textbf{exists } u \in (U_w - \{\star\})\, w R_{\alpha,A[x\mapsto u]} w'\}
\end{array}
$$

Observe that the interpretation of actions depends on the variable assignment.

7.3.5 A proof system for MCL

We give a proof system for MCL, based on sequents $\Gamma \vdash \varphi$. The axioms are: the propositional tautologies, **Inst, EQ, Congr, Undef, Barcan, FrC, Mod, C1-5, Det, Term**, furthermore

?AX $[\varphi?]\psi \leftrightarrow (\varphi \rightarrow \psi)$

;AX $[\alpha;\beta]\varphi \leftrightarrow [\alpha][\beta]\varphi$

+AX $[\alpha+\beta]\varphi \leftrightarrow ([\alpha]\varphi \wedge [\beta]\varphi)$

***AX** $[\alpha^*]\varphi \leftrightarrow (\varphi \wedge [\alpha][\alpha^*]\varphi)$

$\bigcup$AX $[\bigcup x.\alpha]\varphi \leftrightarrow \forall x[\alpha]\varphi$ (x not free in φ)

and the repetition axiom

INF $\{[\alpha^n]\varphi \mid n \in \mathrm{N}\} \vdash [\alpha^*]\varphi$

The proof rules of MCL are: **UG**, necessitation

NEC if $\Gamma \vdash \varphi$ then $[\alpha]\Gamma \vdash [\alpha]\varphi$

modus ponens, weakening, the infinitary cut rule

CUT if $\Gamma \vdash \varphi$ for all $\varphi \in \Delta$ and $\Gamma, \Delta \vdash \psi$ then $\Gamma \vdash \psi$

the deduction rule

DED if $\Gamma, \varphi \vdash \psi$ then $\Gamma \vdash \varphi \rightarrow \psi$

and finally the substitution rule

Subst if $\Gamma \vdash \varphi$ then $(t/x)\Gamma \vdash (t/x)\varphi$

With this last rule, we have to be careful. It is possible to substitute a term at an occurrence in the scope of an action that changes one or more signature elements of that term. Consider $(a/x)([a := t]px)$: it will result in the formula $[a := t]pa$, where a has been brought in the scope of the program $a := t$. By **FrC**, we have $\vdash px \leftrightarrow [a := b]px$; with the unrestricted substitution rule, we would have $\vdash pa \leftrightarrow [a := b]pa$ and also $\vdash pa \leftrightarrow pb$ (via **Mod**), which does not hold in general. Therefore we restrict the substitution rule to *safe* substitutions, where this kind of (usually undesired) dynamic binding cannot occur. See the Appendix for the formal definition of safe substitution.

7.4 Properties of MCL

In this section we present some theorems about MCL and weaker theories. Most proofs are sketched.

Theorem 31 *MCL is a normal multimodal logic, i.e. we have*

$$\vdash [\alpha](\varphi \to \psi) \to ([\alpha]\varphi \to [\alpha]\psi)$$
$$\vdash \varphi \;\Rightarrow\; \vdash [\alpha]\varphi$$

Proof. This follows directly from **MP**, **NEC** and **DED**. □

Theorem 32 *The axiomatisation is sound and strongly complete w.r.t. natural models.*

Proof. Soundness, i.e. the property $\Gamma \vdash \varphi \;\Rightarrow\; \Gamma \models \varphi$, can be proved as usual by induction over the size of a derivation of $\Gamma \vdash \varphi$. For **Subst**, the following substitution properties are used (assuming that (t/x) is a safe substitution for φ and α):

$$\begin{array}{lcl} [\![(t/x)s]\!]_{w,A} & = & [\![s]\!]_{w,A[x\mapsto[\![t]\!]_{w,A}]} \\ w, A \models (t/x)\varphi & \Leftrightarrow & w, A[x \mapsto [\![t]\!]_{w,A}] \models \varphi \\ wR_{(t/x)\alpha,A}w' & \Leftrightarrow & wR_{\alpha,A[x\mapsto[\![t]\!]_{w,A}]}w' \end{array}$$

Strong completeness ($\Gamma \models \varphi \Rightarrow \Gamma \vdash \varphi$) is proved via the construction of maximal consistent sets of formulae in an extension of the language with Henkin constants, along the lines of Goldblatt's proof for the weak completeness of QDL in (Goldblatt 1992, ch. 14). In the resulting model, the worlds are characterised by deterministic programs (not containing $+, ^*, \cup$): an essential property is that every program is equivalent with the (infinite) sum of all deterministic programs contained in it. □

Theorem 33 *MCL is not compact.*

Proof. $\{[\alpha^n]\varphi \mid n \in \mathrm{N}\} \vdash [\alpha^*]\varphi$, but there is no finite subset of $\{[\alpha^n]\varphi \mid n \in \mathrm{N}\}$ which entails $[\alpha^*]\varphi$. □

Theorem 34 *MCL fails to satisfy the interpolation theorem.*

Proof. It is a folklore argument that any consistent logic with a finitary syntax and containing Peano arithmetic refutes interpolation, and it runs roughly as follows.

Beth's theorem (stating that every implicitly definable predicate has an explicit definition) is a consequence of interpolation, so it suffices to give an implicitly defiable predicate which has no explicit definition. MCL contains Peano Arithmetic (see the remark at the end of Section 7.1), so the syntax of MCL can be encoded in MCL, and we can give an implicit definition of a truth predicate. But, according to Tarski's theorem, an explicit truth definition cannot exist (for it leads to contradiction via a diagonal argument). See also (Renardel de Lavalette 1989, 6.4). □

The culprit in the last two theorems is the repetition construct *: we conjecture that compactness, and interpolation hold for MCL minus *. This is evidently the case when Create is omitted, too, since the resulting logic is a definitional extension of first-order logic, as we shall see below.

Now we turn to subtheories. Let MCL^{-c} be MCL without Create, with $\uparrow$ added to the static signature and new, E added to the dynamic signature. Models of MCL^{-c} are of the form $\langle U, I, W \rangle$, where U is the universe, I the interpretation of the static signature elements and W a collection of interpretations of the dynamic signature; in natural models, W contains *all* dynamic interpretations over U. The axiomatisation of MCL^{-c} is like that of MCL, but with the usual axioms and rules for equality and quantification (i.e. not referring to E and $\simeq$). So MCL^{-c} extends first-order logic.

Theorem 35 *MCL can be embedded in MCL^{-c}.*

Proof. The idea is to emulate MCL in MCL^{-c}. For this purpose, we add the unary functions s and l to the static and the dynamic signature, respectively. s is to act as a kind of successor function on the part of the universe that plays the role of the store, and l is used to imitate the localisation A_w of assignment A in world w. The required properties of $\uparrow, \mathsf{E}, \mathsf{new}, s, l$ can be expressed in one MCL^{-c}-formula θ. As an example we give the part of θ which enforces that $\{x \mid sx \neq x\}$ can play the role of the store:

$$\forall xy(sx = sy \rightarrow x = y) \wedge s(\mathsf{new}) \neq \mathsf{new} \wedge$$
$$[(\mathsf{new} := s(\mathsf{new}))^*](s(\mathsf{new}) \neq \uparrow \wedge \neg \mathsf{E}s(\mathsf{new}))$$

Terms, actions and programs from MCL are interpreted in MCL^{-c} via the mapping $^{-c}$. Its nontrivial defining clauses are

$$\begin{array}{lcl} x^{-c} & = & lx \\ (s=t)^{-c} & = & \mathsf{E}s^{-c} \wedge \mathsf{E}t^{-c} \wedge s^{-c} = t^{-c} \\ (\forall x\varphi)^{-c} & = & \forall x(\mathsf{E}x \rightarrow \varphi^{-c}) \\ ([\alpha]\varphi)^{-c} & = & [\alpha^{-c}]\varphi^{-c} \\ \mathsf{Create}^{-c} & = & \mathsf{new} := s(\mathsf{new}); \\ & & \mathsf{E} := \lambda x.\mathsf{E}x \vee x = \mathsf{new}; \\ & & l := \lambda x.\mathsf{if}\ x = \mathsf{new}\ \mathsf{then}\ x\ \mathsf{else}\ lx \\ (\cup x.\alpha)^{-c} & = & \cup x.(\mathsf{E}x?; \alpha^{-c}) \end{array}$$

So all variables in the interpretation occur in the scope of l or E. The interpretation of Create reads: let new refer to the 'next' element in the store, extend E with that element and adapt the localisation function l.

The transformation M^{-c}, w^{-c} of MCL-model M and world w is straightforward, and we have, for all M, all w in M and all φ:

$$\begin{array}{lcl} M^{-c}, w^{-c} \models \theta & & \\ M, w \models \varphi & \Leftrightarrow & M^{-c}, w^{-c} \models \varphi^{-c} \end{array}$$

Finally we claim

$$\Gamma \vdash \varphi \Leftrightarrow \Gamma^{-c}, \theta \vdash \varphi^{-c}.$$

The $\Rightarrow$ part is proved with induction over the derivation of $\Gamma \vdash \varphi$. The $\Leftarrow$ part is proved via contraposition. Assume $\Gamma \not\vdash \varphi$, then (by completeness of MCL) there is a model M with a world w such that $M, w \models \Gamma$ and $M, w \models \neg\varphi$. So there is a model M^{-c} with $M^{-c}, w^{-c} \models \Gamma^{-c}$ and $M^{-c}, w^{-c} \models \neg\varphi^{-c}$ and also $M^{-c}, w^{-c} \models \theta$. So (by soundness of MCL^{-c}) $\Gamma^{-c}, \theta \not\vdash \varphi^{-c}$. □

Theorem 36 *MCL can be embedded in* L_ω, *first-order predicate logic with countably infinite conjunctions.*

Proof. By the previous theorem, it suffices to give an embedding $\cdot^{\blacktriangledown} : \mathsf{MCL}^{-c} \rightarrow \mathsf{L}_\omega$. The embedding uses function substitution $(\lambda x.t/f)$ and predicate substitution $(\lambda x.\varphi/p)$. The essential defining clauses for these substitutions are

$$\begin{array}{lcl} (\lambda x.t/f)fs & = & ((\lambda x.t/f)s/x)t \\ (\lambda x.\varphi/p)ps & = & (s/x)\varphi \end{array}$$

Now the definition of $^\blacktriangledown$. The nontrivial defining clauses are those for formulae $[\alpha]\varphi$:

$$\begin{array}{lcl}
([f := \lambda x.t]\varphi)^\blacktriangledown & = & ((\lambda x.t/f)\varphi)^\blacktriangledown \\
([p := \lambda x.\psi]\varphi)^\blacktriangledown & = & ((\lambda x.\psi/p)\varphi)^\blacktriangledown \\
([\psi?]\varphi)^\blacktriangledown & = & \psi^\blacktriangledown \to \varphi^\blacktriangledown \\
([\alpha;\beta]\varphi)^\blacktriangledown & = & ([\alpha]([\beta]\varphi)^\blacktriangledown)^\blacktriangledown \\
([\alpha+\beta]\varphi)^\blacktriangledown & = & ([\alpha]\varphi)^\blacktriangledown \wedge ([\beta]\varphi)^\blacktriangledown \\
([\alpha^*]\varphi)^\blacktriangledown & = & \varphi^\blacktriangledown \wedge ([\alpha]\varphi)^\blacktriangledown \wedge ([\alpha;\alpha]\varphi)^\blacktriangledown \wedge \ldots \\
([\cup x.\alpha]\varphi)^\blacktriangledown & = & \forall x([\alpha]\varphi)^\blacktriangledown
\end{array}$$

So applying $^\blacktriangledown$ removes all programs with the help of substitution. Proving the correctness of the interpretation is straightforward. □

Theorem 37 *MCL without* Create *and* * *is a definitional extension of first-order predicate logic.*

Proof. This is is an easy consequence of the proof of the previous theorem, by observing that $\varphi^\blacktriangledown$ is finite whenever * does not occur in φ. □

7.5 Extensions

7.5.1 Parallel modifications

When several atomic modification programs affect different signature elements, they can be performed in parallel. E.g., for two function modifications $f := \lambda x.s,\ g := \lambda y.t$ this can be written as $f := \lambda x.s, g := \lambda y.t$. (In the context of evolving algebras, this construct is called the *join*.) It has the following semantics (writing α for $f := \lambda x.s, g := \lambda y.t$):

$$\begin{aligned} R_{\alpha,a} = \{(w, w[f \mapsto \lambda u \in U_w.[\![s]\!]_{w,a[x\mapsto u]}] \\ [g \mapsto \lambda u \in U_w.[\![t]\!]_{w,a[y\mapsto u]}]) \mid w \in W\} \end{aligned}$$

satisfying (z not free in s, t and $f, g \notin \mathsf{sig}(A)$)

$$\begin{array}{l}
[\alpha]fx = z \leftrightarrow s = z \\
[\alpha]gy = z \leftrightarrow t = z \\
A \leftrightarrow [\alpha]A \\
\forall z[\alpha]B \leftrightarrow [\alpha](\forall z B)
\end{array}$$

See (Groenboom and Renardel de Lavalette 1995) for more about this parallel construct.

7.5.2 Logic programming via least fixpoints of predicate operators

The meaning of a logic program H can be defined as the least fixpoint of a continuous predicate operator associated with H, and this can be expressed in MCL as follows. If $\lambda p.\lambda x.A$ defines a continuous predicate operator, then its least fixpoint $\mathsf{fix}(\lambda p.\lambda x.A)$ is definable in MCL as follows:

$$\mathsf{fix}(\lambda p.\lambda x.A)x \leftrightarrow \langle(p := \lambda x.\bot); (p := \lambda x.A)^*\rangle px$$

Now, if the logic program H defines one unary predicate, and has the form

$$\begin{array}{lcl} p(t_1) & \leftarrow & A_1 \\ p(t_2) & \leftarrow & A_2 \end{array}$$

where A_1 and/or A_2 may contain p, then the meaning of H is the least fixpoint of the continuous predicate operator

$$\lambda p.\lambda x.((x = t_1 \wedge A_1) \vee (x = t_2 \wedge A_2)),$$

hence is expressible in MCL.

If H defines more than one predicate, and has the form

$$\begin{array}{lcl} p(t_1) & \leftarrow & A_1 \\ q(t_2) & \leftarrow & A_2 \end{array}$$

where A_1, A_2 may contain p, q, then its meaning is obtained via the program

$$\begin{array}{l} \alpha^H = (p := \lambda x.\bot, q := \lambda x.\bot); \\ (p := \lambda x.(x = t_1 \wedge A_1), q := \lambda x.(x = t_2 \wedge A_2))^* \end{array}$$

by taking $\langle\alpha^H\rangle px, \langle\alpha^H\rangle qy$ for the meaning of H.

7.5.3 Removing objects

Let us now consider the possibility of removing objects with the action $\mathsf{Remove}(t)$. Its intuitive semantics reads: identify $[\![t]\!]$ with the undefined object $\star$. To make this work, the notion of model must be generalised to allow for worlds with local universes of the form $(U \cup V_n) - X$ where X is some finite set. We expect that this can be done in such a way that Remove is both deterministic and terminating. Other expected properties of Remove are:

$$x = y \neq z \leftrightarrow [\mathsf{Remove}(z)]x = y$$

$$[\mathsf{Remove}(t)]p(x) \rightarrow p(x)$$

$$\forall x([\mathsf{Remove}(t)]\mathsf{E}x \leftrightarrow x \neq t)$$

7.5.4 Adding and removing many objects

Create and Remove handle one object at a time. With the repetition construct *, it is possible to create or remove finitely many objects, viz. with the actions Create^* and $(\cup x.\mathsf{Remove}(x))^*$. (Observe that $\mathsf{Remove}(t)^*$ does not work: it has the same effect as $\mathsf{Remove}(t)$.)

If we want more, we can introduce the actions Add and Remove, corresponding with $\delta\uparrow$ and $\delta\downarrow$ from 7.2.4. With Add, it is useful to have the unary predicate New available, which holds for all newly added objects: so we , for example, $\forall x([\mathsf{Add}]\neg\mathsf{New}(x))$.

But other variants are also imaginable: Addinf(adding an infinite number of objects to the universe) and $\mathsf{Remove}(\lambda x.\varphi)$ (removing all objects x satisfying φ). Observe that, slightly paradoxically, we do not have

$$[\mathsf{Remove}(\lambda x.\varphi)]\forall x \neg\varphi(x)$$

to see this, take $\varphi := \neg\exists y.Rxy$ and consider a world with universe $\{a, b\}$ where R is interpreted by $\{(a, b)\}$; then the extension of φ is $\{b\}$, so after $\mathsf{Remove}(\lambda x.\varphi)$ we are left with a world with universe $\{a\}$ where R is empty, so φ holds for a.

7.6 Concluding Remarks

In this paper, we extended first-order logic — the workhorse for the application of logic in computer science, linguistics and artificial intelligence — with features intended for the description, analysis and unification of the numerous dynamic phenomena that occur in these disciplines: modification (of references, situations, contexts, memory states, database contents, information states, etc.) and creation (of pointers, records, referents, assumptions, hypotheses, information items, concepts, etc.). This resulted in the orthogonally designed logic MCL with a sound and complete axiomatisation.

Furthermore, we made a beginning with the unification of logics dealing with dynamics by indicating how QDL and DDL can be embedded in MCL. It will be interesting to try to do the same with DPL and DELḞor DPL, it will be useful to add to MCL expressions $\alpha \leq \beta$ with the intended meaning: all α-alternatives are β-alternatives. Embedding DEL in MCL will be more involved and may require recursively defined actions.

Another direction of research is extension of the action language. Some suggestions: action operators for parallel composition and removal of objects, effects during actions, attemptive actions, actions with so-called modification rights (indicating globally what may be changed by an action and what not, as in COLD).

We end with some more technical problems: prove compactness and interpolation for MCL without repetition, and determine the proof-theoretic strength of MCL (see (Harel 1984, 3.2) for related work on QDL).

Appendix: definition of safe substitutions

Here we define the class of safe substitutions, announced in subsection 7.3.5. The idea is: a substitution is safe when it does not bring signature elements in the scope of actions that may modify them. For this purpose, we introduce the mappings fvar, sig^+, change and mod . $\mathsf{fvar}(\varphi)$ is the collection of free variables occurring in φ, idem for $\mathsf{fvar}(\alpha)$. $\mathsf{sig}^+(t)$ is the collection of extended signature elements (i.e. elements of $\S \cup \{\mathsf{new}\}$) occurring in t. $\mathsf{change}(\alpha)$, an auxiliary mapping for the definition of mod , contains the extended signature elements that are (possibly) changed by α. It is defined by

$$\begin{array}{lcl}
\mathsf{change}(\mathsf{Create}) & = & \{\mathsf{new}\} \\
\mathsf{change}(f := \lambda x.t) & = & \{f\} \\
\mathsf{change}(p := \lambda x.\varphi) & = & \{p\} \\
\mathsf{change}(\varphi?) & = & \emptyset \\
\mathsf{change}(\alpha;\beta) & = & \mathsf{change}(\alpha) \cup \mathsf{change}(\beta) \\
\mathsf{change}(\alpha+\beta) & = & \mathsf{change}(\alpha) \cup \mathsf{change}(\beta) \\
\mathsf{change}(\alpha^*) & = & \mathsf{change}(\alpha) \\
\mathsf{change}(\cup x.\alpha) & = & \mathsf{change}(\alpha)
\end{array}$$

$\mathrm{mod}\ (x,\varphi)$ is the collection of extended signature elements that may undergo modification at some free occurrence of x in φ; similarly for $\mathrm{mod}\ (x,\alpha)$.

$$\begin{array}{lcll}
\mathrm{mod}\ (x, s=t) & = & \emptyset & \\
\mathrm{mod}\ (x, p(t)) & = & \emptyset & \\
\mathrm{mod}\ (x, \neg\varphi) & = & \mathrm{mod}\ (x,\varphi) & \\
\mathrm{mod}\ (x, \varphi\wedge\psi) & = & \mathrm{mod}\ (x,\varphi) \cup \mathrm{mod}\ (x,\psi) & \\
\mathrm{mod}\ (x, \forall x\varphi) & = & \emptyset & \\
\mathrm{mod}\ (x, \forall y\varphi) & = & \mathrm{mod}\ (x,\varphi) & \text{if } y \not\equiv x \\
\mathrm{mod}\ (x, [\alpha]\varphi) & = & \mathrm{mod}\ (x,\alpha) \cup \mathrm{mod}\ (x,\varphi) \cup \mathsf{change}(\alpha) & \text{if } x \in \mathsf{fvar}(\varphi) \\
 & = & \mathrm{mod}\ (x,\alpha) \cup \mathrm{mod}\ (x,\varphi) & \text{if } x \notin \mathsf{fvar}(\varphi) \\
\mathrm{mod}\ (x, \mathsf{Create}) & = & \emptyset & \\
\mathrm{mod}\ (x, f := \lambda x.t) & = & \emptyset & \\
\mathrm{mod}\ (x, p := \lambda x.\varphi) & = & \emptyset & \\
\mathrm{mod}\ (x, \varphi?) & = & \mathrm{mod}\ (x,\varphi) & \\
\mathrm{mod}\ (x, \alpha;\beta) & = & \mathrm{mod}\ (x,\alpha) \cup \mathrm{mod}\ (x,\beta) \cup \mathsf{change}(\alpha) & \text{if } x \in \mathsf{fvar}(\beta) \\
 & = & \mathrm{mod}\ (x,\alpha) \cup \mathrm{mod}\ (x,\beta) & \text{if } x \notin \mathsf{fvar}(\beta) \\
\mathrm{mod}\ (x, \alpha+\beta) & = & \mathrm{mod}\ (x,\alpha) \cup \mathrm{mod}\ (x,\beta) & \\
\mathrm{mod}\ (x, \alpha^*) & = & \mathrm{mod}\ (x,\alpha) \cup \mathsf{change}(\alpha) & \text{if } x \in \mathsf{fvar}(\alpha) \\
 & = & \mathrm{mod}\ (x,\alpha) & \text{if } x \notin \mathsf{fvar}(\alpha) \\
\mathrm{mod}\ (x, \cup x.\alpha) & = & \emptyset & \\
\mathrm{mod}\ (x, \cup y.\alpha) & = & \mathrm{mod}\ (x,\alpha) & \text{if } y \not\equiv x
\end{array}$$

Now we define *safe substitution* by

(t/x) is safe for every term;
(t/x) is safe for formula φ whenever $\mathsf{sig}^+(t) \cap \mathrm{mod}\ (x,\varphi) = \emptyset$;
(t/x) is safe for program α whenever $\mathsf{sig}^+(t) \cap \mathrm{mod}\ (x,\alpha) = \emptyset$.

References

Beeson, Michael J. 1985. *Foundations of Constructive Mathematics*. Berlin: Springer-Verlag.

Blamey, S. 1986. Partial logic. In *Handbook of Philosophical Logic (vol.III)*, ed. D. Gabbay and F. Guenthner. 1–70. Dordrecht: D. Reidel Publishing Company.

Börger, E., and J.K. Huggins. 1998. Abstract State Machines 1988-1998: Commented ASM Bibliography. *Bulletin of the EATCS* 64:105–126.

Feijs, L.M.G., and H.B.M. Jonkers. 1992. *Formal Specification and Design*. Cambridge Tracts in Theoretical Computer Science, Vol. 35. Cambridge: Cambridge University Press.

Feijs, L.M.G., H.B.M. Jonkers, C.P.J. Koymans, and G.R. Renardel de Lavalette. 1987a. Formal definition of the design language COLD-K (Preliminary version). ESPRIT document METEOR/t7/PRLE/7. Eindhoven (the Netherlands): Philips Research Laboratories, Apr. (Final version: August 1989).

Feijs, L.M.G., H.B.M. Jonkers, J.H. Obbink, C.P.J. Koymans, G.R. Renardel de Lavalette, and P.H. Rodenburg. 1987b. A survey of the design language COLD. In *ESPRIT'86: Results and Achievements*, ed. Directorate General XIII. 631 – 644. Elsevier Science Publishers (North-Holland).

Fensel, Dieter, and Rix Groenboom. 1996. MLPM: defining a semantics and axiomatisation for specifying t he reasoning process of knowledge-based systems. In *Proceedings of the 12th European Conference on Artificial Intelligence (ECAI96)*, ed. W. Wahlster, 423 – 427. Budapest.

Fensel, Dieter, Rix Groenboom, and Gera rd R. Renardel de Lavalette. 1998. Modal Change Logic (MCL): Specifying the Reasoning of Knowledge-based Systems. *Data and Knowledge Engineering* 26:243–269.

Gerbrandy, Jelle. 1999. *Bisimulations on Planet Kripke*. Doctoral dissertation, Institute for Logic, Language and Computation, Amsterdam, Jan.

Gerbrandy, Jelle, and Willem Groeneveld. 1997. Reasoning about Information Change. *Journal of Logic, Language and Information* 6:147–169.

Goldblatt, Robert. 1992. *Logics of time and computation*. CSLI Lecture notes, Vol. 7. Stanford: CSLI. (2nd edition).

Groenboom, Rix, and Gerard R. Renardel de Lavalette. 1994. Reasoning about dynamic features in specification languages - a modal view on creation and modification. In *Semantics of Specification Languages*, ed. D.J. Andrews, J.F. Groote, and C.A. Middelburg, 340 – 355. Workshops in Computing. Springer-Verlag.

Groenboom, Rix, and Gerard R. Renardel de Lavalette. 1995. A formalization of evolving algebras. In *Proceedings Accolade '95*, ed. S. Fischer and M. Trautwein, 17 – 28. Amsterdam. Dutch Graduate School in Logic.

Groenendijk, Jeroen, and Martin Stokhof. 1991. Dynamic predicate logic. *Linguistics and Philosophy* 14:39 – 100.

Gurevich, Yuri. 1988. Logic and the challenge of computer science. In *Trends in theoretical computer science*, ed. Egon Börger. 1 – 57. Computer Science Press.

Gurevich, Yuri. 1991. Evolving algebras; a tutorial introduction. *Bulletin of the EATCS* 43:264 – 284.

Gurevich, Yuri. 1995. Evolving algebras 1993: Lipari guide. In *Specification and validation methods*, ed. Egon Börger. Oxford: Clarendon Press.

Harel, David. 1984. Dynamic Logic. In *Handbook of Philosophical Logic*, ed. D. Gabbay and F. Guenthner. 497 – 604. Dordrecht (the Netherlands): D. Reidel Publishing Company.

Hopcroft, John E., and Jeffery D. Ullman. 1979. *Introduction to Automata Theory, Languages and Computation*. Addison-Wesley Publishing Company.

Koymans, C.P.J., and G.R. Renardel de Lavalette. 1989. The logic MPL_ω. In *Algebraic Methods: Theory, tools and applications*, ed. M. Wirsing and J.A. Bergstra. Lecture Notes in Computer Science, Vol. 394, 247 – 282. Springer-Verlag.

McCarthy, J., and P. Hayes. 1969. Some philosophical problems from the standpoint of Artificial Intelligence. In *Machine Intelligence*, ed. B. Meltzer and D. Michie. 463 – 502. Edinburgh University Press.

Pratt, V.R. 1976. Semantical considerations on Floyd-Hoare logic. In *17th annual symposium on foundations of computer science*, 109 – 121. New York. IEEE.

Renardel de Lavalette, Gerard R. 1989. Modularisation, Parametrisation, Interpolation. *Journal of Information Processing and Cybernetics EIK* 25:283 – 292.

Scott, D.S. 1967. Existence and description in formal logic. In *Bertrand Russell, Philosopher of the Century*, ed. R. Schoenman. 181 – 200. London: Allen and Unwin.

Scott, D.S. 1979. Identity and existence in intuitionistic logic. In *Applications of Sheaves*, ed. M.P. Fourman, C.J. Mulvey, and D.S. Scott, Lecture Notes in Mathematics, Vol. 753, 660 – 696. Springer-Verlag.

Spruit, Paul A., Roel J. Wieringa, and John-Jules Ch. Meijer. 1995. Axiomatisation, declarative semantics and operational semantic s of passive and active updates in logic databases. *Journal of Logic and Computation* 5:27 – 50.

Tonino, Hans. 1997. *A theory of many-sorted evolving algebras*. Doctoral dissertation, Delft University of Technology, the Netherlands.

Troelstra, A.S., and D. van Dalen. 1988. *Constructivism in Mathematics, an Introduction (volume 1)*. Studies in Logic and the Foundations of Mathematics, Vol. 121. North-Holland.

Urquhart, Alisdair. 1986. Many-valued logic. In *Handbook of Philosophical Logic*, ed. D. Gabbay and F. Guenthner. 71 – 116. Dordrecht (the Netherlands): D. Reidel Publishing Company.

van Benthem, Johan. 1996. *Exploring Logical Dynamics*. Studies in Logic, Language and Information. Stanford: CSLI Publications and FoLLI.

van Benthem, Johan, and Giovanna Cepparello. 1994. *Tarskian variations — Dynamic parameters in classical semant ics*. Report CS-R9419. Amsterdam: Centrum voor Wiskunde en Informatica.

Veltman, Frank. 1996. Defaults in update semantics. *Journal of Philosophical Logic* 15:221 – 261.

Wirsing, Martin. 1990. Algebraic Specification. In *Handbook of Theoretical Computer Science*, ed. Jan van Leeuwen. Elsevier Science.

8

Model Checking and Deduction for Infinite-State Systems

HENNY B. SIPMA, TOMÁS E. URIBE AND ZOHAR MANNA

8.1 Introduction

Reactive systems are those with an ongoing interaction with their environment. While the relationship between any two given system states can be expressed in first-order logic or a suitable assertion language, properties of non-terminating computations, which are infinite sequences of states, are best expressed using some form of temporal logic.

The two main approaches to verifying temporal properties of reactive systems are *deductive verification* on the one hand, and *model checking* on the other. In the deductive approach, the validity of a given temporal property over a given program is reduced to the general validity of a set of first-order formulas, through the use of *verification rules*. In *model checking*, the state space of the program is systematically explored in search for a computation that violates the property being verified, until such a counterexample is found or it is shown that it cannot exist.

Model checking procedures are usually automatic, while deductive verification often relies on user interaction to identify suitable lemmas and auxiliary assertions. However, model checking is usually applicable only to systems with a finite, fixed number of states, while the deductive approach can verify infinite-state systems and parameterized finite-state systems of arbitrary size.

*This research was supported in part by the National Science Foundation under grant CCR-92-23226, the Advanced Research Projects Agency under NASA grant NAG2-892, the United States Air Force Office of Scientific Research under grant F49620-93-1-0139, the Department of the Army under grant DAAH04-95-1-0317, and a gift from Intel Corporation.

Logical Perspectives on Language and Information.
Cleo Condoravdi and Gerard R. Renardel de Lavalette.

After presenting the computational model of fair transition systems and the specification language of linear-time temporal logic in Section 8.2, we present an overview of deductive verification (Section 8.3) and linear-time temporal logic model checking (Section 8.4). We then present *deductive model checking* (Sipma et al. 1996), which combines the two approaches into a single procedure that retains some of their complementary strengths (Section 8.5). Finally, we discuss related work in Section 8.6.

8.2 Preliminaries

8.2.1 Fair Transition Systems

To carry out formal verification, we need a precise mathematical model of the systems being analyzed. For this, we use *fair transition systems* (Manna and Pnueli 1991) as our computational model for reactive systems. A fair transition system (FTS) $\mathcal{S}$ is a triple $\langle \mathcal{V}, \Theta, \mathcal{T} \rangle$, where $\mathcal{V}$ is a set of variables, Θ is an *initial condition*, and $\mathcal{T}$ is a finite set of *transitions*. A finite set of *system variables* $V \subset \mathcal{V}$ determines the possible states of the system. The *state space*, Σ, is the set of all possible valuations of the system variables, each defining a *system state*.

Fair transition systems allow the description of a wide range of systems, including hardware and software, using the full expressive power of first-order logic. We use a first-order assertion language $\mathcal{A}$ to describe the initial condition Θ and the transitions in $\mathcal{T}$. This assertion language can be augmented with interpreted function symbols and constraints, or specialized to the finite-state case, depending on the system being specified. A formula over the system variables V describes the set of states for which it is true; if a state s satisfies the formula φ, we say that s is a *φ-state*. The initial condition Θ is such an assertion over V, describing the set of *initial states*. A transition τ is described by a *transition relation* $\rho_\tau(V, V')$. This is an assertion over the set of system variables V, indicating their values at a given state, and a set of *primed variables* V', which indicates their values at the next state. $\mathcal{T}$ includes an *idling transition*, *Idle*, whose transition relation is $V = V'$.

Example 1 *Figure 1 shows the transition system* BAK *that represents Lamport's Bakery algorithm (Lamport 1974) for 2-process mutual exclusion. The algorithm owes its name to its resemblance to the procedure in a bakery shop. Initially customers are outside the shop. They take a number to show their interest in being served; the customer with the lowest number is the first one served.* BAK *has four system variables: the (control) variables pc_1 and pc_2 range over the control locations {off, wait, crit}; the (data) variables y_1 and y_2 range over the natural numbers. The transition system has seven transitions, whose actions are schematically shown in the figure. For example, the transition relations for $take_1$ and $enter_1$ are*

$$V: \{pc_1, pc_2, y_1, y_2\}$$

$$\Theta: pc_1 = outside \wedge pc_2 = outside \wedge y_1 = 0 \wedge y_2 = 0$$

$$\mathcal{T}: \{take_1, enter_1, leave_1, take_2, enter_2, leave_2, idle\}$$

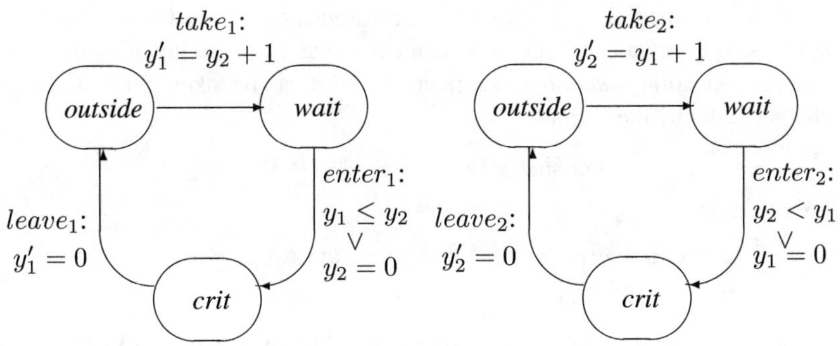

FIGURE 1 Transition system BAK

$$\rho_{take_1} \; : \; pc_1 = outside \wedge pc_1' = wait \wedge y_1' = y_2 + 1 \wedge pres(\{pc_2, y_2\})$$
$$\rho_{enter_1} \; : \; pc_1 = wait \wedge pc_1' = crit \wedge (y_1 \leq y_2 \vee y_2 = 0) \wedge pres(\{pc_2, y_1, y_2\})$$

where $pres(U)$ *stands for* $U' = U$.

Concurrency is modelled by *interleaving*. A *run* is an infinite sequence of states $s_0, s_1, \ldots$ such that s_0 satisfies Θ, and for each $i \geq 0$, there is some transition $\tau \in \mathcal{T}$ such that $\rho_\tau(s_i, s_{i+1})$ is true. For example,

$$\begin{aligned}
&\langle pc_1 : outside, pc_2 : outside, y_1 : 0, y_2 : 0\rangle, \\
&\langle pc_1 : wait, pc_2 : outside, y_1 : 1, y_2 : 0\rangle, \\
&\langle pc_1 : wait, pc_2 : wait, y_1 : 1, y_2 : 2\rangle, \\
&\langle pc_1 : crit, pc_2 : wait, y_1 : 1, y_2 : 2\rangle, \ldots
\end{aligned}$$

is a run of system BAK.

Given a run $s_0, s_1, \ldots$, we say that a transition τ is *taken* at state s_i if $\rho_\tau(s_i, s_{i+1})$ evaluates to true, in which case state s_{i+1} is called a τ-*successor* of s_i. A transition is *enabled* at a given state if it can be taken. Such states are characterized by the formula

$$enabled(\tau) \;\stackrel{\text{def}}{=}\; \exists V'.\rho_\tau(V, V') \;.$$

For example,

$$\begin{aligned}
enabled(enter_1) &= (pc_1 = wait \wedge y_1 \leq y_2) \;. \\
enabled(leave_1) &= (pc_1 = crit) \;.
\end{aligned}$$

The presence of the idling transition ensures that all run prefixes can be extended to an infinite run, since the idling transition is always enabled.

For a formula φ and a transition τ, we define the *weakest precondition* $pre(\tau, \varphi)$ (Dijkstra 1975) and the *strongest postcondition* $post(\tau, \varphi)$ as follows:

$$\begin{aligned}
pre(\tau, \varphi) &\stackrel{\text{def}}{=} \forall V'. (\rho_\tau(V, V') \rightarrow \varphi(V')) \\
post(\tau, \varphi) &\stackrel{\text{def}}{=} \exists V_0. (\rho_\tau(V_0, V) \wedge \varphi(V_0)) \;.
\end{aligned}$$

Intuitively, the weakest precondition of φ with respect to transition τ describes the states that must reach a φ-state after τ is taken. (This is sometimes called the *weakest liberal precondition*, since it is true of those states where τ cannot be taken at all.) Similarly, the strongest postcondition of φ with respect to transition τ describes the set of states that can be reached by taking transition τ from a state that satisfies φ; if τ cannot be taken, then the postcondition is the formula *false* (the empty set of states).

We also use the *Hoare triple* notation,

$$\{\varphi\}\,\tau\,\{\psi\} \stackrel{\text{def}}{=} (\varphi(V) \wedge \rho_\tau(V, V')) \rightarrow \psi(V') \;.$$

This formula is valid if taking transition τ from a φ-state always leads to a state that satisfies ψ. Note that it holds if τ is not enabled at φ-states.

Fairness

Modelling concurrency with interleaving enables a simple encoding of nondeterminism, and abstracts away the relative speed of different processes. However, one then wants to exclude computations where a given process or nondeterministic action is forever ignored (the process never advances or an action never occurs even though it is allowed). To this effect, the transitions in $\mathcal{T}$ can be optionally marked as *just* or *compassionate*. A just (or *weakly fair*) transition cannot be *continually* enabled without ever being taken. A compassionate (or *strongly fair*) transition cannot be enabled infinitely often without being taken (that is, a transition that is enabled infinitely often must be taken infinitely often). A *computation* is a run that satisfies these fairness requirements. In our example system BAK all transitions except $take_1$, $take_2$ and $idle$ are marked as just. Thus, the infinite sequence of states

$$\langle pc_1 : outside, pc_2 : outside, y_1 : 0, y_2 : 0\rangle,$$
$$\langle pc_1 : wait, pc_2 : outside, y_1 : 1, y_2 : 0\rangle,$$
$$\langle pc_1 : wait, pc_2 : outside, y_1 : 1, y_2 : 0\rangle,$$
$$\langle pc_1 : wait, pc_2 : outside, y_1 : 1, y_2 : 0\rangle, \ \ldots$$

is a run of system BAK, but it is not a computation, since the just transition $enter_1$ is always enabled, but never taken.

8.2.2 Temporal Logic

As first pointed out by Pnueli (1977), temporal logic is a convenient formalism for specifying properties of reactive systems. A formula in temporal logic is interpreted over infinite sequences of states. Viewed as a *temporal property*, it describes a set of such sequences. A given system satisfies a property if all of its computations belong to this set.

A model of *linear-time temporal logic* (LTL) is an infinite sequence of states where each point in time has a unique successor. We use the *anchored* version of LTL, where the truth-value of a formula for a given model is evaluated at the initial position of the model. Given a model $s = s_0, s_1, \ldots$, the *future* temporal operators are defined as follows:

$\Box p$ holds at state s_j iff p is true for all states s_i, $i \geq j$;
$\Diamond p$ holds at state s_j iff p is true for some state s_i, $i \geq j$;
$\bigcirc p$ holds at state s_j iff p holds at state $j + 1$;
$p\,\mathcal{U}\,q$ holds at state s_j iff for some $k \geq j$, q holds at state s_k, and p holds at every state s_i, $j \leq i < k$.
$p\mathcal{W}q$ holds at state s_j iff $(p\,\mathcal{U}\,q)$ or $\Box p$ hold at state s_j.

Past versions of these temporal operators are similarly defined. For simplicity, we will restrict our notation and examples to the future fragment of LTL. We do not allow temporal operators to appear within the scope of a quantifier, so all quantification can be thought of as *rigid*; such formulas are known as *state-quantified* formulas (Manna and Pnueli 1995). A formula containing no temporal operators is called a *state formula* or an *assertion*.

For a system $\mathcal{S}$, we say that a formula φ is $\mathcal{S}$-*valid* if all the computations of $\mathcal{S}$ are models of φ (that is, $\mathcal{S}$ satisfies φ).

Example 2 *The mutual-exclusion property for the* BAK *system states that the two processes cannot be simultaneously in their critical section. It is expressed by the LTL formula*

$$\Box(\neg(pc_1 = crit \wedge pc_2 = crit)) \ .$$

Another desirable property of a mutual exclusion algorithm is accessibility*: if a process is waiting to enter its critical section it will eventually be allowed to enter it. This is expressed by*

$$\varphi : \Box(pc_1 = wait \rightarrow \Diamond pc_1 = crit) \ .$$

We will see later that BAK *satisfies both properties. Although accessibility ensures that a waiting process will eventually be allowed to enter its critical section, it does not pose any bound on how many times the other process may go first. The* bounded-overtaking *property, expressed by*

$$\Box(pc_1 = wait \rightarrow pc_2 \neq crit \,\mathcal{W}\, pc_2 = crit \,\mathcal{W}\, pc_2 \neq crit \,\mathcal{W}\, pc_1 = crit) \ .$$

where the waitfor operator $\mathcal{W}$ associates to the right, states that if process 1 is waiting, process 2 is allowed to enter its critical section at most once before process 1 is allowed to enter. Note that the $\mathcal{W}$ (weak until) operator allows any of the intervals to be empty or to extend into infinity. Thus the above formula does not guarantee that process 1 will eventually reach its critical section, like accessibility does.

In *branching-time temporal logic*, points in time can have multiple successors, understood as possible future states. Thus, branching-time models are infinite trees, rather than the linear sequences of LTL models. The logic CTL (*computation tree logic*) of Clarke and Emerson (1981) is interpreted over such models. Since we will focus on LTL, we will not further discuss branching time logics.

A detailed exposition of linear-time temporal logic as a specification language for fair transition systems is found in (Manna and Pnueli 1991). Emerson (1990) presents a survey of branching and linear-time temporal logic.

8.3 Deductive Verification

8.3.1 Verification rules

The classical deductive framework for the verification of fair transition systems is based on *verification rules*, which reduce the proof of temporal properties of systems to checking validity of first-order premises (Manna and Pnueli 1995).

$$
\begin{array}{ll}
 & \text{For an assertion } p, \\
1. & \Theta \rightarrow p \\
2. & \{p\}\,\tau\,\{p\}, \text{ for all } \tau \in \mathcal{T}, \\
\hline
 & \Box p
\end{array}
$$

FIGURE 2 Basic invariance rule.

Figure 2 shows an example of such a verification rule, the *basic invariance rule*: it can be used to prove the $\mathcal{S}$-validity of formulas of the form $\Box p$, where p is an assertion (state formula). The rule states that if p is (1) implied by the initial condition and (2) preserved by all transitions, then we can conclude that p holds in all states of all computations.

When we try to apply this rule, we quickly discover its weakness: most properties we want to prove, albeit $\mathcal{S}$-valid, are not preserved by all transitions. As an example, consider mutual exclusion, which we claimed valid for BAK before:

$$\Box mux : \quad \Box\neg(pc_1 = crit \wedge pc_2 = crit) \ .$$

The verification condition generated for $enter_1$,

$$
\begin{array}{l}
\underbrace{\neg(pc_1 = crit \wedge pc_2 = crit)}_{mux} \wedge \\
\qquad\qquad \underbrace{pc_1 = wait \wedge (y_1 \leq y_2 \vee y_2 = 0) \wedge pc_1' = crit}_{\rho_{enter_1}} \rightarrow \\
\qquad\qquad \underbrace{\neg(pc_1' = crit \wedge pc_2' = crit)}_{mux'} \ .
\end{array}
$$

is clearly not valid. The problem is that the assertion is not strong enough; we say it is not *inductive*. The problem is illustrated in Figure 3, where Σ is the entire state space, p the set of states satisfying p and *acc* the set of states that are accessible by a computation. Clearly the system satisfies p, since the accessible states are a subset of the states satisfying p. However p is not preserved by all transitions, which are drawn as arrows.

To remedy this problem we introduce the *general invariance rule* shown in Figure 4. It relies on finding an auxiliary assertion ψ that is inductive, that is, preserved by all transitions, and that implies the property we want to prove.

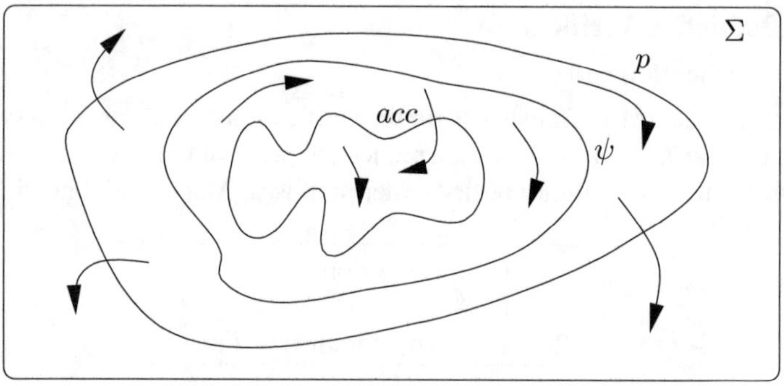

FIGURE 3 Invariants in the state space.

Example 3 *An inductive assertion that implies mutual exclusion for system* BAK *is*

$$\begin{aligned}
\neg(pc_1 = crit \wedge pc_2 = crit) \wedge y_1 \geq 0 \wedge y_2 \geq 0 \wedge& \\
(pc_1 = crit \rightarrow (y_1 > 0 \wedge y_1 \leq y_2)) \wedge& \\
(pc_2 = crit \rightarrow (y_2 > 0 \wedge y_2 < y_1)) \wedge& \\
(pc_1 = wait \rightarrow y_1 > 0) \wedge (pc_2 = wait \rightarrow y_2 > 0)&\ .
\end{aligned}$$

The general invariance rule is *relatively complete*, in the sense that if p is an invariant of a system, then the strengthened assertion ψ always exists (Manna and Pnueli 1995). In fact, the completeness proof shows that *acc* can always be constructed, providing the strongest intermediate assertion. However, this assertion tends to be unwieldy, and in practice simpler assertions suffice. Much research is directed towards finding these intermediate assertions, e.g. (Bjørner et al. 1997). Note that in general the verification of temporal properties of infinite-state systems is undecidable (no algorithm exists that can prove exactly all valid program properties and always terminate, cf. the halting problem for Turing machines).

$$\begin{array}{ll}
 & \text{For assertions } \psi \text{ and } p, \\
1. & \psi \rightarrow p \\
2. & \Theta \rightarrow \psi \\
3. & \{\psi\}\ \tau\ \{\psi\} \text{ for all } \tau \in \mathcal{T}, \\
\hline
 & \Box p
\end{array}$$

FIGURE 4 General invariance rule.

Other verification rules can be used to verify different classes of temporal formulas, ranging from *safety* properties such as the mutual-exclusion and bounded-overtaking properties shown earlier, to *progress* properties, such as accessibility (Manna and Pnueli 1995). These rules are implemented, for example, in the STeP (Stanford Temporal Prover) verification system (Bjørner et al. 1996). Fix and Grumberg (1996) present a complete deductive system for the temporal verification of branching-time temporal properties. Bradfield (1992) presents a deductive proof system for the modal μ-calculus.

These deductive methods are relatively complete and yield a direct proof of any valid property, but can require substantial user guidance to succeed. Furthermore, they do not produce counterexample computations when the property fails.

8.3.2 Graphical Formalisms

Graphical formalisms can facilitate the task of guiding and understanding a deductive proof. *Verification diagrams* (Manna and Pnueli 1994) provide a graphical representation of the verification conditions needed to establish a particular temporal formula. Different types of diagrams are used to prove different classes of temporal properties. The generalized verification diagrams introduced in (Browne et al. 1995) and later extended in (Browne et al. 1996) are applicable to any state-quantified temporal property.

An example of a verification diagram is the *invariance diagram* shown in Figure 5: it represents a formal proof that system BAK satisfies mutual exclusion. An invariance diagram generates three proof obligations, each expressed as a set of first-order verification conditions. The *initial condition* states that all initial states are included in the diagram, that is, Θ is implied by the disjunction of the node assertions. The *consecution condition* ensures that each transition preserves the node assertions or leads to a neighboring node. The initial condition and consecution show that the diagram faithfully represents all runs of the system. The *satisfaction condition,* expressed by a first-order implication for each node, states that each node assertion satisfies the invariant we want to prove.

Comparing the application of the general invariance rule, using the inductive assertion of Example 3, with the invariance diagram of Figure 5, we claim that the diagram provides more insight on why the property holds: it presents a meaningful partition of the state-space, insofar as it is relevant to the property in question, and the transitions between these sets of states. Besides facilitating proofs, verification diagrams can also be used as documentation for a system, describing important properties of its computations.

Another graphical formalism is *deductive model checking*, presented in Section 8.5, in which a diagram is constructed to show that the system does *not* satisfy the negation of the property to be proved. *Fairness diagrams* (de Alfaro and Manna 1996) combine the direct and indirect proof approaches. Here, a

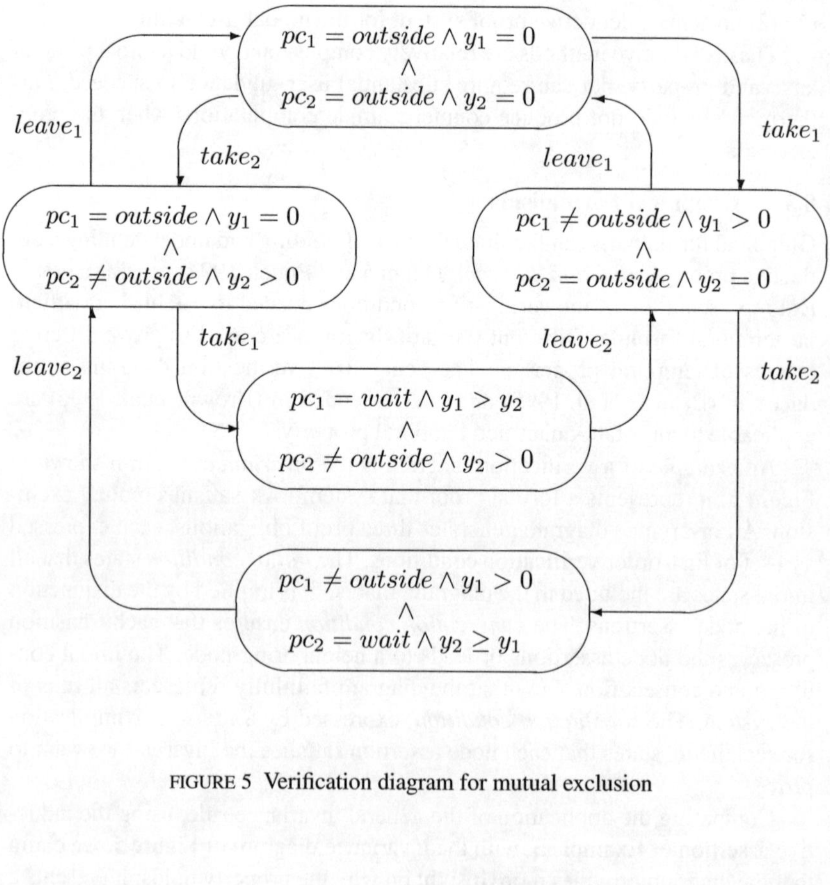

FIGURE 5 **Verification diagram for mutual exclusion**

graphical representation of the transition system is transformed incrementally until a representation is obtained that can be shown to satisfy the specification by algorithmic means. General verification conditions must be proved to justify each transformation step.

(de Alfaro et al. 1997) summarizes the common features of verification diagrams, fairness diagrams, and deductive model checking. They all can describe and verify infinite-state systems using a finite representation that is incrementally constructed, where verification conditions are local and where global properties can be checked algorithmically.

8.4 Model Checking

In contrast to deductive methods, which require the user to find intermediate assertions, model checking is fully automatic. Model checking tests whether the transition graph of the system admits any computations that are a model of the negated specification. We will describe how this is accomplished for specifications expressed by LTL formulas.

8.4.1 Formula Tableau

Given an LTL formula φ, we can construct its *tableau* Φ_φ, a finite graph that describes all of its models. The nodes in the tableau are labeled by *atoms* sets of formulas constructed from the subformulas of φ and the next-state operator. Each atom contains formulas which may hold simultaneously at a state in a computation. Two nodes A_1 and A_2 are connected with a directed edge $\langle A_1, A_2\rangle$ if the formulas in A_2 can hold at a state following one that satisfies the formulas in A_1. An *initial atom* is one whose formulas can hold at the initial state of a model; in particular, it should contain the formula φ. Thus, the atom labeling a node contains the state and temporal formulas that should hold whenever a model of φ reaches this node.

The formula φ is satisfiable only if the tableau Φ_φ admits infinite paths, since models of an LTL formula are infinite sequences of states. Since the tableau itself is a finite graph, to be able to embed a model, it must contain at least one *strongly connected subgraph* (SCS) (a subgraph with at least one edge in which each node is reachable from every other node) that is reachable from an initial node. Furthermore, if a node on a path contains a formula that *promises* that another formula will hold in the future, such as $\Diamond p$ promising p, then that formula must be contained in a later node in the path, if the path is to be a model. Thus, if an SCS node includes $\Diamond p$, and a model is to reside within that SCS, then the SCS must contain a node that includes p. An SCS that contains all formulas that are promised within it is called a *fulfilling* SCS.

Proposition 38 *A formula φ is satisfiable if and only if there is a fulfilling SCS in Φ_φ reachable from an initial node.*

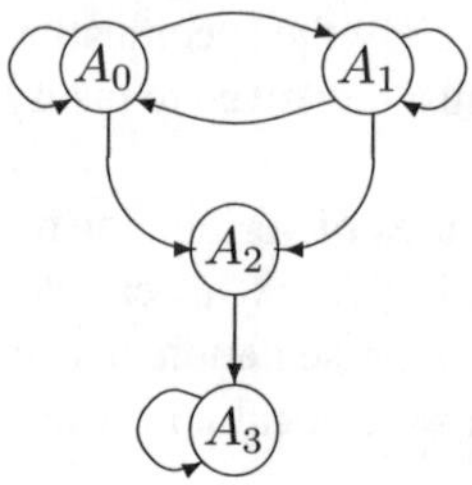

$$\varphi : \Diamond(\overbrace{pc_1 = wait}^{w_1} \wedge \Box\neg\, \overbrace{pc_1 = crit}^{c_1}) \quad (\text{with } p = pc_1 = wait \wedge \Box\neg\, pc_1 = crit)$$

$$\begin{array}{l} A_0 : \{\varphi, \bigcirc\varphi, w_1, p, \Box\neg c_1, \bigcirc\Box\neg c_1, \neg c_1\} \\ A_1 : \{\varphi, \bigcirc\varphi, \neg w_1, \neg p, \Box\neg c_1, \bigcirc\Box\neg c_1, \neg c_1\} \\ A_2 : \{\varphi, \neg\bigcirc\varphi, w_1, p, \Box\neg c_1, \bigcirc\Box\neg c_1, \neg c_1\} \\ A_3 : \{\neg\varphi, \neg\bigcirc\varphi, \neg w_1, \neg p, \Box\neg c_1, \bigcirc\Box\neg c_1, \neg c_1\} \end{array}$$

FIGURE 6 Initial tableau graph for $\Diamond(pc_1 = wait \wedge \Box\neg(pc_1 = crit))$.

Thus, to check whether a temporal formula is satisfiable it suffices to check whether its tableau has at least one fulfilling SCS. In practice it is more efficient to check whether the tableau has at least one fulfilling *maximal strongly connected subgraph* (MSCS) (an SCS that is not contained in any larger SCS), since the number of SCS's is exponential in the size of the graph, while the number of MSCS's is linear in the size of the graph. It is easy to see that a tableau has at least one fulfilling SCS iff it has at least one fulfilling MSCS.

Example 4 *Figure 6 shows the part of a tableau for* $\varphi : \Box(pc_1 = wait \wedge \Box\neg(pc_1 = crit))$ *that is reachable from an initial node. Formula* φ *is the negation of the accessibility property:* $\Box(pc_1 = wait \rightarrow \Diamond pc_1 = crit)$. *The initial nodes of the tableau are* A_0, A_1 *and* A_2, *as their atoms contain* φ. *The tableau has two MSCS's:* $\{A_0, A_1\}$ *and* $\{A_3\}$, *both of which are fulfilling:* $\{A_0, A_1\}$ *contains the promising formula* φ $(= \Diamond p)$, *but also the formula* p *that it promises;* A_3 *does not contain any promising formulas, and thus is trivially fulfilling. We can conclude that* φ *is satisfiable.*

The size of the tableau is exponential in the size of the formula. We can often reduce the size of the tableau (although it still remains exponential in the worst case) by introducing nondeterminism, where sequences of states may be mapped into multiple paths in the tableau, resulting in a so-called *particle tableau* (Manna and Pnueli 1995)

Example 5 *The particle tableau corresponding to the tableau of Figure 6 is shown in Figure 7. It has two MSCS's,* A_0 *and* A_2, *but only* A_2 *is fulfilling. Note that node* A_0 *does not contain any state formulas; it only makes commitments about the future, and not on the present state, and thus any state can be mapped onto it.*

For details on LTL tableau construction, see, e.g. (Kesten et al. 1993) or (Manna and Pnueli 1995).

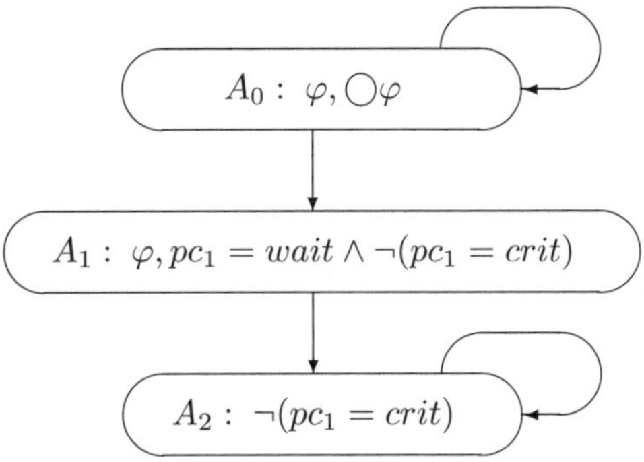

FIGURE 7 Particle tableau for $\varphi : \Diamond(pc_1 = wait \wedge \Box\neg(pc_1 = crit))$.

8.4.2 The Product Graph

In the previous section we saw how to test satisfiability of a temporal formula, by determining whether its tableau admits any models. Similarly, we can check whether a system has any computations that satisfy a given formula, by determining whether the product graph of the tableau and the state-transition graph admits any computations. This is the basis of the LTL model checking procedure: it constructs the product graph of the tableau of the negation of the formula and the state-transition graph, and concludes that the formula is valid of the system if this product graph does not have any computations. If it has a computation, this computation constitutes a counterexample.

More precisely, given a tableau $\Phi_{\neg\varphi}$ and a system $\mathcal{S}$, the *product graph* is a directed graph whose nodes are labeled with pairs (A, s), for an atom A and a state s, such that:

1. For each node (A, s), state s satisfies the state formulas in A.
2. There is an edge from (A, s) to (A', s') if and only if s' is a τ-successor of state s for some transition $\tau \in \mathcal{T}$, and A' is a successor of A in $\Phi_{\neg\varphi}$.
3. A node (A, s) is marked initial if A is an initial atom and s is an initial state.

By construction, sequences of states that follow a path through the product graph are models of the negation of the property (if all promised formulas are fulfilled) and are runs (or run prefixes) of the transition system.

Proposition 39 *System $\mathcal{S}$ has a run satisfying φ iff there is a fulfilling, reachable SCS in the product graph $(\mathcal{S}, \Phi_\varphi)$.*

However, to be a computation of a system, a run has to satisfy the fairness requirements mentioned before: a just transition cannot be continuously enabled without being taken, and if a compassionate transition is enabled infinitely often it must be taken infinitely often. We define an SCS to be *fair* if

justice: every just transition of $\mathcal{S}$ is either taken in the SCS or disabled on some node of the SCS, and

compassion: every compassionate transition is either taken in the SCS or disabled on all nodes of the SCS.

A transition τ is taken in an SCS if there exist two nodes (s_1, A_1), (s_2, A_2) in the SCS such that s_2 is a τ-successor of s_1 and there is an edge between (s_1, A_1) and (s_2, A_2) in the product graph.

Definition 29 A sequence of states $\sigma: \; s_0, s_1, s_2, \ldots$ is a computation of a product graph $(\mathcal{S}, \Phi_{\neg\varphi})$ if there exists a path $\pi: \; (s_0, A_0), (s_1, A_1), (s_2, A_2), \ldots$ in $(\mathcal{S}, \Phi_{\neg\varphi})$ such that (A_0, s_0) is marked initial and π eventually remains in a fair and fulfilling SCS.

Proposition 40 *System $\mathcal{S}$ has a computation satisfying φ iff there is fair and fullfilling SCS in the product graph $(\mathcal{S}, \Phi_{\varphi})$ that is reachable from an initial node.*

Thus, to check whether a system $\mathcal{S}$ satisfies a specification φ, it suffices to check that the product graph $(\mathcal{S}, \Phi_{\neg\varphi})$ does not contain any fair and fullfilling SCS's. As with fulfilment, it suffices to check only MSCS's for justice, since if an MSCS is not just, none of its subgraphs are. However, compassion may have to be checked for all SCS's.

Because the procedure requires the explicit construction of the product graph, it is essentially applicable only to finite-state systems, and in practice only to finite-state systems of limited size. In the following section we present an extension that makes it applicable to infinite-state systems as well.

Example 6 *System* BAK *is an infinite-state system: the integer variables y_1 and y_2 can grow beyond any bound in a computation. Thus, we cannot explicitly represent the transition graph of* BAK, *and therefore we cannot model check this system using the procedure described above. However, it is often possible to abstract an infinite-state system into a finite-state system while preserving the properties of interest. System* BAK *allows an abstraction in which the variables y_1 and y_2 are replaced by the single variable $priority$, which ranges over the finite domain $\{p_-, p_1, p_2, p_{12}, p_{21}\}$, indicating the process of highest* *priority. The mapping can be derived from the diagram shown in Figure 5:*

$$\begin{array}{rcl} y_1 = 0 \land y_2 = 0 & \longleftrightarrow & priority = p_- \\ y_1 = 0 \land y_2 > 0 & \longleftrightarrow & priority = p_2 \\ y_1 > 0 \land y_2 = 0 & \longleftrightarrow & priority = p_1 \\ y_1 > 0 \land y1 \leq y_2 & \longleftrightarrow & priority = p_{12} \\ y_2 > 0 \land y_2 < y_1 & \longleftrightarrow & priority = p_{21} \end{array}$$

The transitions in the abstracted system have to be modified as well, to reflect the mapping. For example, the transition relations for $take_1$ and $enter_1$ now become:

$$\begin{array}{lcl} \rho_{take_1} & : & \ldots\ priority' = (\text{if}\ priority = p_-\ then\ p_1\ else\ p_{21})\ \ldots \\ \rho_{enter_1} & : & \ldots\ (priority = p_1 \lor priority = p_{12}) \ldots \end{array}$$

It can be shown that this abstraction preserves all properties of BAK *that do not mention y_1 or y_2, including mutual exclusion and accessibility. See, for example, (Kesten et al. 1994) for verification rules to establish that a particular abstraction is sound. The transition graph of the resulting abstraction has nine nodes and can easily be constructed.*

Applying the above procedure to check whether BAK *satisfies accessibility, $\square(pc_1 = wait \rightarrow \Diamond pc_1 = crit)$, we obtain a product graph* (BAK, $\Phi_{\neg\varphi}$) *with 17 nodes and 5 MSCS's. One of the MSCS's is not fulfilling, and the remaining four can be shown to be not fair, thus showing that* BAK *satisfies accessibility.*

8.5 Deductive Model Checking

8.5.1 Procedure

Deductive model checking (DMC, for short) is an interactive version of the model-checking procedure described in Section 8.4. It uses first-order formulas to represent (possibly infinite) sets of states, and therefore is, unlike regular model checking, applicable to infinite-state systems.

The computations of the product graph $(\mathcal{S}, \Phi_{\neg\varphi})$ used in model checking are exactly those computations of $\mathcal{S}$ that satisfy $\neg\varphi$. This enabled us to conclude that φ was valid over $\mathcal{S}$ if $(\mathcal{S}, \Phi_{\neg\varphi})$ had no computations, and conversely that any computation of $(\mathcal{S}, \Phi_{\neg\varphi})$ was a counterexample to the validity of φ over $\mathcal{S}$.

The DMC procedure is similar to the regular model-checking procedure, in that it also searches for a $\neg\varphi$-computation of the system. The difference is that its starting point is not the product graph of the state-transition graph and $\Phi_{\neg\varphi}$, but the product graph of an abstraction of the state-transition graph and $\Phi_{\neg\varphi}$. This graph, called a *falsification diagram* represents a superset of the $\neg\varphi$-computations of $\mathcal{S}$, and is then refined until a diagram is obtained that contains no computations. Since we make sure at each refinement step that the computations of $\mathcal{S}$ are preserved, we can conclude that the property φ is $\mathcal{S}$-valid. Alternatively, we may be able to prove that a computation of the diagram is both a computation of $\mathcal{S}$ and a model of $\neg\varphi$, that is, a counterexample which refutes the $\mathcal{S}$-validity of φ. Since we are dealing with infinite-state systems, the general verification problem is undecidable, and thus we are not guaranteed an answer. However, in (Sipma et al. 1998) we show that the set of transformations given is complete (relative to the underlying first-order reasoning) for proving state-quantified temporal properties. That is, if the property is $\mathcal{S}$-valid, then there exists a finite sequence of transformations that produces a diagram with no computations.

We will present and illustrate only some representative transformation rules. A more detailed description of the procedure can be found in (Sipma et al. 1996) and (Sipma et al. 1998).

A *falsification diagram* is a graph whose nodes are labeled by pairs (A, f) where A is an atom and f is a first-order formula, and edges are labeled by sets of transitions. A computation of a falsification diagram is defined similarly to a computation of the product graph.

Definition 30 A sequence of states $\sigma : \ s_0, s_1, s_2, \ldots$ is a computation of a falsification diagram $\mathcal{F}$ if there exists a path $(A_0, f_0), (A_1, f_1), \ldots$ in $\mathcal{F}$ such that s_0 satisfies the initial condition Θ, s_i satisfies f_i for every $i \geq 0$, and the path eventually remains in a fair and fulfilling SCS.

In DMC, nodes are labeled by assertions (representing sets of states), rather than by individual states, so we have to revise the definition of a fair SCS. A transition is considered taken in an SCS of a falsification diagram if it belongs to a set of transitions labeling an edge in the SCS. In a falsification diagram, an SCS is fair if

justice: every just transition of $\mathcal{S}$ is either taken in the SCS or its enabling condition is not implied by the assertion labeling a node in the SCS (that is, the transition is not guaranteed to be enabled), and

compassion: every compassionate transition is either taken in the SCS or its enabling condition is not implied by any of the assertions in the SCS.

To prove that a system $\mathcal{S}$ with transitions $\mathcal{T}$ satisfies the property φ, an initial falsification diagram $\mathcal{F}_0$ is constructed by taking the product of the tableau $\Phi_{\neg\varphi}$ and a graph consisting of a single node, labeled by the assertion *true*, and a single edge, labeled by the set of transitions $\mathcal{T}$, resulting in a graph that is isomorphic to the tableau, except for the edge and node labelings. In addition, we maintain a list $\mathcal{L}$ of potential fulfilling and fair SCS's, initially set to the list of all fulfilling SCS's (in practice we only record the MSCS's).

Example 7 *Figure 8 shows the initial diagram for proving that system* BAK *satisfies accessibility. It is based on the particle tableau shown in Figure 7, and contains the same sets of temporal formulas (not shown here). Its sole fulfilling MSCS is f_2, since the set of temporal formulas belonging to f_0 is not fulfilling, as described in Example 5.*

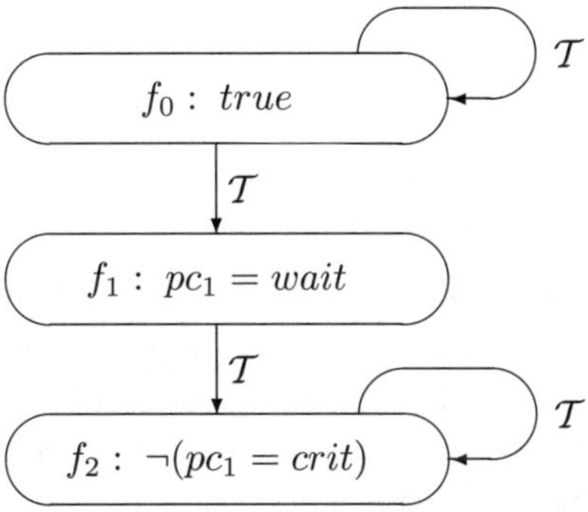

FIGURE 8 Initial falsification diagram for $\varphi : \Diamond(pc_1 = wait \wedge \Box\neg(pc_1 = crit))$.

To show that the property is $\mathcal{S}$-valid we apply transformation rules to obtain a sequence of pairs of ($\mathcal{F}$, $\mathcal{L}$), where $\mathcal{F}$ is a falsification diagram and $\mathcal{L}$ is a list of SCS's in $\mathcal{F}$, until we obtain a pair ($\mathcal{F}$, $\mathcal{L}$) such that $\mathcal{L}$ is empty. An example of such a rule is the *precondition split*, which splits a vertex according to the precondition of an outgoing transition (that is, a transition contained in the label of an outgoing edge). This rule is interactive: the node and transition are supplied by the user.

Precondition split: Given an edge $e = \langle N_1, N_2\rangle = \langle (A_1, f_1), (A_2, f_2)\rangle$, whose edge label includes transition τ, replace (A_1, f_1) by the two nodes

$$\begin{aligned} N_{1,1} &= (A_1, f_1 \wedge enabled(\tau) \wedge pre(\tau, f_2)) \\ N_{1,2} &= (A_1, f_1 \wedge \neg(enabled(\tau) \wedge pre(\tau, f_2))) \end{aligned}$$

and replace e by the two edges $\langle N_{1,1}, N_2\rangle$ and $\langle N_{1,2}, N_2\rangle$ with the same label as e, and, if present, replace $\langle N_1, N_1\rangle$ by the four edges $\langle N_{1,1}, N_{1,1}\rangle$, $\langle N_{1,1}, N_{1,2}\rangle$, $\langle N_{1,2}, N_{1,1}\rangle$, $\langle N_{1,2}, N_{1,2}\rangle$. Simultaneously update all the SCS's in $\mathcal{L}$ that contain N_1.

Note that this transformation rule does not change the set of computations of the falsification diagram. However, it enables the application of other (basic) transformation rules that potentially do reduce it. Some examples of basic rules are

Remove edge label: If an edge $\langle (A_1, f_1), (A_2, f_2) \rangle$ is labeled with a transition τ and the assertion

$$f_1(V) \wedge f_2(V') \wedge \rho_\tau(V, V')$$

is unsatisfiable, remove τ from the edge label.

Empty edge: If an edge is labeled with the empty edge, remove the edge from the diagram.

Unsatisfiable node: If f is unsatisfiable for a node (A, f), or, if a node has no successors, remove the node.

Unjust SCS: If an SCS is not just, remove it from $\mathcal{L}$.

In all these rules $\mathcal{L}$ is updated simultaneously; if an SCS becomes disconnected by the removal of a node or edge, it is replaced by its constituent (fulfilling) MSCS's. These rules can be applied automatically, but may require deductive support for the satisfiability tests.

Example 8 *Figure 9 shows the result of applying a precondition split to node* f_2 *and transition* $take_1$*, followed by the basic transformations.* $\mathcal{L}$ *is updated to* $\{f_{2,2}\}$*. The basic transformations eliminated all transitions from the edges connecting* $f_{2,1}$*, and thus the node could be removed as well.*

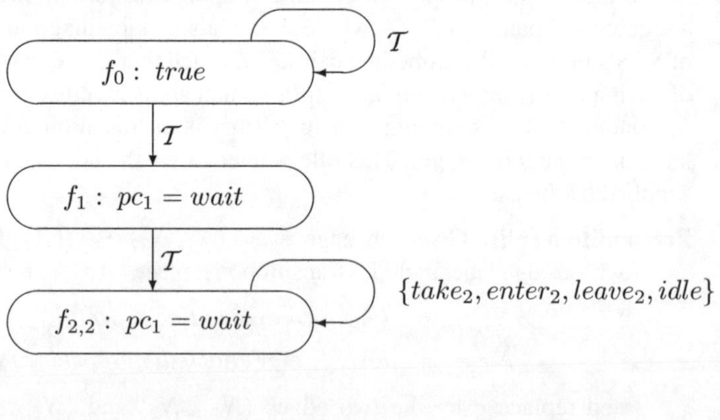

FIGURE 9 Resulting diagram after applying precondition split.

To remove an SCS from $\mathcal{L}$ on the basis that it is not just with respect to some transition τ requires showing that the enabling condition of τ is implied by all assertions in the SCS. To obtain this, we introduce the *enabled split* rule:

Enabled split: Given a node $N = (A, f)$ and a just transition τ, replace N by the two nodes

$$\begin{aligned} N_1 &= (A, f \wedge enabled(\tau)) \\ N_2 &= (A, f \wedge \neg enabled(\tau)) \ . \end{aligned}$$

Example 9 *Figure 10 shows the result of applying an enabled split, followed by (a selective) application of the basic transformation rules. $\mathcal{L}$ now becomes $\{f_{2,2,2}\}$, since $\{f_{2,2,1}\}$ can be shown to be not just with respect to $enter_1$: in the MSCS $\{f_{2,2,1}\}$ the transition $enter_1$ is always enabled, but never taken. With two more enabled splits we obtain a diagram with an empty MSCS list, and we can conclude that system* BAK *satisfies accessibility*

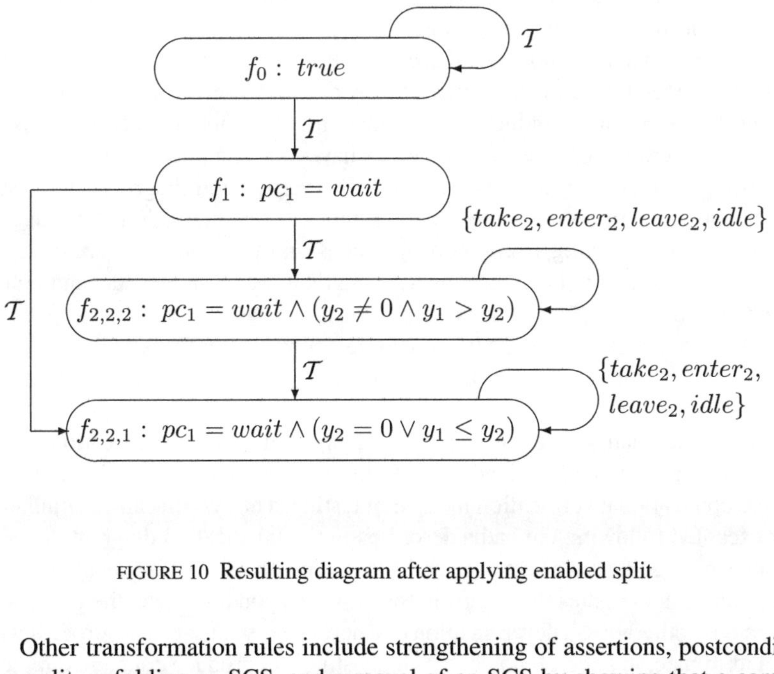

FIGURE 10 Resulting diagram after applying enabled split

Other transformation rules include strengthening of assertions, postcondition split, unfolding an SCS, and removal of an SCS by showing that a computation cannot stay forever in the SCS without leaving it, using well-founded orders. With these last two rules the procedure is relatively complete: if a state-quantified formula holds over a system, then there exists a finite sequence of transformations that produces an empty list $\mathcal{L}$ of SCS's.

8.5.2 Analysis

DMC bridges the gap between modelchecking and deductive verification. On the one hand, for finite-state systems, we can use a finite-state assertion language $\mathcal{A}$, making the satisfiability tests required at the splitting steps and the validity tests required for the fairness tests decidable. In addition, there can only be a finite number of distinct nodes, since every transformation reduces the size of the graphs under consideration or replaces a node with more specific ones (that is, covering fewer states), so the process must terminate.

Proposition 41 *For a finite-state system $\mathcal{S}$, the exhaustive application of transformations terminates, deciding the $\mathcal{S}$-validity of a property φ.*

Standard explicit-state model checking represents the worst-case splitting scenario of DMC, where each assertion is split to the state level, before any nodes are removed. In practice, even without any user interaction, DMC will usually generate considerably fewer nodes than regular model checking, since the basic transformations automatically eliminate portions of the state space that can never contribute to a counterexample. Whether this translates into time savings, of course, depends on how fast these basic transformations can be performed. At the other end, DMC can simulate purely deductive verification, by strengthening all assertions to inductive assertions, making splits unnecessary. As in deductive verification, the strengthenings have to be supplied by the user. The resulting diagrams in this case resemble the verification diagrams discussed in Section 8.3. In between these two extremes, user interaction can assist at various levels, ranging from choosing nodes and transitions for splitting, to providing fairly specific assertions to strengthen or split nodes, depending on the user's understanding of the system.

The soundness of the DMC procedure follows from the fact that at each stage, the falsification diagram represents a superset of the computations of $\mathcal{S}$ that can possibly violate the property being verified. This approximation is refined at each step of the process. Thus, even when a verification effort is not completed, the falsification diagram that is produced can help guide the more conventional verification method of testing. The system can be simulated or executed following the paths described in the falsification diagram: at each node, an outgoing edge is chosen and a transition on its label is executed. If the resulting state satisfies the assertion for the corresponding node, the process is iterated—otherwise, a new transition or a new edge is chosen. This process will not terminate, in general; however, such testing can produce counterexamples, if a fair and fulfilling cycle of states is found.

8.6 Related Work

8.6.1 Abstraction

One way to model check a property φ for a large system $\mathcal{S}$ is to find a simpler system $\mathcal{S}_A$ such that if φ is valid for $\mathcal{S}_A$ then it is also valid for $\mathcal{S}$ (Long 1993). Using *abstract interpretation*, one can require the abstract program $\mathcal{S}_A$ to operate over a domain where the property can be efficiently checked. As a simple example, one could try to reduce an infinite-state program to a finite-state one, as we did in Example 6. A similar method for generating an abstract representation of a possibly infinite state space is presented in (Bouajjani et al. 1990) This is done independently of any particular formula to be verified.

In (Loiseaux et al. 1995), property-preserving abstractions for the μ-calculus are investigated. Dams, Grumberg and Gerth (1993, 1994) present an algorithm for producing abstracted state spaces that preserve various fragments of CTL*. A quotient of the state space is constructed, splitting equivalence classes (sets of states) according to the value of different subformulas. The goal is to obtain an abstracted state space that preserves a given set of formulas; the abstraction is maximized if this set contains only the property to be model checked. (Dams et al. 1994) shows how this quotient construction can be combined with abstract interpretation. A clear and complete description of this line of research is (Dams 1996).

One can think of the DMC procedure as combining the abstraction and model checking phases within a general first-order setting. For instance, it may be possible to do enough splitting and simplification that the model checking of an infinite-state system is reduced to a finite set of finite-state model checking tasks, to which fully automatic methods can be applied.

Real-time systems are always infinite-state. The local model checking algorithm for real-time systems presented by Sokolsky and Smolka (1995) can be seen as a specialized variant of our procedure. It refines a finite representation of an infinite product graph, splitting nodes to satisfy constraints arising from the formula and system being checked.

8.6.2 Other Combinations

Other methods for combining theorem proving and model checking have been proposed. Most of them rely on decomposing the verification effort into subgoals which can be model checked, where the decomposition is justified using deductive methods. Hungar (1993) and Lamport (1993) use (deductive) modular decomposition to reduce the correctness of a large system to that of smaller components that can be model checked. Abstraction is used in (Rajan et al. 1995) and (Dingel and Filkorn 1995) to obtain subgoals that can be model checked, while the correctness of the abstraction is proved deductively.

The PVS system (Owre et al. 1996) includes a decision procedure to model check propositional μ-calculus expressions, which can appear as subgoals in a verification effort. The STeP system (Bjørner et al. 1996) uses deductive verification rules, but can also model check subgoals over the given system specification whenever possible. Pnueli and Shahar (1996) show how deductively obtained invariants can be used to constrain the BDD-based symbolic model checking process.

8.7 Acknowledgements

We thank Nikolaj Bjørner, Anca Browne, Luca de Alfaro, Arjun Kapur and Uri Lerner for their comments.

References

Bjørner, N., A. Browne, E. Chang, M. Colón, A. Kapur, Z. Manna, H. Sipma, and T. Uribe. 1996. STeP: Deductive-algorithmic verification of reactive and real-time systems. In *Proc.* 8th *Intl. Conference on Computer Aided Verification*, Vol. 1102 of *LNCS*, 415–418. Springer-Verlag, July.

Bjørner, N., A. Browne, and Z. Manna. 1997. Automatic generation of invariants and intermediate assertions. *Theor. Comp. Sci.* 173(1):49–87.

Bouajjani, A., J.-C. Fernandez, and N. Halbwachs. 1990. Minimal model generation. In *Proc.* 2nd *Intl. Conference on Computer Aided Verification*, Vol. 531 of *LNCS*, 197–203.

Bradfield, J. C. 1992. *Verifying Temporal Properties of Systems*. Birkhäuser.

Browne, A., Z. Manna, and H. Sipma. 1995. Generalized temporal verification diagrams. In *15th Conference on the Foundations of Software Technology and Theoretical Computer Science*, Vol. 1026 of *LNCS*, 484–498. Springer-Verlag.

Browne, A., Z. Manna, and H. Sipma. 1996. Hierarchical verification using verification diagrams. In 2nd *Asian Computing Science Conf.*, Vol. 1179 of *LNCS*, 276–286. Springer-Verlag, December.

Clarke, E., and E. Emerson. 1981. Design and synthesis of synchronization skeletons using branching time temporal logic. In *Proc. IBM Workshop on Logics of Programs*, Vol. 131 of *LNCS*, 52–71. Springer-Verlag.

Dams, D. 1996. *Abstract Interpretation and Partition Refinement for Model Checking*. PhD thesis, Eindhoven University of Technology, Eindhoven, July.

Dams, D., R. Gerth, G. Döhmen, R. Herrmann, P. Kelb, and H. Pargmann. 1994. Model checking using adaptive state and data abstraction. In *Proc.* 6th *Intl. Conference on Computer Aided Verification*, Vol. 818 of *LNCS*, 455–467. Springer-Verlag, June.

Dams, D., O. Grumberg, and R. Gerth. 1993. Generation of reduced models for checking fragments of CTL. In *Proc.* 5th *Intl. Conference on Computer Aided Verification*, Vol. 697 of *LNCS*, 479–490. Springer-Verlag, June.

Dams, D., O. Grümberg, and R. Gerth. 1994. Abstract interpretation of reactive systems: Abstractions preserving $\forall$CTL*, $\exists$ECTL*, CTL*. In *IFIP Working Conference on Programming Concepts, Methods and Calculi (PROCOMET 94)*, 573–592, June.

de Alfaro, L., and Z. Manna. 1996. Temporal verification by diagram transformations. In *Proc.* 8th *Intl. Conference on Computer Aided Verification*, Vol. 1102 of *LNCS*, 287–299, July.

de Alfaro, L., Z. Manna, H. Sipma, and T. Uribe. 1997. Visual verification of reactive systems. In *Third Intl. Workshop on Tools and Algorithms for the Construction and Analysis of Systems (TACAS 97)*, Vol. 1217 of *LNCS*, 334–350. Springer-Verlag, April.

Dijkstra, E. 1975. Guarded commands, nondeterminancy, and formal derivation of programs. *Communications of the ACM* 18(8):453–457.

Dingel, J., and T. Filkorn. 1995. Model checking of infinite-state systems using data abstraction, assumption-commitment style reasoning and theorem proving. In *Proc. 7th Intl. Conference on Computer Aided Verification*, Vol. 939 of *LNCS*, 54–69, July.

Emerson, E. 1990. Temporal and modal logic. In J. van Leeuwen (Ed.), *Handbook of Theoretical Computer Science*, Vol. B, 995–1072. Elsevier Science Publishers (North-Holland).

Fix, L., and O. Grumberg. 1996. Verification of temporal properties. *J. Logic and Computation* 6(3):343–362.

Hungar, H. 1993. Combining model checking and theorem proving to verify parallel processes. In *Proc. 5th Intl. Conference on Computer Aided Verification*, Vol. 697 of *LNCS*, 154–165. Springer-Verlag.

Kesten, Y., Z. Manna, H. McGuire, and A. Pnueli. 1993. A decision algorithm for full propositional temporal logic. In *Proc. 5th Intl. Conference on Computer Aided Verification*, Vol. 697 of *LNCS*, 97–109. Springer-Verlag.

Kesten, Y., Z. Manna, and A. Pnueli. 1994. Temporal verification of simulation and refinement. In J. de Bakker, W.-P. de Roever, and G. Rozenberg (Eds.), *A Decade of Concurrency*, Vol. 803 of *LNCS*, 273–346. Springer-Verlag.

Kurshan, R., and L. Lamport. 1993. Verification of a multiplier: 64 bits and beyond. In C. Courcoubetis (Ed.), *Proc. 5th Intl. Conference on Computer Aided Verification*, Vol. 697 of *LNCS*, 166–179. Springer-Verlag.

Lamport, L. 1974. A new solution of Dijkstra's concurrent programming problem. *Communications of the ACM* 17(8):435–455.

Loiseaux, C., S. Graf, J. Sifakis, A. Bouajjani, and S. Bensalem. 1995. Property preserving abstractions for the verification of concurrent systems. *Formal Methods in System Design* 6:1–35.

Long, D. E. 1993. *Model Checking, Abstraction, and Compositional Verification*. PhD thesis, School of Computer Science, Carnegie-Mellon University, Pittsburgh, PA, July.

Manna, Z., and A. Pnueli. 1991. *The Temporal Logic of Reactive and Concurrent Systems: Specification.* New York: Springer-Verlag.

Manna, Z., and A. Pnueli. 1994. Temporal verification diagrams. In *Proc. Int. Symp. on Theoretical Aspects of Computer Software*, Vol. 789 of *LNCS*, 726–765. Springer-Verlag.

Manna, Z., and A. Pnueli. 1995. *Temporal Verification of Reactive Systems: Safety.* New York: Springer-Verlag.

Owre, S., S. Rajan, J. Rushby, N. Shankar, and M. Srivas. 1996. PVS: Combining specification, proof checking, and model checking. In *Proc. 8th Intl. Conference on Computer Aided Verification*, Vol. 1102 of *LNCS*, 411–414. Springer-Verlag, July.

Pnueli, A. 1977. The temporal logic of programs. In *Proc. 18th IEEE Symp. Found. of Comp. Sci.*, 46–57. IEEE Computer Society Press.

Pnueli, A., and E. Shahar. 1996. A platform for combining deductive with algorithmic verification. In *Proc. 8th Intl. Conference on Computer Aided Verification*, Vol. 1102 of *LNCS*, 184–195. Springer-Verlag.

Rajan, S., N. Shankar, and M. Srivas. 1995. An integration of model checking with automated proof checking. In *Proc. 7th Intl. Conference on Computer Aided Verification*, Vol. 939 of *LNCS*, 84–97, July.

Sipma, H., T. Uribe, and Z. Manna. 1996. Deductive model checking. In *Proc. 8th Intl. Conference on Computer Aided Verification*, Vol. 1102 of *LNCS*, 208–219. Springer-Verlag.

Sipma, H., T. Uribe, and Z. Manna. 1998. Model checking and deduction for infinite-state systems. To appear.

Sokolsky, O., and S. Smolka. 1995. Local model checking for real-time systems. In *Proc. 7th Intl. Conference on Computer Aided Verification*, Vol. 939 of *LNCS*, 211–224, July.

Index